ECONOMIC AND SOCIAL COMMISSION FOR ASIA AND THE PACIFIC

ATLAS OF MINERAL RESOURCES OF THE ESCAP REGION

VOLUME 15

GEOLOGY AND MINERAL RESOURCES OF AZERBAIJAN

UNITED NATIONS

New York, 2000

ST/ESCAP/2033

UNITED NATIONS PUBLICATION
Sales No. E.00.II.F.21
Copyright © United Nations 2000
ISBN: 92-1-119971-9   ISSN: 1014-5451

PREFACE

Since acquiring membership of the Economic and Social Commission for Asia and the Pacific (ESCAP) in 1992, the Government of Azerbaijan has expressed keen interest in integrating its economy within prospective in Asia and the Pacific and participation of the government in the technical assistance programmes of the Commission in various sectors. As a part of this integration process, the Government of Azerbaijan has requested the ESCAP secretariat to assist in promoting foreign direct investment in the development of oil and gas, mining and mineral-based industries in Azerbaijan. The present volume 15 of the Atlas of Mineral Reserves of the ESCAP Region on geology and mineral resources of Azerbaijan responds to that request.

This publication aims at increased understanding of the complex metallogeny and mineral resources potential of Azerbaijan which have resulted from geodynamic evolution and the complex tectonic and structural setting of the Caucasian mountain system. As in preceeding volumes of this series, there is a brief review of the stratigraphy, magmatism and tectonics of the major structural units of the country, a description of the mineral resources and potential, recent policy initiatives, and the regulatory framework for resource development.

The information contained in this volume is mainly based on a study completed in early 1999 during the consultancy to ESCAP of Dr Khalifa-zade Chingiz Muzaffar oglu, the Head of the Department of the Azerbaijan State Oil Academy, Dr Talat N. Kangarli, the Head of the Department of Ecology and Economy of Natural Resources, the Ministry of Economy of Azerbaijan and Dr Yusif Zamanov, Deputy Chairman of the State Committee on Geology and Mineral Resources of Azerbaijan. The ESCAP secretariat would like to express its appreciation to these experts for their interest in and support of this endeavour. The overall support, assistance and coordination efforts of Dr Chengiz Abasov, the Head of the Department on Foreign Investments of the Ministry of Economy of Azerbaijan in preparing the background study for this publication is also gratefully acknowledged.

The ESCAP secretariat has prepared this publication under its technical assistance programme for countries with economies in transition. It hopes that the publication will generate interest among geoscientists, international petroleum and mining groups and financial institutions in carrying out further research on the geology and mineral resources of Azerbaijan and that it will promote investment in the development of the oil and gas, mining and mineral-based industries of the country.

CONTENTS

CONTENTS *(continued)*

CONTENTS *(continued)*

LIST OF TABLES

CONTENTS *(continued)*

CONTENTS *(continued)*

EXPLANATORY NOTE

The mineral deposits discussed in this publication represent the most important types of mineralization. Soviet nomenclature grades mineralization into mineral deposits, mineral occurrences and mineral showings in decreasing order of significance. Mineral reserve categories in the database of Azerbaijan follow the former Soviet Union resource classification. The table below shows how resource categories in the former Soviet Union correspond to those in the United States of America.

Approximate correspondence of resource categories in the United States of America and the former Soviet Union

Country	Total resources					
United States	Identified resources				Undiscovered resources	
	Demonstrated reserves		Inferred or possible reserves		Hypothetical resources	Speculative resources
	Measured or proved	Indicated or probable				
Soviet Union	Explored reserves		Projected resources			
	A + B	C_1	C_2	P_1	P_2	P_3

Source: Bejanova, M.P. and H.P. Piskorsky, 1989, "Classification of hard economic mineral resources and resources: principles and special features". Paper present to the Seminar on Modern Methods of Mineral Prospecting, Tbilisi. Georgia, 30 October-10 November 1989; United States Bureau of Mines and United States Geological Survey. Principles of a resource/reserve classification for minerals, USGS Circular 831 (Washington, DC, 1980); Astakhov, Denisov, and Pavlov, 1994. "Prospecting and exploration in the Soviet Union", in Hans Landsberg, John Tilton and Rodderick Eggert, eds. *World Mineral Exploration Trends* (Resources for the Future, Washington, DC).

The publication contains many geological terms of Russian origin, which need some guidance for translation. These include words such as aleurolite (siltstone), beresite and beresitization (quartz-carbonate alteration), rogovic (hornfels), listvenite (magnesite schist) and others.

INTRODUCTION

Azerbaijan is located within the southern slopes of the Greater Caucasus and Lesser Caucasus and bordered by the Dagestan Republic of the Russian Federation on the north, Georgia on the northwest, Armenia on the west and southwest, Turkey and the Islamic Republic of Iran on the south and by the Caspian Sea on the east (figure 1).

The territory of Azerbaijan extends over a distance of 680 kilometres from the west to the east and for 520 kilometres from the north to the south. It includes the Nakhchivan Autonomous Republic, which is separated by the Zangezur mountain massif of Armenia. The population of Azerbaijan as of 1 January 2000 was 8,020,000 people.

Azerbaijan is a well-developed agricultural and industrial country. The economy of Azerbaijan is dominated by oil, refinery chemical, petrochemical, metallurgical, mechanical engineering, energy, electronic, light and food industries as well as construction and mining industries. Azerbaijan has also a well-developed network of railroads, motorways and sea links and energy infrastructure.

The territory of Azerbaijan has been systematically mapped and covered by geological and geophysical surveys at the scale 1:100,000. Detailed geological mapping programmes at scales 1:50,000 and 1:25,000 including mineral and petroleum exploration are being currently conducted at the most prospective areas. The country has so far identified 720 deposits and occurrences of fuel and solid minerals, 300 of which have a high potential for development.

The country's most significant deposits are its oil reserves, and a number of foreign firms are involved in projects to develop these reserves. Azerbaijan also has numerous other mineral resources, including such metals as aluminium in alunite, arsenic, cobalt, copper, chromite, iron ore, lead and zinc, manganese, mercury, gold, molybdenum and tungsten, industrial minerals which include barytes, clays, refractory-grade dolomite, gypsum, kaolin, limestone, pyrite, salt, zeolites and semi-precious stones. Around 350 non-fuel mineral deposits have been found so far on the territory of the country including 168 deposits of solid minerals with proven potential for development. Major mining targets for ferrous, ferro-alloy and base metals are located within the western part of the southern slope of the Greater Caucasus and the Murovdog ridge of the Lesser Caucasus. Despite a strong diversified mineral resource base and historical achievements, the mining industry of Azerbaijan is, however, encountering problems in performance, efficiency, transportation and utilization. The industry operates below full capacity and is plagued by outdated technology and equipment, rising production costs, capital, energy and severe infrastructure problems. Attempts to boost domestic minerals supply in the republic so far have progressed slowly because of economic difficulties. The country lacks the financing required to initiate new, large-scale development projects.

In an effort to reinvigorate the mining industry, the Government of Azerbaijan is now encouraging foreign participation in the industry through the use of joint ventures.

Having been closed to foreign investors for decades, the Government of Azerbaijan is undertaking intensive work and making great efforts to attract overseas investment. The Government desires to expand its mineral and energy sectors and improve the efficiency of utilization of raw materials in the country by introducing capital, technology and machinery from abroad. This represents the first massive efforts by the leadership of the republic to seek joint ventures in petroleum and mining sectors and a departure from traditional self-sufficiency principles.

The country's most significant deposits are its oil reserves. Sixty-seven oil and gas deposits have been discovered in Azerbaijan during its 120 years oil and gas industry history. Currently, 37 onshore and 17 offshore fields have been developed in the country, with a total 1,400 million tons of oil and over 450 billion cubic metres

4

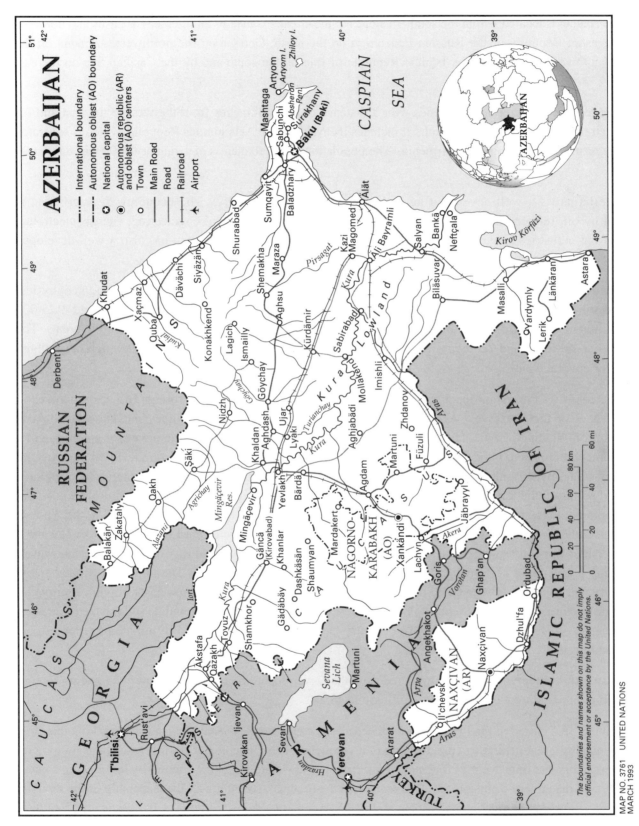

Figure 1. Administrative map of Azerbaijan

MAP NO. 3761   UNITED NATIONS
MARCH 1993

of gas having been extracted from its reservoirs. One hundred forty-five prospective blocks have been found in the Azerbaijan sector of the Caspian Sea containing, according to different estimates, from 4 to 10 billion tons of oil reserves.

Upon acquiring independence in 1991, Azerbaijan has been trying to attract foreign investors to participate in the development of these reserves. Around 50 major petroleum companies are currently engaged in the development of Azerbaijan's oil and gas resources, which will be a significant source of revenue for the country. The last six years have seen several achievements in national oil policy and strategy through the signing of 17 production sharing agreements for offshore hydrocarbon exploration and development in the Azerbaijan sector of the Caspian Sea. The country's crude oil and gas resources are sufficient to increase oil and gas production up to 45-50 million tons a year over the next few years. This in turn will be sufficient to provide a strong basis from which the Government of Azerbaijan can solve the economic and social problems of the country and ensure its sustainable development.

The Government of Azerbaijan supported by international financial and economic institutions has already initiated a series of economic reforms towards (a) liberalization of external economic relations, (b) implementation of the privatization programme, (c) achievement of macroeconomic stabilization and (d) establishment of a friendly environment and incentives for domestic and foreign investment.

During the last six years, Azerbaijan's Parliament has enacted over 60 priority laws to speed up economic reforms and create favourable conditions for foreign investments. The law governing investment activities states that ventures with foreign participation where the share of foreign investment in hard currency, equipment, or raw materials is at least 30 per cent of the registration fund, are exempted from the profit tax. Industrial and construction companies enjoy a five-year tax holiday as of the date of official registration. Foreign investment and direct participation in a wide range of industries are openly invited, especially for exploring, extracting and processing mineral resources. The National Assembly promulgated a new mining law in May 1998 to attract foreign investment for mineral exploration, mining and modernization of existing mines, and processing plants. A set of relevant legislative acts and regulations on land, groundwater, forestry, mineral resources, environment and investment has been translated from the local language to Russian and English and is now available for foreign investors on a commercial basis.

The Government's economic restructuring programme and supporting measures have already enabled Azerbaijan to attract sizeable foreign investment in petroleum exploration and exploitation. The proved geological and mineral potential of Azerbaijan constitutes a favourable basis for the future development of the petroleum and mining industries, and the Government is undertaking further regulatory measures to attract foreign investment to these and other relevant sectors.

I. GENERAL GEOLOGY, TECTONIC SETTING AND METALLOGENIC DEVELOPMENT OF AZERBAIJAN

A. Tectonic and structural setting of Azerbaijan

The territory of Azerbaijan corresponds to the eastern part of the Caucasian segment of the Mediterranean folded belt. Tectonic heterogeneity is a typical feature of the Earth's crust structure in the Caucasian region.

The tectonic setting is characterized by the availability of various structural and formational units with variable degree and nature of deformations, the content of component rocks and the history of geological development.

The polycyclic recurrence of its structural formations is typical for the whole Caucasian region and has been caused by the manifestation of folding phases of the Baikalian, Hercynian and Alpine (including early Kimmerian, Late Kimmerian and Alpine proper) tectono-magmatic cycles. All the above phases are represented in geological and stratigraphic sections of Azerbaijan. However, the actual material enables the observation of geodynamic development of the region only during the Alpine cycle. The description of tectonics and the Alpine geodynamic evolution of the territory of Azerbaijan is based on materials of fundamental geological investigations and research carried out in the territories of Azerbaijan, South Caspian and the whole Caucasian region (Khain, 1984; Gamkrelidze, 1977; Hasanov, 1996; Kangarly and others, 1994; Kangarly, 1997; Knipper, 1975; Kovalev, 1978; Lomidze, 1983; Mansurov, 1998; Milanovsky and Khain, 1963; Mustafayev and others, 1989; Sholpo, 1978).

1. Main tectonic and structural units of Azerbaijan

The main structural units of the Azerbaijan territory are the mountain-folded systems of the Greater and Lesser Caucasus and the dividing Kura intermountain depression (Geology of USSR, Vol. 47, 1972). The Kusari-Devechi fore-deep trough extends along the north-eastern slope of the Azerbaijan part of the Greater Caucasus. The structural formations of the Greater Caucasus and its troughs in the north and south have subsided in the south-eastern direction and disappeared under the recent deposits of the longitudinal depression of the Caspian Sea.

The mountainous orogenic system of the Lesser Caucasus is limited by the Nakhchivan superimposed trough in the south-west; in the south-eastern direction, the system periclinally subsided under the Upper Pliocene-Anthropogene deposits of the Lower Aras superimposed depression. The latter separates structural zones of the Lesser Caucasus from the folding structure of the Talysh mountain, located on the north-eastern slope of the Elburs mountain folded system.

The Elburs system has framed the South Caspian deep water depression from the southwest and south. The modern structure of the region has been formed during the Alpine stage of tectonogenesis in spatial limits, covering the southern flank of the Eurasian continent, Lesser Caucasian belt of Mesotethys and the northern flank of the southern Azerbaijan or Iranian micro-continent. The following main tectonic units from north to south have been distinguished within Azerbaijan:

(a)   *The North-Caucasian plate* constitutes a part of the Scythian platform which has been involved in pericratonic subsidence connected with the foundation and development of the marginal marine trough of the Greater Caucasus. Geomorphologically, the plate corresponds to an uplift of a side range, the northern slope of which has flexurely subsided under Pliocene-Holocene formations of the Gusar-Devechi superimposed trough. The southern boundary of the plate is limited by the Akhti-Nugedi-Gilezi buried fault being reflected on the surface by the Shakhdag-Germian overthrust. The uplift of the side range is represented by the south-eastern extension of the Main Range uplift of the central segment of the Greater Caucasus, where Precambrian and Lower-Middle Palaeozoic metamorphic formations of the North Caucasian plate cropped out at the surface overlying the Lower Middle Jurassic deposits of southern zones.

(b)   *The trough of the southern slope of the Greater Caucasus* corresponds to the linear tectonic axial part of the marginal marine basin, the consolidated crust of which underwent destruction and alternation. On the surface, the trough is represented by the uplift of the watershed range (Tufan tectonic zone) and the Zakatalaj-Kovdag-Sumgait trough. The tectonic units consist of variable age overthrusts, compressed folds and schistose formations. The southern boundary of the trough of the southern slope of the Greater Caucasus is limited by the Zangi-Gozluchay fault.

(c)   *The Transcaucasian plate* is a fragment of the passive margin of the Gondwana which was separated from the continent in a process of Paleotethys' opening and joined the Eurasian tectonic plate as a result of plate tectonic movements during the Hercynian cycle of tectono-genesis. During the Alpine stage of tectono-genesis, the Transcaucasian plate was represented by laminar or island arc system, which separated the marginal sea of the Greater Caucasus from the Lesser Caucasus'offset of Mesotethys. In recent construction, the central part of the plate corresponds to the Kura trough and flank parts take part in building mountain-folded formations of the Greater (Balakan-Vandam tectonic zone) and the Lesser (Artwin-Garabag tectonic zone) Caucasus. The southern boundary of the plate is limited by the Zangezur structural suture, which is represented on the surface by the Girratag overthrust. The overthrust was formed as a result of the closing of the Lesser Caucasian offset of Mesotethys at the beginning of Late Cretaceous in a process of convergence of the Caucasian and southern Azerbaijan tectonic micro-plates. The convergence has resullted in compressing and overthrusting of ophiolites from the root zones of the Zangezur suture in marginal parts of both plates. The Talysh folded system is the most southern segment of the plate within Azerbaijan. It consists of Paleocene-Miocene formations and underwent riftogenesis during the Eocene-Oligocene period.

(d)   *The south Azerbaijan plate* constitutes a sialic massif of the Gondwana origin. The massif is the integral part of the Anatolian-Iranian region with a complex geologic and tectonic structure. On the territory of Azerbaijan, the plate on its northwest is represented by the Aras trough filled by the platform Palaeozoic-Mesozoic formations. The northeastern segment of the south Azerbaijan plate underwent tectonic destruction and rifting, which ended in the Oligocene (Khain, 1984, Kangarly, 1999).

2. Structure of major tectonic zones and units of Azerbaijan

(a)   Mountain-folded system of the Greater Caucasus

The global plate tectonics theory has received much attention from the geosicentific community during the past two decades in attempts to interpret the Mesozoic-Cenozoic geodynamics of the Greater Caucasus (Gamkrelidze, 1977; Kangarly, 1982; Kangarly and others, 1994; Kangarly, 1997). According to this theory, the Greater Caucasus is considered as a complex folded-overthrust tectonic unit originated and formed within spatial limits covering the flanks of the Transcaucasian continental plate in the south and the north Caucasian plate in the north. The rift depression has been formed as a result of their movement. The major elements of the modern structure of the Azerbaijan part of the Greater Caucasus are three tectonic zones differing by heterogeneity of substratum, uneven conditions of rock formation and heterogeneity of the Alpine cover. From north to south, these tectonic zones are (i) the uplift of the Side Range of the Greater Caucasus, (ii) the south slope trough; and (iii) the Balakan-Vandam uplift (figure 2).

These tectonic zones consist, in turn, of a number of structural sub-zones, overthrusting each other southwards. The latter triggered the formation of variable in age overthrusts, which are the main structural elements of the region.

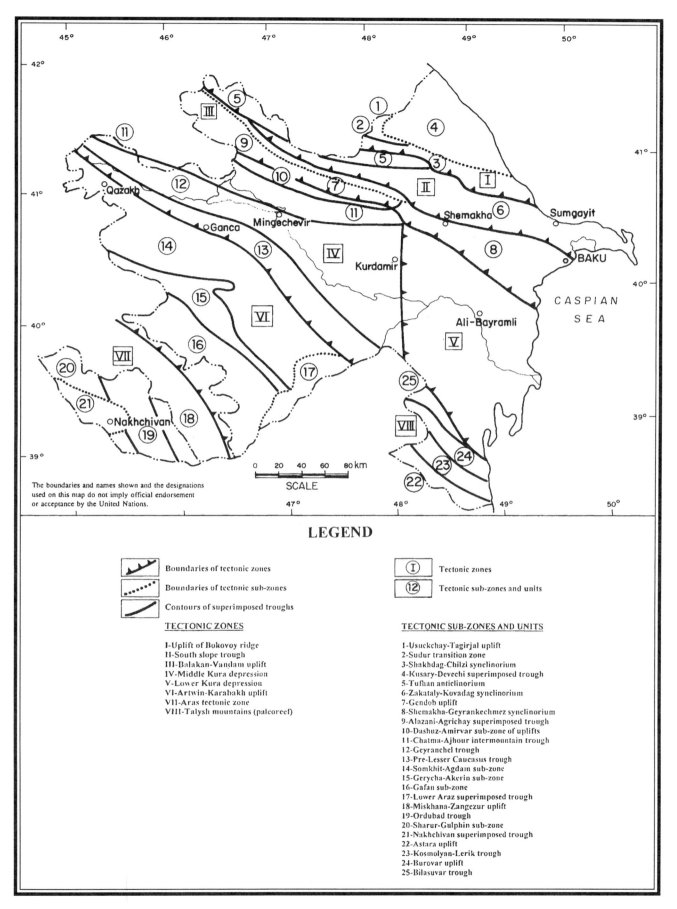

Figure 2. Schematic tectonic setting of Azerbaijan

The uplift of the Side Range is located on the southeastern extension of the central uplift of the Greater Caucasus and has a subplatform basement which corresponds to the Tersk-Caspian segment of the North Caucasian plate. On the territory of Azerbaijan, the Mesozoic structures of the anticline and northern slope of the uplift of the side range have flexurely subsided along the Samur fault to a south-eastern direction to a depth from 3,000 to 5,000 metres spartially coinciding with the Kusary-Devechi superimposed trough. The latter was formed in the Middle Pliocene representing the western closure of a large north Absheron depression of the Middle Caspian aquatoria. Three tectonic stages have affected the formation of the consolidated Pre-Jurassic basement of the trough. The Khachmaz tectonic stage corresponds to the uplifted flank of the Scythian platform, where 200 metres of andesite has been traced as a result of deep drilling to a depth of more than 5,000 metres. Andesites overlie the crystalline schists of the Permian-Triassic age. The Quba tectonic stage corresponds to the subsided Tersk-Caspian segment of the platform, and the Tufan tectonic stage constitutes the substratum of the southern slope trough. The tectonic boundary between the last two stages is traced along the Akhti-Nugedi-Gulezi fault, where an amplitude of 32-35 kilometres of tectonic overthrusting and overlapping has been observed (Kangarly and others, 1994). On the surface, the fault is represented by a series of flaky overthrusts. The Shakhdag-Germian overthrust limits the outcropped Mesozoic formations of the uplift of the Side Range from the south. On the surface, the Mesozoic formations of the tectonic zone of the side range have pronounced three sub-zones (Kangarly, 1982), which are as follows:

(i)   *The uplifted Usukhchay-Tairdal sub-zone* represents a mega-anticline deeping southward and being complicated along the wings by shallow folding. The anticline is composed of relatively shallow-water sandstones and argillites of the Lower-Middle Jurassic age;

(ii)   *The transition Sudur sub-zone* is located on the southern wing of the above sub-zone and represents a synclinorium structure being complicated by linear folds. The synclinorium is composed of evaporates and carbonaceous formations of the Upper Jurassic-Neocomian dominated by facies of continental shelf and barrier reef;

(iii)   *The subsided Shakhdag-Khizi sub-zone* represents the south most structural unit of the Side Range of the Greater Caucasus. The trough is composed of carbonaceous-terrigenous-clayey formations of the Upper Jurassic-Cretaceous age dominated by facies of continental slope and foothill.

The trough of the southern slope of the Greater Caucasus is represented by sub-zones of the watershed range in the north and Zakataly-Kovdag-Sumgayit in the south. The sub-zone of the watershed range or Tufan sub-zone is traced by continuous development of the Lower-Middle Jurassic sandy-clayey terrigeneous formations with additional sub-zone or Upper Jurassic flyschoid strata in the southern area. The Tufan sub-zone is characterized by a rather tense folding and consists of linear, strongly compressed, frequently isoclinal upright folds. The sub-zone in its south-eastern pericline is tectonically pinched out along the western Caspian fault and, in the southern wing, it is overthrusted into the northern flank of the Zakataly-Kovdag-Sumgayit sub-zone along the Malkamud upthrust.

The Zakataly-Kovdag-Sumgayit sub-zone originated on the extreme west of Azerbaijanian part of the southern slope of the Greater Caucasus and subsequently extended to the coast of the Caspian sea (figure 2).

The sub-zone is a flysch trough composed of terrigenous-carbonaceous-clayey formations of the Upper Jurassic-Neocomian in the western segment of the sub-zone. The stratigraphic sequence has undergone an intensive folding resulting in the appearance of shallow strongly compressed isoclinal folds overturned to the south. On the east, the section is supplemented by the Upper Cretaceous flysch and in the near shore area by deposits of the Paleocene-Miocene. Here, the comb-shaped folding has been accompanied by intensive tectonic fracturing.

The Duradja tectonic block crops out along the south flank of the western segment of zone in the narrow suture of the Zangi fault. The block is made up of the Jurassic rocks overthrusted on the Upper Cretaceous rocks of the southern Balakan-Vandam tectonic zone (Kangarly and others, 1994; Kangarly, 1997). The age of overthrusting is the Late Senonian (Laramian phase of tectonogenesis), and the amplitude is to 30 kilometres on the east, in the area of Geychay river.

The Durudja block is tectonically overlapped by the Bascal-Pirekishkul allochthonous complex of the Shtir and Attic phases of tectogenesis. The complex includes the sedimentary formations from the Barremian-Aptian to Miocene overthrusted along the Zangi fault on the Tertiary series of the Shemakha-Jeyrankechmaz trough with an amplitude of around 25 kilometres. On the east, the allochthonous complex subsided under the Pliocene-Quaternary deposits of the Absheron periclinal trough. Regionally, the eastern extension of the trough of the southern slope has been traced within the Caspian Sea as the Absheron-Fore-Balakhan trough. The trough transfers eastward into the Fore-Balakhan folded zone of western Turkmenistan.

The Balakhan-Vandam uplift crops out in the foothills of the southern slope of the Greater Caucasus and represents the northern structural flank of the Transcaucasian plate. The basement of the uplift corresponds to the Vandam tectonic stage of Pre-Jurassic. The Alpian volcanogenic-sedimentary formations of the uplift extend far to the north subsiding under the southern wing of the trough of the southern slope. On the west, the Balakhan-Vandam tectonic zone represents a geoanticlinal uplift. The arc of the anticline includes the Bajocian volcanogenic formations and Neocomian flyschoid strata. The limbs of the anticline arc composed of volcanogenic-sedimentary formations of the Upper Cretaceous complicated by comb-shaped folding. Most of the arc and the southern wing of uplift is overlaid by recent continental formations of the Alazan-Agrichay superimposed depression. A chain of geophysical anomalies being interpreted as buried intrusions and paleovolcanoes are overlaid by detrital deposits. The Mesozoic core of the Balakhan-Vandam uplift is flexurely subsiding in the area of the Girdimanchay-Akhsuchay watershed along the Girdimanchay zone of latitudinal faults. The southeastern extension of the uplift represents a wide Shemakha-Jeyrankechmaz depression mainly composed of terrigenous-clayey sediments of the Paleocene-Pliocene. The sediments are marked by shallow, frequently inversed overthrusting southward and the presence of sharp and isoclinal folds. Gentle overthrusts of the Rodan phase of folding in the Middle Pliocene have complicated the internal structure of the trough, and doubled a thickness of the Cenozoic deposits. At the same time, in the Valakh phase of tectono-genesis, the southern flank of the trough cuts tectonically the northern flank of the Lower Kura trough along the Adjichay-Alyat overthrust with an amplitude of allochthonous overlapping reaching 15-20 kilometres.

(b)   Kura intermontain depression

The Kura depression occupies the eastern subsided part of the Transcaucasian plate and includes the Middle and Lower Kura troughs separated by the Talysh-Vandam buried meridional uplift. On the east, the Kura depression opens up and subsides into the Caspian sea. The Pre-Jurassic basement of the Kura depression subsided bench-like from flanks to the axis eastwards. The depression is a superimposed structure, wherein the sedimentary cover consisting of molasses series uncomfortably overlies sedimentary and volcanogenic complexes of dislocated sediments of Mesozoic and Paleogene (Shikhalibeyli and others, 1984).

The Middle-Kura trough incorporates the following structural units:

(i)   *The Dashuz-Amirvar sub-zone* of uplifts mostly developed in the suture zone of the Alazani-Agrichay fault separating the trough from the northern Balakan-Vandam uplift. The sub-zone is composed of Pliocene-Anthropogenous deposits with xenoliths of the Eocene flysch in several areas. On the surface, the sub-zone consists of a chain of echelon-like brachy-anticlines wherein the northern wings overthrusted on the southern wings with overlapping amplitude up to 1.5-2.0 kilometres. In the west, on the territory of Georgia, the amplitude of overthrusting sharply increases with a formation of allochthonous flakes occurring in the basement of tectonic cover of Kakhetia. The latter overthrusted on the northern flank of the Upper Kura trough as a result of the Shtir, Attick and Rodan phases of folding during the Miocene-Middle Pliocene.

(ii)   *The Chatma-Adjinour sub-zone* is composed of the Oligocene-Pliocene molasses and has a complicated scaly-overthrusting structure in combination with sharp, overturned to the south anticlines and gentle overthrusts formed during the Valakh phase of folding in the Late Pliocene-Early Pleistocene. The amplitude of overthrusted transformations varies from a range of 25-20 kilometres on the west to a range of 6-10 kilometres on the east of the sub-zone.

(iii)   *The Geyranchel sub-zone* is located on the west of the Middle Kura trough being separated from the above Chatma sub-zone by the Eriktar zone of overthrusts and composed of the Upper Pliocene-Quaternary deposits. The sub-zone incorporates three anticlinoria developed on the background of a regional subsidence.

(iv)   *The Fore-Lesser Caucasian foredeep* is limited in the northeast and southwest by the Kura and Fore-Lesser Caucasian buried faults respectively and filled by molasse formations of the Paleogene and Neogene-Anthropogene. While the Pliocene-Quaternary deposits have experienced gentle and quiet subsidence, the underlying Paleogene-Mesozoic formations have been subjected to the brachy-anticlinal uplifting.

The Lower Kura trough is separated from the Middle Kura depression by the western Caspian submeridional fault spatially conciding with the Talysh-Vandam Mesozoic uplift (figures 2 and 3). The roof of Cretaceous formations occurs at a depth from 3,000 to 3,500 metres and the Pre-Jurassic basement has been traced at an approximate depth of 9,000 metres. The thickness of the Meso-Cenozoic stratigraphic sequence within the Lower Kura trough has increased remarkably towards the Caspian coast where a half of a total thickness from 16 to 20 kilometres belongs to the Pliocene-Quaternary formations. On the northeast, the Lower Kura trough is limited by the Lengebiz-Alyat zone of uplifts, being in turn fringed by the Adjichay-Alyat overthrust.

The transversal cross-section of the trough indicates some anticlinal and synclinal structures overlain by the recent detrital sediments. The density of tectonics in the trough tends to increase with a depth. The anticlinoria are complicated by extended upthrust-overthrusts.

(c)   Mountain-folded system of the Lesser Caucasus

The mountain-folded system of the Lesser Caucasus represents a zone of collisional jointing of the Transcaucasian and South Azerbaijanian (Iranian) plates, formed in the process of subduction of the oceanic crust of the Lesser Caucasian arc of Mesotethys (Khain, 1984; Geology of the USSR, 1972; Karyakin, 1989; Hasanov, 1985, 1996; Knipper, 1975). The continental plates are separated by the Girratag tectonic suture spatially conciding in the modern geological structure with the northern Zangezur deep-water trench. At the beginning of Late Cretaceous, the edges of converging plates have formed the northern Amasia-Geychy-Hakera and the southern Vedi melange zones. The latter is located on the territory of Armenia.

The Artwin-Garabag uplift represents the southern structural flank of the Transcaucasian plate spartially corresponding to the northern ridges of the Lesser Caucasus. The uplift has developed during the Alpine stage of tectono-genesis in the geodynamic regime of volcanic island arc. In the southeast, the uplift's structures have subsided under the Oligocene-Quaternary deposits of the Lower Aras superimposed north-east-trending trough. The latter has transformed into the Kura intermountain depression. In the west, the uplift's structures are traced in the northern part of Armenia, the south of Georgia and on the territory of Turkey in the Artwin ranges of the Eastern Pontian mountains.

Southwards, the Artwin-Garabag uplift incorporates three major structural sub-zones described below:

(i)   *The Somkhit-Agdam sub-zone* represents a complex echelon-like fold-block structure consisting of a number of relatively simple anticlinoria and synclinoria. The antichinoria are Shamknor, Gey-gel, Murovdag and Agdam, and the synclinoria are Guzukh, Dashkesan, Agdjakend and

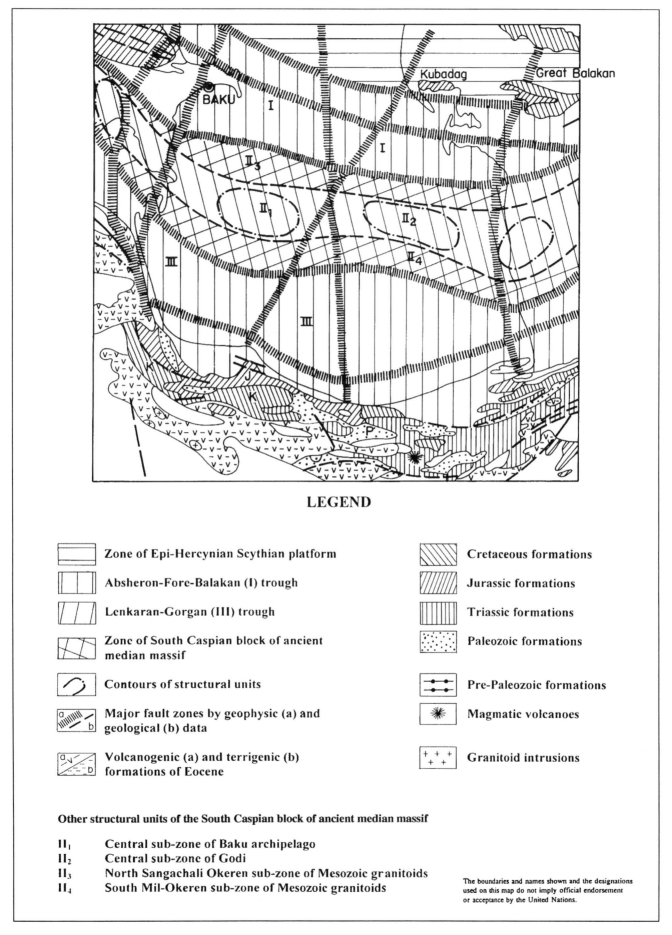

LEGEND

Zone of Epi-Hercynian Scythian platform		Cretaceous formations	
Absheron-Fore-Balakan (I) trough		Jurassic formations	
Lenkaran-Gorgan (III) trough		Triassic formations	
Zone of South Caspian block of ancient median massif		Paleozoic formations	
Contours of structural units		Pre-Paleozoic formations	
Major fault zones by geophysic (a) and geological (b) data		Magmatic volcanoes	
Volcanogenic (a) and terrigenic (b) formations of Eocene		Granitoid intrusions	

Other structural units of the South Caspian block of ancient median massif

II_1 Central sub-zone of Baku archipelago
II_2 Central sub-zone of Godi
II_3 North Sangachali Okeren sub-zone of Mesozoic granitoids
II_4 South Mil-Okeren sub-zone of Mesozoic granitoids

The boundaries and names shown and the designations used on this map do not imply official endorsement or acceptance by the United Nations.

Figure 3. Schematic tectonic setting of Mesozoic-Eocene formations in the South Caspian depression

Agdara. The tectonic structures are composed of Mesozoic volcanogenic and sedimentary-volcanogenic formations. The sub-zone gradually rises along the strike in a northwestern direction where the rocks of basement are outcropped in the erosional windows at the surface. The northern part of the sub-zone has monoclinaly subsided under the Cenozoic deposits of the Fore-Lesser Caucasian trough. The southwestern segment of the sub-zone, complicated by an overturned folding on the south, overlays the formations of the Geychay-Garabag sub-zone along the Murovdag overthrust.

(ii)   *The Geychay-Garabag sub-zone* is composed mainly of the Jurassic and Cretaceous (Albian-Upper Senonian) sedimentary-volcanogenic formations assembled in relatively simple compressed folds. Southwards, the transversal cross-section sequentially delimits the Touragachay and Khodjavend synclinal structures, Garabag uplift and Saribaba trough. The contacts between these structural units are tectonic. The southwestern boundary of the sub-zone is limited by the Lahyn-Bashlibel abyssal fault.

The distinguishing feature of the sub-zone structure is the development of the extended Amasia-Geychay-Hakera allochthonous ophiolite belt forming the tectonically-complex covers within its southwestern segment. The tectonic covers are overthrusted within the Touragachay and Saribaba structures and are underlied by the rocks of a thick olistostrome series, composed mainly of erosional rocks of the ophiolite association. The time of formation of the tectonic covers extends from the Late Senomanian to the Early Santonian. The neo-autochthone sedimentary-volcanogenic formations of the Late Santoniam-Eocene equalize the structural plan of autochthone and allochthonous flakes.

(iii)   *The Gafan sub-zone* is composed of sedimentary-volcanogenic and volcanogenic formations of the Jurassic, Cretaceous and Paleogene, followed by volcanogenic and continental formations of the Neogene-Anthropogene. The northeastern flank of the sub-zone is complicated by the underlying of each other Lachyn and Starotag anticlinal uplifts being separated by the narrow Khuzabirt synclinorium. A wide Gochaz trough occupies the central area of the sub-zone being overlapped on the northwest by the Kelbadjar superimposed trough filled by the Eocene-Anthropogenous deposits. The extreme southwestern structural unit of the sub-zone is the Gafan dome-folded uplift. All these sub-zones are complicated by folding and tectonic faults.

The Aras tectonic zone or micro plate is isolated in the southwest from the above Gafan sub-zone by the Girratag fault. The Upper Jurassic-Cretaceous formations of the Gafan sub-zone are overthrusted along the Girratag fault in the south by the Devonian and Permian deposits, as well as by the Early Devonian volcanic rocks and the Eocene granitoids. A zone of overthrust is being marked by flows of ophiolite melange of the Zangezur ophiolite zone being traced on the north-west in the areas of the Geicha lake and Barum ridge, where it transfers into the ophiolites of the Amasia-Geycha-Hakera zone and is being observed as the continuing ophiolite belt on the territory of Turkey.

The following structural units have been distinguished within the Aras tectonic zone to the southwest from the Girratag fault:

(i)   *The Miskhana-Zangezur sub-zone* represents a narrow horst-uplift, the most part of which is located on the territory of Armenia. The metamorphic rocks of the Pre-Cambrian crystalline basement are exposed in the Miskhana, Nyuvedi, and Garadag (in the Islamic Republic of Iran) massifs and are transgressively overlain by the Devonian formations, carbonaceous formations of the Upper Cretaceous and the Eocene volcanogenic formations. Within the Nakhchivan part of Azerbaijan, the uplift is represented by the southwestern monoclinal subsiding wing composed of the Upper Cretaceous and Eocene formations and being complicated by two anticlinal folds. The above stratigraphic sequence has been intruded by the largest on the Lesser Caucasus Megri-Ordubad granitoid batholith of the Eocene-Miocene age and smaller intrusive granitoid bodies. In the southwest, the sub-zone is limited by the Ordubad abyssal fault.

(ii)   *The Ordubad sub-zone* represents a reef-related trough originated in the Early Jurassic on the southwestern segment of the Miskhana-Zangezur uplift. The sub-zone underwent periods of active volcanic activity in the Early Jurassic, Early Cretaceous and Eocene-Oligocene, alternating with the periods of quiet sub-aerial sedimentation. Linear folding of Pre-Miocene age complicated by the Miocene-Pliocene folding of near-latitudinal direction is typical to this zone. In the southwest, the sub-zone is limited by the Aznabyurt-Nekhram abyssal fault.

(iii)   *The Sharur-Djulfa sub-zone* in the Nakhchivan part of Azerbaijan contains the northwestern (Sharur) and the southeastern (Djulfa) structural units separated by the young Nakhchivan superimposed trough. Submarine sedimentary deposits of the Devonian-Triassic age represent a platform cover of the northern shelf of the Gondwana. The Devonian-Triassic sequence is followed by the Middle-Upper Jurassic stratigraphic interval of minor thickness. The tectonic structure of the sub-zone is rather complex, being characterized by superposition of folded structures of variable order, age and strike as well as by a wide development of tectonic faults and fractures and associated plicated dislocations.

(iv)   *The Nakhchivan superimposed trough* originated as an independent structure at the end of the Oligocene-Early Miocene, and developed in lagoonal conditions with accumulations of variegated clays and evaporites. The sub-zone is characterized by folding with development of dome-shaped and brachiophore uplifts of variable limbs adjusting to the contours of the depression. The origin and development of the Nakhchivan superimposed trough is being associated with movements along the abyssal fault in the northeastern area of the trough.

(d)   Zone of the Talysh mountain

The zone of the Talysh mountain represents a zone of the lateral transition from the mountain-folded system of the Iranian Elburs to the Lower Kura depression. The zone represents a paleo-reef superimposed on the Cretaceous volcanic island arc of the southern flank of the Transcaucasian tectonic plate. The Talysh tectonic zone is mostly composed of the Middle and Upper Eocene subalkaline and alkaline volcanites of andesite-basalt composition. The underlying Paleocene-Lower Eocene tuffogenous flysch and the Danian limestones are exposed in the south of the zone northward. The folding system of the Talysh mountain incorporates the following structural units (Azizbekov and others, 1979): (a) the Astara uplift composed of the Cretaceous-Paleocene formations; (b) the Kosmolyan-Lerik trough containing the Eocene sequence; (c) the Burovar uplift composed of the Upper Eocene formation being cut in the north-east by the Pre-Talysh abyssal fault; (d) the Biyasuvar trough filled by molasse of the Middle and the Upper Miocene; and (e) the South Mugan uplift subsided under modern detrital deposits. These structural units are characterized by a moderately-compressed folding, complicated in the northeast by thrusts towards the Lower Kura depression.

(e)   South Caspian depression

The Caspian depression mainly belongs to the superimposed structures of the Earth crust, which appeared during the orogenic stage of development of the Alpian folding area (Geology of the USSR, 1972). The South Caspian depression belongs to the system of the Kura and Transcaspian intermountain troughs being separated from the Middle Caspian depression by the uplift of the Absheron trough (figure 3).

The Fore-Elburs trough in the Islamic Republic of Iran limits the South Caspian depression from the south. According to the geophysical data, the thickness of the Earth crust within the depression varies in sublatitudinal direction from the maximum thickness of 40-45 kilometres in the southern and northern parts of the depression to a range of 30-40 kilometres in its central part. The depression represents a transition lateral zone between the Kura and Transcaspian intermountain troughs. The Alpian sedimentary cover reaching a thickness of up to 20 kilometres, consists of the Mesozoic-Eocene and Oligocene-Holocene formations. The Oligocene-Holocene stratigraphic interval of sandy-clayey composition includes three zones of variable thickness and extent caused by regional tectonics and ancient and young folding. These zones and the deposits were accompanied by the formation of the volcanic Baku archipelago and zones of lateral and latitudinal folding. Some anticlines within the South Caspian depression are associated with inherited uplifts, and sedimentary and diapiric faults are associated with ruptures and occurrences of mud volcanism.

According to the geophysical data, three major structural units have been distinguished within the buried Mesozoic-Eocene formations southwards: the Absheron-Pre-Balakhan trough, South Caspian uplift and Lenkaran-Gorgan trough (figure 3). The Absheron-Pre-Balakhan trough is considered to be the southeastern continuation of the trough of the southern slope of the Greater Caucasus corresponding to the Mesozoic reefogenous marginal marine basin between the Scythian platform and Transcaucasian plate. The uplift of the South Caspian depression is the marine continuation of the Transcaucasian plate being tectonically complicated in the north and south by the Sangachali-Okurch and Mil-Okeren zones of intensive magmatic activity respectively. These zones represent axial parts of buried extensions of the Balakhan-Vandam and Artwin-Garabag island arc uplifts. The Lenkoran-Gurgan trough reflects the location of tectonically-overlapped formations of the Lesser Caucasian branch of the Mesotethys from the north and south.

B. Geodynamic development of Azerbaijan

The description of the regional geodynamic development of Azerbaijan during the Alpine tectono-magmatic cycle is based on the concept of new global tectonics or the mobilists' concept which provides a new interpretation of the foundation of the Earth crust (Adamiya, and Shavishviti, 1979; Geology of Azerbaijan, 1997; Hasanov, 1985, 1996; Kangarly, 1982; Yusufova and Zamanov, 1998). According to this concept, the Meso-Cenozoic history of the Mediterranean fold belt has passed through the oceanic, transition and continental stages.

1. Oceanic stage (Late Triassic-Late Aalenian)

The southern Azerbaijan massif represented a passive continental margin of the Gondwana of the Atlantic type at the end of the Hercynian cycle of tectono-genesis (Carboniferous-Early Triassic). The accumulation of terrigenous-carbonaceous deposits was accompanied by the formation of volcanic belts of the Andian type on the southern margin of Eurasia including the Transcaucasian tectonic plate. The Early Kimmerian collision of the Gondwana's fragments from the northern platform at the end of the Triassic has resulted in the closure of the Paleotethys and low marginal seas in the Transcaucasus. Simultaneously, the Mesotethys has opened in the south as a result of the Gondwana's shelf collapse and a sequential separation of the southern Azerbaijan micro-continent. Later on, the Mesotethys was developed in conditions of extension and spreading of the oceanic crust.

In the Early Jurassic, the process of extension and rifting during the ancient Kimmerian phase of tectono-genesis has extended to the southern continental margin of Eurasia. The foundation of the Greater Caucasian basin in the north was accompanied by destruction and alternation of continental crust, manifestations of tholeiite-basalt magmatism in the axial part of the trough and outflows of the calc-alkaline magma in the offshore and continental areas of the northern Caucasian and Transcaucasian plates.

In the south, the process of riftogenesis was accompanied by an intensive basaltic magmatism and led to a separation of the southern Azerbaijanian micro-continent from the continental margin and the opening of the Lesser Caucasian offset of the Mezotethys. Simultaneously, the Jurassic-Neocomian formations of effusive-radiolarite series have accumulated on the oceanic bed of the Mezotethys. The south-western margin of the southern Azerbaijanian micro-continent has moved to the south entering into the regime of active continental margin of the Andian type with an intensive volcanism. The volcanism has indicated the generation of the subduction zone being accompanied by the subsidence of the oceanic crust of the main oceanic basin northward under this continental plate.

During the Lias-Aalenian stage of tectono-genesis, a vast sedimentary basin of the marginal sea type has been formed on the site of the Greater Caucasus as a result of a separation of the Transcaucasian and the northern Caucasian plates. In the axial rift depression of the sedimentary basin with suboceanic crust, the magmatism has been pronounced through outflows of calc-alkaline magma of the basalt-andesite-dacite-rhyolite association and injection of small intrusions of gabbro-diorite composition. The marginal sea has separated from the Lesser Caucasian oceanic basin partly flooded by water of the Transcaucasian plate with non-volcanic island arc on its southwestern segment.

2. Transition stage (the end of Aalenian-Miocene)

At the end of the above oceanic stage, the geodynamic setting was characterized by a prevalence of uneven and fragmental tectonic clustering being accompanied by the formation of secondary spreading zones. The transition stage on the Caucasus includes (a) the pre-collision epoch of generation and development of island arcs continued until the Middle Cretaceous and (b) collision epoch of closure of oceanic basins and collision of continental plates.

The beginning of the transition stage of the Alpian tectono-genesis is signified by the radical change of geodynamic setting at the end of the Aalenian-beginning of the Bajocian. The extension forces in the northern part of the Tethys have been replaced by the lateral compression along the south flank of Eurasia apparently associated with a continious non-reimbursable extension of the Lesser Caucasian oceanic basin. The start of a mechanism of intercontinental accretion within the limits of marginal continental sea indicated the beginning of reapproachment of the Transcaucasian and northern Caucasian plates and the underthrust of suboceanic crust under the northern continental margin. The clustering of sedimentary material continued in the northern part of the Early Jurassic trough and on the southern flank of the North Caucasian plate during the Pre-Bajocian sub-stage of tectono-genesis. The non-volcanic island arc divided the marginal sea into a deep water southern trough and shallow water basin on the north.

The accumulation of reef limestones along the southern flank of the Transcaucasian plate in the Late Jurassic has been accompanied by a weak subduction limestone-alkaline volcanism with a maximum intensity during the Kimmeridge period. The Lesser Caucasian oceanic basin in the Late Jurassic and beginning of the Cretaceous has been continuously expanding while the southern Azerbaijanian micro-continent was flooded by a shallow sea.

The Late Kimmerian tectonic activization at the end of Jurassic-beginning of the Cretaceous promoted the intensification of blocks' clustering of the Earth crust. The process of subduction was followed by outflows of andesite-basalt magma in the Upper Cretaceous in the front and injection of numerous granitoid intrusions in the Jurassic volcanic back-arc of the Lesser Caucasus under the conditions of carbonaceous sedimentation. The strengthening of tangential compression on the north was followed by the rising and draining of barrier reefs in the southern wing of the northern Caucasian plate and non-compensate warping of substrate of marginal sea. The detrital material of non-volcanic island arc was supplied both to the northern neritic zone and in the southern direction where the accumulation of a "wild" flysch on the continental slope occurred.

The beginning of a collision epoch is reflected in the structural reconstruction during the Austrian phase of tectono-genesis on the boundary of Lower and Upper Cretaceous when the first signs of common compression appeared. The latter has resulted in spontaneous tectonic activization along the jointing underthrust of the Transcaucasian and northern Caucasian plates. During the Aptian stage, the tectonic activization has been accompanied by lateral reduction of the Pre-Mesozoic substrate and formation of powerful shearing stress along the line of the northern barrier reef. The tectonic reconstruction has resulted in overthrusting of the

Malm-Neocomian carbonaceous beds and their displacement from the margin of the continental shelf to the south with allochthonous overlapping of "wild" flysch of the continental slope of the marginal sea. In the Middle Senonian-Early Santonian, the process of spreading within the Lesser Caucasian oceanic basin discontinued. The convergence of the Caucasian continental margin with the southern Azerbaijanian micro-continent has completed by a closure of the Lesser Caucasian offset of the Mesotethys. The migration of the micro-continent to the north towards paleo-island arc of the southern segment of the Transcaucasian plate has been accompanied by a bi-polar overthrust of ophiolite covers from the axial part of the basin within both continental plates, which was completed in the Early Santonian. In the middle of the Senonian stage of tectono-genesis, the Earth crust of the Lesser Caucasus represented a gigantic tectonic "breccia" consisting of the fragments of pre-collision structures.

In the Albian-Senonian, the island arc volcanism was observed along the whole territory of the Transcaucasian plate. While volcanic manifestations of andesite-liparite composition dominated in the southern and central parts of the plate, the volcanism of sub-alkaline-basic composition developed the northern sector of the plate in the Balakhan-Vandam tectonic zone. Magmatism of tectonically-overlapped northern wing of the Balakhan-Vandam tectonic zone has been earmarked by the transition of small sub-alkaline intrusions to the allochthonous Lower-Middle Jurassic shales of the south flank of the marginal sea. The shales have been overthrusted southward in the process of the Bajocian-Bathonian period of intercontinental accretion.

The similar sequence of events occurred within the basic oceanic basin of the Mesotethys where the phase of cover folding was completed in the Maastrichtian; the collision between the Aravian margin of the southern continent and the southern Azerbaijanian micro-continent, however, was continued, judging by the involvement of the Miocene sediments in the ophiolite melange.

In the Late Senonian-Middle Oligocene, spatially-disconnected zones of compression and extension of the same age have been formed under conditions of rotatory movement of fragments of paleo-structures against the background of convergence of the Aravian-African and Euro-Asia continents. These zones have been observed in the eastern part of the Lesser Caucasus by the superimposed and volcanically-active Gochaz, Gadrug and Aldjalin rift troughs in the Late Senonian, as well as the Ordubad and Talysch troughs in Paleogene. A slight differentiation of composition of volcanic rocks in the above troughs from calc-alkaline to alkaline has been likely caused by a composition and thickness of the underlying Earth crust. The riftogenesis in the Ordubad trough was completed by the formation of the Megri-Ordubad granitoid batholith and its smaller intrusions.

In the northern margin of the Transcaucasian plate, a volcanism of trachy-basalt and andesite-basalt composition was pronounced in the Late Senonian. The volcanism is apparently confined to subsidence calderas of volcanoes of central type. Magmatic activity of the latter was completed by injecting the Paleogene intrusions of syenite-diorite composition.

The basic structures of the Lesser Caucasus with the formation of vast onshore areas have been formed as a result of the Late Eocene-Oligocene diastrophism. In the Late Oligocene-Early and Middle Miocene, the onshore areas were intensively washed out under the conditions of reduced tectonic activity, thus supplying terrigenous material in the northern and southern directions.

The period of secondary extension on the Lesser Caucasus at the turn of the Early and Late Senonian has triggered an activization of a mechanism of inner-continental accretion. The formation of compression zones within the Upper Cretaceous basin of the Greater Caucasus has been developed under the influence of reinforced underthrusting of the Transcaucasian plate under the northern Caucasian margin of the Scythian platform. As a result of the underthrusting, the Upper Jurassic-Cretaceous flysch complex of the trough of the marginal sea has been moved away from its Middle-Jurassic plastic basement and overthrusted on the Early Senonian formations of the northern flank of the Transcaucasian plate. In the west, the overthrusting has also involved the underlying Lower-Middle Jurassic formations. The same process has been developing along the northern flank of the flysch trough where the Early Senonian deposits have been tectonically overlaid by the Upper Jurassic-Cretaceous complex of continental slope of the northern Caucasian plate. The transition period from the Cretaceous to Paleogene is signified by shoaling of the Greater Causcasian basin. The subsequent period of the transition stage of development in the same region is characterized by weak and moderate tectonic movements.

3. Continental stage (Late Miocene-Quaternary)

From the end of Miocene, the region enters into the new orogenic stage of development being dominated by vertical movements of the blocks of the Earth crust under the influence of the Aravian wedge intruding in the northern direction.

In the Lesser Caucasus, the orogenic process of mountain formation and folding was followed by an active sub-aerial volcanism and formation of volcanic-plutonic complexes in the Miocene-Early Pliocene-Holocene time. The chemistry of magma of strato-volcanoes was transformed from the calc-alkaline to the alkaline composition during that time. The growing uplifts of the Lesser Caucasus and the Talysh mountain have been fringed and separated by the superimposed Nakhchivan, Lower Aras and Kura southern Caspian amagmatic troughs originated during the Late Oligocene-Early Miocene time. The intensive activization of tangential compression at the beginning of the continental stage of development (Shtir and Attick phases of tectono-genesis) resulted in the secondary overthrusting of deposits of the rest of the marginal marine basin southward. A multi-stage complex of allochthonous flaky sheets overlying the Oligocene-Miocene formations of the northern flank of the Transcaucasian plate has been developed. A follow-up migration of impulses of deformation southwards caused the formation of cover-overthrust structures in the Cenozoic deposits of the northern wing of the Transcaucasian plate through the south-eastern submergence of the Balakhan-Vandam uplift and the northern flank of the Kura trough during the Rodan and Valakh phases of tectono-genesis. The general tangential compression setting was completed by mountain-building and shifting of a prism of the central uplift of the Greater Caucasus along the young subvertical faults and formations of compensate troughs on its northern and southern peripheries.

C. Stratigraphy

The description of stratigraphy and lithology of Azerbaijan is based on long-standing extensive geological field research and investigations, which have been carried out by Azerbaijanian and other geologists over the past four decades, (Ali-zade and others, 1978; Azizbekov and others, 1979; Geology of Azerbaijan, 1997; Geology of Azerbaijan, 1998; Geology of the USSR, 1972; Agayev, 1990; Azizbekov, 1961; Hasanov, 1967, 1973; Khalilov, 1978; Shikhalibeyli, 1956, 1966; Shikhalibeyli and others, 1984).

The stratigraphic evolution of Azerbaijan has a long history. The exposed rocks in the country cover practically the entire stratigraphic succession from the Precambrian to the Recent. The oldest group of rocks constitutes the Proterozoic crystalline basement, which is overlain by alternating sequences of classic and carbonate lithologies of the Upper Proterozoic, Palaeozoic, Mesozoic and Cainozoic systems. The Upper Proterozoic and Palaeozoic stratigraphic intervals are represented mainly by marine sedimentation. The Mezo-Cainozoic sequences are dominated by continental clastic sediments. These contain in places significant volcanic components in the Proterozoic and younger rock formations. The majority of stratigraphic intervals have been proved paleontologically. Considerable lithofacial changes within some stratum are determined by substantial conditions of their formation.

1. Precambrian – Cambrian

The Baikalian crystalline basement crops out within the territory of Azerbaijan in the core of the Shamknor uplift of the Somkhit-Agdam sub-zone of the Lesser Caucasus. The sequence of metamorphic schists in the Asrikchay river basin has been found to be similar to the fauna-proved Precambrian and Lower-Middle Cambrian formations of the Dzirul massif in the neighbouring Georgia. Upwards, the section consists of crystalline schists followed by phyllites containing thin interlayers of quartzose sandstones and lens-shaped interbeds of marbles. The above stratigraphic section of 170 metres thick is transgressively overlaid by basal conglomerates, sandstones and tuffites of the Hettangian and Sinemurian stages of the Lower Jurassic age. The Pazmarin metamorphic complex and associated magmatic rocks have been delineated within the Zangezur horst-uplift of the Aras tectonic zone. The metamorphic rocks have been found to be enclosed in the body of the Megri-Ordubad batholith and re-presented by gneiss-shales, amphibolites, metabasites and metakeratophyres. Boulders and blocks of Precambrian mylonites, gneiss-schists and double-mica gneisses have been also observed in tectonic breccia and conglomerates of the Upper Jurassic on the southern slope of the Greater Caucasus.

Metamorphic rocks of Azerbaijan are well correlated with the Precambrian metamorphic formations of the Western Transcaucasus of southern Azerbaijan and the eastern part of the Islamic Republic of Iran.

2. Palaeozoic

The distribution of the Palaeozoic formations on the territory of Azerbaijan is rather limited and mainly confined to the Sharur-Djulfa sub-zone of the Aras tectonic zone. Two isolated outcrops of volcanomictic rocks of Middle-Upper Carboniferous have been also mapped on the northern slope of the Lesser Caucasus within the Shamkir uplift of the Somkhit-Agdam sub-zone. Deep drilling in the extreme northeast of Azerbaijan has identified quartz plagioporphyres of the Permian-Triassic age at a depth of 4,700 metres in the part of pericratonal subsidence of the Scythian platform.

(a) Ordovician system

The Ordovician sequence within the Sharur-Djulfa uplift is represented by an alternation of black coaly and graphitized limestones, clayey shales, calcereous-siliceous and quartzose sandstones and quarzite-sandstones with a total thickness of 1,414 metres. The sequence is overlaid by fauna-proved formations of the Middle Devonian. The Ordovician cross-section is well correlated with corresponding deposits of southern Azerbaijan and Turkey.

(b) Devonian system

The Devonian deposits overlie the formations of the Ordovician age disconcordantly and contain only the middle and upper sections. The stratigraphic interval of 2,200 metres thick is subdivided into the Eifelian, Givetian (Middle Devonian), Franskian and Famenian stages of geological evolution. The sedimentary rocks of the *Eifelian stage* are represented by dark-grey crystalline limestones interbedded by pelitomorphous, breccia-like oolitic, shaly and sandy limestone, quartzose sandstones, quarzite-sandstones, quarzite and coaly calcereous argillites. The sequence of the *Givetian stage* is composed of the rocks of the Sadarak and the upper Danzik series. The Sadarak series includes the crystalline organic-rich limestones interbedded by breccia-like shaly and sandy limestones, clayey and marly shales, calcareous quartzite-sandstones and quartzites. The Danzik series is represented by quartzose sandstones, quartzite-sandstones, quartzites and calcereous dolomites. The *Franskian stage* of sedimentation is characterized by alternation of marly and clayey shales with crystalline pelitomorphic, breccia-like, shaly and sandy limestones, quartzite-sandstones, quartzites and phathanites. The *Famenian stage* of development is represented by alternation of organic crystalline and sandy limestones and bituminous clayey shales with interbeds of oolitic and shaly limestones.

(c) Carboniferous system

The Carboniferous system is represented by its lower section, which consists of the Turnaisian and Viseian stages of development with a total thickness 450 metres. *The Turnaisian stage* of sedimentation includes the Etrensky, Lower and Upper Turnaisian stratigraphic intervals consisting of alternating brecciated, sandy and pelitomorphic limestones, clayey shales and quarzites. The *Viseian stage* is represented by alternation of brecciated organic and siliceus limestones.

(d)   Permian system

The formations of the Permian system overlie disconcordantly sedimentary rocks of the Carboniferous system, being represented by its lower and upper sections with a total thickness 550 metres. The distribution of the Permian rocks is rather limited. *The Lower Permian* stratigraphic interval incorporates rocks of the Sakmarian and Artinsky stages of development composed of massive and foliated crystalline, pelitomorphic, dolomitic, sandy and clayey-bituminous varieties of limestones. *The Upper Permain* section is subdivided into the Guadelupian and Gilfian stages of sedimentation composed of clayey, siliceous-bituminous and shaly limestones and sandy shales. The upper most section is dominated by sandy limestones interbedded by calcereous conglomerates, dolomitic limestones and dolomites.

3. Mesozoic

(a)   Triassic system

The Permian period was completed in the Caucasus region by a total regression. However, the sea and marine conditions of sedimentation have been retained in separate mostly subsided areas including the Aras tectonic zone, where the transition from the Permian to the Triassic is quite gradual. The total thickness of the Triassic formations in the Sharur-Djulfa sub-zone reaches a range of 1,500-1,600 metres. The Triassic stratigraphic interval is subdivided into the lower, middle and upper sections. The Triassic sequence is overlaid by the Jurassic and more younger formations with a hiatus. *The Lower Triassic* is represented by the Indsky and Olenekian stages of sedimentation composed of alternation of marly, clayey, sandy, oolitic and dolomitic varieties of limestones. *The Middle Triassic* interval includes the Anisian and Ladinian stages of sedimentation consisting of alternation of marly and clayey limestones. The limestone section on the top of this sequence has been replaced by pelitomorphic and crystalline dolomites with injections of diabases and diabase porphyrites. *The Upper Triassic* section is represented by the Norian stage of development composed of alternation of micaceous argillites with bands of quartzose sandstones, sandy argillites and carbonaceous shales.

(b)   Jurassic system

The beginning of the Jurassic period opened a new stage in the development of the eastern part of Caucasus, where erosion cropped out various horizons of the Jurassic section overlying disconcordantly the underlying formations of variable age including those of the Lower Palaeozoic.

The Jurassic deposits play a substantial role in the formation of all structural elements of the Greater and Lesser Caucasus. According to the results of deep drilling, a thick Jurassic sequence is known to exist within the Kura intermontane trough, where they are traced under the molasse formation. The Jurassic formations reach a considerable thickness in all major structural units of the Greater and Lesser Causasus being represented in various combinations of sedimentary and volcanogenic rocks. These deposits are intensively metamorphozed, crumpled into folds, fractured by faults, cleavaged and dissected by numerous intrusions and their derivatives of basic, intermediate and acid composition. The description of the Jurassic succession is given along major tectono-structural units of Azerbaijan.

(i)   The Greater Caucasus

The accessible sections of the Lower Jurassic incorporate the formations of the Sinemurian, Pliensbachian and Toarcian series of sedimentation which are outcropped within uplifted north-western blocks of the Azerbaijanian part of region. The sequence is represented by alternation of bands of phyllitic and clayey shales, sandstones and aleurolites in combination with volcanogenic rocks of the spilite-diabase formation. The latter are represented by horizons of pillow lava, sills and dykes. The total thickness of the Lower Jurassic rocks is 3,400 metres.

The Middle Jurassic formations concordantly overlie the rocks of the Lower Jurassic in the watershed and wide areas of the northern slope of the Greater Caucasus range. In the southeast, the Middle Jurassic rocks have subsided under younger formations not reaching the Caspian coast. The Middle Jurassic succession includes the formations of all suites of the Aalenian stage as well as those of the Bajocian and Bathonian stages. The lower section of the Middle Jurassic stratigraphic interval is dominated by shaly argillites and clayey shales saturated by concretions and lenses of clayey siderite and interbeds, horizons and bands of sandstones and aleurolites. The upper part of this stratigraphic interval represents a terrigenous flysch, expressed by a rhythmic alternation of sandstones, aleurolites and argillites. The total thickness of the Middle Jurassic rocks outcropped in the surface reaches 3,500-3,700 metres. The above Jurassic rocks have been traced by drilling at various depths along the Caspian coast in the Kusary-Devechy trough, where they disconcordantly overlie volcanogenic rocks of the Permian-Triassic age. The latter is being corresponded to the epi-platform complex of the southern flank of the Scythian platform. The volcanogenic facies of the Bajocian stage, known as a porphyrite suite, have been mapped along the foothill of the southern slope of the Greater Caucasus within the Balakan-Vandam tectonic zone corresponding to the northern flank of the Transcaucasian plate. The suite consists of porphyrite tuff-breccia and tuff-sandstones with a thickness from 80 to 100 metres.

The Upper Jurassic rocks concordantly overlie the above Middle Jurassic succession in the watershed part and on the southern slope of the Greater Caucasus. The cross-section represents a terrigenous and terrigenous-carbonaceous flysch with a total thickness from 1,200 to 1,300 metres. On the northern slope of the Side Range in the Sudur sub-zone, the Upper Jurassic rocks overlie disconcordantly the eroded surface of the Aalenian stage of sedimentation. The latter is represented on the base by subcontinental sulphate-terrigenous rocks of 120 to 200 metres thick overlaid by organic-rich reef limestones of carbonaceous formation of continental shelf. The thickness of limestones varies from 150 to 900 metres.

Southwards, in the Shakhdag-Khizi sub-zone, the Upper Jurassic succession is represented by the lithofacies of continental slope; the terrigenous flysch consists of rythmic alternation of conglomerates, gritstones, sandstones and argillites disconcordantly overlying the Middle Jurassic sequence. The total thickness of the Upper Jurassic stratigraphic interval reaches 1,000 metres.

According to the data of deep drilling, the Upper Jurassic interval is missing within the Kusary-Devechi trough, where younger formations disconcordantly overlie the Middle Jurassic rocks.

(ii) Kura trough

The Jurassic cross-section of the Kura trough has been studied based on the materials of a deep drilling in the Saatly and Djarli areas. The Middle Jurassic (Bajocian-Bathonian) sequence is composed of volcanogenic rocks of andesite-basalt composition interbedded by inlayers of terrigenous rocks. The thickness reaches 4,700 metres. The Upper Jurassic succession is represented by carbonaceous complex genetically related to the reef sedimentation of open basin. The thickness of the Upper Jurassic interval in the Kura trough varies from 670 to 700 metres.

(iii) The Lesser Caucasus

The accessible cross-section of the Jurassic deposits within the Lesser Caucasus consists of the rocks of terrigenous-tuffaceous, volcanogenic-sedimentary and carbonaceous facies. The disribution of the Lower Jurassic formations is limited by small outcrops in the Somkhit-Agdam sub-zone and in the Djulfa uplift of the Aras tectonic zone on the northern and southern slopes of the Lesser Caucasus respectively. The Lower Jurassic section in the Somkhit-Agdam sub-zone is represented by all stages and starts with a basal series of quartzose conglomerates and sandstones overlying disconcordantly the Palaeozoic metamorphic schists 3,000 metres thick. The overlying section consists of clayey-sandy shales with interbeds of tuff-sandstones and tuffs with a total thickness of 170 metres. The Nekhram cross-section of the Lower Jurassic succession in the Aras tectonic zone includes flows of basalts, mandelstones and diabase porphyrites of total thickness of 269 metres.

The Middle Jurassic deposits are widely spread over the whole territory of the Lesser Caucasus. The rocks of the Lower Aalenian suite concordantly follow the Tarsky section in the Shamkhir uplift and consist of 120 metres-thick band of sandy-clayey shales interbedded by siliceous sandstones. In the Aras zone, quartzose sandstones and aleurolites with interbeds of limestones, tuffs and tuff-sandstones overlie disconcordantly the basalts of the Lower Jurassic of a total thickness 35 metres. The rocks of the Bajocian suite of the Lesser Caucasus transgressively overlie the deposits of the Lower Aalenian and consist of a complex association of lava and volcanoclastic rocks represented by volcanic breccia, aglomerate tuffs, tuff-breccia, tuff-conglomerates, tuff-sandstones, pyroxene, plagioclase and diabase porphyrites. The upper part of the Bajocian suite is made up of quartzose plagioporphyres and their volcanoclasts. The total thickness exceeds 3,200 metres. In the Aras tectonic zone, the Bajocian suite incorporates sandy limestones, sandstones, sandy and marly clays with a total thickness of up to 220 metres.

The Bathonian cross-section is dominated by effusive-pyroclastic rocks: lava, tuff-conglomerates, tuff-breccia and tuff-sandstones. The topmost part of the section represents an altenation of clays, argillites and sandstones of up to 1,500 metres thick. In the Araz zone, the Bathonian deposits of 50 metres thick overlie concordantly the Upper Bajocian section of interbedded clayey limestones and calcereous clays.

The Upper Jurassic sequence is represented by volcanogenic-sedimentary and carbonaceous lithofacies of the Kellovian, Oxfordian, Kimmeridgian and Tithonian suites. The volcanogenic-sedimentary deposits are composed of porphyrites and their pyroclasts: tuff-sandstones, tuff-breccia and tuff-conglomerates. The interbeds and bands of argillites, sandstones and gritstones are less representative. The rocks of carbonaceous facies are massive organic limestones and dolomites. The total thickness of the Upper Jurassic stratigraphic interval reaches 2,500 metres. In the Aras zone, the Upper Jurassic sandstones of the Kellovian suite of 200 metres thick conformably overlie the rocks of the Bathonian suite.

(c)   Cretaceous system

The Cretaceous deposits are characterized by a substantial lithofacial differentiation, however, separate types of deposits remain facialy unchanged over vast areas and are typical for certain stratigraphic horizons.

Lower Cretaceous

(i)   The Greater Caucasus

The formations of all stages of the Lower Cretaceous stratigraphic interval are widespread over vast areas of the Greater Caucasus. Shallow-marine lithofacies with a primary development of organic and oolitic limestones in the bottom part and sandy-clayey rocks in the upper part of the section are typical to the Sudur sub-zone of the Side Range. The thickness of the limestone section here varies from 500 to 600 metres. The sandy-marly-clayey deposits of the Barremian, Aptian and Albian suites have been transected by drilling in the Kusary-Devechi trough. Southward, in the Shakhdag-Khizi sub-zone, the Lower Cretaceous section of more than 2,200 metres thick is subdivided into carbonaceous-terrigenous flyschoid and substantively clayey series. The cross-section of the Lower Cretaceous starts with basal conglomerate-breccia of the Berriassian suite followed by a chaotic and complex alternation of olistostromes and olistolites of limestones of the Sudur lithofacies. Within the Zakatally-Kovdag-Sumgait sub-zone on the southern slope and southeastern subsidence of the Greater Caucasus, the Lower Cretaceous formations conformably overlie the Upper Jurassic flysch facies with a total thickness exceeding 3,500 metres.

The section is subdivided into three series: (a) terrigenous-carbonaceous flysch (Berrissian-Valanginian), (b) terrigenous-clayey (Hauterivian-Lower Aptian) and (c) carbonaceous-terrigenous flyschoid (Upper Aptian-Albian). In the Balakhan-Vandam tectonic zone, the Berrissian interval of the Lower Cretaceous is also represented by carbonaceous-terrigenous flysch from 1,400 to 1,600 metres thick. Psammolites of the flysch contain tuff material. The Albian sequence from 300 to 650 metres thick, is dominated by flyschoid alternation of argillites, tuff-sandstones, sandstones, siliceous marls, tuffs, tuffites with rare flows of porphyrites and andesites. The role of volcanogenic material in the cross-section is increasing.

(ii)   Kura trough

The Lower Cretaceous volcanogenic-sedimentary section from 1,100 to 1,200 metres thick has been transected by drilling in the interval of the Hauterivian-Aptian suites. The cross-section starts in the base with andesites and hornblende porphyrites, subsequently followed up by the section of alternation of tuffs, tuffites and sandstones of clayey-argillites series with interbeds of sandstones and limestones. The cross-section ends up with a series of tuffs, tuff-aleurolites and tuff-sandstones.

(iii)   Lesser Caucasus

The Lower Cretaceous formations within the Lesser Caucasus are mainly distributed in the Somkhit-Agdam, Geychay-Garabag and Gafan structural sub-zones. The formations are mainly represented by the Berrissian-Barremian carbonaceous and the Aptian-Albian terrigenous-carbonaceous-tuffogenous formational types. The Lower Cretaceous rocks overlie in most areas the Jurassic sequence transgressively, except the internal troughs of the central part of the Lesser Caucasus mountains where the gradual transition from the Tithonian suite of the Jurassic to the Berrissian suite of the Cretaceous is noticeable. In the Somkhit-Agdam and Gafan sub-zones, the Lower Berrissian-Hauterivian suites of the Lower Cretaceous are missing. The thickness of the Lower Cretaceous stratigraphic interval varies in a great extent from a range of 20-318 metres in the northeast through 350-1,534 metres in the central part and to 1,800 metres in the southwest of the Lesser Caucasus mountains.

Carbonaceous rocks are represented by silicified crystalline, sandy and, more rarely, clayey limestones with a mixture of tuffogenous material and inlayers of tuffites and tuf-sandstones. The Barremian-Lower Aptian sequence within the Gafan sub-zone consist of volcanogenic-reef rocks with organic constructions from reefs, bioherm, biostrome and lagoonal facies of reef environment represented by alternation of limestones, marls, argillites and tuff-sandstones. The upper part of the Lower Cretaceous section of the Lesser Caucasus is represented by alternation of tuff-sandstones, tuff-gritstones, tuff-conglomerate-breccia, tuffites, limestones, sandstones, marls, argillites with occasional flows of porphyrites. In the Aras zone, the Lower Cretaceous section is composed of 300 metres thick lava flows of basalts and andesite porphyrites of the Albian age transgressively overlying sandstones of the Cellovian suite.

(b)   Upper Cretaceous

The Upper Cretaceous stratigraphic interval is dominated by carbonate formations caused by the largest sea transgression of the Alpine cycle after a short marine regression at the end of the Early Cretaceous period. The Upper Cretaceous rocks are widely distributed in all structural zones of Azerbaijan and are represented by limestone-marly, terrigenous-carbonaceous flysch and volcanogenic-sedimentary formational types. Purely terrigenous rocks have only been found in the Senomanian base suite of the Upper Cretaceous.

(i)   The Greater Caucasus

The Upper Cretaceous rocks are confined to the same structural zones as the Lower Cretaceous formations. The sedimentation process on the northern slope of the Greater Caucasus range within the Sudur and Shakhdag-

Khizi sub-zones has experienced a long hiatus. As a result, various suites with basal conglomerates in the base overlie the eroded surface of the Lower Cretaceous and even the Upper Jurassic. The terrigenous-carbonaceous and carbonaceous flyschoid section of the Upper Cretaceous on the northern slope is typically represented by alternation of limestones, marls, sandstones and clays. The thickness of the succession is increasing in the sub-latitudinal direction from a range of 50-80 metres on the northwest to a range of 800-1,200 metres on the southeast.

According to the drilling data within the Kusary-Devechi structural zone, the Upper Cretaceous rocks transgressively overlie the formations of the Lower Cretaceous and Middle Jurassic with a maximum total thickness over 1,200 metres.

On the south-eastern submergence and southern slope of the Greater Caucasus range within the Zakataly-Kovdag-Sumgayit sub-zone, the Upper Cretaceous stratigraphic interval is characterized by the prevalence of flysch deposits, the absence of hiatuses and considerable thickness reaching 2,200 metres. The cross-section starts at the base with the terrigenous flysch of the Lower Senomanian consisting of alternation of sandstones and clays. The section is followed upwards by the terrigenous-carbonaceous flysch represented by alternation of sandstones, limestones, marls, clays, aleurolites, rarely gritstones and conglomerates with a presence in separate horizons of interbeds of combustible shales and bentoni clays. Southwards, in the Balakhan-Vandam structural zone, the Upper Cretaceous volcanogenic-sedimentary section starts with the transgressive Senomanian suite composed of tuff-conglomerate-breccia, tuff-sandstones and tuffites interbedded by argillites and clays and rare inlayers of andesite and basalt porphyrites. The following section of the Upper Cretaceous is composed of tuffaceous sandy-clayey flysch represented by alternation of sandstones, tuff-gritstones, argillites, marls, limestones, jaspers, tuffs and tuffites. The total thickness of the Upper Cretaceous section in this zone varies from 1,000 to 1,200 metres.

(ii) Kura trough

The Upper Cretaceous cross-section in the Kura trough transected by a large number of drilling wells is missing some intervals, litholigically variable and composed of volcanogenic, terrigenous-tuffogenous and carbonaceous formational rock types. The lower part of the section is represented by alternation of the Senomanian and Conician tuff-sandstones, limestones, tuffites and clays. The cross-section is followed upwards by volcanogenic series of andesite and andesite-basalt porphyrites, tuff breccia and tuffites replaced by alternation of the Santonian dolomites, sandstones and the Campanian tuff-sandstones and carbonaceous rock series. The section ends up with a 1,000 metres thick series of andesite porphyrites, transforming into tuff-lava with pockets of tuffs. The total thickness of the Upper Cretaceous stratigraphic interval reaches 2,800 metres.

(iii) The Lesser Caucasus

The Upper Cretaceous deposits are widespread in the Lesser Caucasus region and take part in the formation of all structural units, including the Aras tectonic zone. Most of sections are characterized by a continuity and rich paleontological proof of stratigraphic stages, sub-stages and zones. Lithologically, the Upper Cretaceous section is roughly subdivided into mainly volcanogenic type of deposits in the bottom part and carbonaceous type in the top of the section. The boundary between these two sub-sections is being traced between the Lower and Upper Santonian suites.

The Senomanian deposits have mostly developed in central part of the Lesser Caucasus with some remnants in the foothill zone. The section is represented by rocks of argillite-clayey, argillite-sandy-calcareous and sandy-clayey facies. The distribution of the Turonian deposits is confined to some areas of the Geycha-Garabag and Aras zones being represented by rocks of argillite-marly or argillite-sandy lithofacies.

The deposits of the Coniacian suite have a wide distribution being represented by sedimentary and volcanogenic-sedimentary types of rocks. The sedimentary section is represented by alternation of limestones, sandstones, tuff-sandstones, marls and clays. The second sub-section of 1,000 metres thick consists of porphyrites and their volcanoclasts with a rare interbeds of sandstones and limestones. In the Aras zone, the Upper Coniacian is exceptionally composed of limestones with rare interbeds of aleurolites and marls.

The Santonian deposits of the Upper Cretaceous have also a wide distribution and represented by rocks of terrigenous (clays, marls, sandstones), volcanogenic-sedimentary (tuffs, tuff-sandstones, tuff-breccia, porphyrites, mandelstones, basalts) and carbonaceous (limestones and marls) facies.

The Campanian stage is dominated by widely developed limestones and marls with interbeds of benthonic tuffs and clays, containing in some areas volcanogenic formations in the base part of the suite.

The rocks of the Maastrichtian suite have been found in all structural zones of the Lesser Caucasus. The section consists of carbonaceous rocks lithofacially close to those of the Campanian suite. The total thickness of the Upper Cretaceous stratigraphic interval in the Lesser Caucasus varies from 1,800 to 3,000 metres.

4. Cenozoic

The Cenozoic deposits are widely developed on the territory of Azerbaijan and represented by rocks of the sedimentary, sedimentary-volcanogenic and volcanogenic lithofacies. These rocks are involved in mountain constructions of the Greater and Lesser Caucasus and in the formation of superimposed basins of modern foothill and intermontane troughs including the southern Caspian trough.

(a)   Paleogene system

The Paleogene deposits on the territory of Azerbaijan are distributed in the areas of the southeastern end of the Greater Caucasus, Middle Kura depression, foothills of the Lesser Caucasus, Aras tectonic zone and Talysh Mountain.

(i)   The Great Caucasus

The Paleogene formations are well represented in the geological cross-sections of the northern slope of the Greater Caucasus range, except the Sudur and Shakhdag-Khizi sub-zones, where they have a limited distribution. The complete cross-sections of the Paleogene age have been transected by drilling in the Siazan monocline, Kainardja and Fore-Caspian area of the Kusary-Devechi trough. In the Shakhdag-Khizi sub-zone, the Paleogene rocks have been retained in two western areas. In the Budug trough, the stratificated section of the Danian-Eocene interval is represented by alternation of calcareous clays, marls and calcareous sandstones, 25-30 metres thick inlayers of quartzose sands and sandstones in the middle part of section. The thickness of this interval is 440 metres. On the east, in the areas of periclinal subsidence of folded structures, the Paleogene formations transgressively overlie the Barremian-Lower Aptian deposits. The deposits of the Datsky suite are missing; the thickness of the transgressive Oligocene formations is increasing in the part of the section. The cross-section is mostly composed of sandy and calcareous clays with beds of sandstones and marls. The total thickness of this interval varies from 350 to 740 metres.

The Paleocene sandstones and clays, the Eocene clays, marls and limestones and the Oligocene clays retained in the Sudur sub-zone. These rocks of up to 300 metres thick transgressively overlie various horizons of the Lower-Cretaceous in sporadic areas. A more persistent section of the Paleogene is observed along the southern flank of the Kusary-Devechi trough in the Siazan monocline, where it is mainly represented by clays with interbeds of sandstones, aleurolites and marls with a total observed thickness of up to 1,000 metres. According to the drilling data, the thickness of the Paleogene deposits in the central part of the trough exceeds 400 metres and in the Fore-Caspian trough, they are disappearing.

Within the southeastern submergence of the Zakataly-Kovdag-Sumgayit sub-zone of the southern slope of the Greater Caucasus, the Paleogene rocks retained in the cores of the Upper Cretaceous synclines. The sequence is represented by alternation of clays, sandstones, marls, limestones with in increasing role of clayey material in the upper part of the section. The maximum total thickness of deposits reaches 1,900 metres.

The thickness of the Paleogene deposits varies from 1,200 to 2,500 metres within the Absheron peninsula and Shemakha-Jeyrankechmaz depression located on the eastern subsidence of the Mesozoic core of the Balakhan-Vandam zone. The thickness increases in the south and eastern directions. The Paleogene is represented by all stages and suites and is similar to the section of the northern Azkataly-Kovdag-Sumgayit sub-zone.

(ii)   Kura trough

The Paleogene deposits in the Kura trough have been transected by numerous wells at various depths of the middle part of the trough to the west from the confluence of the Kura and Aras rivers up to the border with Georgia. The Paleogene is represented by its all sections and stages and has a total variable thickness from 720 to 2,860 metres. The Paleocene-Lower Eocene section is represented by alternation of limestones, marls and clays with interbeds of sandstones. The Middle Eocene section of 460 metres thick consists of clays with beds of sandstones, marls, limestones and tuffs. The upper part of the section is composed of a series of clays, 1,730 metres thick, with interbeds of sandstones.

(iii)   The Lesser Caucasus

The Paleogene deposits in the foothills of the Lesser Caucasus are spread in isolated areas of the fore-deeps filled by carbonates of the Upper Cretaceous. According to lithological parameters and distribution of fauna and flora, the Paleogene deposits are subdivided into near-shore shallow water and relatively deep water types of facies. In the northeastern foothills, the Paleogene is represented by all sections and stages with a total thickness from 980 to 1,760 metres. The lower part of the Datsky-Middle Eocene section has a carbonaceous character and consists of alternation of limestones, marls, sandstones, clays and aleurolites. The upper part of the section consists of alternation of clays, sands and sandstones.

The deposits of the Iprian stage are outcropped on the south-eastern subsidence of the Lesser Caucasus where they transgressively overlie carbonates of the Upper Cretaceous. The Paleogene section from 1,100 to 1,400 metres thick has a carbonaceous-terrigenous character and is represented by alternation of clays, limestones, aleurolites, sandstones, conglomerates with interbeds of aleuro-tuffites in the Middle-Eocene interval.

In the central mountainous part of the Lesser Caucasus, the Paleogene deposits are widely spread in the Kelbadjar trough and the Shakhdag syncline and represented by rocks of carbonaceous, shaly, sandy-clayey, tuffogenous, volcanogenic-sedimentary and volcanogenic facies. The total thickness varies from 1,070 to 2,655 metres in the first and from 1,140 to 3,860 metres in the second troughs.

Within the Aras tectonic zone, the Paleogene deposits are widely developed in the Ordubad trough where they conformably overlie the Upper Cretaceous formations. The total thickness varies from 2,000 to 4,320 metres being represented by rocks of terrigenous, terrigenous-carbonaceous, tuff-sedimentary and volcanogenic facies. The complete sections of the Paleogene are confined to the deepest areas of the trough. The Middle Eocene deposits are spread mainly in the areas of hiatus in sedimentation. The Paleocene section is represented by alternation of clays, marls, sandstones, and conglomerates from 250 to 730 metres thick. The above section is dominated by tuff-conglomerate-breccia, tuff-gritstones, porphyrites, tuff-sandstones, aleuro-tuffites with beds of clays, marls and limestones.

(iv)   Talysh Mountain

The Paleogene formations occupy a predominant position within the Talysh tectonic zone. The section is composed of volcanogenic and volcanogenic-sedimentary varieties of rocks with a total thickness from 5,000 to 8,000 metres. The cross-section starts with the Paleocene formations represented by alternation of argillites with interbeds of marls and clayey limestones, aleuro-tuffites and bedded tuffites. The section is followed by a complete interval of the Eocene volcanogenic and volcanogenic-sedimentary rocks and the Oligocene sequence represented by clays, sandstones, aleurolites and conglomerates with an insignificant admixture of tuff material.

(b)   Neogene system

The Neogene deposits occupy more than 70 per cent of the territory of Azerbaijan and consist of rocks of the marine, lagoonal, continental and subaerial volcanogenic lithofacies. The maximum thickness of the Neogene deposits have been observed on the southern slope of the Shemakha-Jeyrankechmaz depression and south-eastern periclinal subsidence of the Absheron peninsula of the Greater Caucasus and Kura trough.

(i)   The Greater Caucasus

On the northern slope of the Shakhdag-Khizi sub-zone, the Neogene deposits retained in the Budug trough where they are represented by shaly limestones of the Sarmatian stage, continental-marine shingles and conglomerates of the Middle Pliocene and clays and sandstones of the Upper Pliocene with a total thickness of 580 metres.

On the south-eastern subsidence of this zone in the Caspian coast, the rocks of the Tarkhan stage of the Middle Miocene transgressively overlie the rocks of the Gadim horizon of the Oligocene section. The Caucasian, Sakaraul and Kazaknur regional stages of the Lower Miocene are missing in the cross-section. The stratified interval of the Middle Miocene-Middle Pliocene consists of alternation of clays and sandstones with rare interbeds of dolomites and gritstones of a total thickness 900 metres. The Meotian and Pontian stages of this stratigraphic interval are missing. Within the Kusary-Devechi trough, the complete Neogene section has been observed only in the Siazan monocline. In the Fore-Caspian part of the trough, many sub-divisions of the Miocene had not been deposited or washed out according to the drilling data. The total thickness of the Miocene marine clays, sands and sandstones varies from 190 to 1,600 metres. The Pliocene deposits of the trough are represented by continental shingles and conglomerates on the west and by marine clays, sands and sandstones and their transitional varieties on the east. The total thickness varies from 2,000 to 4,200 metres.

On the southern slope, the Neogene deposits represent the basic part of the geological cross-section of the Shemakha-Jeyrankechmaz sub-zone and the Absheron periclinal trough. Here, the Miocene deposits are transgressively overlaid by formations of the Pontian stage of the Lower Pliocene which are disconcordantly overlaid by deposits of the Middle-Upper Pliocene. Within the Shemakha-Jeyrankechmyaz sub-zone, the Miocene has a complete section and consists of clays with interbeds of siderites, marls, and sandstones in its bottom part. The section is followed mainly by clays interbedded by sands, sandstones, sometimes conglomerates and volcanic ash in the upper part. The thickness of the section is more than 3,000 metres. The Pliocene is represented by alternation of clays, limestones and sandstones of the Pontian stage and clayey-sandy rocks of the Balakan, Archagil and Absheron stages containing inlayers of volcanic ash. The total thickness of the Pliocene section exceeds 4,600 metres.

Within the Absheron peninsula, the Miocene section has a thickness of 1,400 metres represented mainly by clays with interbeds of sandstones, marls, rare dolomites and volcanic ash in the top part of the section. The main part of the Pliocene deposits of 3,940 metres thick consists of clays, sandstones, aleurolites and clays of the Balakhan stage. The rest of the section is primarily composed of clays with interbeds of limestones, sandstones and volcanic ash. The total thickness of the Pliocene section is 5,560 metres.

(ii)   Kura trough

The accessible sections of the Neogene deposits contain the rocks of marine, continental-marine and continental facies. The Miocene formations represented by its all sub-divisions have been mainly studied on the territory of the Middle Kura depression, where they are composed of marine lithofacies, mainly clays with interbeds of sandstones and limestones. The thickness of these deposits in the interval of the Sakaraul-lower part of the Upper Sarmatian exceeds 3,400 metres. Deposits of the Upper Sarmatian-Meotician interval of 400 metres thick are represented by continental clays and sands with interbeds of brown coal and volcanic ash.

The deposits of the Pontian stage of the Lower Pliocene are outcropped along the northern flank of the Middle Kura depression and represented by marine clays and limestones from 250 to 300 metres thick on the east and by rocks of the continental fluvial and delta formations lithofacies on the west. The thickness of the latter is 200 metres.

The deposits of the Balakhan stage of the Middle Pliocene are widely developed within the Lower Kura depression and Baku archipelago and have a large thickness from 5,500 to 6,000 metres. They differ from coeval deposits of the Gobustan and Absheron peninsula by well-sorted sediments and are represented by a thick series of clays interbedded with sand and aleurolites. Within the Middle Kura depression, the Balahkan stage is outcropped along its northern flank in the Adjinour region and represented by alternation of continental conglomerates, sandstones and clays of 800 metres thick transgressively overlying a washed-out surface of the Pontian stage.

The deposits of the Akchagyl and Absheron stages of the Upper Paleocene occupy the whole Kura depression and eastern Georgia. Within the Lower Kura depression and southern Caspian trough, the Upper Pliocene is presented by marine relatively deep water shaly clays with interbeds of sands and volcanic ash. The total thickness varies from 600 to 2,000 metres. In the Middle Kura depression, marine sediments have been retained only in its axial part, being filled by sandy clays, sandstones, shales and conglomerates. Toward the north and the south, these deposits transform into rocks of fresh water and continental facies. The thickness of the section in the northern part of the depression varies from 2,500 to 3,000 metres and that of the sandy-clayey section in the south varies from 200 to 300 metres. Numerous interbeds of volcanic ash are typical sections of the formations of the Pliocene.

(iii)   The Lesser Caucasus

On the south-eastern subsidence of the Lesser Caucasus, the Lower-Middle Miocene stratigraphic interval is primarily represented by rocks of the near shore-marine and clayey-sandy lithofacies with beds of shingle material and interbeds of conglomerate-breccia in some horizons. The thickness of this sequence is 545 metres. The above Miocene section is followed on the top by a 40 metres thick bed of continental sandstones and clays of the Concodian stage. Deposits of the Lower and Middle Pliocene are missing here and the Upper Pliocene section with basal conglomerates transgressively overlie various horizons of the Cretaceous, Paleogene and Miocene. The Upper Pliocene section starts in the base with clays interbedded by sands, sandstones and volcanic ash of the Akchagyl stage of a maximum thickness 600 metres. The section is followed by the formations of the Absheron stage of 250 metres thick containing conglomerates, shingles, sandstones and clays with thin beds of volcanic ash.

In the highly mountainous part of the Lesser Caucasus, in the Saribaba and Gochaz troughs and the Kelbadjar superimposed trough, the Neogene section is represented by volcanogenic formations of the Lower and Upper Pliocene. The Pontian stage of the Lower Miocene consists of covers of andesites, dacites, their tuffs, tuff-breccia, conglomerates with interbeds of sandstones and clays with a total thickness 300 metres. The Akchagyl stage of the Upper Miocene is represented by volcanic lava.

In the Aras tectonic zone, the Miocene deposits are developed in lagoonal-continental and lagoonal-marine environment being represented by alternation of sandstones, tuff-sandstones, aleurolites, clays, limestones and marls in the lower part and mainly clays and sandstones with beds of gypsum and rock salt in the upper part of the section. The transition from the Lower to the Middle Miocene and from the Middle to the Upper Miocene are characterized by a hiatus in the sedimentation. The total thickness of the Miocene section in the Aras tectonic zone varies from 800 to 2,200 metres.

The volcanogenic formations of the Pontian stage of the Lower Miocene of 800 metres thick consist of andesites, basalts, and their breccia. The section overlie disconcordantly the deposits of the Miocene and more ancient rocks. Continental boulder-shingle deposits of the Absheron stage of the Upper Pliocene complete the Neogene section in the Aras tectonic zone.

(iv)   Talysh Mountain

The accessible sections of the Neogene sequence are represented by the Sakaraul-Upper Sarmatian formations of the Miocene and the Upper Pliocene. The Miocene section starts at the base with alternation of conglomerates, sandstones and clays. The middle part of the section consists of conglomerates being replaced by interbeds of marls. The upper part of section is dominated by clays with interbeds of sandstones. The total thickness of the Miocene deposits exceeds 2,400 metres. The Pliocene deposits are not outcropped on the surface and have only been transected by drilling in the foothill of the Talysh mountain. Clays of the Akchagil stage of the Upper Pliocene of 220 metres thick transgressively overlie the rocks of the Upper Sarmatian stage being overlaid by continental formations of the Quaternary age.

5. Quaternary system

The Quaternary deposits are widely developed in the Kura depression, south-eastern part of the Gobustan, Kusary-Devechi trough, the Caspian depression and on the southern slope of the Lesser Caucasus. The Quaternary section is represented by the Pleistocene and Holocene formations of marine and continental facies. The Pleistocene formations are mostly distributed in the eastern part of Azerbaijan and the Holocene sediments are more developed in the central and western parts of the country.

(a)   Pleistocene

The Pleistocene deposits almost everywhere are represented by the lower, middle and upper sub-stages and overlie the underlying Neogene formations with angular disconcordance. Marine deposits are distributed exclusively in depressional zones, including the Caspian aquatorium.

The Lower Pleistocene in its base part is composed mainly of clays and sandy-aleurolite material in the archy parts of the uplifts; separate sections are represented by sands or conglomerates. The follow-up sub-section of the Lower Pleistocene consists of clays and sandstones with interbeds or shingles, conglomerates, volcanic ash and shells. The upper part of the section is dominated by shales interbedded by sandy loams and clays.

The Middle Pleistocene deposits overlie the above Lower Pleistocene formations almost everywhere with hiatus and angular disconcordance. The section is dominated by sandy-clayey and detrital sediments with an increasing thickness westward.

The Upper Pleistocene deposits have been mostly observed in the low-lying areas and terraces on the flanks of the Kura-Aras depression, in the Absheron peninsula and Kusary-Devechi lowlands. The contact with underlying deposits is disconcordant. The section in its base part starts with conglomerates followed by sands and shales. The following part of the section is composed basically of alternation of clays, sands and sandstones, rare shales, shingles and conglomerates. Interbeds of volcanic ash are present in the upper part of the section on the east. The thickness of the Pleistocene marine formations depends on their location and varies to a great extent reaching a maximum thickness of up to 1,000 metres.

Continental formations are widely developed in the near shore parts of the Kura-Aras depression and within the Kusary-Devechi lowland where they are represented by delluvial, proluvial-alluvial and allurial sediments. Fluvial terraces are mostly developed in the Azerbaijanian part of the Greater Caucasus and the Kusary-Devechi foredeep trough where 13 accumulative and erosional terraces have been delineated. From three to five accumulative terraces have been distinguished in the Adjinour region along the northern flank of the Kura trough; eight accumulative terraces are determined in the Lesser Caucasus.

Colluvial deposits are widely spread on the slopes and glacial deposits in the highly-mountainous zones of the Greater and Lesser Caucasus. Volcanogenic formations are developed within the Garabag volcanic highland and adjacent areas of the Lesser Caucasus represented by lava of andesites-basalts, tuff-breccia and ash beds. Chemogenic deposits are widely developed within the Aras zone of the Nakhchivan superimposed through where they are represented by travertines. The thickness of continental deposits normally varies within a range of 10-50 metres reaching up to 300 metres in some places.

(b)   *Holocene*

The Holocene deposits continuously overlie the Kura-Aras and Kusary-Devechi lowlands and have a widespread distribution in other regions of Azerbaijan.

Marine deposits are mainly spread in the near shore strip and at the bed of the Caspian sea and in the Kura depression. These deposits are usually observed in the accumulative terraces and facially represented by clays and sands with shales and interbeds of mud breccia of mud volcanoes. The thickness of deposits varies from 5 to 160 metres.

Continental deposits have a wider distribution than the marine sediments being represented by alluvial, alluvial-proluvial, deluvial, lacustrine-alluvial and mud volcanic formations. The thickness of deposits varies within a range from 5 to 60 metres. Mud volcanic deposits are developed in the areas of intensive manifestation of mud volcanism and represented by loose clays with debrises of rocks from the Cretaceous to Quaternary age. The thickness of these deposits varies to a great extent from 30 to around 300 metres depending on the power of eruption and size of mud volcanoes.

D. Magmatism

The prolonged and complex geological evolution has determined not only the heterogenous tectonic structure of the territory of Azerbaijan but also a multiple re-emergence of igneous activity, both intrusive and extrusive, at different time slices throughout the stratigraphic column. Magmatic formations of the Alpine tectono-magmatic cycle are widespread in the tectono-magmatic zones of the Greater and Lesser Caucasus. Distribution of magmatic rocks of the Hercynian cycle is limited and magmatic formations of the Baikalian cycle are missing on the territory of Azerbaijan.

The following description of magmatic formations of Azerbaijan is based on extensive research, field work and numerous publications of Azerbaijanian and Russian geologists (Abdullayev, 1963; Abdullayev and Mustafaev, 1984; Abdullayev and others, 1988, 1991; Afanasiev and others, 1968; Azizbekov, 1961; Azizbekov and others, 1979; Azizbekov and Kashkay, 1952; Azizbekov and Hadjiyev, 1969; Borsuk, 1979; Geology of Azerbaijan, 1999; Geology of the Greater Caucasus, 1976; Geology of the USSR, 1964, 1968, 1970, 1972; Hasanov, 1985; Hasanov and Aliyev, 1981; Karyakin, 1989; Kashkay, 1947; Kashkay and others, 1970; Lomidze, 1977, 1981, 1983; Mustafayev, 1977; Paftengols, 1970; Shikhalibeyli, 1966; Shikhalibeyli and others, 1984; Sokolov, 1983).

1. Hercynian tectono-magmatic cycle

Magmatic formations of the Hercynian cycle are represented by gabbro-diabase rocks of small intrusions, sills and dykes found to occur between the Devonian siliceous limestones of the Sharur-Djulfa uplift of the Aras tectonic zone. Debris of granitoid rocks have been found also among basal conglomerates in the base of the Lower Jurassic in the Shamkhor uplift of the Somkhit-Agdam tectonic zone of the Lesser Caucasus and in the southern flank of the Tufan tectonic zone of the Greater Caucasus.

2. Alpine tectono-magmatic cycle

The Alpine tectono-magmatic cycle of development in the Caucasus covers the geological interval from the Jurassic to Quaternary and is subdivided into the oceanic, transition and continental stage of the Earth crust formations. Volcanogenic and intrusive formations of this cycle are characterized by variable composition and genesis.

(a)   Formations of oceanic stage

(i)   Volcanogenic formations

The rocks of the Early Jurassic basalt formation are outcropped in the zone of junction of the Sharur-Djulfa uplift and the Ordubad trough of the Aras tectonic zone along the tectonic contact with dolomites of the Upper Triassic. Formation is represented by lava and pyroclastic facies of almond-shaped and mandelstone basalts and diabase porphyrites.

The Middle Jurassic-Early Cretaceous spilitic-diabase rock association forms allochthonous plates of ophiolites within the Saribaba and Touragachaly structures of the Geychay-Garabag sub-zone spatially associated with rocks of gabbro-peridotite intrusive formation. The formation is mainly composed of lava covers and flows interbedded by tuffs. It consists of spilites, spilite-diabase, diabase, basaltic porphyrites and, rarely, trachybasaltic andesite porphyrites. Sub-volcanic facies are represented by radial and ring dykes composed of trachybasalts and diorites porphyrites. Secondary alteration process caused by metamorphism is reflected by albitization, epidotization, chloritization of plagioclase and chloritization and epidotization of pyroxenes.

The Early Jurassic formation of sodium basalts takes part in the structure of the western part of the Tufan sub-zone of the trough of the southern slope of the Greater Caucasus composed of sandy-shales of the Lower-Middle Jurassic. The formation is represented mainly by tholeiitic lava basalts metamorphosed from the initial greenstone regeneration to complete spilitization. Sub-volcanic facies are represented by dykes and sills composed of diabases, dolerites and, rarely, olivine dolerites.

(ii)   Intrusive formations

The gabbro-peridotite association forms the ophiolite zones of the Lesser Caucasus being traced as continuous chain of hyperbasite and gabbro lens-shaped outcrops in the Shakhdag, Saribaba and Touragchay troughs of the Geychay-Garabag structural sub-zone. The formation is subdivided into peridotite and gabbro sub-formations composed of serpentinized peridotites, dunites and pyroxenites and less-developed hornblende gabbro, norites and gabbro-diorites respectively. Hyperbasites have undergone methasomatic secondary alteration pronounced through serpentinization, listvenitization and rodingitization.

(iii)   Formations of small intrusions

The Middle Jurassic andesite-dacite-rhyolite formation replaces the formation of sodium basalts of the Greater Caucasus and is being controlled by deep-seated faults. The formation is represented by dykes, sills and stockworks composed of a continuous series of rocks from andesite to rhyolite.

(b)   Formations of transition or pre-collision stage

(i)   Volcanogenic formations

Volcanogenic formations of the pre-collision stage are mainly distributed in the Somkhit-Agdam and, to a lesser extent, in the Geychay-Garabag and Gafan sub-zones of the Artwin-Garabag uplift of the Lesser Caucasus as well as in the Aras, Balakhan-Vandam and Talysh tectonic zones.

Rocks of the Bajocian spilite-diabase formation are distributed in isolated areas of the southern slope of the Greater Caucasus within the Balakan-Vandam tectonic zone. The rocks of this formation are mostly widespread in neighboring Georgia, where the lower horizons of the formation are composed of spilites and avgiteplagioclase porphyrites. Porphyrites occur as lava flows, inlayers and sub-volcanic bodies in the environment of pyroclasts composed of tuffs, tuffites, tuff-breccia and tuff-sandstones in the upper part of the formation. Secondary alteration is pronounced through intensive chloritization, albitization and carbonitization.

The Bajocian andesite-basalt-plagio-liparite formation is subdivided into the Lower Bajocian andesite-basalt and the Upper Bajocian plagioliparite sub-formations. Rocks of andesite-basalt sub-formation are widely developed in the Lesser Caucasus within the Shamkhor and Murovdag uplifts of the Somkhit-Agdam sub-zone. The sub-formation is represented by alternation of rocks of volcanogenic-rudaceous and lava facies with intrusion of sills and dykes. Pyroclastic material consists of volcanic breccia, aglomerates and tuffs, tuff-breccia, tuff-conglomerates, tuffites and tuff-sandstones. Rocks of lava facies are represented mainly by flows of basalt, andesite-basalt, diabase porphyrites and, to a lesser extent, andesite porphyrites. The most commonsecondary alteration processes are propylitization, albitization, chloritization, sericitization, calcitization and zeolitization. Plagioliparites represent products of acidic magma in pyroclastic lava and sub-volcanic facies confined mainly to the Shamkhor, Geygel, Murovdag and Agdam uplifts of the Somkhit-Agdam sub-zone. Subvolcanic facies are represented by extrusive domes and near-surface bodies of plagiogranite-porphyres. Rocks of lava facies are represented by plagioliparites. Secondary alteration processes are propilitization and secondary silicification.

Rocks of the Bathonian andesite-basalt formation are widespread in the Lesser Caucasus within the Shamkhor, Dashkesan, Agdjakend, Murovdag, Agdam, Garabag and Lachyn structures. The formation is represented mainly by rocks of volcanogenic-rudaceous facies composed of volcanic breccia, agglomerate tuffs, tuffites, tuff-breccia and tuff-sandstones. Andesite, basalt and andesite-basalt porphyrites are the rocks of lava facies. Rocks of subvolcanic facies are confined to dykes, sills, extrusives and endogenous domes of diorite-porphyrites, gabbro-basalts and diabasic porphyrites. The process of autometamorphism has caused secondary alteration expressed by uralitization and chloritization of pyroxenes and albitization, sericitization and epidotization of plagioclases.

Volcanogenic rocks of the Kimmeridgian basalt-andesite-dacite formation have been developed within the Somkhit-Agdam zone both in the uplifted and subsided blocks. Volcanites of andesite-dacite composition have been found to occur along the north-eastern margin of the Shamkhor uplift, in the area of the south-eastern submergence of the Murovdag uplift and on the south-western flank of the Agdam uplift. The formation is mainly represented by rocks of pyroclastic, lava and sub-volcanic facies. The latter facies is presented by epidote-hornblende quartzose diorites. Volcanites of basic composition are represented by basalts, andesite-basalts and andesites found to occur in the structures of the Dashkesan and Agdjakend troughs. Rocks of the formation have been exposed to propilitization with the development of albite-epidote-carbonate-sericite association in andesite-dacite group and carbonate-chlorite-zeolite association in andesite-basalt group.

Volcanogenic rocks of the Valanginian-Hauterivian andesite-basalt formation occur in the area of the north-western submergence of the Shamkhor uplift and in the eastern part of the Gafan sub-zone. The formation consists of rocks of lava, pyroclastic and subvolcanic facies of a monotonous andesite-basalt composition. Secondary alteration is pronounced by albitization, epidotization of plagioclase and chloritization of pyroxene.

(ii)   *Intrusive formations*

The intrusive rocks of the Middle Jurassic plagio-granite formation have been found to occur in the Shamkhor uplift of the Somkhit-Agdam sub-zone within a volcano-plutonic association composed of products of the Late Bajocian volcanism and the Atabek, Gilenbiz and Gariblin granitoid massif. Albitization and epidotization are typical secondary alteration processes. In the Atabek granitoid massif, the pneumatolitic hydrothermal metamorphism has resulted in formation of greisens with an intensive tourmaline mineralization.

The rocks of the Middle-Late Jurassic gabbro-plagiogranite formation occur within the large Bulbulduzi massif, intruding the core of the Lachyn uplift of the Gafan sub-zone. The massif is a part of the Shalfa-Lachyn group of intrusives composed of rocks of the initial gabbroid phase of magmatism (gabbro, gabbro-diorites and quartz-diorites) and, to a large extent, of rocks of a following plagiogranite phase of magmatism (plagiogranites, quartz, diorites, granodiorites, adamellites and granites). Secondary alterations are represented by albitization, sericitization, epidotization of plagioclases and chloritization of non-ferrous metals.

The intrusive rocks of the Late Jurassic-Early Cretaceous gabbro-diorite-granodiorite formation are widely distributed within more than thirty intrusive massifs of the Somkhit-Agdam sub-zone. These include the Gabakhtapa, Dashbulag, Barum and Novo-Gaorelovka granitoid massifs within the Shamkhor uplift, the Gedabek, Dashkesan, Zurnabad and Uchtapa massifs in the territory of the Dashkesan trough, the Goshgardag, Irac-Manuk and other massifs in the Murovdag uplift and the Mekhmana massif within the Agdam uplift. Quartz diorites, granodiorites and adamellites are the most widespread intrusive rock types. Intrusive bodies have been exposed to auto-metamorphism pronounced by albitization, sericitization, epidotization of plagioclase, chloritization of biotites and amphibolites, uralitization of pyroxenes and often skarn formation.

(iii) Formations of small intrusions

The distribution of *the rocks of the Late Jurassic gabbro-diorite-plagiogranite formation* concides spatially with that of the Lower-Middle Jurassic magmatic formations in the trough of the southern slope of the Greater Caucasus. The formation is represented by dykes, sills and stockworks controlled by zones of abyssal faults. Petrographically, the rocks are characterized by an extremey variable composition from gabbro to porphyry and aplitic plagiogranites.

The rocks of the Late Jurassic gabbro-diabase formation constitute large inlayered bodies exposed in the central part of the Khodjavend trough of the Geychay-Garabag sub-zone and in the area of the south-eastern submergence of the Gochaz trough of the Gafan sub-zone of the Lesser Caucasus. The intrusive bodies have a porphyry appearance and are composed of plagioclase and monoclinal pyroxene and secondary minerals like chlorite, epidote, calcite and magnetite.

(c) Formations of transition stage (collision epoch)

(i) Volcanogenic formations

The rocks of the Albian andesite-basalt formation occur as isolated outflows in the western flank zone of the Ordubad trough of the Aras tectonic zone where they are spatially associated with the Lower Jurassic basalt formation. The facial analysis of the rocks suggests that the initiation of formation started with eruption of lava flows of andesite-basalt and basalts with a follow-up transition to andesites.

The rocks of the Late Cretaceous basalt-andesite-dacite-liparite formation have been mapped in the Qazakh, Agdjakend and Agdara troughs, the Shamkhor uplift of the Somkhit-Agdam sub-zone and in the Gochaz trough of the Gafan sub-zone. The formation has been subdivided into the Conician-Santonian andesite-basalt and the Upper Santonian liparite-dacite sub-formations. Volcanites of the first sub-formation are represented by rocks of pyroclastic facies in the lower part of the stratigraphic section followed by basalts of lava facies. The stratigraphic section is intruded by subvolcanic dykes and stockworks of basalt composition. The second sub-formation is represented by rocks of subvolcanic and pyroclasitc facies, composed of dacites, liparite-dacites and trachyliparites. Rocks of both sub-formations have been subjected to metamorphism pronounced by zeolitization and albitization of plagioclases and chloritization and uralitization of pyroxenes. On the whole, regional metamorphism is characterized by the development of the albite-chlorite-laumontite-leonhardite association.

Rocks of the Santonian trachybasalt formation occur in the Khodjavend trough of the Gafan sub-zone and represented by lava and pyroclastic facies corresponding to olivine basalts, andesite-basalts, trachyandesites and their almond-shaped varieties. Rocks of subvolcanic facies are exposed as extrusives and necks of the same composition. Rocks of this formation have been exposed both to autometamorphism and regional metamorphism resulting in the formation of albite, chlorite and serpentine.

The Late Cretaceous trachyandesite-basalt formation has been mainly developed in the eastern part of the Vandam tectonic zone of the southern slope of the Greater Caucasus. The formation has been subdivided into volcanoclastic, lava and subvolcanic facies. Volcanomiktes-tuff-sandstones and tuff-alerurolites have been found as well. The most widespread rocks of this formation are andesite, trachyandesite, trachyandesite-basalt porphyrites and, to a lesser extent, basaltic and diabase porphyrites and their almond-shaped varieties. Rocks of volcanoclastic facies are represented by lithoclastic and crystalloclastic tuff-breccia and aglomerate tuffs. Rocks of the formation have been exposed to auto-metamorphic changes pronounced by iddingsitization of olivine, chloritization, epidotization and sericitization of plagioclase and chloritization.

Rocks of the Early-Middle Eocene basalt-andesite-dacite formation have developed in the south-eastern part of the Ordubad trough of the Aras zone being represented by volcanoclastic of up to 60-70 per cent of the total volume and lava facies: basalts, andesite-basalts, andesites and dacites. Metamorphism is pronounced by chloritization, epidotizaiton, zeolitizaiton, calcitizaiton and kaolinizaiton and formation of secondary quarzites and alunites in tectonic zones.

Rocks of the Middle Eocene andesite formation are distributed in the Shakhdag and Saribaba troughs of the Geychay-Garabag sub-zone, Kelbadjar supeimposed trough of the Gafan sub-zone and in the Ordubad trough of the Aras tectonic zone. Within the first sub-zone, the formation is represented by alternation of lava flows and sheets with interbeds of pyroclastic and tuffaceous-sedimentary rocks. Rocks of subvolcanic facies are confined to domes and dykes composed of andesites and andesite-dacites. Within the Ordubad sub-zone, the formation consists of pyroclastic flows of andesites. Regional metamorphism is pronounced by chloritization and calcitization on non-ferrous minerals and albitization, sericitization and zeolitization of plagioclase.

The Middle Eocene trachyandesite-basalt formation has a limited distribution within the Qazakh trough of the Somkhit-Agdam sub-zone and facially represented by lava, volcanoclastic and subvolcanic rocks composed of andesites, trachyandesites, trachybasalts and trachydolerites. Secondary alteration process of middle and lower temperature propylitization is typical for rocks.

Rocks of the Eocene alkali basalt formation occur in the Astara and Burovar uplifts and the Lerik trough of the Talysh tectonic zone. The formation has been subdivided into the Early-Middle Eocene trachyandesite-picrite-trachybasalt and Late Eocene trachyandesite-trachybasalt sub-formations. The first sub-formation is composed of leucite-sanidine tuffs of trachyandesites, volcanic conglomerate-breccia of andesite-basalts and basalts, lava and pyroclasts of picrite-trachybasalt and leucite basanites, tuffaceous rocks, autoclastic lava and volcanic breccia of trachyandesite and basalts and trachyandesites. The second sub-formation consists of lava and pyroclasts of trachyandesites-basalt and leucite trachyandesites, lava and pyroclasts of alkaline vitrobasalts and trachytoidal viterbites. The series of rocks of this formation are the products of original olivine-basalt magma.

The Oligocene andesite-dacite formation has been formed as a result of explosive volcanism along the western flank of the Ordubad trough of the Aras tectonic zone. The formation incorporates tuff-conglomerate-breccia and tuff-lava of andesites and andesite-dacites in the base section, gritstones and tuff-breccia in the middle stratigraphic internal, and tuff-sandstones and tuff-conglomerates in the upper section.

The Late Oligocene-Early Miocene trachyandesite formation has the same spatial distribution as a previous one and is composed of alternating ash tuffs of trachyandesites and volcanic breccia of andesites and trachyandesites. The process of autometamorphism is reflected by apatization of femic minerals.

(ii)   Intrusive formations

The Paleogene syenite-diorite formation is confined to the Buynuz intrusive massif located in the core of the Gendob uplift of the Balakhan-Vandam tectonic zone of the southern slope of the Greater Caucasus. The intrusive massif is mainly composed of basic varieties of alkaline gabbro, gabbro-syenites and syenite-diorites. Secondary alteration processes are pronounced by sericitization and carbonitization of plagioclases, chloritization of hornblendes and biotites.

The Late Eocene-Oligocene gabbro-peridotite-gabbro-syenite formation has a limited distribution in the Talysh zone represented by stockworks and linear elongated bodies of lherzolites, gabbro, orthoclase-biotite gabbro, gabbro-teschenites and gabbro-syenites. Dykes and sills derivatives consist of picrite-basalts and lamprophyres of gabbro-syenite composition. Metasomatic processes are pronounced by biotization, amphibolization and serpentinization of rocks.

The Late Eocene-Oligocene gabbro-granodiorite-granite formation is represented by adamellitic intrusive massif of the Megri-Pordubad batholith and its Khazaryurt satellite. The generation of the intrusive massif has passed four subsequent stages: main intrusive phase (granites, adamellites), phase of additional intrusive (granite-porphyries, granodiorite-porphyres), aplites and aplite-granites and dykes of several generations from granodiorite-porphyres to lamprophyres. The intrusions of this formation are accompanied by formations of numerous skarns in contact zones with carbonaceous environment.

Rocks of the Oligocene gabbro-diorite-granodiorite formation have limited distribution on the intersection of the Geychay-Garabag and Gafan sub-zones. The formation is represented by relatively small intrusive bodies composed of gabbro, gabbro-diorite, diorite, tonolite, basalt, granodiorite, adamellite, granites, and porphyry grano-diorite. The intrusions of this formation are accompanied by contact metamorphism on silicate rocks with formation of various facies of hornfels.

Rocks of the Late Eocene-Early Miocene granite-granosyenite formation occur in the Dalidag pluton in the central part of the Lesser Caucasus composed mainly of quartz syenites, granites, granodiorites and quartz diorites. Secondary alteration processes are reflected by sericitization, albitization of plagioclase and chloritization of hornblende and biotite. Contact metamorphism is accompanied by formations of endo-and exo-skarns.

Rocks of the Late Eocene-Early Miocene gabbro-diorite-granodiorite formation are confined to small layered and irregular intrusive bodies within the Gochaz and Saribaba troughs of the Geychay-Garabag sub-zone. The bodies are mainly composed of quartz diorites, facially transiting into gabbroids, granodiorites, monzonites and quartzose syenites. Secondary alteration is replicated by development of syenite, kaolin, epidote, carbonate, chlorite and other post-magmatic minerals on basic rock-forming minerals.

Rocks of the Late Oligocene-Early Miocene gabbro-monzonite-granodiorite formation occur in the Aras zone. The formation is presented by three intrusive massifs composed of gabbroides, monzonites and porphyry granitoids within the Megri-Ordubad batholith and the Lyakiyatakh-Sakkarsu intrusive complexes. A wide development of dyke fields and belts is typical for this formation. Contact metamorphism and metasomatism in exo-contact zones of intrusives were accompanied by formation of hornfells and high-alumina secondary quarzites.

(iii)   Formations of small intrusions

Rocks of the Late Cretaceous formation of sub-alkaline gabbroids are hosted by terrigenous-shaly rocks of the Lower-Middle Jurassic of the Tufan sub-zone of the trough in the southern slope of the Greater Caucasus. The formation is represented by deeply-eroded plutonic lens-shaped bodies composed of gabbro-diabase, diorites, gabbro-syenites, syenite-diorites, augite syenites and sub-alkaline gabbroids.

The Eocene gabbro-diabase formation is represented by small stockworks and layered bodies hosted by rocks of the Middle Eocene andesite formation of the Shakhdag trough of the Geychay-Garabag sub-zone. Porphyry rocks of gabbro-ophite structure are composed of plagioclase and monoclinal pyroxene. Autometamorphism is represented by sericitization and carbonitization of plagioclase and chloritization of pyroxene.

The Early Miocene diorite-teschenite formation has developed on the eastern flank of the Nakhchivan depression of the Aras zone. The formation includes layered intrusive bodies, composed of watergezite diorites and diorite teschenites. Skarns and hornfels are widespread in contact zones with host rocks.

(d)   Formations of the continental stage

(i)   Volcanogenic formations

The Miocene-Pliocene andesite-dacite-liparite formation is widely developed within the Kelbadjar superimposed trough and the Gafan uplift of the Lesser Caucasus. The formation has been formed during two stages of volcanic activization. The Late Miocene stage comprises lava and pyroclasts of liparites, dacites-liparites, andesite-dacites and trachyliparites, sub-volcanic formations of porphyrites and quartzose diorite porphyrites. The Middle Pliocene stage is composed of lava and tuffs of andesite and andesite-dacite. Secondary alteration processes are reflected by albitization, chloritization, sericitification, silicification and carbonitization.

Rocks of the Early Pliocene andesite formation are mainly developed in the north-eastern part of the Ordubad trough of the Aras zone. The formation is represented by lava and volcanic tuffs of basalts, andesite basalts, andesite and andesite-dacite. Post-volcanic alteration nearby volcanic centres are reflected by zeolitization, carbonitization, montmorillization, kaolinizaiton, alunitization and silification.

The Late Pliocene trachyandesite-basalt formation is developed within the Gochaz trough of the Gafan zone being dominated by the development of thick lava flows. The formation is composed of basalts, andesite-basalts and trachyandesite-basalts.

Rocks of the Quaternary andesite-basalt formation are widely distributed within the Gafan uplift and the Kelbadjar and Gochaz troughs of the Gafan sub-zone. The formation is represented by numerous lava cones, flows and covers of andesite-basalt of the Early Pleistocene, Middle Pleistocene, Late Pleistocene and Holocene age.

(ii)   Formations of small intrusions

The Miocene-Pliocene diorite-porphyrite and Early Pliocene andesite-dacite formation of the Aras zone are represented by numerous intrusive and extrusive bodies accompanied by dykes and sills.

E. Regional metamorphism

Regional metamorphism on the territory of Azerbaijan has mostly been pronounced through propylite, zeolite and greenstone facies. All rocks of volcanogenic formations have been exposed to processes of late magmatic replacement which did not completely change the mineralogical, chemical composition and structural peculiarities of rocks. Propylitization which is a post-volcanic metasomatic process has affected all volcanogenic rocks of the Lesser Caucasus, and particularly those of the Jurassic and Eocene age. According to mineral associations of post-volcanic replacement, two facies of propylitization have been determined in the Jurassic volcanites. A high temperature propylitizaiton is represented by epidote, zoisite, chlorite, albite quartz and prehnite calcite. A group of middle temperature propylitization process consists of chlorite, albite, sericite and carbonate.

Low temperature late magmatic replacement processes have affected all volcanogenic formations of Azerbaijan. The albite-chlorite-laumontite-leonhardite facies consists of albite, chlorite, heulandite, desmine, natrolite, laumontite, clinoptilolite, mordenite, calcite, quartz and chalcedony. Metamorphism of volcanic rocks of the Conician-Santonian age in the Qazakh and Agdjakend troughs and rocks of trachybasalt formation of the Khodjavend trough has resulted in zeolitization of lava and volcanic tuffs. Manifestations of regional metamorphism of zeolitic facies have been traced in the Early-Middle Eocene basalt-andesite-dacite formation of the Talysh mountain and in the Middle Eocene flyschoid volcanogenic-sedimentary association in the Ordubad trough. The greenstone muscovite-chlorite phase of regional metamorphism is slightly pronounced through phyllitizaiton of the Lower Jurassic shales in the watershed part of the main ridge of the Greater Caucasus.

F. Metallogeny of Azerbaijan

The complex geological evolution of Azerbaijan has in many cases resulted in favourable conditions for the formation of hydrocarbon and mineral resources, metallic and non-metallic alike.

1. Basic metallogenic epochs

The territory of Azerbaijan covers the eastern part of the metallogenic provinces of the Greater and Lesser Caucasus, incorporating the mineral deposits of the Hercynian, Kimmerian and Alpine metallogenic epochs (Abdullayev, 1963; Abdullayev and Mustafayev, 1984; Azizbekov and Kashkay, 1952; Geology of the USSR, 1964; Geology of the USSR, 1976; Mustafayev and others, 1989).

The most widespread ore formations of the Kimmerian and Alpine metallogenic epochs were formed during the Alpine tectono-magmatic cycle of development. A small number of mineral deposits are related to the Hercynian metallogenic epoch; no deposits of the Baikalian poch have been found on the territory of Azerbaijan.

Horizons of bauxite-bearing rocks have been formed during the Hercynian metallogenic epoch within a long break in sedimentation from the Lower Carbonaceous to Upper Permian on the south-west of Azerbaijan in the Aras zone. The mineralization of the Early Permian age was found among siliceous-carbonaceous-terrigenous formations of the platform's cover. Galenite-sphalerite mineralization was formed in limestones of the Givetian stage of the Middle Devonian in paragenetic association with gabbro-diabase.

The Kimmerian metallogenic epoch corresponds to the initial stage of the Alpine tectono-magmatic cycle represented by mineral deposits and occurrences of oceanic and pre-collision stages of ore genesis.

The Aalenian oceanic stage of the Lower Jurassic is characterized by formations of deposits and occurrences of chromite ores associated with the Lower Jurassic gabbro-peridotite-pyroxenite formation and sulphide-polymetallic and copper-pyrrhotite ores of the Greater Caucasus found to occur in the Early-Middle Jurassic shale rocks being spatially and paragenetically associated with non-differentiated tholeiitic basalts.

In the Somkhit-Agdam and Gafan sub-zones on the Lesser Caucasus, the beginning of the Bajocian and Bathonian pre-collision stage of ore genesis is marked by formation of massive sulphide deposits associated spatially and genetically with acidic varieties of plagiogranite-porphyries, and gold-sulphide quartz and gold-copper-sulphide mineralization associated with rocks of the basalt-andesite-dacite series.

The Late Jurassic-Early Cretaceous period of the oceanic stage of ore genesis within the Somkhit-Agdam sub-zone is earmarked by formation of porphyry copper deposits paragenetically coupled with small intrusions of plagiogranite massif. The deposits of magnetite skarn, alunite, cobalt, barite, barite-copper-polymetallic and vein quartz-polymetallic formations are associated with the Dashkesan intrusive massif of gabbro-diorite-granodiorites. Mineralization of gold-copper-sulphide and gold-bearing-metasomatic formations was formed in paragenetic association with gabbro-diorite-plagiogranites. Within the Gafan sub-zone, gold-sulphide-quartz mineralization of the Late Jurassic-Early Cretaceous age is associated with andesite-basalt formations.

The Alpine metallogenic epoch is characterized by the formation of various types of endogenous deposits of collision and continental stages of ore genesis concentrated within the metallogenic province of the Lesser Caucasus. The Late Cretaceous period of the collision stage is marked by the formation of exhalation-sedimentary manganese ores, associated with subvolcanic liparite-dacitees and localized in the Santonian sedimentary-volcanogenic interval. Quartz-polymetallic and gold-sulphide-quartz mineralizaiton is associated with the Coniacian-Santonian subvolcanic co-magmatic rocks of basalt-andesite-liparite composition.

The Paleocene-Eocene period is characterized by the development of occurrences of sulphide-polymetallic and copper-polymetallic formations associated with the Early Eocene subvolcanic facies of andesite-dacite porphyrites. Gold-sulphide-quartz mineralization is connected with the Middle Eocene andesite-dacite-rhyolites. Gold-sulphide-quartz and gold-bearing metasomatic mineralization has been found in association with volcanites of basalt-andesite composition of the Middle Eocene age. Manganese occurrences are coupled with the Middle Eocene volcanism.

The Oligocene-Miocene period of collision stage of ore genesis is marked by the formation of copper-molybdenum, tungsten, polymetallic and gold-sulphide-quartz deposits and occurrences associated with the Late Eocene-Early Miocene cycles of magmatism in the Megri-Ordubad and Dalidag plutons of granitoids.

The Pliocene-Holocene period of the continental stage of ore genesis is associated with the formation of mercury, antimony and arsenic deposits and occurrences hosted by subvolcanic andesite-dacites as well as occurrences of copper-bearing quartz veins, volcanogenic copper and manganese mineralization in andesite-dacite aglomerate lava.

2. Metallogenic setting

Metallogenic zoning is based on the tectonic position of ore-bearing areas and spatial location of mineral deposits and occurrences. Basic units of zonation are metallogenic zones subdivided into ore regions, districts and potential ore-bearing areas. Ten metallogenic zones and eighteen ore regions have been identified on the territory of Azerbaijan along the major metallogenic epochs (figure 4).

(a)   Metallogenic zones of the Hercynian epoch

The Sharur-Djulfa zone corresponds to the uplifts of the Aras tectonic zone of the Lesser Caucasus and represents itself as a modern projection of the Paleozoic and Triassic deposits in the south-west of Azerbaijan. The zone hosts bauxite-lead-zinc mineralization concentrated within the Gyumushlug ore region. Bauxites occurrences are associated with redeposition of lateral weathering crust in the Lower Carboniferous. Lead-zinc mineralization of vein type is confined to anticlinal folds in limestones of the Givetian age fragmented by a network of faults of pre- and post-ore formational stages.

(b)   Metallogenic zones of the Kimmerian epoch

(i)   Metallogenic province of the Greater Caucasus

The Saribash zone is located in the north-west of the most uplifted part of the Tufan tectonic sub-zone of the Greater Caucasus, composed of the Lower-Middle Jurassic shales with inlayered intrusions of diabase and gabbro-diabase. The sequence is overturned southward by linear and brachyform folds. The zone is subdivided into the northern and southern sub-zones separated by co-sedimentary upthrust-overthrusts which control sub-intrusive and intrusive bodies of variable age. The Saribash zone includes the Zakataly-Balakan and Qazakh ore regions. The Zakataly-Balakan ore region corresponds to the uplifted block, the same name and includes the Djikhikh-Gizildara and Filizchay-Attagay ore zones hosting the Filizchay, Kasdag, Katekh, Djikhikh, Gizildara, Kasmala, and Mazimchay sulphide-polymetallic and copper-pyrrhotite deposits and occurrences. Copper-

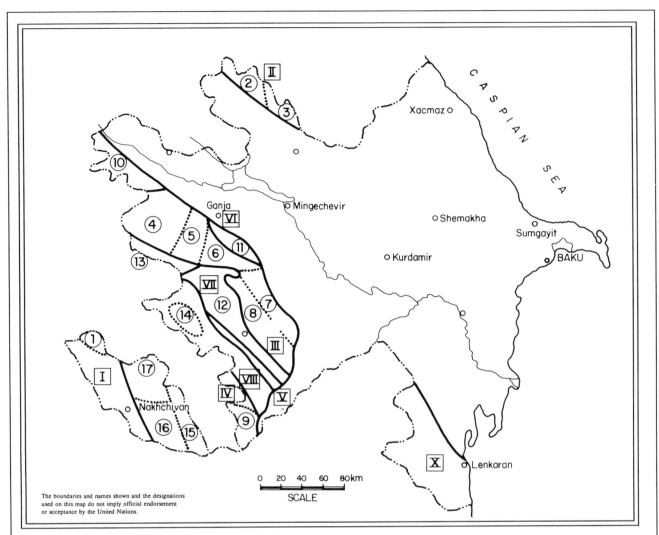

LEGEND

⋯⋯ Boundaries of metallogenic zones	
⟋ Boundaries of metallogenic regions, districts and ores areas	

METALLOGENIC ZONES	ORE DISTRICTS AND DEPOSITS
I-Sharur-Gulphin	1. Gumushlug
II-Saribash	2. Zakataly-Balakand
III-Somkhit-Agdam	3. Qakh
IV-Gafan	4. Gedabek
V-Lachyn	5. Dashkesan
VI-Kazakh-Ganja	6. Murovdag
VII-Geychay-Akera	7. Mekhmana
VIII-Kelbadgar-Bochaz	8. Karabakh
IX-Ordubad-Zangezur	9. Vejnali
X-Talysh	10. Jazajg
	11. Agdjakend
	12. Shorbulag-Levchay
	13. Shakhdag
	14. Dalidag
	15. Ordubad
	16. Darridag-Paradash
	17. Shakhbuz (perspective)

Figure 4. Schematic metallogenic setting of Azerbaijan

pyrrhotite mineralization is controlled by tectonic faults and their intersections. The major ore controlling factor of sulphide-polymetallic mineralization is the structural environment represented by longitudinal upthrust-overthrusts and folds with complicated cores and the northern limbs of large brachyform anticlines.

(ii) Metallogenic province of Lesser Caucasus

The Somkhit-Agdam zone corresponds to the tectonic sub-zone of the same name occupying the north-eastern slope of the Lesser Caucasus. The zone is composed of the Jurassic terrigenous and volcanogenic-sedimentary formations with rare outcrops of metamorphic rocks of the Pre-Cambrian crystalline basement.

The Dashkesan, Gedabek and Mekhmana polyfacial intrusive massifs are confined to abyssal faults controlling various types of mineralization. Massive sulphide deposits of the hydrothermal-metasomatic type are associated with the Late Bajocian volcanism pronounced at the initial stage of pre-collision period of ore genesis. Deposits and occurrences of magnetite skarn, arsenic, cobalt, porphyry copper, alunite as well as occurrences of veined polymetallic quartz-copper-barite polymetallic, gold-copper-sulphide, metasomatic gold-bearing barite and hematite types of hydrothermal genesishave been formed during the final stage of the pre-collision period in paragenetic connection with the Late Jurassic-Early Cretaceous gabbro-diorite-granodiorite formation.

The Gedabek ore region is located in the western part of the Somkhit-Agdam zone and hosts hydrothermal deposits and occurrences of copper-sulphide, copper-arsenic, veined gold-copper-polymetallic, alunite and hematite types.

The Dashkkesan ore region occupies the central part of the Lesser Caucasus metallogenic zone and hosts deposits and occurrences of sulphide, vein quartz-copper-gold, barite-copper-polymetallic, arsenic cobalt, skarn-magnetite alunite and titano-magnetite types.

The Murovdag ore region is confined to the southern flank of the Somkhit-Agdam zone and includes occurrences of barite-copper-polymetallic, porphyry copper, barite, quartz-copper, gold-copper-sulphide and sulphide types of mineralization.

The Mekhmana ore region hosts predominantly deposits and occurrences of polymetallic copper-sulphide, sulphide, barite and porphyry copper vein types of mineralization.

The Garabag ore region concides with the tectonic sub-zone of the same name located between the Murovdag and Mekhmana ore regions. The region hosts mineralization of massive copper-sulphide, magnetite-sulphide and quartz-copper types.

The Gafan ore zone occurs in the extreme south-east of the Gafan tectonic sub-zone of the Lesser Caucasus being composed of the Upper Bajocian plagioliparites, Upper Jurassic-Lower Cretaceous andesite and terrigenous-carbonaceous rocks as well as rocks of the Lower Cretaceous terrigenous formation.

The Vezhnali ore region of the Gafan metallogenic zone on the territory of Azerbaijan hosts occurrences of copper-sulphide and gold-sulphide quartz and quartz-copper of pre-collision stage of ore genesis. *The Lachyn ore district* is located on the north-east of the Gafan tectonic sub-zone and is composed of rocks of the Bathonian sedimentary-volcanogenic, the Upper Jurassic terrigenous-carbonaceous and the Aptian-Albian terrigenous formations. The axial part of the district is intruded by granodiorites and quartz-diorite massifs of the Upper Jurassic age. The district hosts mineralization of copper-sulphide type as well as mercury and arsenic occurrences.

(c) Metallogenic zones of the Alpine epoch

The Qazakh-Ganja metallogenic zone incorporates the western Qazakh and eastern Agdajakend ore regions located on the north-eastern flank of the Somkhit-Agdam sub-zone. *The Qazakh ore region* is composed of the

Upper-Jurassic, Cretaceous, Paleogene and Miocene-Pliocene deposits injected by the Cretaceous and younger intrusions. The region hosts occurrences of polymetallic, mercury gold-sulphide-quartz and magnetite-manganese types of mineralization. The Upper Cretaceous liparite-dacite formation of the *Agdjakend ore region* hosts magnetite-manganese deposits.

The Geychay-Hakara metallogenic zone corresponds to the tectonic sub-zone of the Lesser Caucasus. This synclinal suture zone is composed of thick volcanogenic-sedimentary formations from the Middle Jurassic to Recent age with prevalence of rocks of the Upper Cretaceous and Upper Eocene terrigenous-volcanogenic series. The zone hosts mineralization of chromites, mercury-antimony-arsenic as well as poor skarn-magnetite and copper-polymetallic mineralization. Deposits and numerous occurrences of chromites, nickel and cobalt were formed in the oceanic stage of ore genesis and paragenetically are associated with the Lower Jurassic ultrabasites.

Occurrences of magnetite skarn, gold-sulphide-quartz and copper-polymetallic vein types were formed during the Paleocene-Eocene stage of collision period of ore genesis. The occurrences are spatially associated with the Eocene gabbro-diorite-granodiorite intrusive massif. Mercury mineralization is spatially and paragenetically associated with subvolcanic andesites, andesite-dacites and granodiorite-porphyres confined to the continental stage of ore genesis.

The above types of mineralization of the Geychay-Hakara metallogenic zone are mostly distributed within the Shorbulag-Levchay and Shakhdag ore regions. Occurrences of chromite, mercury, antimony-mercury and arsenic are developed within the first region. Mineralization of copper-polymetallic, skarn-magnetite and, rarely chromite vein type mineralization is typical to the Shakhdag zone.

The Kelbadjar-Gochaz zone constitutes a part of the Gafan tectonic sub-zone composed of carbonaceous-terrigenous and sedimentary-volcanogenic formations of the Albian, Senomanian, Senonian, Middle Eocene and Miocene-Pliocene age and volcanogenic formations of the Pliocene-Recent stratigraphic sequence. The axial part of the trough is intruded by granitoid polyphase massif of the Late Eocene-Early Pliocene age, consisting of several intrusions of syenite-diorite and granite-granodiorite composition.

The Dalidag ore region corresponds to the Kelbadjar trough and hosts occurrences of copper-molybdenum and polymetallic types of continental stage of ore genesis. Mineralization of copper-molybdenum type is genetically coupled with the Late Eocene-Early Pliocene polyphase granitoid massif of granite-granosyenite composition. Polymetallic mineralization is spatially associated with the above copper-molybdenum mineralization.

The Ordubad-Zangezur metallogenic zone occurs within the Aras tectonic zone in the Ordubad trough and, partially, in the south-western wing of the Zangezur uplift. The zone is hosted by carbonaceous-terrigenous, terrigenous, volcanogenic-sedimentary and volcanogenic formations of the Jurassic, Upper Cretaceous, Eocene-Oligocene and Pliocene age. The zone incorporates mineralization of collision and continental stages of the Alpine epoch. The collision stage of ore genesis is characterized by formation of (a) sulphide-polymetallic hydrothermal veins paragenetically associated with subvolcanic bodies of andesite-dacites and dacite porphyrites of Early Eocene age; (b) gold-sulphide-quartz and gold-bearing metasomatic occurrences associated with volcanites of basalt-andesite composition and small intrusions of granitoids; and (c) copper-molybdenum, porphyry copper, and skarn-sulphide-cobalt mineralization coupled with the Megri-Ordubad pluton. The continental stage of ore genesis is associated with the Early Pliocene volcanism of andesite-dacite, diorite-porphyrite small intrusions, extrusives and dykes hosting hydrothermal deposits and occurrences of copper and antimony-arsenic of quartz vein type and exhaulation mineralization of mangetite and native copper. The Ordubad-Zangezur metallogenic zone on the territory of Azerbaijan consists of the Ordubad, Darridag-Paradash and Shakhbuz ore regions.

The Ordubad ore region occurs in the area of the western part of endo-exo-contact of the Megri-Ordubad pluton, known to host deposits and occurrences of molybdenum, copper-molybdenum and copper-polymetallic ores. The mineralization is spatially confined to the local brachy-anticlines with subvolcanic structures elongated as echelon-like chain parallel to the contact of the pluton. The endo-exo-contact areas of the pluton host deposits and occurrences of molybdenum, porphyry copper, lead-zinc, skarn sulpho-arsenide-cobalt and manganese types.

The Darridag-Paradash ore region is located westward of the Ordubad ore region and composed of the Eocene, Oligocene and Miocene-Pliocene volcanism of andesite-dacite, dacite, and rarely, diorite and dolerite. The region hosts small occurrences of copper-polymetallic ores, more later occurrences of mercury-antimony-arsenic mineralization as well as numerous manifestations of native copper of exhaulation-sedimentary genesis.

The Shakhbuz prospective ore region is located northward from the Darrydag-Paradash region and composed of andesites of the Upper Eocene and andesite-dacites of the Lower Pliocene. Arsenic and mangetite mineralization is associated with subvolcanic formations of the Early-Pliocene volcanism. The region has been found to be prospective for discovery of antimony-arsenic and mercury deposits.

The Talysh prospective zone corresponds to the tectonic zone located on the south of Azerbaijan and links the tectonic structures of the north-western submergence of the Elburs with the Lesser Caucasus. Mineralization of exogenous and endogenous types has been distinguished within this zone. The exogenous mineralization is represented by titano-magnetite sands and tuffaceous rocks of the Eocene. The endogenous mineralization is represented by accumulations of pyrite, chalcopyrite, galenite and sphalerite and rare elements. A potential prospectivity of the zone is defined by favourable geological conditions for the formation of deposits of hydrothermal and exhaulation sedimentary type.

3. Major ore formations and genetic types

(a)   Skarn-magnetite formation

The major Dashkesan, South Dashkesan and Damir deposits and occurrences of skarn-magnetite formation are concentrated within the Dashkesan ore region of the Somkhit-Agdam metallogenic zone. The deposits have been formed during a completion stage of pre-collision period confined to the carbonaceous-sedimentary-volcanogenic and volcanogenic series of rocks of the Upper Jurassic injected by the Dashkesan and Zurnabad intrusive massifs of the same age. Magnetite skarn deposits are localized in a close proximity to contacts of the intrusive massif. Ore bodies of a bed form belong to massive, disseminated and skarn types of ores. Magnetite ores contain substantial amounts of cobalt. Skarn-magnetite deposits with sulphide mineralization are subdivided into early contact-metasomatic skarn-magnetite and hydrothermal arsenic-cobalt formational types.

(b)   Titano-magnetite formation

This formational type is represented by the North Dashkesan deposit of titanium-magnetite ores hosted by the Bathonian tuff-sandstones. The deposit has been traced as a continious extended ore zone located in the northern part of the Dashkesan ore region of the Somkhit-Agdam zone. The deposit has been formed during the initial phase of the pre-collision stage.

(c)   Chromite formation

The Geydara deposit and forty chromite occurrences are associated with the Geychay-Garabag metallogenic zone. The mineralization was formed during the oceanic stage of ore genesis and genetically linked with ultrabasites. Segregation and hystero-magmatic types of chromite mineralization have been distinguished. The segregation type of mineralization is represented by schlieren chromite and the magmatic type by lens-shaped schlieren chromite ore bodies hosted by dunites.

(d)   Alunite formation

The formation is represented by the Zagik deposit of the Dashkesan ore region and the Seifali alunite occurrence of the Gedabek ore region of the Somkhit-Agdam zone. Alunite and pyrophyllite mineralization is related to hydrothermal-metasomatic low temperature type. The mineralization is spatially and paragenetically associated with skarn-magnetite formation. The alunite and pyrophyllite mineralization was formed by metasomatic reworking of pyroclastic rocks of the Upper Kimmeridgian age under conditions of high oxygene inflow. The layered structure of the deposit was caused by selective metasomatic substitution of rocks of volcanogenic series.

(e)   Polymetallic formation

The deposits and occurrences of polymetallic formation are located in the Gedabek, Qazakh-Gandja, Mekhmana, Dashkesan, Gyumushlug and Ordubad ore regions of the Lesser Cauacsus. The mineralization is characterized by a variable time interval of formation and spatial distribution and related to the vein hydrothermal type. The Mekhmana polymetallic deposit occurs in the Mekhmana ore region of the Somkhit-Agdam zone. The deposit was formed during the initial phase of pre-collision stage ore of genesis and confined to the Bajocian quartz plagioporphyres. Steeply dipping quartz-carbonaceous veins contain galenite, sphalerite, and chalcopyrite and pyrite in small quantities.

(f)   Massive sulphide-polymetallic formation

The Filizchay, Katekh and Kasdag deposits and numerous occurrences of this formational type are concentrated in ore regions of the Saribash metallogenic zone of the Greater Caucasus. The Ordubad ore region of the Ordubad-Zangezur zone hosts also the Agdara small deposit of this formational type. The massive sulphide-polymetallic mineralization within the Greater Caucasus is mainly located in the Filizchay-Attagay ore zone. The mineralization is structurally controlled by deeply-seated upthrusts and overthrusts. Thick layered deposits of massive sulphide ores are located within uplifted blocks in substantially clayey deep-water shales of the Lower-Middle Jurassic. The deposits have been formed during the oceanic stage of ore genesis and are related to the hydrothermal-sedimentary and hydrothermal-metasomatic types. Lead, zinc and copper are the basic ore components.

The Agdara deposit of the Ordubad ore region has been formed during the Paleocene-Eocene period of the collision stage of tectogenesis and is related to the hydrothermal-metasomatic type. The deposit is hosted by the Lower Eocene volcanites of basalt-andesite-dacite subformation. The mineralization is localized in secondary quarzites as layered-lens-shaped massive ores and vein-disseminated occurrences.

(g)   Copper-molybdenum formation

Copper-molybdenum mineralization is concentrated within the Ordubad and Dalidag ore regions of the Lesser Caucasus. Within the Ordubad ore region, the formation is represented by the small Paragachay deposit and several occurrences. The mineralization was formed during the Oligocene-Miocene phase of the collision stage of ore genesis. The molybdenite, pyrite, chalcopyrite and magnetite mineralization has been found to occur in quartz veins and stockworks localised in marginal parts of intrusive massifs. The mineralization is being controlled by tectonic faults of various limbs. Within the Dalidag ore region, the vein type mineralization is genetically associated with exocontacts of the Late Eocene-Early Pliocene granitoid intrusions.

(h)   Gold-copper-sulphide formation

Gold-copper-sulphide mineralization has been found in the Mazimchay deposit within the Balakan-Zakataly ore region of the Greater Caucasus as well as in the Gedabek and Gizilbulag deposits and the Agkend occurrence of the Lesser Caucasus. Mineralization has been formed during the pre-collision stage of ore genesis and is confined to the Bajocian terrigenous formations on the Greater Caucasus and Bajocian quartz porphyres, gabbro-diorites and plagioliparites in the Lesser Caucasus. Ore bodies of stockwork and lens-shape and hydro-thermal genesis contain pyrite, chalcopyrite, sphalerite, rarely galenite, arsenopyrite, magnesite and other minerals. The deposits of this formational type in the Lesser Caucasus contain mineable reserves of precious metals.

(i)   Gold sulphide-quartz formation

The deposits and occurrences of this formational type have been found across the whole territory of the Lesser Caucasus. Within the Somkhit-Agdam metallogenic zone, the mineralization was formed during the initial stage of pre-collision period and the Late Cretaceous stage of collision period of ore genesis. The mineralization is confined to tectonic faults in volcanogenic formation of basalt-andesite-dacite composition. Ore bodies of hydrothermal genesis are represented by vein and fissure-disseminated types of mineralization. On the territory of the Geychay-Garabag zone, hydrothermal veins of this formational type are genetically associated with gabbro-diorite-granodiorite massifs of the Eocene-Oligocene age localized in exocontact zones of intrusions.

Within the Gafan zone, the mineralization has been formed during the final phase of pre-collision stage and the Paleocene-Eocene phase of continental stage of ore genesis in genetic linkage with andesite-basalt and andesite-dacite-ryolite formations of magmatic rocks. Ore-bearing bodies of vein and stockwork type are confined to exocontacts and alkaline parts of magmatic intrusives complicated by fissures, fractures and linear faults.

On the territory of the Ordubad ore region of the Ordubad-Zangezur metallogenic zone, the mineralization was formed during the final phase of collision stage of ore genesis in association with granitoid intrusions and volcanic structures of andesite-basalt composition. Ore bodies are represented by veins, columnur bodies and irregular zones of mineralization. Noble metals, pyrite, chalcopyrite, galenite, sphalerite, rarely molybdenum and antimonite are typomorphic minerals for this formational type.

(j)   Gold-bearing-metasomatic formation

The mineral deposits and occurrences of this formational type are distributed within the Somkhit-Agdam and Ordubad-Zangezur metallogenic zones of the Lesser Caucasus. Mineralization on the territory of the first zone is confined to the final phase of pre-collision stage of ore genesis and associated with magmatic bodies of gabbro-diorite-plagiogranite composition. Within the Ordubad-Zangezur zone, the mineralization was formed during the Paleocene-Eocene period of collision stage of ore genesis being genetically associated with basalt-andesite formation. Mineralization in both zones is structurally controlled by zones of intensive tectonic faults, fractures and fissures pronounced in magmatic rocks. Ore bodies are mainly represented by stockworks containing noble metals, pyrite, chalcopyrite and sphalerite.

(k)   Porphyry copper formation

Porphyry copper mineralization is distributed within the ore regions of the Lesser Caucasus and have been formed during two stages of ore genesis. Porphyry copper deposits of the Gedabek and Murovdag ore regions are confined to the Bajocian plagiogranites and quartz porphyres or the Bathonian effusive-pyroclastic series intruded by dykes of diorite porphyrites. Ore bodies are represented by veins, stringers, clustered impregnated zones of hydrofermal type containing pyrite, chalcopyrite, rarely galenite, magnetite and molybdenite. Porphyry copper mineralization of the Ordubad ore region has been formed during the final phase of continental stage of ore genesis being represented by stockworks, stringers and impregnated bodies in endocontact zones of monzonite intrusive massif. Two types of porphyry copper mineralization have been distinguished, namely (i) quartz-magnetite with molybdenum and chalcopyrite, and (ii) quartz-chalcopyrite with molybdenite and pyrite.

(l) Mercury, antimony and arsenic formations

Mercury and associated antimony and arsenic mineralization are concentrated mainly within the Shorbulag-Levchay ore region of the Gechay-Garabag metallogenic zone of the Lesser Caucasus. The mineralization of this formational type has been found in the Shorbulag, Agkara, Agyatag, Chilgyazchay (mercury), in the Levchay antimony-mercury small deposit and more than 100 mineral occurrences. The mineralization has been concentrated during the continental stage of ore genesis to be related to the telethermal genetic type. The mineralization is associated with eruptive rocks hosted by jasperoid, argillite-carbonaceous, clayey-siliceous and calcic rock types. Ore bodies of lens and vein types contain mineralization pronounced as insets, stringers, shallow nests and selvages. Tectonic zones and faults of various limbs control the mineralization of this formational type. Cinnabar is the main mineral of mercury mineralization being sporadically accompanied by chalcopyrite, galenite, sphalerite, realgar and arsenopyrite. Cinnabar, antimonite, realgar, associated pyrite, sphalerite and orpiment are considered to be the main ore minerals of mercury mineralization.

Within the Darridag-Paradish ore region of the Ordubad-Zangezur metallogenic zone, the Darridag deposit and occurrences of antimony-arsenic ores are confined to fractured and alteration zones. The mineralization here is associated with recent andesite-dacite subvolcanic bodies of stockwork and stringer types containing realgar, orpigment, antimonite, rarely cinnabar and pyrite.

II. MINERAL DEPOSITS AND OCCURRENCES OF AZERBAIJAN

The territory of Azerbaijan covers a part of the Mediterranean Alpine belt of Eurasia, being characterized by complex geologic and tectonic structures and numerous formational types of mineral concentrations and hydrocarbon accumulations within folded systems of the Greater and Lesser Caucasus, Kura intermountain depression and Talysh Mountain.

Azerbaijan is very well endowed with mineral deposits. More than one billion tons of crude oil has been produced in the Absheron peninsula and Azerbaijan sector of the Caspian Sea over the last 100 years. Large reserves of oil and gas have been concentrated in producing horizons of the Lower Pliocene. Oil and gas fields have been also discovered in the Miocene, Oligocene and Eocene horizons of the Shemakha-Gobustan, Lelakh-Agdjabedi and Ganja regions and in the watershed of Kura and Gabirri rivers. Nearly 350 mineral deposits of metallic, non-metallic minerals, construction materials and drilling brines with mineable reserves have been explored in the country (Geology of the USSR, 1976; Shekinsky and others, 1998; Zamanov and others, 1998). The mineral resources of the country are subdivided into fuel, metallic and non-metallic minerals and construction materials.

Major deposits of ferrous metals occur in the Murovdag ridge of the Lesser Caucasus. Large reserves of cobalt and iron ore have been discovered in the South Dashkesan magnetite deposit and the Alabashli hematite deposit within the Azerbaijanian part of the Lesser Caucasus. The Filizchay, Katekh and Kasdag sulphide-polymetallic deposits on the western part of the southern slope of the Greater Caucasus contain large mineable reserves of zinc, lead, copper, associated silver, gold, cobalt, selenium, tellurium and bismuth. Copper-pyrite and porphyry copper ores are known to exist in the Khar-Khar deposit in the Kedabek region of the Lesser Caucasus and in the Mekhmana deposit in the Karabakh ridge. The Dashkesan ore region hosts numerous deposits and occurrences of cobalt ore with large mineable reserves. The Paragachay molybdenum deposit is associated with the Ordubad intrusive pluton in the Nakhchivan Autonomous Republic of Azerbaijan. The Ordubad intrusive massif also hosts numerous deposits and occurrences of mercury-antimony ore, gold, silver and other associated metals. Some deposits of noble metals and mercury are localized in the Gedabek region of the Lesser Caucasus. Large mineable reserves of zeolites and bentonites have been discovered in the Qazakh trough. The Dagkesaman and Gasan-Su sulphide-polymetallic and gold deposits have been explored in the Qazakh trough recently. The Lesser Caucasus region hosts large mineable reserves of dolomite, barite and limestones. The Nakhchivan and Negrom deposits of the Nakhchivan trough contain unique reserves of rock salt. The Nakhchivan Autonomous Republic and other regions of the Lesser Caucasus host also large reserves of raw materials for cement production as well as facing and dimension stones. The Karabakh ridge hosts several deposits of optical materials. Large reserves of dolomites and quartz sands have been explored in the Gobustan and Gubadag districts. Mineral water springs and therapeutic muds are known to exist in the Absheron peninsula, Neftchala and other regions of the Lesser and Greater Caucasus. The total cost of recoverable reserves of 28 kinds of mineral resources excluding hydrocarbons has been estimated at 36.3 billion US dollars. Around 40 per cent of these recoverable reserves are being exploited. Mining and processing of deposits of precious and base metals is being carried out by the state-owned mining enterprises.

The proved geological potential of Azerbaijan constitutes a favourable basis for the future development of the mining industry. The Government is undertaking regulatory measures to attract foreign investment to the mineral sector.

A. Fuel resources

1. Oil and Natural Gas

Azerbaijan started the industrial exploitation of hydrocarbon resources in 1871 in the Absheron peninsula. By the end of nineteenth century, around 10 million tons of crude oil had been produced from the Surakhan, Sabunchi, Ramani and Bibi-Eibat old fields. At the beginning of the twentieth century, an 850 kilometres-long Baku-Batumi pipeline was built by the Swedish millionaire Nobel to transport Azerbaijan oil to the western countries. After the First World War and the formation of the USSR, the oil industry of Azerbaijan was nationalized and a Baku-Batumi pipeline was partially destroyed and lost its economic and political significance. A well-established oil, gas, petrochemical industries with supporting oil machine manufacturing industries, research institutions and trained personnel were created in the country during the existence of the former Soviet Union (Alikhanov, 1968; Aliyev and others, 1985; Ali-zade and others, 1966).

(a) Tectonic setting of major oil-gas perspective territories

At present, large reserves of hydrocarbon fuels have been explored not only on the Absheron peninsula and Azerbaijan shelf of Caspian sea, but also in the Fore-Caspian lowland, Shamakha-Gobustan region, Middle and Lower Kura depression, Ganja region and in the west of Azerbaijan.

The potential to increase reserves in the known deposits and discover new oil and gas fields in Azerbaijan is quite high depending on newly emerging technologies and methodologies in petroleum exploration. Several schemes of oil-gas zonation have been worked out during the last 25 years in Azerbaijan based on a methodology of the Geological Department of the Ministry of Oil and Gas Industry of the former USSR. The results of this work have been published in the monograph entitled "Oil-gas-bearing provinces of the USSR". The latest oil-gas zonation of the petroliferous basins of Azerbaijan was worked out in 1985 (Aliyev and others, 1985).

The petroliferous and potentially petroliferous basins of Azerbaijan are located within the southern Caspian oil-gas-bearing province. Tectonically, the basins are confined to the recent depression zones of the Caucasus-Kopetdag mobile belt characterized by a considerable thickness of the Meso-Cenozoic sedimentary rocks up to more than 20 kilometres. According to the recent oil-gas zonation scheme, seven petroliferous basins have been delineated on the territory of Azerbaijan (figure 5).

A brief description of the geological structure, conditions of production and exploration of major oil and gas fields is given below. Some comments on prospective areas and horizons of each oil-gas-bearing basin are given in conclusion.

Absheron oil-gas-bearing region

The region occupies the Absheron peninsula and aquatorium of the adjacent shelf of the Caspian Sea, limited by the Kyapaz uplift on the east. Tectonically, the region represents a periclinal trough of mountain-folded system of the Greater Caucasus limited from the west by the Yashlyn abyssal fault. The thickness of sedimentary cover within the region varies from 15 to 20 kilometres. The region is characterized by the development of the Absheron type of productive series section. Reservoirs are well absorptive sands with high values of viscosity and permeability. Rhythmic alternation of sandy reservoirs and clayey caps and favourable structural conditions enabled hydrocarbons saturation of the whole productive series section on the Absheron peninsula and the adjacent shelf aquatorium. Recent geophysical and drilling exploration has resulted in a discovery of new unique oil fields within the Azeri, Chirag and Kyapaz structures. More than fourty oil-gas-bearing deposits have been delineated in the sections of the Balakhan-Sabunch-Ramani, Surakhani and Bibi-Eibat productive structures.

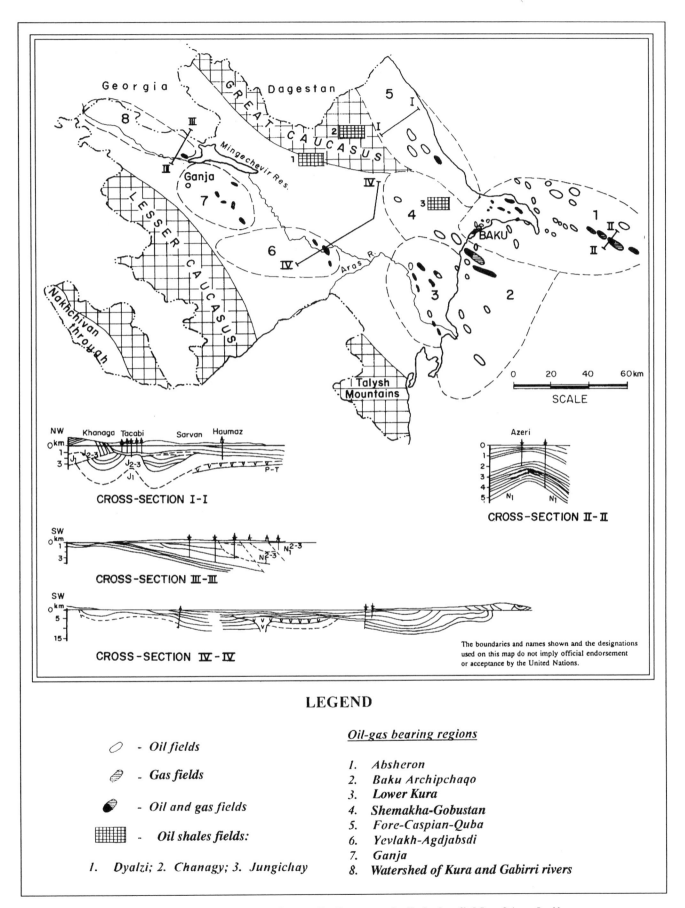

LEGEND

$\oslash$ — *Oil fields*

$\oslash$ — *Gas fields*

◐ — *Oil and gas fields*

▦ — *Oil shales fields:*

1. Dyalzi; 2. Chanagy; 3. Jungichay

Oil-gas bearing regions

1. *Absheron*
2. *Baku Archipchaqo*
3. *Lower Kura*
4. *Shemakha-Gobustan*
5. *Fore-Caspian-Quba*
6. *Yevlakh-Agdjabsdi*
7. *Ganja*
8. *Watershed of Kura and Gabirri rivers*

Figure 5. Petroliferous basins and oil, gas and oil shales fields of Azerbaijan

The average thickness of the productive series within the Absheron oil-gas-bearing region varies from 1,200 to 1,400 metres. The increased thickness of a range 3,600-4,200 metres and more was traced in uplifted tectonic structures and within the Bakhar, Zirya and Bina-Govsan synclines. In the area of the Shakh deniz oil deposit, the thickness of productive series proved by drilling is more than 5,000 metres.

The cross-section of productive series of the Lower Pliocene within the Absheron petroliferous region is subdivided into the upper Surakhani, Sabunchi and Balakhan suite, "hiatus suite" and fore-Kirmaki clayey suite, the Lower Kirmaki sandy suite, Kirmaki suite, Lower Kirmaki and Kala suites. There are grounds to believe that in the more subsided zones of the Absheron petroliferous basin, more ancient beds of productive series will be met below the Kala suite.

Tectonically, the Absheron oil-gas-bearing region has a complex structure, characterized by development of folds of various limbs due to superposition of the Mesozoic, Paleogene-Miocene and Pliocene-Quaternary structural stages on each other. The folding of the Mesozoic structural stage has a sub-latitudinal orientation and is more clearly pronounced in shallow zones of the North Absheron uplifts. The sub-latitudinal Mesozoic folding is also traced in structures of more recent complexes of the Buzovna-Mashtaga uplift. The rocks of the Paleogene-Miocene and Upper Cretaceous stratigraphic sections are outcropped in the north-western part of the Absheron region. South-eastward, these sections sharply subsided to a considerable depth of up to seven kilometres. In the central part of the Absheron peninsula, the amplitude of subsidence over a distance of 75 kilometres from the Djorat to Bakhar oil fields is more than 5,000 metres on the base of productive series.

The northern Absheron zone of uplifts of sub-latitudinal extent constitutes the large tectonic element of the Absheron oil-gas-bearing region. This zone includes the Goshadash, Agburun deniz, Absheron bank, Garabag, Gilavar, Dan-Ulduzu, Ashrafi, Nakhchivan and Aypara-Arzu uplifts. In the western part of this zone, the Lower-Upper Cretaceous strata have been struck by drilling in shallow depths at the areas of the Agburun deniz and Absheron bank deposits. In the Gilavar area, the surface of the Mesozoic strata subsided to a depth of more than 4,000 metres. Small oil reserves have been proved in the Kirmaki suite and these of gas-condensate in the Kala suite of the productive horizon of the Absheron deposit. Future prospects of petroleum potential in the northern Absheron zone of uplifts are associated with further detailed petroleum exploration of the major oil-gas-bearing productive series. The Darvin bank-Pirallakhigadasi-Gyurgyan deniz structural units of sub-meridianal direction and the Khazri, Chilov, Palchig pilpilasi and Neft-Dashlari structural units of north-west-south-eastern direction of the Absheron archipelago join in the south the northern Absheron zone of uplifts. The structures of the Absheron archipelago are separated from the northern Absheron zone of uplifts by the Pirallakhi syncline. Within the Absheron archipelago, a significant part of productive series section is developed and outcropped at the bottom of the sea up to the Kala suite of the Chilov basin. Petroleum exploration of revealed anticlinal structures within the Absheron archipelago identified large hydrocarbon reserves. The discovered oil deposits are localized in the lower section of productive series. Gas-condensate deposits are found only in the Janub subsided structure. Further exploration work on productive series is required.

The major structural element of the Absheron oil-gas-bearing region is the Azerbaijan sector of the Absheron-Fore-Balakhan archy threshold, stretching in sub-latitudinal direction to the north-east from the Neft-Dashlari zone. The top of productive series within the threshold sharply subsided to a depth of 1,000-1,200 metres and amplitude of subsidence in regard to the Neft-Dashlari zone is 3,000 metres along the top of the "hiatus" suite. The first deep-water multilayered Gunashli field was discovered following petroleum exploration work. The Azeri, Chirag and Kyapaz prospective structures were delineated and prepared by seismic detailed works for a deep exploration drilling. In 1988, these prospective structures were explored from semi-submersible platform.

Further exploration in the shallow water part of the Azeri, Chirag and Kyapaz prospective structures showed large oil and gas accumulations in the Balakhan suite (VI, VII, VIII, IX, X, XI horizons) and "hiatus" suite of the upper section of productive suite. According to AMOCO estimates, the recoverable reserves of hydrocarbons in only two Azeri-Chirag fields are accounted at 655 million tons. In November 1997, a strong gusher of oil with a daily well discharge from 1,800 to 3,000 tons was obtained from the floating Koroglu platform that proved the forecasts of Azerbaijanian specialists and foreign experts.

The "Caspian-Geophysics" company has conducted during the years 1997-1998 a detailed three-dimensional seismic exploration in the eastern part of the northern Absheron zone of uplifts in the foreign concession areas over the Garabag, Dan Ulduzu and Ashrafi and Nakhchivan structures. In the drilled wells of the Garabag and Ashrafi structures, commercial oil, gas and gas-condensate flows of productive series were obtained from the lower section of the productive series. Calculated oil and gas reserves have not been, however, proved of these two structures at present. Up to now, total oil and gas-condensate reserves of the Garabag field is estimated at 30 million tons.

The Koun-Shabandag-Lokbatan uplifts of the western Absheron anticline and the Kirmaki-Bakhar uplifts of the Central Absheron anticline as well as adjacent synclinal troughs with oil-bearing fragmented uplifts are the basic structural units of the Absheron peninsula and major targets for the nearest oil exploitation. The Paleogene-Miocene deposits and the whole cross-section of the productive series including the Kirmaki suite are outcropped in the western Absheron in most structures of diapiric type.

The revealed oil fields are basically associated with stratigraphic and tectonically-screened types of traps found in the Binagady-Chakhnaglyar, Sulutapa, Atashkyah-Shabandag and Yasamal valley structural units. South-westwards, the cross-section of the productive series becomes more clayey, folding bend subsides, a depth of occurrence of regional oil-gas-bearing suites increases, oil deposits are substituted by the Lokbatan, Puta and Gushkhana gas-oil and the Karadag gas-condensate structures. The Bibi-Eibat fold of the south-western Absheron region joints the Atashkyah uplift through a shallow saddle-like trough. The Bibi-Eibat oil deposits have been developed since 1871. More than 40 productive layers were delineated in the cross-section of the productive series in the Balakhan-Sabunchi-Ramani deposit. Oil deposits are basically confined to the archy, tectonically-screened types of traps.

The main structural unit of the Absheron petroliferous basin is the central Absheron anticline, which stretches in submeridional direction over a distance of more than 75 kilometres from Kirmaki on the north to Shakh deniz on the south. Considerable parts of hydrocarbon resources of this oil-gas-bearing region are concentrated in this zone. Oil production had been realized in the Balakhan-Sabunchi-Ramani deposits since 1871. The thickness of productive series varies from 1,200 metres in the Kirmaki region to 3,000 metres and more in the Shakh deniz region. All structures involved into exploration of this zone appeared to be commercial oil-gas-bearing. Revealed deposits are basically confined to the archy, tectonically-screened and stratigraphic traps. The ratio of liquid and gaseous hydrocarbons within this zone is variable. Southwards, oil deposits are substituted by oil-gas and gas-condensate deposits.

The most prospective and largest structure of this zone is Shakh deniz. Following the completion of the contract with British Petroleum in February 1999, two exploratory wells with a projected depth of 5,500 metres were installed on the archy part of the Shakh deniz structure, where opening of multi-layered field with oil-gas-condensate deposits is to be expected. Gas resources of this structure are estimated at 1 trillion cubic metres.

Thus, the Absheron oil-gas-bearing region in spite of more than one hundred years of oil production is still the most prospective area for the enhancement of hydrocarbon reserves and the development of the oil and gas industry in Azerbaijan. Fifty prospective structures have been discovered by petroleum exploration work in the region over a long period of time. Thirty-five structures underwent deep exploration drilling resulting in the discovery of recoverable oil and gas reserves in thirty structures.

Oil-gas-bearing region of the Baku archipelago

This petroliferous region covers a structural zone of the western shelf of the southern Caspian Sea within minus 200 metres isobath. Twenty four small uplifts have been discovered by seismic exploration (figures 5 and 6). This region is not considered to be an independent tectonic element and represents a marine continuation of structures of the Jeyrankechmaz and lower Kura depressions. The Baku archipelago is characterized by active neo-tectonic movement, manifestations of mud volcanism and intensive dislocations of local uplifts complicated by a series of longitudinal and cross faults.

Prospective areas of the central and northern parts of the Baku archipelago contain a complete upper section of the productive series exposed by deep prospecting drilling. The underlying rocks of the Pontian and Upper Diatom productive series were struck by singular wells in the fore-arc areas of the Sangachali deniz and Duvanni deniz structures.

The cross-section of the productive series within the Baku archipelago is more clayey in comparison with that in the Absheron region. Total thickness of sandy beds varies from 25 to 30 per cent of the upper section of the productive series. The upper sections of V-VII horizons (according to Garabag separation) are sandier. Thickness of the upper section of the productive series within the Baku archipelago varies from 3,000 to 3,500 metres.

The deep prospecting drilling in thirteen local structures of the Baku archipelago identified the Sangachali deniz, Duvanni deniz, Bulla adasi gas-condensate-oil and the Bulla deniz gas-condensate deposits. Recoverable reserves of oil and gas have been also proved for the VII horizon of the productive series in the Duvanni deniz, Garasu, Alyat deniz and 8 March deposits. Horizons V, VI and VIII of the productive series are the basic oil-gas-bearing objects. The above deposits are related to the tectonically-screened type and have a significant height in their hydrocarbon cross-section.

Further prospects of the oil and gas industry and enhancement of hydrocarbon reserves in the Baku archipelago is coupled with detailed petroleum exploration of "8 March" and the Alyat deniz deposits and suites of the lower section of the productive series within existing oil and gas deposits.

New discoveries of large oil and gas fields within the Khazri, Inam, Alov, Nakhchivan and Kurdashi prospective structures are expected following the petroleum exploration programmes under signed contracts with AMOCO, Lukoil, Exxon, AZHIB and Itochu oil companies. At present, detailed three-dimensional seismic exploration is conducted by a leading Caspian Geophysics company within the above structures to prepare them for a deep exploration drilling. The Gizilagach, Talysh deniz and Lenkaran deniz new large structures have been recently identified by seismic exploration in the lowest areas of the Baku archipelago. The detailed seismic exploration work on the Talysh deniz and Lenkaran structures are currently being conducted by Total and Elf-Aqutaine French company.

Lower Kura oil-gas region

Tectonically, this region is a part of the Southern Caspian depression. It represents an intermountain trough of the same name limited on the south-west by the Talysh-Vandam gravitational maximum and on the north and the north-east by the Lengebiz-Alyat zone of uplifts. On the east and south-east, the region stretches to the South Caspian Sea. The thickness of sedimentary cover within the Lower Kura oil-gas-bearing region reaches 20 kilometres. More than six kilometres of cross-section falls into the Pliocene-Quaternary stratigraphic sequence. The territory of the region has been systematically mapped and studied by regional and detailed geological and geophysical exploration and drilling. Seventeen prospective structures were delineated within the Lower Kura petroliferous region subdivided into the Kalamadin-Kharami-Mishovdag-Byandoyan and Kyurovdag-Neftchala anticlinal zones. Two buried uplifts were located within the Mugan-Salyan (Padar) and Karagala (Kyursangi) synclines. The structures extend in the northwest-southeast direction and, in most cases, are strongly dislocated

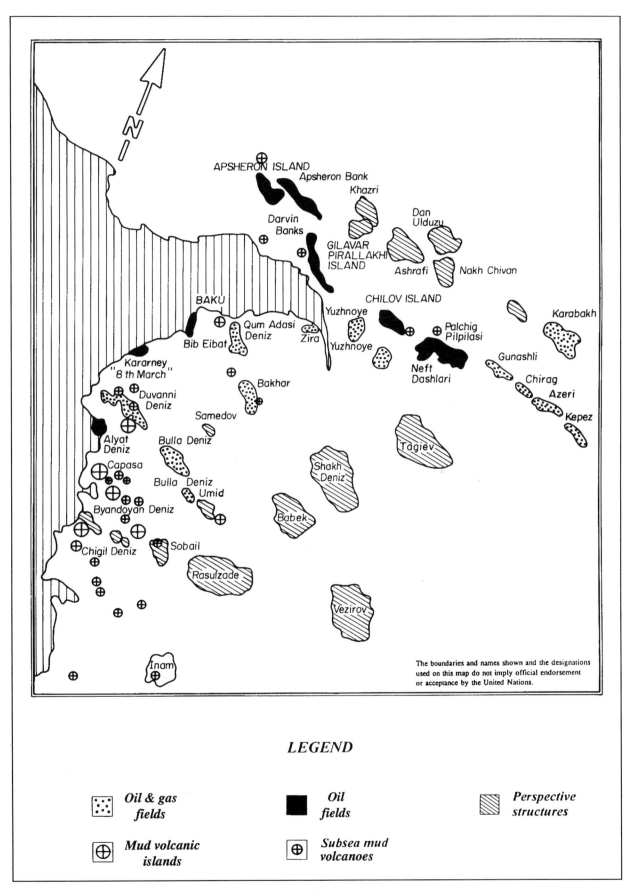

Figure 6. Location of oil and gas fields in Azerbaijan sector of the Caspian Sea

and complicated by mud volcanism. The hydrocarbon productive series crops out on the surface in the archy areas of the most uplifted Kalamadin, Beyuk and Kichik Kharami, Babazanan structural units. In the adjacent synclines, its upper roof submerges to a depth of 3,000 metres and more. Deep prospecting drilling of all revealed local structures of the Lower Kura petroliferous basin has enabled the identification of nine new oil and gas-condensate deposits. Commercial oil and gas discharges were obtained on other structures from various intervals of the productive series. The Kyurovda deposit is the most remarkable one among the discovered deposits. The Kyursangi, Mishovdag and Karabakhli deposits contain hydrocarbon reserves of medium size; the Kalmas, Prisagat, Neftchala and Kalamadin deposits have small reserves.

The hydrocarbon productive series contains a significant part of proved oil and gas reserves and is considered to be the major oil-gas-bearing complex of the exposed part of the cross-section. Small deposits with recoverable reserves were found in the stratigraphic intervals of the Akchagil and Absheron stages. The productive series has been completely transected by deep drilling in all revealed structures including underlying rocks in the areas of the Kalamadin, Beyuk and Kichik Kharami, Kalmas, Pirsagat and Byandovan structures; its maximal thickness reaches more than 4,000 metres. Suites of the upper group represent the productive series across most of the territory of the Lower Kura depression. The shortening of this stratigraphic interval has developed along the north-west and the south-west directions and was noticed in the areas of the Pirsagat and Byandovan structures. It suggests that the complete cross-section of the hydrocarbon productive series will be developed in the Karagala syncline including the Kyursangi structure. In this respect, the hydrocarbon potential of these structures is sharply increasing. The stratigraphic types of traps in the bottom part of the productive series on the inverted wings to the Karagala syncline are being investigated now.

The known cross-section of the productive series in the Lower Kura oil-gas-bearing region is lithologically represented by irregular alternation of sandy aleurolite and clayey rocks. Sands and sandstones are heterogeneous, and grouped in 20 sandy horizons. Thicker beds of sandstones from 600 to 800 metres are distinguished in the upper part of the section. This section represents the main oil-gas-bearing interval in the Lower Kura depression.

Southeastwards, the cross-section of the productive series becomes more clayey and capacity and filtration properties of reservoirs worsen. Over 60 per cent of the initial potential resources of hydrocarbons were found in the Lower Kura oil-gas-bearing region. By density of estimated resources, this petroliferous basin remains the most prospective onshore oil-gas-bearing region. Further prospects of resource enhancement depend on the results of detailed petroleum exploration in the areas of the Kyursangi oil and gas field and structural units of the Karagala syncline along the Alyat ridge.

Recently, the State Oil Company and the Government of Azerbaijan have signed a US$550 million contract with "Frontier Research Company" of the Untied States of America on the development of hydrocarbon resources of the Kyursangi and Karabakhli fields including detailed petroleum exploration.

The Shemakha-Gobustan petroliferous basin

Tectonically, this basin represents a marginal trough of more than 100 kilometres extension superimposed on rocks of the southern flank of the south-eastern subsidence of the Greater Caucasus mega-anticlinorium. Thick accumulation of plastic clayey formations of the Paleogene-Miocene interval in the Central and South Gobustan structures characterize the basin. The synclines are densely dislocated and fractured by faults and complicated by mud volcanoes. The thickness of the sedimentary cover varies from 15 to 20 kilometres. In the Central and South Gobustan, the Cretaceous deposits submerge sharply to a significant depth and the Mesozoic folding stage is overlaid by the Paleogene-Miocene cover.

The Tertiary deposits are represented by a complete stratigraphic interval from the Paleocene to the Upper Pliocene with a total thickness of over 8,000 metres. The Paleogene deposits of up to 3,000 metres thick are represented, mainly, by clayey formations with thin beds of sandy-aleurolitic rocks, fractured dolomites and marls. The Miocene deposits are composed mainly of interbeds of sands sandstones and aleurolites.

Seven sandy seams are distinguished in the cross-section of the Upper Maikop. The thickness varies from 700 to 800 metres in the south-east of the Gobustan synclines. These benches are of practical interest from the viewpoint of hydrocarbon potential. The Pliocene deposits of 500 metres thick are developed only in the south-east of the Gobustan structure within the Jeyrankechmaz depression and represented by sandy-clayey rocks with organogenic limestones in the upper part of the section. The Lower Maikop section of the productive series of 3,500 metres thick on extreme south-east is characterized by a dominant clay content of the section and course-grained sandstones and aleurolites rocks. Six tectonic zones have been distinguished in the Shemakha-Gobustan region according to structural-tectonic setting vis-a-vis the northern Gobustan, Shemakha, central Gobustan, south-western Gobustan, Jeyrankechmaz and Alyat ridge zones. Complex folding of the Cretaceous deposits and intensive development of tectonic dislocations characterize the northern Gobustan zone.

The Shemakha zone is bounded on the west by the Bascal cover and is represented by structures of the Paleogene-Miocene stage. The zone contains numerous narrow and elongated arches. The elongated Paleogene-Miocene anticlinal zones of the south-eastern direction are developed in the central Gobustan. In the south-western Gobustan, the anticlinal belts extend in the latitudinal direction. The fractured rocks of the Paleogene-Miocene are outcropped in the archy parts of the structures.

The Jeyrankechmaz depression is represented by the Pliocene structures forming the tectonic belts of different directions. The structure of these belts is complicated by tectonic faults. The elongated uplifts of the south-eastern direction are traced in the Alyat ridge zone. These uplifts are composed of the Paleogene-Miocene and Pliocene deposits. The specific feature of the region is an intensive development of mud volcanic activity within its borders. Over 110 anticlinal structures were discovered within the Shemakha-Gobustan region in the Mesozoic, Paleogene-Miocene and Pliocene-Quaternary structural stages.

The petroleum potential of the region is pronounced by surface oil-gas shows as mud volcanoes, oil discharges and gushers witnessed during the drilling of the Adjiveli, Ragim, Cheildag, Shikhgaya, Anart, Miadjik, Utalgi, Touragai, Koturdag, Solahai and other oil fields. However, the petroleum exploration work, which has been carried out for a long period of time, did not lead to great discoveries.

The only Umbaki small oil and gas deposit was discovered in the Upper Maikop and Chokrak sandy interval. The Duvanni, Dashgil and Kyanizadag small deposits were found within the productive series. Major targets of petroleum exploration in the Shemakha-Gobustan region are associated, first of all, with carbonaceous reservoirs of the Upper Cretaceous in the central and southern Gobustan. In the Jeyrankechmaz depression, the hydrocarbon potential is associated with thick seams of sandstones of the Maikop and Chokrak suites bearing the recoverable oil-gas reserves of the Umbaki field. These suites submerge to considerable depths of over 4,000 metres and are overlaid by the Upper Miocene-Pliocene cover.

Fore-Caspian-Quba petroliferous basin

Tectonically, this basin includes the north-eastern wing of the south-eastern end of the Greater Caucasus mega-anticlinorium and the adjacent south-eastern part of the Tersk-Caspian front trough. The onshore length of the basin from the north-west to the south-east is up to 130 kilometres. The width is 50 kilometres. The width of the water area adjacent to the basin from the north-east is up to 60 kilometres. The total area of the onshore basin is 6,500 square kilometres including that with petroleum potential of 4,700 square kilometres. The thickness of the sedimentary cover in the basin is up to 10,000 metres.

The oil-gas-bearing suites of the Fore-Caspian-Quba basin contain sandy-aleurolitic interbeds and fractured carbonaceous rocks playing the role of reservoirs. Interbeds of sandy-aleurolitic rocks of a variable thickness from several centimetres to a range of 1-5 metres often occur in the sandy-clayey flysh of a total thickness up to 50 metres. Reservoirs of such type were developed in the sections of the Valanginian, Hauterivian, Albian, Maastrichtian, Danian, Sumgaitian, Kounian and Maijopian suites as well as in the Chokrak horizon and in the

Sarmatian suite. During the Aalenian and Bajocian internals, sandy-aleurolitic rocks have formed a monolithic bed up to 60 metres thick in separate areas. Fractured carbonaceous reservoirs have been developed during the Valanginian-Hauterivian-Maastrichtian and Danian intervals of the Mesozoic section. Tectonically, the Khizi zone is separated on the south from the Dibrar-Yashma zone. On the north-east, the Shakhdag-Khizi zone is bounded by the narrow Tengi-Beshbarmag zone composed of the Mesozoic deposits. These deposits are covered on the north-eastern flank by the Tertiary deposits of the Siazan monocline.

The Kusary-Devechi trough is situated to the north-east from the Tengi-Beshbarmag zone. The Cenozoic deposits of this trough overly formations of the Kainardja fore-deep trough and Pre-Samur tectonic zone, represented by the buried Gusar-Khachmaz and Yalama-Khudat Mesozoic structural uplifts. On the east, within the aquatorium of the Caspian Sea shelf, the Kusary-Devechi trough transects the south-western flank of the northern Absheron Cenozoic trough. Altogether, thirty anticlinal structures have been discovered within the Fore-Caspian-Quba region. Exploration work had been carried out on some of them, however, further detailed geophysical exploration is needed.

The exploration drilling have identified 17 structures in the Fore-Caspian-Quba region containing recoverable resources of oil and gas in the Tertiary and Upper Cretaceous formations. Six prospective deposits, namely the Chandagar-Zorat, Siazan-Nardaran, Saadan, Amirkhanli, Zaglik-east and Zaglik-Tengialti were delineated along the Siazan monocline. In addition, industrial flows of oil and gas were obtained at the Shurabad and Begimdag-Tegchay deposits from the Mesozoic formations.

Currently, within the Fore-Caspian-Quba petroliferous basin, exploitation of oil fields along the Siazan monocline is carried out on the Chandagar-Zorat, Siazan-Nardaran, Saadan, Amirkhanli, Zaglik (Zaglik-east) and Zeiva (Zaglik-Tengialti) deposits. The first four deposits of the Maikop suite and Chokrak horizon are in the preparatory stages for the exploitation. Oil production in separate wells is carried out from the deposits of the Upper Cretaceous, Sumgait and Koun suites. At the Zaglik and Zeiva deposits, oil is produced from the Lower Maikop, Koun, Sumgayit and the Upper Cretaceous intervals by joint exploitation using one filter.

The deposits under exploitation within the Siazan zone are associated with monoclinal occurrence of the Paleogene Miocene and Upper Cretaceous beds, often overturned to the north-east. The deposits are in bedded stratigraphically, lithologically and tectonically screened. The main targets of development are the sandy horizons of the Lower Maikop suite represented by alternation of sands layers from 15 to 25 centimetres thick, aleurolites, clays and marls. The total thickness of sandy seams of the upper horizons (I, II, III) is from 30 to 35 metres and that of the lower bed (IV-V) from 40 to 48 metres. The width does not exceed 300 metres. Oil occurrences of the Lower Cretaceous at the Begimdag-Tegchai and Shuraabad areas are tectonically-screened and lithologically limited.

According to estimates, limited resources of oil and gas in the Fore-Caspian-Quba region concentrate in some zones of the Siazan monocline and in the south-eastern part of the Quba trough. Substantial oil-gas resources are supposed to be in the Fore-Samur tectonic zone, aquatorium of the Caspian Sea shelf, in Tengi-Beshbarmag zone and in the south-eastern part of the Khizi zone.

The immediate petroleum exploration targets are the north-western continuation of the Siazan monocline in the Paleogene and the Upper Cretaceous deposits and in the south-eastern part of the Kainardja trough within the Talabi, West Kainardja and Kainardja uplifts. The Tengi-Beshbarmag zone and the south-eastern edge of the Khizi zone are prospective for search of oil and gas deposits in the Cretaceous and Jurassic deposits. Primary targets of exploration work are the Afurdja, Atachay-Gilgilchay, Beshbarmag, Shuraabad, Keshai, Begimdag-Tegchay and Sitalchay uplifts.

The hydrocarbon prospects of the Pre-Samur tectonic zone are associated with the Jurassic deposits occurring in depth interval from 3 to 7 kilometres. The oil and gas deposits of stratigraphic and lithologic types can also be identified in the Cretaceous and Paleogene-Miocene stratigraphic intervals. The Yalama, Khudat,

Shirvan, Imamgulikend, Kusary, Khachmaz and other uplifts have been recommended for exploration drilling. Within the aquatorium of the Fore-Caspian-Quba region, the main prospects of oil-gas resources are associated with the Jurassic, Cretaceous and the Paleogene-Miocene deposits.

The State Oil Company of Azerbaijan Republic "SOCAR" has signed a contract with the Russian Oil Company "Lukoil" for the exploration and development of oil fields in the Jurassic and Cretaceous deposits of the Yalama structure.

The Ganja petroliferous basin

In the past, this petroliferous basin included the territory to the south from the Shamkhoy nose up to Aras river on the south-east and Kura river on the north-east. Tectonically, it corresponded to the south-west flank of the Evlakh-Agdjabedi trough. The north-eastern flank of this trough supposed to be a member of the Adjinour petroliferous area.

The extensive geological research work, geophysical exploration and deep drilling conducted over the last 25 years have changed the understanding of the structure of the Evlakh-Agdjabedi trough and its flank systems. It was discovered that the Mesozoic fold basement of the Cenozoic sedimentary cover has subsided downstairs from the Lesser Caucasus in the north-eastern direction along the extended Fore-Lesser Caucasian fault. This enabled to localize the Ganja petroliferous basin only within the Lesser Caucasus superimposed trough limited on the north-east by the deep fault of the same name, and to consider the Evlakh-Agdjabedi trough as the independent oil-gas bearing region.

The Pre-Lesser Caucasus superimposed trough is characterized by heterogeneous structure of the Mesozoic basement of the Cenozoic sedimentary cover proved by the presence of numerous gravitational local anomalies apparently reflecting the projections of eroded surface of the Mesozoic stage of folding. The surface of the Mesozoic deposits submerges in the north-eastern direction to a depth from 4,000 to 4,500 metres. The presence of inter-formational breaks and discordance of the Mesozoic, Paleogene-Miocene and Pliocene-Quaternary structural settings characterize the trough. This complex structural setting makes it difficult to estimate resources and to plan further petroleum exploration in variable morphological types of traps, prospective for the industrial accumulations of hydrocarbons.

The whole territory of the basin has been covered by the systematic geological mapping of large-scale, detailed gravity, seismic and electro-sounding exploration surveys. Deposits of the Mesozoic, Paleogene-Miocene and the Upper Pliocene-Quaternary stratigraphic intervals take part in the geologic structure of the basin. The Jurassic deposits have a wide development in the adjacent zones of the Lesser Caucasus and are represented by the volcanogenic-sedimentary and sedimentary formations (argillites, clayey shales and various coarse rocks).

The Upper Cretaceous deposits are widely developed in the Ganja region and represented by volcanogenic and carbonaceous facies. Deep drilling at the Yalimamedli, Gazanbulag, Terter, Borsunli, Gyulludja, Agdjabedi, Bilasuvar and other deposits has transected the sequence. These deposits constitute the main oil and gas resources in the Ganja region. Massive fractured limestone of the Campanian-Maastrichtian interval is of special interest in the search for industrial oil and gas accumulations. In the Bilyasuvar deposit, the opened thickness of the Upper Cretaceous interval is over 2,000 metres. Only rocks of volcanogenic facies represent the sequence.

The upper part of the Upper Cretaceous section represented by the Santonian-Maastrichtian formations is composed of limestone from 160 to 180 metres thick in the archly arcs and up to 800 metres on the north-eastern wing of the uplift.

In the area of the Gazanbulag deposit, the lower part of the section of the Upper Cretaceous of 750 metres thick is represented mainly the volcanogenic rocks. The upper part of 80 metres thick, consists of limestone and marls. The Paleogene-Miocene rocks were proved by drilling on considerable part of the basin being represented mainly by clayey rocks with rare interbeds of sandy-aleurolitic and carbonaceous formations. The near shore-shallow water deposits of the Upper Pliocene transgressively overlie rocks of older series.

The exploration works in the Ganja basin were begun in 1930 in the Naftalan area, where small reserves of known medical oil in the Maikop deposits had been developed as far back as the second half of the nineteenth century. The exploration works carried out till 1940 have failed and a search for oil deposits was resumed in post-war years. A range of deposits in sandy reservoirs of the Eocene foraminifa beds and the Oligocene-Miocene of the Maikop suite were discovered as a result of these works and brought into development in the Naftalan, Gazanbulag, Adjidara and Terter prospective areas. The amount of exploratory drilling in the Ganja petroliferous basin was reduced later on owing to low oil debit of tested wells and little capacities of the Paleogene-Miocene reservoirs. Small oil deposits were identified in the Gazanbulag, Adjidara, Naftalan and Terter areas from ten deposits covered by exploratory drilling. Industrial oil flows were obtained from the Dalimame dili, Borsunly, Gedakboz and other deposits.

It is worthwhile to mention that for a long time the main targets of petroleum exploration in the Ganja region were the Lower Tertiary deposits. However, it has been recently found that the real prospects of this region for oil and gas discoveries are associated with the Mesozoic deposits, in particular, carbonaceous reservoirs of the Upper Jurassic and Upper Cretaceous. With this in view, re-evaluation of oil and gas prospects of the Ganja petroliferous basin is necessitated. Further petroleum exploration should focus on detailed mapping of the Mesozoic structure, including exploration and sampling of the fractured carbonaceous reservoirs.

The Yevlakh-Agdjabedi petroliferous basin

This petroliferous basin of over 150 kilometres long and 60 kilometres wide represents a deep trough of the same name with a thickness of the sedimentary cover up to 16 kilometres. On the north-east, the basin is bounded by the Saatly-Geychay zone of buried uplifts, composed of volcanogenic formations and transgressively overlaid by various rocks of the Paleocene-Miocene stratigraphic interval.

The south-western border of the basin is the Fore-Lesser Caucasian deep fault. On the north-west, the basin is bounded by the Shamhor Paleozoic structural nose and by the Aras deep fault on the south-east. This fault joints the Evlakh-Agdjabedi downlifted block with the Bilasuvar-Garadonli cross uplift. The surface of the Mesozoic deposits in the Evlakh-Agdjabedi trough submerges to a depth from 6,000 to 7,000 metres and elevates to 4,000 metres on the north-eastern flank.

Despite a considerable amount of geologic and prospecting work being carried out in Evlakh-Ahdjabedi trough, beginning from 1960, a complete understanding of its geologic structure and evaluation of hydrocarbon resources is still lacking. Regional and detailed exploration seismic works, carried out on the north-eastern flank of the trough, distinguished a range of buried uplifts, representing the Mesozoic erosion noses of the Mesozoic volcanogenic formations.

The industrial oil flows, which have been obtained from the volcanogenic formations of the Upper Cretaceous in early 1970s, have triggered a new stage of petroleum exploration and deep prospecting drilling within the Evlakh-Agdjabedi trough on the Muradkhanli, Zardob, Mil, Shirinkum and Amirarkh buried Mesozoic structures. In the Muradkhanli area, the contours of hydrocarbons area in volcanogenic formations has been widened. Small oil deposits were distinguished in the Eocene, Maikop and Chokrak horizons. Recoverable oil and gas resources have been also identified in the volcanogenic formations of the Zardob deposit. An important result of the prospecting works in the Evlakh-Agdjabedi trough is the obtaining of industrial oil flows at the Amirarkh, Shirinkum and Shihbagi deposits. A thick series of Mesozoic formations, represented by the terrigenous-carbonaceous and volcanogenic rocks, take part in the geologic structure of the region. Older Lower Cretaceous and Jurassic formations are represented by rocks of volcanogenic facies transected by deep drilling in the area of the Kurdamir gravitational maximum along the Terter Saatly, Djarly, Tpesorte and Karadjali deposits.

At the Saatli area, the super-deep well SG-1 has transected a 4.5 kilometres thick sequence of andesites, basalts and dacites of the Lower-Middle Jurassic age. Here, the Upper Jurassic sequence of 350 metres thick is represented by effusive formations of the lower part of the Callovian-Oxfordian stages and coral organogenic limestone in the upper part of the Oxfordian-Tithonian section. Drilling in the majority of Mesozoic structural noses transected the Upper Cretaceous rocks.

On the north-eastern flank of the Evlakh-Agdjabedi trough and in the Kyurdamir region in the areas of the Karadjali, Terter, Djarli, Amirarkh, Zardob, Muradkhanli, Mil and other structural units, the Upper Cretaceous section consists of volcanogenic-sedimentary and carbonaceous rocks. The thickness of carbonaceous formations of the Upper Cretaceous within the Evlakh-Agdjabedi trough varies from 300 to 400 metres in the flank parts to 1,400 metres in the submerged zones. The appropriate lithology and considerable thickness of the Upper Cretaceous carbonaceous formation make it attractive for further detailed petroleum exploration. The Upper Cretaceous deposits are overlaid transgressively by various seams of the Paleogene-Miocene formations in the flank zones of the Evlakh-Agdjabdi trough.

The Paleogene deposits were identified by drilling in all explored areas being represented, mainly, by clayey rocks with interbeds of marls, limestones, sandstones and tuff-sandstones. The Oligocene-Lower Miocene formations of the Maikop suite are also represented by dark-grey, brownish-grey clayey rocks with intrusions of numerous siderite, calcite-dolomite and, rarely, pyrite concretions. Their thickness reaches 2,500 metres in more submerged zones of trough; on its flank areas the thickness of the Maikop suite sharply reduces. The Middle-Upper Miocene deposits of 1,400 metres thick are represented by all the stages of the sedimentation process.

Zone of pinching out of separate stratigraphic intervals of the Paleogene-Miocene section have been traced by seismic and drilling data on the slopes of the Cenozoic structural noses along the north-eastern flank of the trough. In this connection, the search for non-structural traps of various morphologic types in the Paleogene-Miocene deposits is of considerable interest.

According to the data of prospecting works in the Evlakh-Agdjabedi trough, recoverable oil and gas reserves were identified in the Upper Cretaceous volcanogenic and carbonaceous reservoirs and terrigenous-carbonaceous rocks of the Eocene, in the Maikop suite and Chokrak horizon. Large oil and gas deposits, however, have not been found there. All the discovered fields similar to the Ganja basin, turned out to be small and confined to the heterogeneous reservoirs.

The main prospects for oil and gas discoveries in the Evlakh-Agdjabedi trough are associated with the Upper Cretaceous carbonaceous formations. The accumulation and filtration capacities of the fractured carbonaceous reservoirs of the Upper Cretaceous in some areas of the Evlakh-Aghdjabedi trough were proved by a high debit of groundwater (1,500-2,000 cubic metres per second) in the drilling wells in the areas of the north-eastern flank of the Muradkhanli, Djarli and Tertch structures as well as on the south-western flank of the Sovetlyar and other structures.

The petroliferous basin of the watershed of Kura and Gabirri rivers

The basin occupies an area of 2,700 square kilometres in the western part of Azerbaijan. It is bounded on the north by the Gabirri river basin, on the south by the Fore-Lesser Caucasian deep fault, and on the east by the Mingechevir reservoir. Tectonically, it represents the south-western flank of the Gabirri trough with a thickness of sedimentary cover of up to 12 kilometres. The basin has been studied by all methods of geophysical exploration, detailed geologic mapping, structural analysis and deep drilling. The gravimetric survey in the watershed of the Kura and Gabirri rivers distinguished a range of local gravity anomalies, which reflect the Mesozoic buried structures. The limbs of some of the structures do not coincide with the azimuth of the Caucasian structures, apparently owing to an eroded surface of the Pre-Cenozoic basement. Since the 1960s, the regional and detailed seismic surveys in the basin have been carried out up to a depth of 6 kilometres. In spite of considerable amount of geologic-geophysical exploration works, the geologic structure of this region remains uncertain due to a discordance of separate structural stages during various time slices. Structural units of the Pliocene-Quaternary structural stage in the Jeyrankechmaz depression cropped out on the surface, in some cases, do not find their reflection in the structures of the Paleogene and Mesozoic interval. Structural discordance was noticed between the Cretaceous-Paleogene and Neogene-Quaternary structural stages as well as between the folding of the Upper Pliocene-Quaternary and Miocene deposits expressed in integration of older structural elements with a depth. The surface of the Mesozoic deposits in the watershed of the Kura and Gabirri rivers is much deeper than in the Pre-Lesser Caucasian superimposed trough and varies from 4,500 metres on the south-west to 7,500 metres on the north-east of the basin. Over forty asymmetrical, in some cases overturned anticlinal structures complicated by longitudinal faults of overthrust type, were discovered in the watershed of the Kura and Gabirri rivers on the Neogene-Quaternary structural stage. Over twenty structures in the Paleogene-Upper Cretaceous interval have been seismically surveyed to enable exploration drilling.

The discovery of the first Tarsdallyar oil field and industrial oil flows in the Gyurzundag and Damirtepe-Udabno areas from the Middle Eocene deposits bring this region into the category of highly potential oil and gas-bearing basins of Azerbaijan.

The Eocene oil-bearing section from 1,000 to 1,300 metres thick transected by drilling in some areas of the Kura and Gabirri watershed is represented by clays with interbeds of sandstones and aleurolites in the lower part, by the alternation of clays, clayey marls, sandstones and tuff-sandstones of tuff-breccias in the middle part, and by clays with rare interbeds of sandstones and aleurolites in the upper part of the section. The Maikop suite and the Upper Miocene formation contain mainly clayey rocks with interbeds of sandstones and marls, and are not of practical interest.

Currently, the major oil and gas-bearing sequence with industrial recoverable reserves was identified in the Eocene deposits, characterized by development of the favourable terrigenous and volcanogenic-sedimentary reservoirs. Nearly a half of the estimated oil resources are associated with these deposits in this petroliferous basin. Further petroleum prospects in the watershed of the Kura and Gabirri rivers are associated with the Upper Cretaceous fractured limestone supposed to contain large accumulations of hydrocarbon fuel.

(b)   Hydrocarbon reserves

Azerbaijan is one of the oldest centres of the world's oil industry. As mentioned above, the industrial production of oil and gas on the Absheron peninsula begun in 1871. Azerbaijan is also a leader in the production of oil and gas in the Caspian Sea aquatorium. Azerbaijanian geologists and oilmen developed the Pirallakhi, Qum adasi, Darvin bank and the famous Neft Dashlari offshore oil fields of the Caspian Sea in 1948. A total of one billion of crude oil had been produced from the onshore areas of Azerbaijan by 1989. According to estimates of the SOCAR national oil company, the total recoverable reserves of oil and gas in Azerbaijan are 9.6 billion tons. Around 1.8 billion tons of oil and gas had been produced from onshore and offshore areas of Azerbaijan by 1 January 1998. The total remaining reserves of oil and gas estimated up to a depth of seven kilometres are 7.8 billion tons, including 6.0 billion tons in the offshore fields of the prospective structures of the Azerbaijan sector of the Caspian Sea. Around one billion tons of oil, gas and gas-condensate are concentrated in the Gyunashli, Chirag, Azeri and Kyapaz deposits of the Absheron archipelago (figures 6 and 7). From 15 to 20 hydrocarbon reservoirs were distinguished in the geologic sections of the productive series of each of these fields. Around 70 per cent of the reservoirs were accumulated in oil-bearing horizons of the Balakhan and "hiatus" suites. Despite over a century of oil production on the Absheron peninsula, this petroliferous basin still possesses substantial hydrocarbon reserves. By the rate of hydrocarbons' production, the Lower Kura depression ranks the second after the Absheron peninsula. The distribution of reserves within both petroliferous basins is shown in table 1.

**Table 1. Distribution of reserves of crude oil in the petroliferous basins of the Absheron peninsula
and Lower Kura lowland of Azerbaijan**

Unit: Thousand tons

Oil fields	Total estimated reserves	Ultimate recoverable reserves	Cumulative production at the end of 1998
Absheron peninsula:			
Bibi-Eibat	324 561	169 935	159 711
Balakhan-Sabunchi-Ramani	331 807	708 205	348 053
Surakhany	210 740	118 259	113 904
Binagady	68 344	36 111	31 556
Chakhnaglyar	17 968	9 819	7 798
Sulutapa	33 557	11 692	6 517
Atashkyah	3 362	1 135	0 993
Shabandag	4 171	2 086	1 307
Garachukhur	88 196	41 793	36 004
Buzovna-Mashtaga	79 136	36 088	28 843
Kala	124 462	67 401	57 766
Zira	5 591	3 120	2 571
Lower Kura lowland:			
Kyursangi	100 092	30 860	5 420
Garabali	47 008	7 292	5 440
Prisagat	5 846	1 502	0 717
Neftchala	156 500	32 250	13 350
Kyurovdag	159 832	42 527	34 812
Total:	**2 137 549**	**960 123**	**841 512**

The ultimate recoverable reserves of natural gas in Azerbaijan amount to 1 trillion cubic metres and total estimated reserves are in a range from 2 to 7 trillion tons. The Garadag gas field remains the largest onshore field and the Bahar, Bulla-adasi, Bulla deniz gas fields offshore.

According to three-dimensional seismic exploration work and prospecting drilling, the large reserves of natural gas and condensate are expected in the prospective structure of Shakh deniz. The latest estimates of the British Petroleum corporation indicate 700 billion cubic metres of gas, 200 million tons of gas-condensate and from 100 to 120 million tons of gas-condensate and from 100 to 120 million of crude oil reserves in the Shakh-deniz petroliferous field. The Garagag prospective structure drilled by the Caspian International Company (CIPCO) contains 30 billion cubic metres of natural gas.

2. Combustible shales

About fifty occurrences of combustible shales are known to exist on the territory of Azerbaijan. Most of occurrences are located in the eastern part of the Greater Caucasus in the Quba and Vandam – Lagich zones as well as on the south-eastern submergence of the Gobustan-Absheron zone of the Caucasus within the Gobustan and Absheron regions (Khalifa-Zade and Sultanov, 1968; Zamanov, 1989). Outcrops of combustible shales are also known in the Nakhchivan Autonomous Republic. The known occurrences of shales are localized in the Paleogene-Miocene formations.

The State Amalgamation "Kavkazugolgeologia" has studied the occurrences of combustible shales in Azerbaijan in 1950s. The limited reserves of these occurrences, however, did not justify the detailed geologic and geophysical exploration at that time. The Energy Institute studied the combustible properties of shales later on to extract natural gas to supply to the rural population. The Institute of Soils and Agrochemistry studied the possibilities of using these shales as organic fertilizer for cotton plants and other agricultural crops. The Experimental Laboratory of Geochemistry of Baku State University has identified the presence of rare metals in combustible shales (Khalifa-zade and Sultanov, 1968). The Amalgamation "Kavkazugolgeologia" studied the Dialli, Hanagya, Jangichai and Hirdalan groups of combustible shales (Arutyunova and Juze, 1968). The Dialli occurrence of the Ismaill region and the Hanagya occurrence of the Quba region were recognized as more prospective according to quality and technological properties of shales.

The Dialli occurrence

The host shale series of the Dialli occurrence is represented by the alternation of combustible shales with clayey aleurolites and dark-grey clays enriched by organic matter. Combustible shales of the Upper Sarmatian age outcrop along the creek of the same name, approximately two kilometres to the north-east of Dialli village.

The shale series extends over a distance of 2,000 metres with a total thickness of 80 metres. Four seams of combustible shales with a thickness from 0.5 to 1.5 metres were distinguished in the host rocks. These beds contain thin seams of dark-grey clays with imprints of the Sarmatian macriides. Because of the thinness of the combustible shales in this occurrence, it had not been studied by special mining openings and prospecting wells. The calorific value of shales from the Dialli occurrence varies from 1,800 to 3,000 kcal/kg. The total estimated resources are 25 million tons.

The Hanagya occurrence

This occurrence was firstly described by R.G. Suleimanov in 1948. The occurrence outcrops near Hanagya and Alich villages of the Quba region. The occurrence is hosted by the shale series from 30 to 40 metres thick extending over a distance of 25 kilometres in forested and mountainous areas. The stratigraphic position of the shale series of the Hanagya occurrence is very similar to that the combustible shales of the Dialli occurrence proved by *Mactra subcaspia species* fauna in dark-grey clayey seams. According to Khalifa-zade and Sultanov, 1968, the shale series occurs transgressively on grey clays with interbeds of organogenic-detrital limestones of the Middle and Lower Sarmatian Suites. Based on enrichment by rare micro-elements and heating capacity, the combustible shales of Azerbaijan can be used in agriculture as organic mineral fertilizer and as fuel and raw material for extracting gas, tar and construction materials.

B. Metallic minerals

1. Ferrous and ferro-alloy metals

The deposits and occurrences of iron, chromite and manganese ore are known to exist on the territory of Azerbaijan, however, the only iron ore deposits contain proved mineable reserves (Kashkay, 1947; Mustafabei and others, 1964; Mustafaev and others, 1989). The titanium occurrences have been found in magnetite-bearing sandstones.

(a)   Iron ore

Iron ore formations play a substantial role in the metallogeny of Azerbaijan. Genetically, deposits of iron ore have been subdivided into segregation-magmatic, contact-metasomatic (magnetite skarn mineralization), hydrothermal-metasomatic (hematite mineralization), and sedimentary genetic types. The contact-metasomatic and hydrothermal-metasomatic types are the most prospective types of mineralization.

The proved mineable reserves of iron ore are concentrated within the Dashkesan ore region of the Somkhit-Agdam metallogenic belt. The Dashkesan group of iron ore deposits is located in the Dashkesan region extending for 40 kilometres to the south-west of Ganja city. The motor highway and railway link the Dashkesan,

South Dashkesan, Damir deposits and series of small deposits and occurrences close to Dardara village and on the slopes of the Ponakh-Chermez mountain. The Dashkesan deposit has been known from times immemorial. However, up to 1917, iron ore has been mined by primitive methods and geological data was sporadic.

The mineable reserves of the Dashkesan deposit were estimated for the first time in 1933 and recalculated in 1954. The additional mineral exploration of the deposit from 1954 to 1966 has resulted in a discovery of the South Dashkesan iron ore deposit. At the beginning of the 1970s, exploration of the northern area of the Dashkesan deposit was conducted. Mineable reserves of iron ore have been approved by the State Commission on Reserves of Economic Minerals of the former USSR. Total reserves of iron ore of all categories were estimated at 278 million tons. The industrial exploitation of the Dashkesan deposit was initiated in 1954. The Azerbaijanian ore mining and processing enterprise was established. The iron ore deposits of the Dashkesan group have served as the source of raw materials for the metallurgical industry of the Transcaucasus. Iron concentrate was supplied until 1991 to the Rustavi metallurgical combinate in Georgia. The proved mineable reserves of the Dashkesan group of iron ore deposits accounted for 234 million tons providing 90 years life cycle of the mine based on annual mining capacity.

Magnetite skarns

The Dashkesan group of iron ore deposits is confined to the Dashkesan syncline, located in the central axial part of the Dashkesan synclinorium, with pronounced intensive volcanic activity in the Bathonian and Kimmeridgian (figure 8). The transition from the syncline to adjacent anticlines are fixed mainly by bends of beds and outcrops of the Upper Bajocian deposits represented by quartz porphyry and their tuffs with interbeds of tuff-sandstones. The deposits of the Bathonian stage from 450 to 800 metres thick are composed of rocks of tuffogenous and tufogenous-effusive formations.

The Upper Jurassic formations are represented by a thick series of volcanogenic and sedimentary rocks of the Callovian and Kimeridgian stages. Tectonically, the ore region is confined to the jointing zone of the Murovdag and Shamkhor anticlinoriums of the general Caucasian direction and the Shamkhor and Pantdag cross-Caucasian uplifts. Combination of the two folded constructions forms the gentle Dashkesan synclinorium hosting various mineralization.

Two systems of the north-western and north-eastern faults complicated the structure of the ore region and served as the channels of intrusive magmatism. The Jurassic sedimentary formation was intruded by the polyphase and polyfacial Dashkesan intrusive massif confined to the abyssal fault along the axial part of the Dashkesan syncline. The deposits and occurrences of iron ore, cobalt, sulphide-arsenide, sulphides, alunite, pyrophyllite, kaolinite and other mineralization of the region are genetically and spatially associated with this intrusive massif. Four phases of intrusion of magmatic rocks were delineated. The first phase is represented by gabbro, gabbro-diorites, syenite-diorites and other basic magmatic rocks of neck and stock shapes. The most widespread rocks of the second phase outcrop on the area of more than 25 square kilometres and are represented by granodiorites, adamellites and banatites. Aplites and alaskites of the third phase have a limited distribution. The fourth phase of the intrusion is represented by numerous extended dykes of diabase porphyres and diabase. Cobalt mineralization of the ore region is paragenetically associated with these dykes. The iron ore mineralization is also associated by some geoscientists with these dykes. The intrusion of magmatic rocks was accompanied by contact-thermal metamorphism of volcanogenic-sedimentary rocks. Metamorphic rocks are represented by hornfels, metasomatites and marbles.

The rocks of hornfels facies are represented by pyroxene-scapolite, albite-pyroxene-xcapolite, pyroxene-plagioclase, amphibole-pyroxene-plagioclase, biotite-pyroxene-plagioclase and biotite feldspartic varieties developed both above and under iron ore deposits. The thickness of hornfells and metasomatites varies from a range of 20-30 metres to 50 metres. They are developed on volcanogenic rocks in contact zones of gabbroids and quartz diorites.

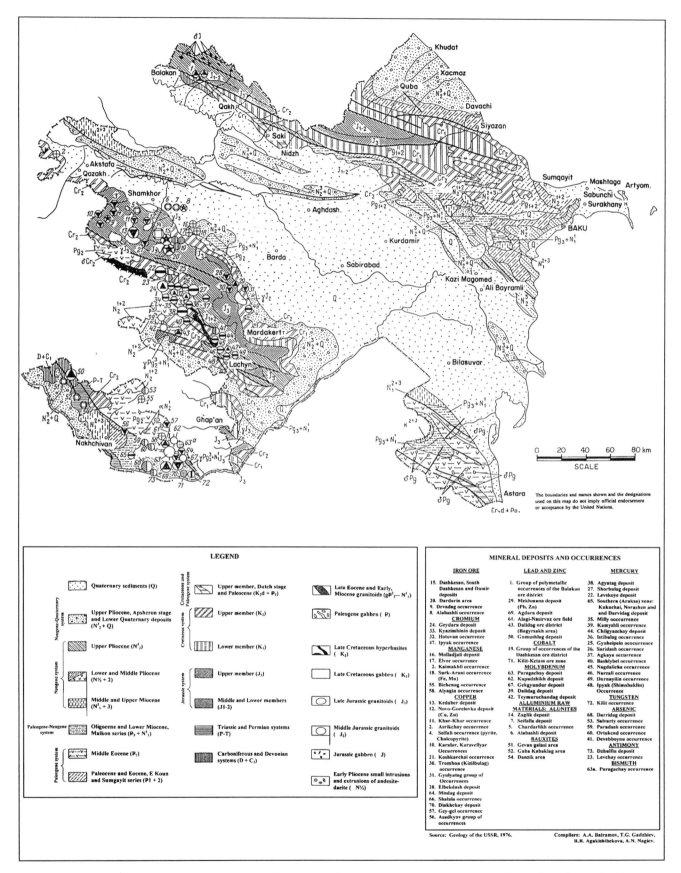

Figure 7. Schematic geological map of ferrous, ferro-alloy and base metals deposits of Azerbaijan

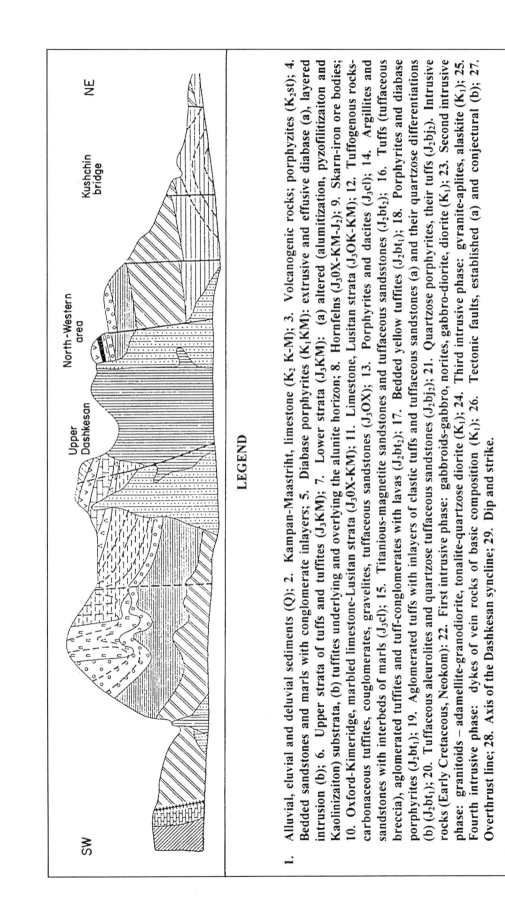

LEGEND

1. Alluvial, eluvial and deluvial sediments (Q); 2. Kampan-Maastriht, limestone (K_2 K-M); 3. Volcanogenic rocks; porphyzites (K_2st); 4. Bedded sandstones and marls with conglomerate inlayers; 5. Diabase porphyrites (K_1KM): extrusive and effusive diabase (a), layered intrusion (b); 6. Upper strata of tuffs and tuffites (J_3KM); 7. Lower strata (J_3KM): (a) altered (alumitization, pyzofilitizaiton and Kaolinizaiton) substrata, (b) tuffites underlying and overlying the alunite horizon; 8. Hornfelns (J_30X-KM-J_2); 9. Skarn-iron ore bodies; 10. Oxford-Kimeridge, marbled limestone-Lusitan strata (J_30X-KM); 11. Limestone, Lusitan strata (J_3OK-KM); 12. Tuffogenous rocks-carbonaceous tuffites, couglomerates, gravelites, tuffaceous sandstones (J_3OX); 13. Porphyrites and dacites (J_3cl); 14. Argillites and sandstones with interbeds of marls (J_3cl); 15. Titaniuos-magnetite sandstones and tuffaceous sandstones (J_2bt$_2$); 16. Tuffs (tuffaceous breccia), aglomerated tuffites and tuff-conglomerates with lavas (J_2bt$_1$); 17. Bedded yellow tuffites (J_2bt$_1$); 18. Porphyrites and diabase porphyrites (J_2bt$_1$); 19. Aglomerated tuffs with inlayers of clastic tuffs and tuffaceous sandstones (a) and their quartzose differentiations (b) (J_2bt$_2$); 20. Tuffaceous aleurolites and quartzose tuffaceous sandstones (J_2bj$_2$); 21. Quartzose porphyrites, their tuffs (J_2bj$_2$). Intrusive rocks (Early Cretaceous, Neokom): 22. First intrusive phase: gabbroids-gabbro, norites, gabbro-diorite, diorite (K_1); 23. Second intrusive phase: granitoids – adamellite-granodiorite, tonalite-quartzose diorite (K_1); 24. Third intrusive phase: gvranite-aplites, alaskite (K_1); 25. Fourth intrusive phase: dykes of vein rocks of basic composition (K_1); 26. Tectonic faults, established (a) and conjectural (b); 27. Overthrust line; 28. Axis of the Dashkesan syncline; 29. Dip and strike.

Source: Geology of the USSR, 1976.   **Compiler: M.A. Cashkay**

Figure 8. Schematic geological cross-section of the Dashkesan ore district

Marbles and marbled limestones have been formed by thermal and contact metamorphism of limestones. According to their chemical and physical properties, they meet the requirements of ornamental stones and flux limestones. The new Dashkesan deposit of white marble is being quarried now and the Khoshbulag deposit of flux limestones with reserves of more than 57 million tons has been explored near the Dashkesan iron ore deposits.

Magnetite skarn deposits of the Dashkesan group are concentrated in the northern and southern zones of exocontacts of intrusive massifs. The massifs of latitudinal direction are spatially confined to the abyssal fault passing the axial part of the Dashkesan syncline. The Dashkesan and South Dashkesan deposits of submeridional direction are separated by the Goshgarchay river into the western and eastern parts (figures 9 and 10).

The Damir iron ore deposit is located to the south-east from the South Dashkesan gabbroid massif of submeridional direction. According to lithofacial analysis, the magnetite skarn mineralization is hosted by the rocks of calcareous series of the top sections of the Oxfordian-Lower Kimmeridgian age. The mineralization is localized in the near shore lithofacies, where the volume of limestones varies from 0 to 30 per cent.

This carbonaceous formation hosts the major part of the Dashkesan deposit and the eastern area of the South Dashkesan deposit containing around 60 per cent of identified reserves of the Dashkesan ore region. The thickness of magnetite scarns reaches a range from 100 to 200 metres. Calcareous tuff-sandstones of the base of limestone strata have been subjected to scarn formation and partial replacement by magnetite. The mineralization of this interval occurs as isolated lenses from two to four metres at a depth from 300 to 450 metres and does not present any economic interest.

The character of localization of magnetite skarn mineralization is variable. In the north-western area of the Dashkesan deposit, magnetite skarn mineralization overlies the marbled limestones. Its thickness gradually increases reaching 60 metres by simultaneous reduction of the thickness of limestones. In the north-eastern area, the mineralization occurs between hornfells and keratinized tuffites of the Callovian-Oxfordian series and volcanogenic series of the Kimmeridgian age. Similar types of occurrence were observed within the Damir iron ore deposit.

In general, magnetite skarn mineralization of the Dashkesan group of deposits is represented by 8-10 monoclinal stratified beds concordant by strike and dipping with host rocks. The maximum distance of skarns from the contours of the main intrusive massif is 2.5 kilometres. The length of magnetite skarn deposits varies from 1,900 to 4,000 metres in separate areas. The width of the deposit normally corresponds to the length, and in plan, the deposits have an isometric shape. The thickness of deposits varies from 4 to 40 metres reaching a range from 100 to 200 metres. Magnetite skarn deposits are characterized by a complicated integral structure due to a wide range of magnetite content from 0 to 90 per cent and a great variety of skarn types.

Five major types of magnetite skarns were distinguished. The widely distributed garnet-bearing-skarns contain garnet, epidote, chlorite, calcite, quartz, andalusite, magnetite and pyrite. The garnet-magnetite skarns constitute the major part of iron ore deposits of the Dashkesan group. The pyroxene-garnet skarns are developed in the Dashkesan and South Dashkesan deposits being mainly represented by garnet and pyroxene. Chlorite, quartz, calcite, epidote and ferrum hydrooxide are the secondary minerals. The garnet-actinolite skarns differ from the others by a high content of grossularite in garnet and a presence of actinolite. In these skarns, magnetite usually fill the inter-grain space. The pyroxene-dashkesanite skarns are characterized by a presence of dashkesanite-chlorium-containing alkaline amphibole. Basic minerals are dashkesanite, pyroxene and garnet. Secondary minerals are epidote, chlorite, ortite, magnetite, zoisite and others. Magnetite ore within magnetite skarn deposits can occur in the top and base sections of the mineralized bed. However, the major accumulations of magnetite were found in the central section.

The stratified and lens-shaped deposits of economic value of up to 60 metres thick extend from 100 to 2,000 metres. Massive deposits are subdivided into massive magnetite ores containing up to 90 per cent of magnetite and sulphide-magnetite ores containing up to 20 per cent of sulphide minerals. The content of iron

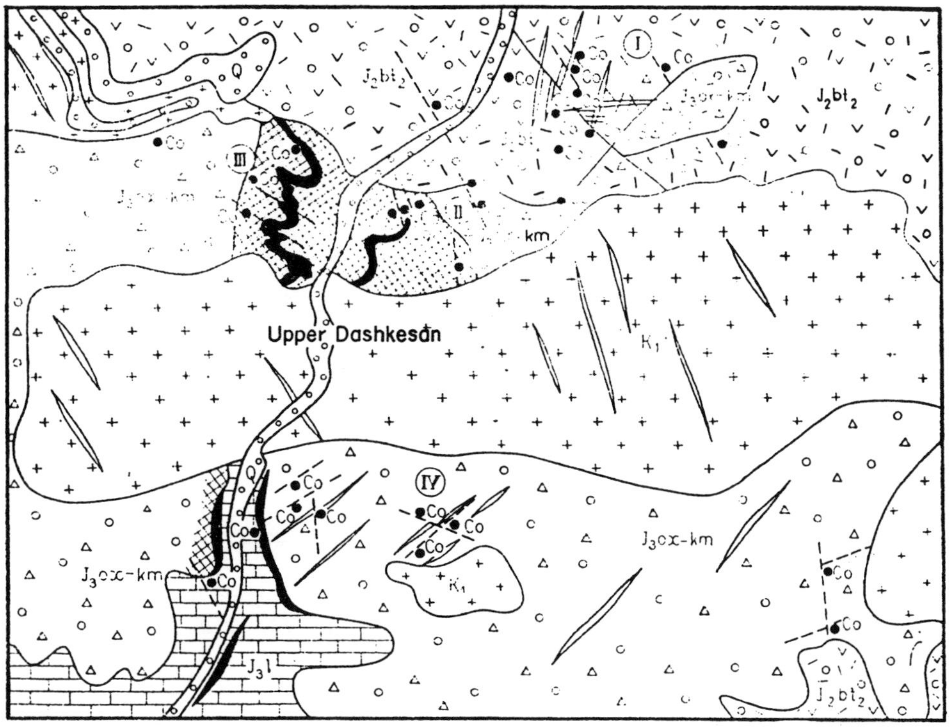

LEGEND

⬚	Quaternary fluvial deposits
⬚	Lower Cretaceous intrusive rocks (K₁)
⬚	Vein rocks of basic composition (K₁)
⬚	Marbled limestones of Lusitan age (J₃Lz)
⬚	Tuffs, lime tuffs, tuff-sandstones, pebbles, siltstones of Oxford-Kimmerian age (J₃oxf + km)
⬚	Tuffs, tuff-breccia, tuff-pebbles and tuff-sandstones alternating by separate flows of andesite and andesite-dacite porphyrites of the Upper Bathian age (J₂bt)
⬚	Hornfels
⬚	Cobalt-bearing tectonic zones
⬚	Scarn-iron fields
●Co	Occurrences of cobalt mineralization; I-northern cobalt deposits, II-north-eastern iron-cobalt deposits; III-north-western cobalt-bearing iron ore field; IV-southern iron-cobalt deposit.

Figure 9. Geological map of the central area of the Dashkeasn ore district

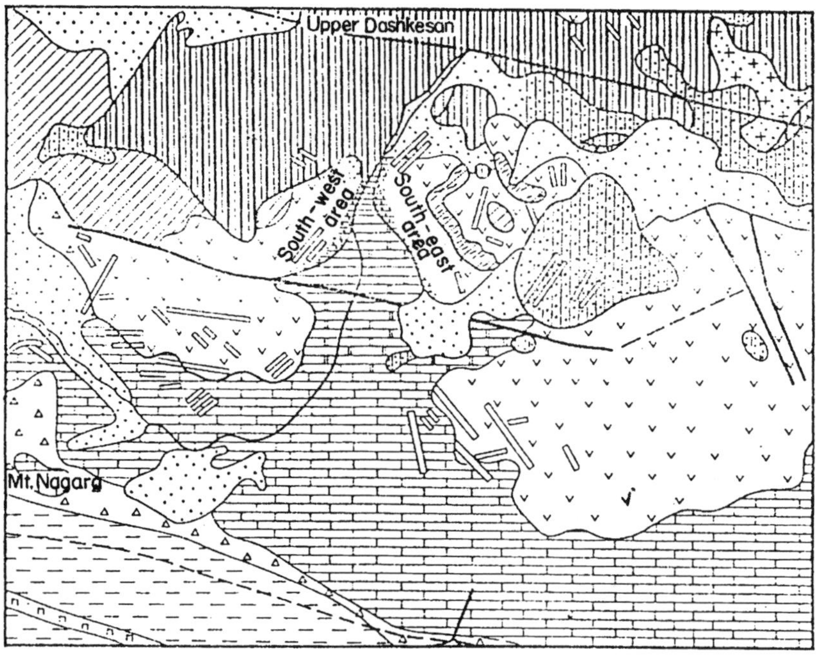

LEGEND

| | Quaternary fluvial-alluvial deposits |

Lower Cretaceous - Upper Jurassic formations (K_1-J_3)

| | Extrusive and effusive diabases - diabase-porphyrites, stratified intrusive rocks of Lower Cretaceous - Kimmerian age (K_1-J_3^{km}) |

| | Suite of tuffs and tuffites (J_3^{km}) |

| | Hornfelns of Kimmerian age |

| | Scarn-iron-ore mineralization in volcanic rocks |

| | Marbled limestones (Lusitan strata) of Oxford-Kimmerian age (J_3^{oxf+km}) |

| | Limestones (J_3^{oxf-km}) |

| | Tuffogenous rocks: limestone, tuffites, pebblestones, siltstones (J_3^{oxf}) |

| | Mudstones, sandstones with inlayers of marl (J_3cl) |

| | Gabbro-norite, gabbro-diorites of the first intrusive phase of Lower Cretaceous (K_1F_1) |

| | Granitoids (adamellites-granodiorites, tonalities-quartzose diorites) of the second intrusive phase of Lower Cretaceous (K_1F_1) |

| | Granite-aplite alaskites of the third intrusive phase of Lower Cretaceous (K_1F_3) |

| | Dykes of the fourth intrusive phase of Lower Cretaceous (K_1F_4) |

| | Tectonic faults (established and conjectural) |

| | Axes of the Dashkesan syncline |

Source: Kashkay, 1964.

Figure 10. Geological map of the southern iron-cobalt area of the Dashkesan deposit

ore in massive magnetite ores varies from 45 to 60 per cent. The texture of the ore is massive, slaggy and finally porous. The sulphide minerals of disseminated texture and irregular shapes in the north-western area of the deposit contain 50 per cent of chalcopyrite, 40 per cent pyrite, 5 per cent chalcozine as well as rare bornite, sphalerite and arsenopyrite. The sulphide ores of the north-eastern part of the deposit contain from 70 to 95 per cent pyrite, up to 15 per cent chalcopyrite, from 5 to 7 per cent arsenopyrite, up to 5 per cent galenite, rare sphalerite and bornite.

The massive magnetite ores of the South Dashkesan deposit contain up to 12 per cent of sulphides being represented by a range of 70-80 per cent of pyrite, up to 10 per cent of chalcopyrite, cobaltine, rare pyrrhotite arsenopyrite, glaucodote, bornite, sphalerite and galenite. Sulphide-magnetite ore contains arsenic, vanadium, titanium, cobalt, zinc, manganese, tin, magnesium, copper, lead, molybdenum, nickel, silver, gallium, cadmium, bismuth, indium and zirconium.

The deposits of the disseminated type also form beds and lenses and gradually transit into massive magnetite ores. The ores contain from 40 to 70 per cent magnetite, up to 25 per cent garnet, from 5 up to 30 per cent calcite, up to 1 per cent quartz, epidote, rare hematite, chlorite, dashkesanite and actinolite. Manganese, gallium, tin, molybdenum, vanadium, titanium, copper, zinc, cobalt and nickel were assayed in sulphide part of disseminated types of ores. The iron content in this type of ores reaches 30 per cent.

Garnet-magnetite skarns are widely developed in all iron ore deposits of Azerbaijan representing a transition type between massive and disseminated deposits. The skarns contain from 30 to 40 per cent magnetite, up to 60 per cent of garnet, calcite, chlorite, rare epidote and quartz. The iron content varies from 15 to 25 per cent. Copper, silver, zinc, nickel, cobalt, also zirconium, chromite, rare gallium, vanadium, indium and molybdenum were also identified in ore skarns. By cobalt content, the ores of the above types have an economic significance irrespective of magnetite content. Cobalt-bearing skarns are subdivided into cobalt-bearing pyrite ores with a cobalt content of more than 0.04 per cent and primary cobaltine ores with a variable cobalt content from 0.041 to 0.925 per cent and up to 3 per cent. The average cobalt content is 0.132 per cent.

The contours of mineable iron ores in magnetite skarns are defined by the content of dissolved iron distinguishing massive magnetite ores with iron content of more than 45 per cent, magnetite skarns from 30 to 45 per cent of iron content and ore skarns with iron content from 15 to 25 per cent. The share of massive magnetite ores of skarn type of total reserves varies from 30 to 50 per cent, that of reach magnetite skarns from 10 to 40 per cent, poor magnetite skarns from 6 to 13 per cent and ore skarns from 2 to 4 per cent. Despite available infrastructure and sufficient mineable reserves of cobalt-bearing iron ore in the Dashkesan group of deposits, the open cast mining production has been sharply reduced owing to a low demand after a break-up of the former Soviet Union.

Smaller deposits of magnetite skarns are known to exist on the territory of the Gedabek and Ordubad ore regions. The Novo-Ivanovka occurrence is located within a range of 4-5 kilometres to the north-west from Novo-Ivanovka village of the Gedabek region. The mineralization is confined to the contact zones of the Somkhit-Agdam limestones of the Upper Cretaceous age and volcanogenic-sedimentary rocks of the Eocene intruded by the Post-Middle-Eocene granitoids of gabbroid and syenite-diorite phase. Small ore bodies contain fine-grained magnetite with admixture of pyrite. The iron content varies from 9 to 58.2 per cent and cobalt from 0.015 to 0.02 per cent. The cobalt mineralization is paragenetically associated with pyrite. The occurrence is of no economic interest.

The Bashyurd occurrence of magnetite skarns is located in the Ordubad region of the Nakhchivan Autonomous Republic. Genetically, mineralization is associated with adamellite phase of the Megri-Ordubad intrusive massif. The mineralized lenses from three to six metres thick are traceable over a distance of 120 metres. The occurrence has not been investigated in detail.

Hematite ore

Hematite ore is khown to exist in the Dashkesan ore region, being represented by the Alabashli deposit and a number of small occurrences. The deposit is located westward from Gyandja city close to the Alabashli railway station. The deposit is hosted by the Middle Jurassic volcanogenic and the Upper Cretaceous sedimentary formations overlaid by the Quaternary deposits. The Middle Jurassic volcanics are represented by tuff-sandstones, tuff-breccia and tuff-conglomerates of the Bathonian stage exposed to hydrotermal alterations. The upper section of the Cretaceous system is represented by the formations of the Lower Coniacian, Turonian and Santonian stages transgressively overlapping volcanogenic rock series of the Bathonian stage. The formations are complicated by a series of tectonic faults of various orientation. The mineralized zone of the Alabashli hematite deposit subsided concordantly with enclosing rocks and has a moderate dipping of $15°$-$20°$. The mineralized zone is broken by faults defining the terrace structure of the deposit. The ore body occurs in the form of stratabound beds.

The ores are represented by massive red hematite and fine-and coarse-crystallic hematite of steel-grey color. Ore texture is impregnated and laminated, sometimes banded and breccia-shaped. Main ore minerals are hematite, hansmannite, hydroferrum oxide, pyrite and chalcopyrite. The associated minerals are quartz, cericite, chlorite, epidote, calcite, alunite and kaolinite. The chemical assay of samples shows 25 per cent of Fe_2O_3, 47 per cent of SiO_2, 1 per cent of TiO_2, a range of 0.12-0.74 per cent of sulphur, from 0.4 to 2.0 per cent of CaO, from 0.04 to 0.08 of Cr_2O_3, from 0.02 to 0.029 of zinc, 0.019 of copper, from 0.012 to 0.2 of water-dissolved salts, all indicating the siliceous type of mineralization.

Hematite ores of the Alabashli deposit after enrichment on chemical composition and density can be used as a weighting ingredient of drilling muds. The proved reserves of hematite ore are estimated at 580,000 tons. The geological prospecting and geophysical exploration works in the vicinity of the deposit indicate additional reserve potential in the south-eastern flank of the deposit. The stratabound hematite mineralization of up to 60 metres thick has been proved to be hosted by rocks of volcanogenic series. Besides the Alabashli deposit, the Shamkhor uplift also hosts typical hydrothermal manifestations of hematite of veinlet type in acid intrusions being characterized by monomineral composition.

The Chardakhli hematite occurrence is located within 2-3 kilometres westward from the Alabashli deposit and confined to a contact zone of the Atabek-Slavyan plagiogranite intrusive massif with quartz porphyrites, where hematite mineralization is represented by stringers and lenses. Ore bodies are small and of a little economic value. A maximum content of ferrum in hematite ore is 60 per cent.

The Atabek hematite occurrence is confined to the endogenious contact zone of the Atabek intrusive massif of plagiogranites, which were transformed into secondary quatzites. Mineralization is represented by vertically dipping veins and lenses. Similar manifestations of hematite mineralization are developed in various parts of the contact zone of the plagiogranite intrusive massif. This type of hematite mineralization has not been studied in detail.

The titanium-magnetite-bearing mineral sands placers were observed along the coast of the Caspian sea in the south-eastern part of Azerbaijan up to the border with the Islamic Republic of Iran.

Magnetite sandstones

Numerous occurrences of magnetite sandstones are concentrated in the Somkhit-Agdam metallogenic belt (Dashkesan, Shamkhor, Khanlar ore regions) and stratigraphically confined to the volcanogenic series of the Bathonian age. More than twenty outcrops of magnetite sandstones were traced over a distance of 85 kilometres along the coastal line of the Lower Bathonian palaeo-sea. The occurrences in the form of beds and lens-shaped bodies have a variable thickness from 0.5 to 2 metres and are traced over a distance from 10 to more than 1,000 metres.

The main ore minerals are magnetite, titanium-magnetite, ilmenite, rare hematite-ilmenite, hematite and martite. Hypergene magnetite, goethite, hydrogoethite and siderite are rare. Among sulphides, rare grains of pyrite and chalcopyrite are found. The content of magnetite in the form of rolled and angular grains from 0.1 to more than 1 milli-metre varies from 30 to 90 per cent. According to the content of ore grains, reach (70-80 per cent) and poor (20-35 per cent) types of magnetite ore have been distinguished. The grade of titanium-magnetite which is the second ore mineral in titanium-bearing magnetite sandstones varies from 3 to 4 per cent. The content of ilmenite is from 2 to 3 per cent. Chlorite is the basic cementing mineral, while quartz, plagioclase, pyroxene, epidote, actinolite and zircon are found as separate grains. The content of these cementing minerals varies from a range of 1-5 per cent to 30-50 per cent and the quantum of cementing mass varies from a range of 3-12 to 20-25 per cent.

The content of Fe_2O_3 in magnetite sandstones varies from 47.8 to 75.7 per cent, that of metallic ferrum from 33.4 to 53.0 per cent and V_2O_5 from 0.36 to 0.46 per cent. A method of magnetitic separation from magnetite sandstones is applied to obtain enriched iron ore concentrate grading 60 per cent of Fe_2O_3 and from 0.47 to 0.57 per cent of V_2O_5. The flotation method enables the extraction of 55 per cent of magnetite concentrate from the initial quantity of magnetite ore. The content of TiO_2 in magnetite concentrate varies from 9.6 to 10.68 per cent. The percentage of extraction of titanium varies from 43 to 64 per cent. The presence of titanium and vanadium in magnetite sandstones indicates the possibility of using these ores as metallurgical raw materials for high quality steel. Favourable geological conditions suggest a discovery potential of large deposits of magnetite sandstones in various regions of the north-eastern slope of the Lesser Caucasus.

(i)   Magnetite-bearing sands

Titanium placers of magnetite-bearing sands are traced along the coast of the Caspian Sea over a distance of 52 kilometres from Lenkaran to Astara city representing iron ores of sedimentary type. The width of placers varies from 50 to 300 metres. Further south, these sands are observed on the Iranian coast of the Caspian sea. The mineral composition of the sands is represented by magnetite (21.5 per cent), titanium magnetite (63.2 per cent), hematite (2 per cent), chromite (0.5 per cent), quartz and feldspar (12.8 per cent).

(ii)   Chromites

The deposits and occurrences of chromites are confined to the ultrabasic rocks of the ophiolite belt of Azerbaijan. The total extent of the ophiolite belt within the Transcaucasus is 260 kilometres, from which 160 kilometres falls into Azerbaijan's territory. Tectonically, the ophiolite belt of Azerbaijan is confined to the Geycha-Garabag tectonic zone of the Lesser Caucasus. Petrologically, ultrabasic rocks of the ophiolite belt are represented by peridotites (harzburgite), dunites and pyroxenites, all reworked into serpentinites by metamorphism. While all massifs of ultrabasic socks of the ophiolite belt of Azerbaijan are chromite-bearing, the majority of deposits and occurrences of chromite ores are confined to outcrops of dunites and, more rare, harzburgites. The major chromite mineralization in the Azerbaijanian part of the ophiolite belt was found within the Geydara and Kyazimbinin-Gavrilov deposits as well as the Zaydara, Nikolayev, Khotavan and Ipak groups of occurrences.

The Geydara chromite deposit is one of the known chromite deposits in the Transcaucasus located in the watershed of the Soyutluchai and Istibulag rivers at an altitude of 2,290 metres above sea level. The deposit occurs on the contact of strongly serpentinized harzburgites with the massif of gabbro-amphibolites, which is hosted on the north-east by volcanogenic-sedimentary sequence of the Santonian age. The ore bodies of the Geydara deposit are confined to a lens-shaped massif of serpentinized dunites elongated in parallel with an archy contact of peridotites and gabbro-amphibolites. The length of the dunite massif is 350 metres with a variable thickness from 0.5 to 15 metres. Contacts of dunites with enclosing peridotites are gentle and rare. Chromite ore bodies of economic interest are represented by isolated nests of oval, and rarely, lens-shaped form, being located as a chain along the strike of dunites. Some elongation of ore nests along the strike and dip is observed.

Minor cromite ore nests or bodies nearby the massive ore bodies are met in the form of spheroids, veinlets and fracture fillings. A disseminated type of cromite mineralization is rare.

Five groups of ore bodies were distinguished within the Geydara cromite deposit. The most prominent ore zone on the south-east of the deposit contains around 40 nests of cromite ore. Chemical assay shows a range of 43.1 to 52.2 per cent of Cr_2O_3, 12.5-16.4 per cent of FeO, 5.77-5.94 per cent of SiO_2, 0.17-0.37 per cent of CaO, 0.01-0.03 per cent of SO_3, 0.01-0.02 per cent of P_2O_5 and ratio of CrO to FeO from 3.0 to 5.2 per cent.

Single nests of massive chromite in harzburgites are rarely found. Singular ore lenses of impregnated and nodular chromite are widespread and typical in the Nikolayev, Kazimbina, Gavrilov, Ipak and other occurrences. The length of cromite ore lenses varies from 8 to 70 metres and the thickness from 2 to 7 metres. Major minerals of cromite ore bodies are chrome-spinel, olivine and serpentine, and secondary minerals are chromium silicates (chrome-chlorites, chrome-diopside, chrome-garnet), pentlandite, millerite, magnetite, native copper, carbonates of magnesium and calcium, talc and opal. Chemical composition of ore-forming chrome-spinels depends on the composition of host rocks. Chrome-spinel ore bodies which occur in harzburgites have an increased content of alumina from 22.52 to 22.66 per cent and decreased content of chrome oxide from 39.2 to 39.74 per cent whereas chrome-spinels of ore bodies hosted by diorites contain from 10.39 to 17.01 per cent of Al_2O_3 and from 50.52 to 58.54 per cent of Cr_2O_3.

Massive impregnated ores with a high grade of Cr_2O_3 and a favourable Cr_2O_3: FeO ratio are suitable for the production of ferro-chrome, metallic chrome and chrome salt. Lower grade cromite ores are used for refractory purposes.

Massive chromite ores of deposits and occurrences of Azerbaijan are characterized by the following average composition: from 42 to 54 per cent of Cr_2O_3, from 6 to 17 per cent of FeO, from 6 to 11 per cent of Al_2O_3, from 0.13 to 0.16 per cent of CaO, from 16 to 20 per cent of MgO, from 0.005 to 0.02 per cent of P_2O_5, and from 0.01 to 0.02 per cent of SO_3. Vanadium, zinc, cobalt and nickel are associated ore minerals. Technological properties of massive cromite ore meet the highest requirements of the metallurgical industry and can be used for the production of ferro-alloys. Cromite ores of impregnated and nodular types grading from 18 to 39 per cent of Cr_2O_3 and from 8 to 18 per cent of FeO can also be used for metallurgical purposes after appropriate enrichment. Field tests have proved it is possible to obtain concentrates grading more than 50 per cent of Cr_2O_3 and more than 16 per cent of FeO. While mining and technological conditions of cromite ore development are generally favourable, additional mineral exploration and mineral economics works are required to determine their development.

The ophilolite belt of Azerbaijan constitutes a part of the large Pontian ophiolite belt extending through northern Turkey, Armenia and Azerbaijan with known cromite deposits being exploited in Turkey. The proven reserves of the cromite deposits in Turkey vary from a range of 5,000-20,000 tons to more than 200,000 tons. The similarity of the geological environment and tectonic regimes suggests a potential for discovery of new medium-size cromite deposits in Azerbaijan.

(iii)   Manganese

Only small deposits and occurrences of manganese ore are known to exist in the Somkhit-Agdam and Araz tectonic zones of the Lesser Caucasus, on the southern slope of the Greater Caucasus and in the northern Gobustan. All occurrences of the Somkhit-Agdam tectonic zone are hosted by the Upper Cretaceous volcanics being characterized by exhalation-sedimentary and hydrothermal types of mineralization. The most known mineralization in this tectonic zone are the Molladjali deposit and Elvar occurrence in the Agdjakend trough and the Dashsalakhli occurrence in the Gazakh trough of the Lesser Caucasus.

The Molladjali deposit is located close to the same village in favourable mining and geographical conditions. The deposit is hosted by volcanogenic and sedimentary rocks of the Upper Cretaceous: andesite-basalts and tuffs of the Conician and Lower Santonian stages, clayey-sandy horizon of the Upper Santonian stage, and marly limestones of the Campanian-Maastrichtian stages. Stratiform beds of ferro-manganese ore occur in sandy-clayey rocks of the Upper Santonian stage on a contact with limestones of the Campanian stage. Ore bodies are elongated in the north-western direction conformable with enclosing rocks, and are traced as fragmented occurrences. The mineral composition of manganese ores shows a vertical upward zonation from siliceous manganese and ferro-manganese varieties to more pure manganese ore in the middle of the mineralized section. The ferro-manganese content, however, prevails towards the topmost sections. The deposit is subdivided into the north-western, central and south-eastern areas.

In the north-western area, ferro-manganese beds are represented by several separated ore bodies from 0.3 to 3.0 metres thick and from 45 to 90 metres long. The total extent of this mineralized zone is more than 700 metres. Chemical assay of ore shows from 0.3 to 16.71 per cent of MnO, from 20.4 to 42 per cent of FeO and 1.54 per cent of P_2O_5. In the south-eastern area, the ore-bearing horizon contains two beds with a thickness from 0.2 to 0.5 metres in the lower part and from 0.5 to 1.0 metres in the upper part being separated by strongly limonitized sandy clays. North-westward, the thickness of the upper ore bed increases to 4 metres. The grade of manganese varies within a range from 0.4 to 32 per cent.

Major ore minerals are psilomelane, pyrolusite, manganite and hydro-ferrum oxide. Other minerals are quartz, chalcedony and calcite. The Molladjali deposit belongs to a volcanogenic-sedimentary genetic type, where a deposition of ferro-manganese ores obviously occurred in the near-shore zone of the marine basin in the process of the Upper-Cretaceous volcanism. The favourable geological environment suggests a potential for existence of new buried manganese deposits under limestones of the Upper Creataceous age.

The Elvar occurrence of ferro-manganese ore is located westward from the Molladjali deposit close to Elvar village. The occurrence is hosted by porphyrites and tuffs of the Conician-Upper Santonian stage overlain by coarse-grained clayey and calcareous sandstones of the Upper Santonian stage and followed by limestones of the Campanian stage. Lenses and nodules of ferro-manganese ore are confined to clayey sandstones of the Upper-Santanian stage, which corresponds to the clayey-sandy manganese ore-bearing horizon of the Molladjali deposits. Ore bodies of more than one metre thick are represented by numerous lenses and beds extending over a distance from 30 to 400 metres. The grade of manganese is 34 per cent and that of FeO is from 10 to 15 per cent. Ore minerals are pyrolusite, ramsdellite and manganite in limited quantity, psilomelane and hydro-ferrum oxides. The occurrence has been poorly studied due to its small size. The favourable geological setting for localization of manganese mineralization coupled with a presence of known occurrences suggests a potential for discovering new deposits and occurrences in larger concentrations within the Agdjaryn trough.

The Dashsalakhli occurrence is located westward from Dashsalakhli village in the Gazakh region. The occurrence is hosted by volcanics and volcanogenic-sedimentary rocks of the Upper Coniacian-Lower Santonian and volcanogenic and pyroclastic rocks of the Upper Santonian stages. This sequence is overlain transgressively by limestones of the Companian-Maastrichean stage. The ore horizon contains several beds of almost pure aggregate of manganese minerals among tuffites and tuff-sandstones of the Upper Santonian underlaid by a sequence of bentonite clays, tuffites and tuff-lava.

The thickness of the ore-bearing bed is twelve metres including four metres of mineralized beds and lenses of ferro-manganese ore. The content of manganese is from 1.8 to 3.62 per cent, FeO from 16 to 19 per cent and cobalt from 0.005 to 0.664 per cent. Manganese minerals are vernadite, pyrolusite and manganite. By its size, the Dashsallakhli occurrence is of little economic interest. However, the presence of manganese and some other small manifestations of manganese mineralization within the Gazakh trough suggests some prospects for a discovery of larger concentrations of manganese ore of volcanogenic or volcano-sedimentary origin.

In the Araz tectonic zone, there are also known to exist several manifestations of manganese mineralization. The most typical is the Alyagi occurrence located in the Ordubad region close to the Alyagi village. The mineralization is localized in volcanics of the Middle Eocene and represented by bed-like lenses. Some ore intervals from 50 to 350 metres long each with an average thickness of 2 metres are traced over a distance of 3.6 kilometres. The maximum thickness reaches 8 metres. The content of manganese varies within a wide range with an average grade of 17.8 per cent. Mineralization is represented by braunite substituted by hausmannite and pyrolusite. The occurrence belongs to the exhalation-sedimentary type. The prospects for discovery of large deposits of manganese ore within the Araz tectonic zone are coupled with favourable lithofacies of the Pliocene, Oligocene and Eocene rocks of exhalation-sedimentary type, which are genetically linked with synchronous volcanism.

There are also known to exist some manifestations of manganese mineralization on the southern slope of the Greater Caucasus. The mineralization here is confined to zones of intensive tectonics and hydrothermal alteration. The mineralization, however, has not been studied in detail and the prospects are unknown.

There are high prospects for the discovery of new large manganese deposits in the Northern Gobustan region on the south-eastern subsidence of the Greater Caucasus. The region by geologic and tectonic settings is similar to those in the world-class Mangishlag, Chiaturi and Nikopol manganese deposits. Manganese mineralization here occurs in the form of powdery coatings, crusts, crowns and concretions of pyrolusite. The region, however, remains unexplored and requires an extensive mineral exploration programme to judge its potential.

2. Non-ferrous and light metals

(a)   Lead and zinc

The lead/zinc deposits of Azerbaijan are characterized by variable genetic and morphological types being hosted by a wide spectrum of the Phanerozoic formations from the Devonian (Gyumushlug deposit) to the Miocene-Pliocene age. Artisanal mining and processing of lead/zinc ores existed in the nineteen century at the Mekhmana deposit of the mountainous Garabag and the Gyumushlug deposit of the Nakhchivan Autonomous Republic. The geological prospecting and mineral exploration from 1950 to 1954 resulted in the discovery of the Agdara lead/zinc deposit in the Lesser Caucasus, a number of occurrences in Nakhchivan Autonomous Republic and in the Dalidag intrusive massif in the Kelbadjar region. The discovery of the Filizchai large deposit on the southern slope of the Greater Caucasus in 1958 triggered intensive exploration work for base metals mineralization in this previously unexplored region and follow up discovery of the Kasdag, Katekh and Sagator deposits in Azerbaijan, the Gizildara and Gurdul deposits in Dagestan, occurrences of copper-zinc ores within the Azerbaijan territory of the southern slope of the Greater Caucasus and also in adjacent areas of Dagestan. The base metals deposits in the Lesser Caucasus of hydrothermal type are generally of small size. The Agdara base metals deposit has been exploited until depletion and mining operations at the Gyumushlug deposit were ceased owing to political instability in the Nagorny Karabakh.

The metallogenic province of the Greater Caucasus

All known deposits and occurrences of base metals are hosted by the Lower and Middle Jurassic tectonic zone of mountainous folded system of the Greater Caucasus (Agayev, 1990; Akberov and others, 1982; Geology of the USSR, 1976; Hasanov, 1982; Kurbahov, 1982; Kurbanov and others, 1967; Shirinou, 1982). The geological investigations and tectonic analysis of this tectonic zone distinguished southward the Metlyuta-Akhtichay, Tufan, Katekh-Gyumbulchay and Zakatala-Kovdag tectonic subzones. These subzones of a deep thrust-over thrust nature have served as boundaries of structural-facial zones in the early geosynclinal stage, and currently represent large tectonic transversal elements of thrusting mature. The Jurassic tectonic zone of the mountainous system of the Greater Caucasus has experienced an intensive magmatism being represented by subvolcanic, hypovolcanic and hyper-abyssal bodies of gabbro and gabbro-diabases, as well as by subvolcanic and hypovolcanic intrusions of dacites, liparites-dacites, liparites, and more rarely, by andesite-basalts and basalts.

The major structural control of mineralization in this tectonic zone belongs to transversal tectonic elements which divide longitudinal zones into a number of large transversal terrace uplifts and subsided blocks. On the recent erosional level, the cross-cutting blocks are expressed as the north-north-eastern or the north-north-western vertical flexures being complicated by fragmented faults of a thrust-upthrust nature of the same directions.

These surficial cross-cut structures in the Paleozoic basement have been proved by geophysical data, where the uplifted blocks are reflected by magnetic and gravimetric extremes and subsided blocks by distinct negative anomalies. As a result of geological-geophysical investigations, the Balakhan-Zakatala, Kakh and Ismalin uplifted blocks from west to east within the metallogenic zone of the Greater Caucasus were delineated. These uplifted transformal blocks are being separated by a series of subsided blocks of which the Sheki block is the largest one.

Massifs of intrusive rocks form extended belts along abyssal fractures which are considered as borders of structural-formational zones. Based on mutual intersections, grade of metamorphism and relation to folded structures, three stages of intrusive activity have been distinguished. The earlier stage of magmatic rocks, which were subjected to folding and green schist metamorphism, are represented by dykes and bedded bodies of diabases. The second stage of magmatism is represented by dykes, stocks and rarely sills of gabbro-diabase, andesite-basalt, dacite porphyrites and liparite-dacite porphyres.

The detailed mineralogical analysis of massive pyrite mineralization indicates a presence of copper sulphides, pyrite-polymetals and copper-pyrrhotite subformations. It has been proved that sulphides of sulphide-polymetallic subformation are substituted by sulphides of copper-pyrrhotite subformation. The distribution patterns of this mineralization type within the metallogenic province of the Greater Caucasus indicate the following results. The minimum concentration of massive pyrite ores was found within the Tufan and Katekh-Gyumbulchay tectonic zones. The deposits of sulphide-polymetalic and copper-pyrrhotite subformations form individual, spatially separated metallogenic zones. The deposits of copper-pyrrhotite subformation are concentrated in the northern part of the Tufan zone and ores of sulphide-polymetalic composition were found only as relicts in certain isolated blocks being almost completely substituted by chalcopyrite-pyrrhotite association. Localization of mineralization and morphology of deposits are defined by dykes and stratabound bodies of basic and acid composition.

Intrusive bodies, which are confined to the same faults, play a role of ore-controlling screen, sometimes being exposed to a partial substitution by sulphide ores. Hydrothermal-metasomatic changes in case of dykes substitution are presented by facies of quarzites and that in terrigenous rocks by carbonates, quartz and rarely, by sericite. A zone of a predominant concentration of copper-pyrrhotite ores is followed southward by a zone of sulphide-polymetallic ores. This type of mineralization is being controlled by deep faults of overthrusting nature, the factor which defines a scale of mineralization and morphology of enclosed ore bodies. The typical example is the Filizchay deposit where sulphide-polymetalic ores are confined to the large fault-overthrust complicating the northern limb of the Koroichai anticline of a trunk structure.

The Filizchay deposit

The Filizchay deposit of base metals is hosted by terrigenous deposits of the Upper siderite and Khinalug suites of the Middle Jurassic which are crumpled into a large overturned to the south the sublatitudinal Karabchay anticline. The morphology of the ore deposit is rather simple being represented by a stratabound lens-like ore body with swells and pinches along the dip and strike of the ore body (figures 11 and 12). The ore body is dipping to the north at 40°-45° and on the top horizons at 60°-70° up to a vertical dipping. Unlike the roof, where the deposit is characterized by sharp and well-pronounced contours, its base has a more complicated structure.

Mineral composition of the ore body is quite monotonous comprising mainly of pyrite followed by sphalerite, galenite and pyrrhotite. Chalcopyrite, marcasite, arsenopyrite, magnetite and secondary copper

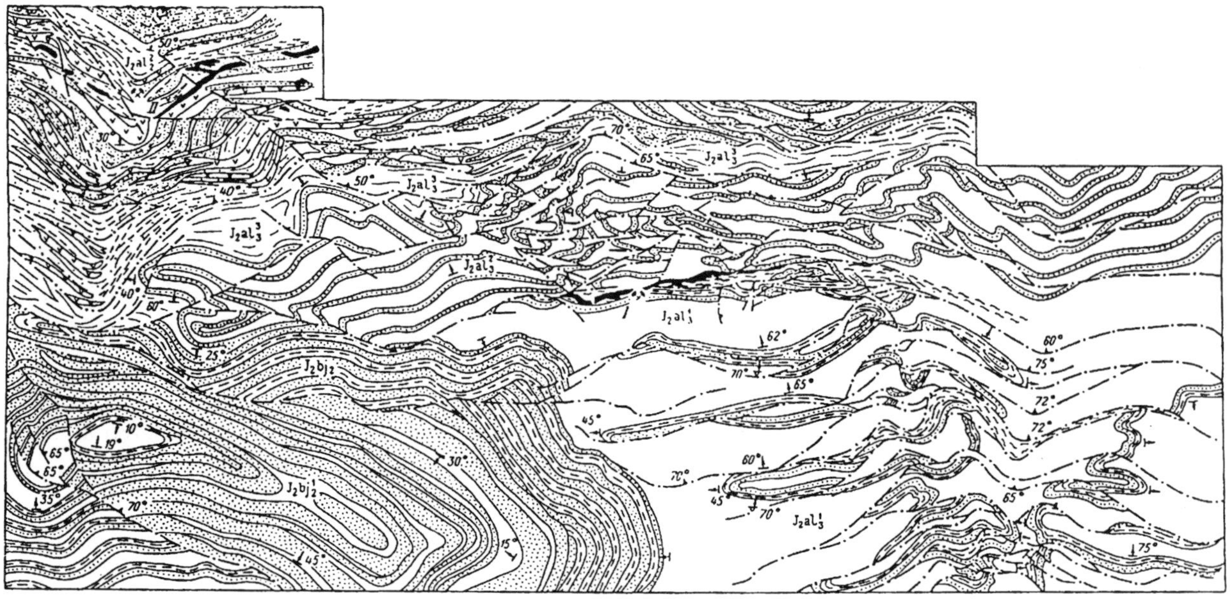

LEGEND

Middle Jurassic, Atashkyah suite (Middle Aalen):

First layer: fine-grained bedded sandstones with thin inlayes (1-20 cm) of siltstones and shales (J_2^{aal1})

Second layer: alternation of fine bedded and fine-grained sandstones and shales (J_2bj_2)

Third layer: fine-bedded and grained sandstones with beds shales ($J_2{}^{aal2}{}_2$)

Fourth layer: monotonous shales interbedded with siltstones and fine-grained clayey sandstones (J_2^{aal2})

Upper siderite suite (Upper Aalen):

Lower layer: clayey shales interbedded with inlayers of flysch sandstones ($J_2aal_2{}^1$)

Middle layer (sandy shales): rythmic alternation of medium and fine-grained sandstones and shales ($J_2aal_2{}^3$)

Upper layer: monotonous clayey shales with rare inlayers of fine grained siltstones ($J_2aal_3{}^1$)

Jimi, suite (Middle Baios

Rythmic alternation of fine-grained sandstones, siltstones and shales (J_2bj_2)

Lower layer: massive fine bedded medium and coarse-grained sandstones with inlayers of shales (J_2bs_2)

Intrusive rocks:

Andesites, andesite-dacites and porphyrites

Gabbro-diabase

Diabase and gabbro-diabase

Diabase and diabase-porphyrites

Faults:

Major faults

Secondary faults and fractures

Stratiform pyrite-polymetallic deposits

Fine bedded shales

Strike and dip elements

Source: Geology of the USSR, 1976

Compiled by: Kurbanov N.K., Romanov V.I., Sulfugarov S.V., Isayev B.M., Hasanov M.A.

Figure 11. Lithological-structural map of the Fylizchai pyrite-polymetallic deposit

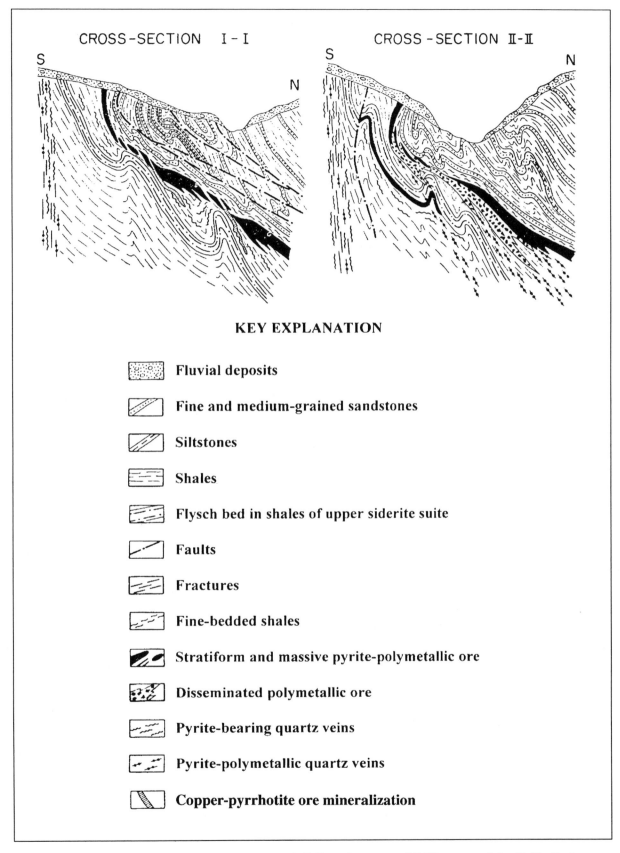

Figure 12. Cross-sections of the central (I-I) and eastern (II-II) areas of the Fylizchai pyrite-polymetallic deposit

sulphides are found in small quantities. The cementing minerals are carbonates, quartz, and to a lesser extent, chlorite and sericite. The ore contains more than twenty rare minerals.

Five types of ore have been distinguished within the Filizchay deposit based on the texture of the ore, namely (a) banded pyrite and pyrite-sphalerite-galenite; (b) massive pyrite; (c) impregnated pyrite and pyrite-sphalerite-galenite; (d) streaky and fracture fillings of pyrite, pyrite-sphalerite-galenite and pyrrhotite and (e) massive copper-pyrrhotite.

The banded ores occur in a hanging side of the deposit and occupy most of the volume of the ore body. Massive pyrite ores with a minor admixture of chalcopyrite, sphalerite and galenite are found together with banded ores and form lens-shaped areas in the top and bottom sections of the ore body.

The impregnated and disseminated pyrite-sphalerite-galenite type of ores occurs in the eastern part of the deposit forming the bodies of rather complicated form. This type of ores is characterized by a coarse-grained pyrite segregation of up to 1.0-1.5 centimetres of cubic and irregular form on the background of cementing material. Textural varieties of impregnated ores are defined by quantitative correlation of pyrite, cementing minerals and content of polymetalls sulphides. Two extreme textural members are impregnated ores grading from 60 to 70 per cent of pyrite and ores grading from 20 to 30 per cent of pyrite.

The veinlets and fracture fillings ores are developed in a lying side of the ore body on the eastern flank of the deposit and extend beyond its limits up to 2.0 kilometres. This type of ore is overlain by banded and impregnated ores. Three textural varieties of mineralization are parallel to schistosity, net-like-breccia and brecciated ores. The thickness of separate stringers and veins varies from 0.5 centimetre to 0.5 metre.

Later massive pyrrhotite ores are developed exclusively in the eastern part of the deposit forming a single vein-shaped body located in a hanging side of massive pyrrhotite and partially among the impregnated and banded ores. Massive textural varieties prevail in the surficial part of the ore body; more abyssal horizons of the ore body are dominated by breccia texture being cemented by fine-grained pyrrhotite.

The deposit has been explored in detail by profile drilling and audits at four exploration levels. The reserves of the upper part of the deposit explored by underground mining openings and drilling were calculated by Category B_2 and the lower part explored by drilling by Category C. The technological types of ores include the primary ore (97.3 per cent), mixed (2.2 per cent) and oxidized ore (0.5 per cent). Technological properties of ores have been studied in laboratories and two semi-industrial tests on selected flotation indicate a feasibility of obtaining 67.7 per cent of copper concentrate, 65.2 per cent of lead concentrate and 86.1 per cent of zinc concentrate. Technology of complex reworking of pyrite concentrate enabled to obtain 90.3 per cent of lead, 92.0 per cent of zinc, 84.7 per cent of gold, 84.6 per cent of silver, 72.1 per cent of cobalt, 72.2 per cent of cadmium, 29.7 per cent of indium and 10.4 per cent of selenium. The deposit is planned for development by underground mining. The proven reserves of the deposit, the data on which are unavailable, were approved by the State Commission on Reserves of the former Soviet Union in 1983.

The Kasdag pyrite-polymetallic deposit

The Kasdag pyrite-polymetallic deposit is located to the north-west from the above Filizchay deposit (Hasanov, 1982). All ore zones of the deposit are confined to the Kekhnamedan abyssal upthrust-overthrust. The deposit is hosted by the Lower Siderite suite of the Middle Jurassic being represented by alternations of sandstones, sandy-clayey shales and clayey shales. This sequence overlies the upper clayey series of the Khinalug suite dipping to the north at a variable angle from 20° to 65° (figure 13). The deposit is tectonically controlled by the Kekhnamedan fault which is separated into crushed and schistose zones of various degree being exposed to hydrothermal metamorphism and sulphide mineralization. These structural units host dykes and sills of basic, intermediate and acid composition, which have been formed in two stages. Sills and dykes of the early stage

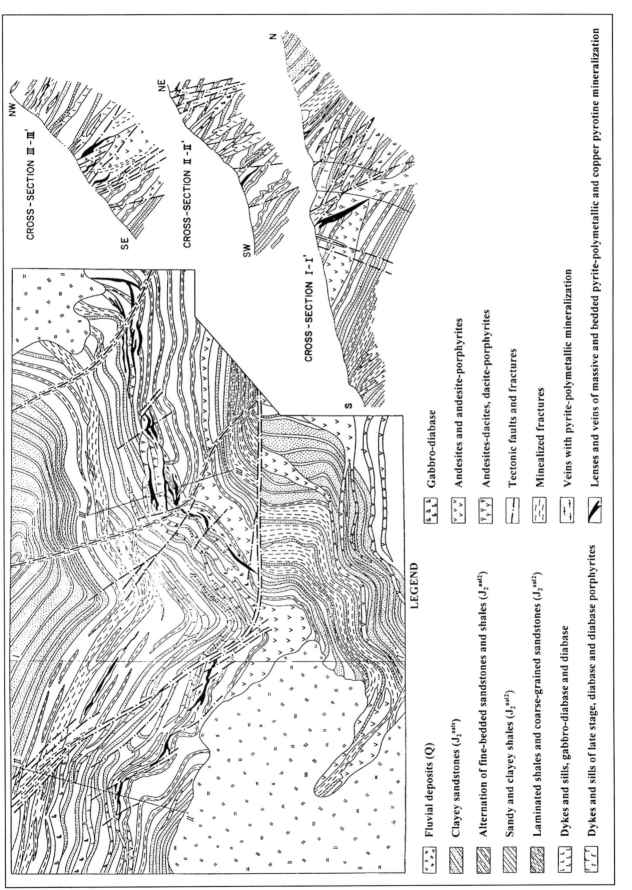

LEGEND

Fluvial deposits (Q)	
Clayey sandstones (J_2^{aal5})	
Alternation of fine-bedded sandstones and shales (J_2^{aal2})	
Sandy and clayey shales (J_2^{aal2})	
Laminated shales and coarse-grained sandstones (J_2^{aal2})	
Dykes and sills, gabbro-diabase and diabase	
Dykes and sills of late stage, diabase and diabase porphyrites	

Gabbro-diabase	
Andesites and andesite-porphyrites	
Andesites-dacites, dacite-porphyrites	
Tectonic faults and fractures	
Mineralized fractures	
Veins with pyrite-polymetallic mineralization	
Lenses and veins of massive and bedded pyrite-polymetallic and copper pyrotine mineralization	

Figure 13. Geological map and cross-sections of the Kasdag pyrite-polymetallic deposit

are represented by diabases and gabbro-diabases hosted by schistose rocks. The later stage of intrusive magmatism includes diabases, gabbro-diabases, andesite-porphyrites, andesite-dacites, dacites and liparite-dacites.

Based on intensity of mineralization, the deposit has been subdivided into several mineralized zones. The most prominent zones I and IV have been traced in sublatitudinal direction parallel to each other over a distance of more than 2,000 metres. Comparatively shallow ore zones of up to 60 metres deep are represented by a series of subparallel ore-bearing fractures up to 50 metres long. These fracture-filling zones form an echelon-like mineralized zones from 50 to 300 metres long and occurring from each other at a distance from 30 to 50 metres. The detailed mineral exploration within the most prospective zone I has revealed mineralized beds, lenses and veinlets with an average thickness from 2.5 to 5 metres and a maximum thickness from 10 to 16 metres in their swellings. The ore bodies are composed of banded and massive ores of sulphide-polymetallic and copper-pyrrhotite composition, which are found in equal ratios. The stringer-impregnated type of mineralization of same composition prevails in other parts of the deposit. The major role in localizing mineralization belongs to the above-mentioned dykes and sills, which were exposed to an intensive hydrothermal-metasomatic alteration preceeding the mineralization. These dykes and sills are considered to be the screens for large ore deposits. The presence of numerous shallow veins composed of all known mineral associations in all types of dykes indicates their preceeding formation in relation to major mineralization time.

Massive, banded and stringer-impregnated types of ores are the prevailing textural types of mineralization in the Kasdag deposit. The banded type of mineralization includes mineral associations of copper-pyrrhotite and sulphide-polymetallic composition. Hydrothermal alterations of host rocks at the Kasdag deposit which are accompanying or preceeding mineralization are different from those in the Filizchay deposit. Unlike the Filizchay deposit, the hydrothermal alterations here are pronounced with the same intensity in hanging and lying sides of ore bodies. Differing from the Filizchay deposit, where the major hydrothermal alteration is carbonization, quartzatization, chloritization and sericitization create a metasomatic column of facies of secondary quarzites around the ore bodies of the Kasdag deposit. Five ore bodies in the form of mineralized beds and lenses have been explored by drilling and audits within the Kasdag deposit. Ore bodies have been traced and contoured on five horizons at a depth from 1,800 to 2,100 metres level. The major ore-forming minerals are pyrrhotite, sphalerite, galenite, chalcopyrite, pyrite and rare arsenopyrite and cabaltite. Major metals are zinc, lead, copper, sulphur, silver and associated cadmium and gold.

Technological properties and ore enrichment have been studied through five laboratory and two semi-industrial tests. Technological processing of admixture of massive and veined ores was tested in semi-industrial conditions and proved to be effective in extraction of up to 82.2 per cent of copper, 86.3 per cent of zinc and 77.7 per cent of lead. Silver, cadmium and gold can be extracted as by-products using an appropriate metallurgical regime. The deposit is planned to be exploited by underground mining. The deposit is regarded as additional raw material base to the Filizchay deposit. The reserves at $C_1 + C_2$ category have been approved by the State Commission on Reserves of the former Soviet Union.

The Katekh polymetallic deposit

The Katekh deposit occurs in the Katekh-Gyumbulchay ore-bearing tectonic zone to the south from the Kasdag deposit (Kurbanov, 1982). Numerous clayed siderite and pyrite concretions from 1 centimetre up to 1.5 metres size are hosted by flyschoid sandy-clayey formation of the Aalenian suite being subdivided into two large rhythms with regressive and transgressive structures.

All known mineralized zones of the deposit are localized within the archy part of the Katekh anticline being located between transversal and longitudinal faults (figure 14). Three genetic types of sulphide mineralization are (a) diagenetic, (b) sulphide-polymetallic and (c) polymetallic mineralization of vein type. The most prospective are the latest two types. By texture, the mineralization is subdivided into massive, impregnated, vein, and rudaceous ores. All these types of ores are spatially associated with each other and localized in the

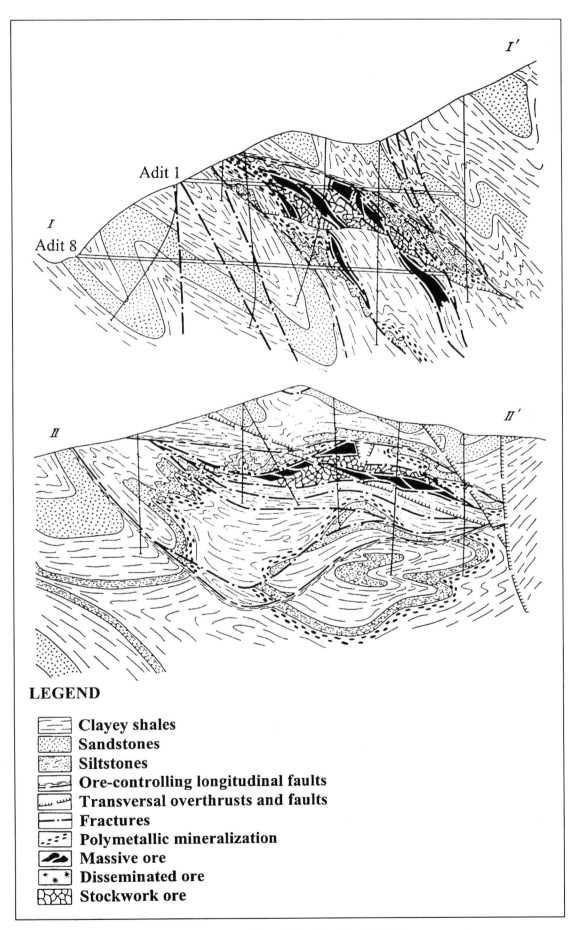

Figure 14. Transversal (I-I) and longitudinal (II-II) cross-sections of the Katekh polymetallic deposit

same ore zones being controlled by faults limiting the tectonic wedge. This tectonic wedge hosts three ore-bearing zones.

The first most southern zone hosts a lens-shaped ore body in a hanging side of the ore zone. It consists of shallow and clustered lens-shaped boulders of massive ores separated by clayey shales. On extent and upwards, massive ores gradually transit into fragmented pyrite ores. The widespread disseminated impregnated ores frequently superimpose the diagenetic pyrite and siderite-pyrite concretions of fragmented-shape and pyrite ores. The most latest and less developed stockwork type of mineralization transects all other types of mineralization.

The second echelon-like ore zone is located northward from the first ore zone and hosts the ore body of lens-shaped form. It nearly joins the third ore zone by a series of stockworks on the western flank (figure 14). It integral structure is completely similar to that of the first zone.

The third most northern ore zone is characterized by a complicated morphology, being defined by a combination of lateral and transversal faults in pre-mineralization time. As a result, the ore body has a complicated lens-shaped and fragmented block structure.

The major morphological type of sulphide deposits of the Katekh deposit are lens-shaped bodies complicated by longitudinal and cross-cutting ore-controlling faults. Pyrite, galenite, sphalerite, chalcopyrite, arsenopyrite, secondary copper sulphides, marcasite and pyrrhotite are the basic ore-forming minerals. Lead, zinc, silver, copper, gold and cadmium are the major metals of commercial value.

Technological properties including enrichment of ores of the Katekh deposit have been studied on seven samples in laboratory conditions. Application of a scheme of collective-selective floatation enabled to obtain tradeable commodity concentrates with extraction of lead up to 85.5 per cent, 85.8 per cent of zinc, 33.2 per cent of copper, 76.2 per cent of gold and 65.5 per cent of silver. The ore reserves of the Katekh deposit on $C_1 + C_2$ category have been approved by the State Commission on Reserves of the former Soviet Union. The deposit was planned to be exploited by underground mining.

The Sagator polymetallic deposit

The Sagator deposit is located within a distance from 10 to 12 kilometres northward from the Filizchay deposit. The deposit is hosted by terrigenous formations of the Pleinsbachian and Toarcian suites of the Middle Jurassic. The deposit is confined to the development of aleuro-clayey series represented by intercalation of fine-bedded aleurolite-sandstones, clayey shales and aleurolites.

Two natural ore types are massive copper-zinc and vein-type copper-pyrrhotite mineralization. Sphalerite, chalcopyrite and pyrrhotite are the basic ore-forming minerals. Lead, zinc, silver, cobalt and cadmium are the major metals of commercial value. Separate technological tests of three samples have been conducted on vein and massive ores as well as on admixture of these types of ore in a ratio 1:1. An appropriate technological scheme and ore enrichment regime enabling to extract up to 86.8 per cent of copper and 68.1 per cent of zinc have been developed and recommended. The ore reserves have been evaluated by appropriate mineral exploration grid at category C_2.

The metallogenic province of the Lesser Caucasus

Polymetallic deposits and occurrences of the Lesser Caucasus are known to exist within the Somkhit-Agdam, Ordubad-Zangezur and Sharur-Djulfa metallogenic belts (Aliev, 1976; Geology of the USSR, 1976; Kerimov and others, 1986; Kerimov, 1962).

The Somkhit-Agdam metallogenic belt

This metallogenic belt hosts one hydrothermal polymetallic deposit and numerous occurrences of vein type containing lead, zinc and barite mineralization. The sporadic lead – zinc mineralization is mainly pronounced in small occurrences consisting of single veins or a series of small quartz and quartz-carbonaceous veins.

The Mekhmana base metals deposit

The Mekhmana copper-lead deposit is the only deposit of commercial significance in this metallogenic belt. The deposit is located near Mekhmana village of the Garabag region. The artisanal mining of this deposit is recorded since the end of the nineteenth century.

The deposit occurs in a complex of volcanogenic-sedimentary rocks from the Middle Jurassic to the Upper Cretaceous and is hosted by the Middle Jurassic sedimentary rocks. The main structural unit of the deposit is a large anticlinal fold of the north-north-western direction (figures 15 and 16). The structure of the deposit and mineralization is controlled by a deep-seated tectonic fault being a channel of multiple magmatic activity during the Middle-Late Jurassic time. The magmatic series is represented by gabbro-diabase magma and subvolcanic intrusions of quartz porphyres of the Upper Bajocian, small intrusions of diorite-porphyres of the Late Jurassic and finally quartz ore veins of the Mekhmana deposit. The youngest intrusive rocks are the Late Jurasic dykes of diorite-porphyrites in the eastern part of the deposit being localized in fragments of more late tectonic downthrusts. Around thirty ore-bearing quartz veins of the Mekhmana deposit are concentrated in a narrow strip of sublatitudinal direction corresponding to a bending area of anticlinal fold and localized in fracture fillings. The veins' volume is usually filled up by calcites, quartz and ore-forming minerals intermixed with enclosed hydrothermally-altered rocks. Ore minerals are mainly represented by galenite and sphalerite, which are closely associated with quartz and carbonates. Chalcopyrite, pyrite, marcasite, chalcosine, bornite and secondary copper sulphides have a lesser distribution. Galenite and sphalerite in quartz veins and veinlets are met in the form of strips from 5 to 10 centimetres thick, large and small nests, stringers and impregnations. The most typical banded texture of ores is followed by breccia, colloform, looped and impregnated textures. As a rule, structure of ore accumulations is coarse-grained. Based on the content of lead and zinc, the ores have been divided into predominantly lead ores, predominantly zinc ores, and mixed lead-zinc ores. Associated metals are cadmium, silver, selenium and tellurium.

The Mekhmana deposit belongs to mesothermal type of hydrothermal deposits. Ore-bearing veins show a close spatial connection with small intrusions, where a time interval between magmatic activity and hydrothermal process was very limited. Only four viens out of thirty polymetallic veins have been found to be prospective based on reserves and grade of enclosed base metals. Technological enrichment tests of four samples in laboratory conditions have proved that the ores are easily enrichable by a method of selective floatation with a lead extration from 94 to 97 per cent and zinc extraction from 70 to 78 per cent.

Mining-geological and hydrogeological conditions of exploitation are favorable. The deposit was explored by trenches and prospecting shafts. The reserves of the deposit can be increased through additional mineral exploration of unexplored existing veins and discovery of new mineralization.

The Ordubad – Zangezur metallogenic belt

This belt is a typical representative of the Late Alpine stage of development of the Lesser Caucasus, wherein various ore formations, typical to the early and orogenic stages of geosynlinal development are present. All large polymetallic deposits are associated with a late stage of belt's development and concentrated within the western margin of the Megri-Ordubad granitoid massif. The deposits are typical examples of sulphide formation genetically linked with volcanites being the constituent part of a single volcano-plutonic complex. Small deposits and occurrences of sulphide-polymetallic type within the Ordubad ore region are spatially and genetically

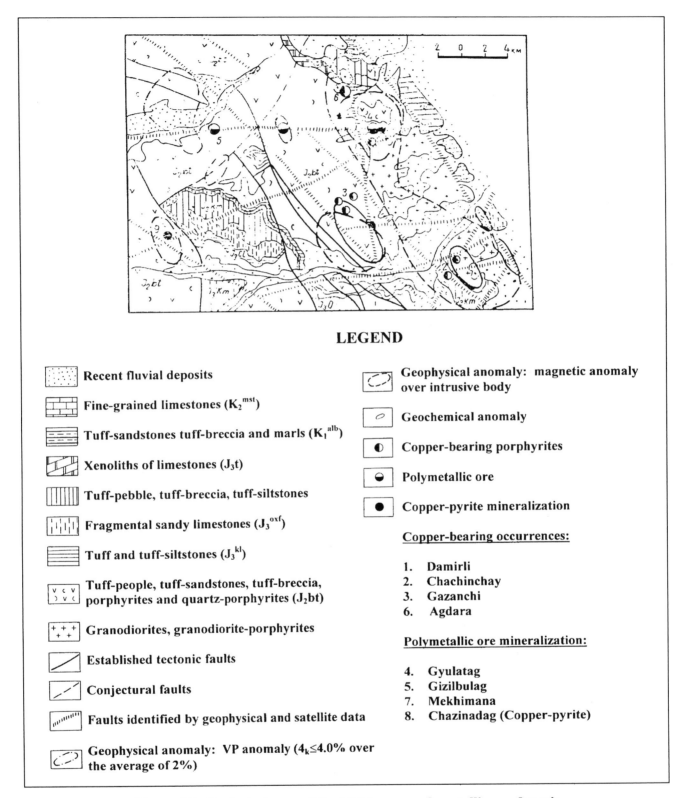

LEGEND

⬚	**Recent fluvial deposits**
▦	**Fine-grained limestones (K$_2^{mst}$)**
▤	**Tuff-sandstones tuff-breccia and marls (K$_1^{alb}$)**
▨	**Xenoliths of limestones (J$_3$t)**
▥	**Tuff-pebble, tuff-breccia, tuff-siltstones**
▥	**Fragmental sandy limestones (J$_3^{oxf}$)**
▤	**Tuff and tuff-siltstones (J$_3^{kl}$)**
▦	**Tuff-people, tuff-sandstones, tuff-breccia, porphyrites and quartz-porphyrites (J$_2$bt)**
⊞	**Granodiorites, granodiorite-porphyrites**
▱	**Established tectonic faults**
▱	**Conjectural faults**
▱	**Faults identified by geophysical and satellite data**
▱	**Geophysical anomaly: VP anomaly (4$_k$≤4.0% over the average of 2%)**

◯	**Geophysical anomaly: magnetic anomaly over intrusive body**
⬭	**Geochemical anomaly**
◐	**Copper-bearing porphyrites**
◗	**Polymetallic ore**
●	**Copper-pyrite mineralization**

Copper-bearing occurrences:

1. Damirli
2. Chachinchay
3. Gazanchi
6. Agdara

Polymetallic ore mineralization:

4. Gyulatag
5. Gizilbulag
7. Mekhimana
8. Chazinadag (Copper-pyrite)

Figure 15. Geological map of the Mekhmana polymetallic ore deposit

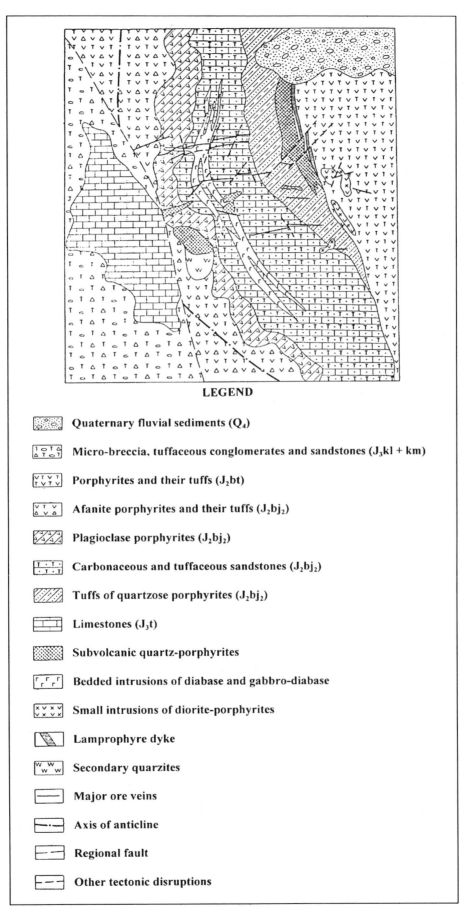

LEGEND

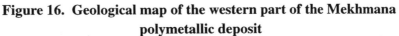

Quaternary fluvial sediments (Q_4)

Micro-breccia, tuffaceous conglomerates and sandstones ($J_3kl + km$)

Porphyrites and their tuffs (J_2bt)

Afanite porphyrites and their tuffs (J_2bj_2)

Plagioclase porphyrites (J_2bj_2)

Carbonaceous and tuffaceous sandstones (J_2bj_2)

Tuffs of quartzose porphyrites (J_2bj_2)

Limestones (J_3t)

Subvolcanic quartz-porphyrites

Bedded intrusions of diabase and gabbro-diabase

Small intrusions of diorite-porphyrites

Lamprophyre dyke

Secondary quarzites

Major ore veins

Axis of anticline

Regional fault

Other tectonic disruptions

Figure 16. Geological map of the western part of the Mekhmana polymetallic deposit

associated with the areas of hydrothermal-metasomatic alterations in enclosing volcanogenic rocks of the Lower Eocene which form a single basalt-andesite-liparite-dacite formation. The most intensive concentration of sulphide-polymetallic ores are linked with sulphate-fumarole fields of the central type being the products of post-magmatic activity of acid volcanites in subsequently differentiated basalt-andesite-liparite-dacite formations.

In spite of a common presence of sulphide mineralization in volcanites of acid composition, a distribution pattern of massive sulphide deposits is irregular. Large deposits of pyrites and pyrite-polymetallic ores are confined to local uplifts being expressed by closely converged volcanic structures of various types. The most typical are volcanic dome extrusions which are synchronous with volcanism of subvolcanic bodies. The tectonic and magmatic control of sulphide mineralization within this metallogenic belt has been studied in detail within the Agdara sulphide-polymetallic deposit in the north-western part of the belt.

The Agdara sulphide – polymetallic deposit

The deposit is confined to the northern part of the core of the Agdara archy uplift which is composed of typical volcanic brachyanticlines appeared on the site of extrusive structures and volcanic domes (figure 17). The core of the fold is composed of rocks of eroded pipes and pre-pipe facies. Wings and the eastern periclinal hinge of the old consist of more younger basic volcanites. Sulphide-polymetallic mineralization is concentrated within the core of the southern periclinal hinge of brachyanticline. The mineralization is controlled by a wide subvertical zone of intensive tectonic reworking. The core of ore-enclosing brachyanticline is intruded by subvolcanic bodies of liparite-dacite exposed to intensive hydrothermal-metasomatic alteration of secondary quarzites and propyllites.

Mineral exploration in the southern part of the brachyanticline has revealed massive sulphide mineralization underlied by secondary quarzites and overlapped by sedimentary-volcanogenic sequence. Two morphogenetic types of sulphide-polymetallic mineralization are stratabound massive and streaky-impregnated ores which occupy various structural positions, though spatially are closely associated with each other.

The stratabound bed of massive sulphides varies in thickness from 0.2 to 4.5 metres and has been traced from the surface to a 65 metres depth, where it reaches a range of 120-130 metres length. Bend of the ore body on dip and extent repeat those of overlapping and enclosing sedimentary-volcanic rocks. Along the strike, the ore body has a sharp contacts with underlying secondary quarzites. The roof structure of the deposit is more complicated. The morphology of streaky ores developed in a base of bed-shaped ore deposit is rather complicated.

Sulphide stringers from 1 millimetre to 1.5-2.5 centimetres form a complicated stockwork inside of areas of mineral concentrations where they coat fragments of mono-quarzites and sericite-quartzose rocks.

Major ore-forming minerals are pyrite (80 per cent), sphalerite (3-4 per cent), galenite (3 per cent) and chalcopyrite. The volume of bed-shaped deposit is composed of sphalerite (70-75 per cent), pyrite (5 per cent), chalcopyrite (10 per cent) and galenite (20-30 per cent). A certain vertical zonation in localization of sulphides is expressed by a prevailance of ferrum, copper and lead sulphides in the lower part of the ore body and a volumous domination of zinc and lead sulphides in the massive ores of the deposit upward. Secondary minerals are tennantite, tetraedrite, stromeyenite, bornite, molybdenite, chalcosine, cerussite and covellite. The cementing minerals are quartz, sericite, alunite, barite, calcite and chlorite. The formation of stringer-impregnated ores has occurred in two stages, where the initial stringers of quartz-pyrite-chalcopyrite and molybdenite composition have been cross-cut by stringers of quartz-calcite and sphalerite-galenite composition. The deposit has been worked out and closed due to its depletion.

The Sharur-Djulfa metallogenic belt

The polymetallic mineralization within this metallogenic belt is known to exist in the Gyumushlug and Darridag-Paradash regions. The Gyumushlug ore region is situated in the area of the Paleozoic terrigenous-

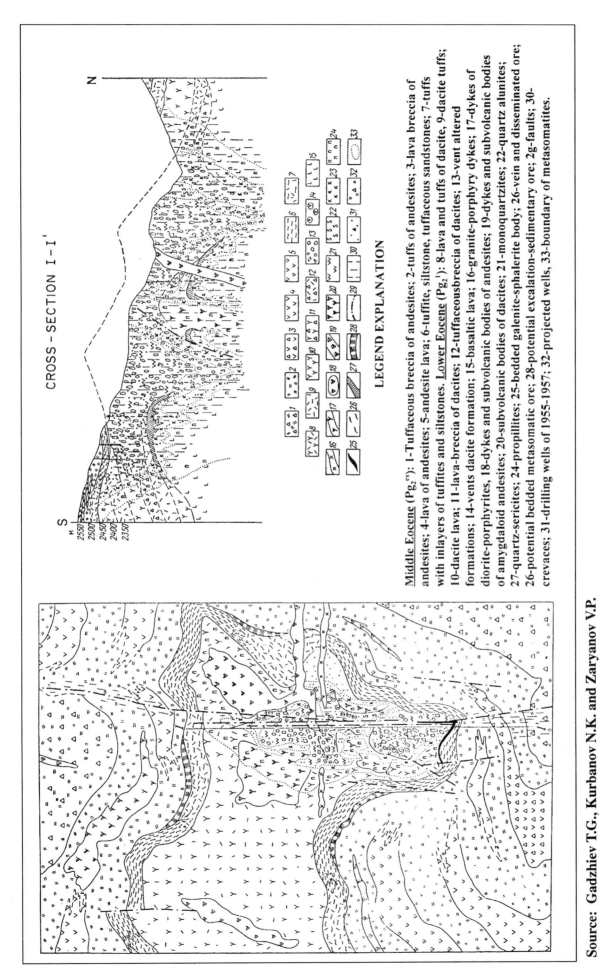

CROSS – SECTION I – I'

LEGEND EXPLANATION

<u>Middle Eocene (Pg₂ᶜˢ):</u> 1-Tuffaceous breccia of andesites; 2-tuffs of andesites; 3-lava breccia of andesites; 4-lava of andesites; 5-andesite lava; 6-tuffite, siltstone, tuffaceous sandstones; 7-tuffs with inlayers of tuffites and siltstones. <u>Lower Eocene (Pg₂¹):</u> 8-lava and tuffs of dacite, 9-dacite tuffs; 10-dacite lava; 11-lava-breccia of dacites; 12-tuffaceousbreccia of dacites; 13-vent altered formations; 14-vents dacite formation; 15-basaltic lava; 16-granite-porphyry dykes; 17-dykes of diorite-porphyrites, 18-dykes and subvolcanic bodies of andesites; 19-dykes and subvolcanic bodies of amygdaloid andesites; 20-subvolcanic bodies of dacites; 21-monoquartzites; 22-quartz alunites; 27-quartz-sericites; 24-propillites; 25-bedded galenite-sphalerite body; 26-vein and disseminated ore; 26-potential bedded metasomatic ore; 28-potential excalation-sedimentary ore; 2g-faults; 30-crevaces; 31-drilling wells of 1955-1957; 32-projected wells, 33-boundary of metasomatites.

Source: Gadzhiev T.G., Kurbanov N.K. and Zaryanov V.P.

Figure 17. Geological map of the Agdara polymetallic deposit

carbonaceous complex development and hosts the known Gyumushlug lead-zinc deposit and the Danzik and Sadarak small occurrences.

The Gyumushlug polymetallic deposit

The deposit was discovered at the end of the nineteenth century and has been exploited by the "Alagez" Joint Stock Company during a period from 1908 to 1916. The deposit is confined to the south-western limb and core of the Gyumushlug anticline made up by limestones, clayey shales, marly limestones and sandstones of the Givetian and Fransnian stages of the Devonian age. The Gyumushlug anticline has a complex tectonic structure due to intersection of lateral and transversal tectonic faults forming a clear block or mosaic structure (figures 18 and 19).

The mineralization is strictly confined to limestones of the Givetian stage being localized in pre-ore meridional brecciated zones and also in inter-layer space of limestones favorable for ore deposition. Structural and lithological factors have defined the existence of two morphological types of mineralization, namely, steeply-dipping cross-cutting ore zones and stratobound mineralized beds.

Altogether, twenty four steeply-dipping ore zones with a variable thickness from 0.4 to 6 metres have been found in the deposit and only eight zones have been proved to be of an industrial importance. Clayey shales played a screening role in the formation of ore bodies enabling the localization of mineralization in the topmost sections of the limestone sequence. Industrial concentrations of lead and zinc have been found only in the lower horizons. The mineralization spreads towards from the fractures of a range of 25-30 metres with a thickness of stratified mineralized lenses from 1 to 11.0 metres. Veins, nests, lens-shaped veins being accompanied by the areal of impregnated ores are distinguished in both morphological types of ores. The main initial ore minerals are galena and sphalerite; secondary minerals are pyrite, chalcopyrite and secondary copper sulphides; rare minerals are boulangerite, boutnonite and argenite; associated minerals are smithsonite, cerussite, limonite, covellite, chalcosine, anglesite and malachite; vein minerals are quartz, barite, calcite, rarely ankerite, dolomite and gypsum.

The mineralization has concentrated in three stages being separated by the periods of tectonic movements. These stages are the main sulphide ore-forming stage, the galena-barite stage, and the galena-carbonate stage. According to texture peculiarities, massive, gneissose, brecciated, streaky and impregnation ores have been distinguished. While massive ores have localized in ore zones and adjacent areas of stratabound mineralization streaky and impregnated ores have been met in the peripheral parts of ore bodies. The cemented, subgraphical, emulsioned and replacement types of ore structures are distinguished. According to chemical composition, three industrial types of ores, namely the prevailing lead type and lead-zinc types have been identified. The polymetallic ores of the Gumushlug deposit are typical hydrothermal formations being concentrated under conditions of shallow depths and low temperatures.

The deposit has been explored by underground mining in combination with drilling. The reserves have been estimated on a category $B + C_1$. The deposit has been exploited since 1955, and up to now, the reserves of the I, II and III ore areas have been nearly worked out (figure 19). The ore-processing capacity of the Gumushlug processing plant used to be at around 50 tons per day. The detailed geological prospecting and mineral exploration have identified further prospects of sulphide mineralization in the south-eastern flank of the IV ore zone of the deposit (figure 20). The reserves here have been estimated on a category C_2 and the underground mining is visible from a single shaft. At present, the exploitation works have been suspended due to technical reasons. The remaining reserves as of 1 January 1991 on category C_1 were 133,000 tons of ore or 5,800 lead metal.

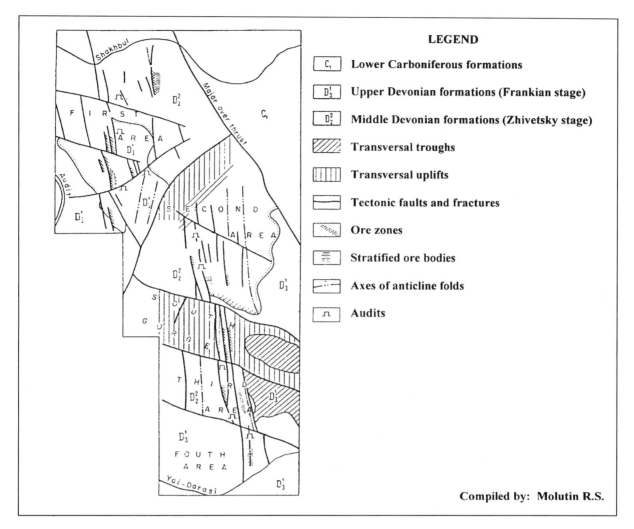

Figure 18. Tectonic setting of the Gyumushlug polymetallic deposit

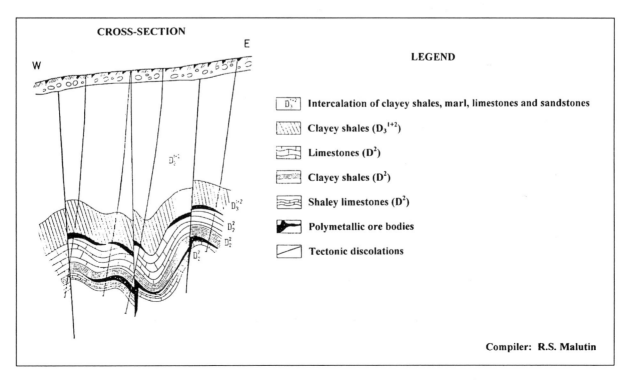

Figure 19. Cross-section of the polymetallic ore body at area IV of the Gyumushlug deposit

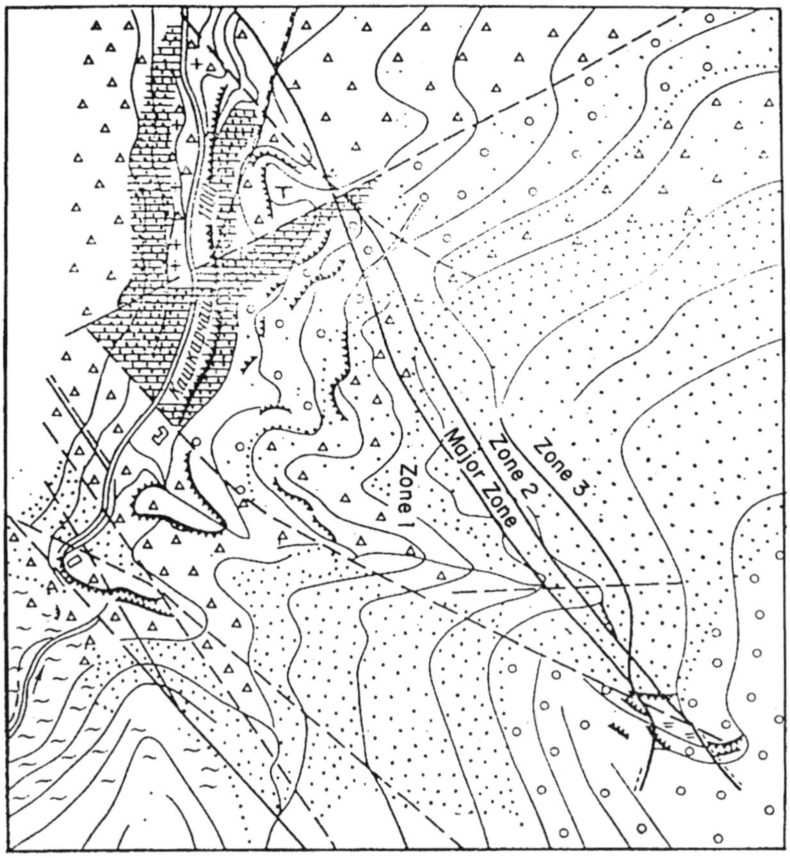

LEGEND

~~	Tuff-breccia and tuff-sandstones
°₀°	Tuff-conglomerates
::::	Silty and quartzose tuff-sandstones
△ ˙ △	Tuff-breccias and tuff-conglomerates with interbeds of tuff-sandstones
° ° °	Tuff-conglomerates with interbeds of tuff-sanstones and tuff-breccias
△ ˸ △	Aglomeratic tuff-breccias of porphyrites and tuff-conglomerates
⸫⸫	Quartzose tuff-sandstones
+ △ +	Tuff of quartz porphyrites
	Dykes of diabase and gabbro-diabase
	Post-ore tectonic faults
	Tectonic zones with dykes of diabase
˙ T	Elements of dip and strike

Figure 20. Geologic map of the "North" cobalt deposit

(b) *Cobalt*

Cobalt mineralization is closely associated with magmatic activity and has been found in many tectonic zones of Azerbaijan (Geology of the USSR, 1976). The cobalt deposit of the Dashkesan ore region is paragenetically associated with the Dashkesan polyphase granitoid massif of the Upper Jurassic age. The deposit has been studied in details by mineral exploration and has been partially worked out in the Somkhit-Agdam zone. Cobalt mineralization has also been observed in sulphide ores of the Goshgardag and Chanakhchi occurrences (Bajocian-Bathonian), hematite ore of the Novo-Ivanovka occurrence (Eocene) and others. In the Geychay-Garabag tectonic zone, the prospects of cobalt mineralization are associated with hyperbasites and magnesite schists of the Late Cretaceous. In the Aras tectonic zone, cobalt mineralization is associated with skarns of the contact area of the Megri-Ordubad pluton of granitoids of the Early Eocene-Late Pliocene age. On the southern slope of the Major Caucasus ridge, cobalt mineralization has been found within the southern limb of the western part of the Tufan anticlinorium. Cobalt mineralization here occurs as isomorphic admixture to pyrite-coper-polymetalic ores of the deposits of the southern slope of the Greater Caucasus.

The Dashkesan ore region of the Somkhit-Agdam metallogenic belt

The Dashkesan ore region is hosted by the Middle and Upper Jurassic sedimentary, volcanogenic-sedimentary and volcanic rocks. These rocks are intruded by the Dashkesan polyphase granitoid massif, the exocontacts of which host metamorphic and contact-metasomatic rocks, hornblendes marbles as well as barren and mineralized skarns.

Numerous dykes of mainly diabase diorite and plagioclase porphyrites have been found in the Jurassic sedimentary rocks containing the intrusive massif. The presence of dykes inside of the granitoid massif is very rare. The main tectonic element is the Dashkesan anticline of the west-north-western direction and associated numerous tectonic dislocations of variable age. Cobalt mineralization is also known to occur in the form of cobalt sulpho-arsenide in the Dashkesan deposit of iron ore and in hydrothermal ore bodies beyond the skarns zones in the North deposit. Cobalt mineralization has been also found in a dispersed form in magnetite and as isomorphic admixture in pyrite.

By structural – morphological features and mineral associations, the following types of cobalt deposits and occurrences have been identified: (a) steeply-dipping zones with sulpho-arsenic cobalt mineralization (the North deposit of the Dashkesan ore region); (b) lenses and nests of sulpho-arsenic cobalt concentration in magnetite skarns (the North-Eastern iron ore deposit); (c) steeply-dipping zones bearing lenses and nests sulpho-arsenic cobalt mineralization (Amamchay area); and (d) lenses and nests of cobalt-pyrite and sulpho-arsenic cobalt mineralization in magnetite skarns (the South Dashkesan and Damir deposits).

The "North" cobalt deposit

The "North" deposit is situated directly to the north from the Dashkesan intrusive massif (figure 20). Cobalt mineralization is localized mainly in steeply-dipping crushed zones along dykes of diabase porphyrites. Cobalt mineralization is confined to the rocks of hydrothermal alteration widely developed in tectonically-reworked zones. The distribution of cobaltite and other sulpho-arsenides of cobalt is uneven. There are known to exist 18 ore zones including the major ore zone from 300 to 350 metres long, and a variable thickness from 0.25 metre to more than 10 metres. Contacts between lateral host rocks and the major ore zone are clear with well-expressed slide planes. The hydrothermal alteration processes are represented by chloritization and kaolinisation. Sulpho-arsenides of cobalt have been concentrated unevenly, being met as the impregnations of lenses and small streaks. The average content of cobalt in ore is 0.5 per cent. The major ore zone has been explored to a depth of 400 metres. The concentration of cobalt is increasing from the surface until a 150 metres depth and, then it is decreasing until 280 metres deep. Mineral exploration indicated a presence of gold mineralization along a strike of the major ore zone thus increasing its economic potential.

The cobalt grade within other ore-bearing zones of the deposit varies from traces to 15 per cent. Unlike the major ore zone, the ore zones in the rest of the deposit are not accompanied by dykes. Most of the cobalt mineralization occurs intermixed with glaucodites, pyrite and chalcopyrite in steeply-deeping fissure veins and fillings. In some places, mineralization is found in a form of impregnations of tuffaceous sandstones. All the cobalt-bearing zones are associated genetically and, some times spatially, with the major ore zone, being confirmed by a similar mineral composition.

The North-Eastern deposit

This cobalt deposit is situated within the north-eastern part of the iron ore deposit of the Dashkesan ore region. It is represented by numerous lenses, nests, streaks and rare impregnations of cobaltite in the upper section of the Dashkesan iron ore deposit. The sulpho-arsenic cobalt mineralization in the form of interrupted ore bodies of lens and nest morphology was found in a tectonically-reworked zone of the north-eastern direction. Cobalt mineralization is associated with tectonically-related dykes, veins and fissures.

The South Dashkesan deposit of cobalt-bearing magnetite skarns

Cobalt-bearing pyrite and sulpho-arsenic-cobalt mineralization is associated with magnetite skarns from 40 to 50 metres thick (figure 21). Cobalt-bearing pyrite mineralization is represented by twelve lenses of an average size 50 x 50 metres each. The minimum cut-off grade of ore is 0.04 per cent of cobalt. Lenses of cobalt-bearing pyrite are concentrated among hematite-and magnetite-bearing garnet skarns being enriched by pyrite and chalcopyrite. The crystallization time of cobalt-bearing pyrite is close to a period of formation of magnetite. Cobalt content in magnetite skarns varies from traces to 0.015 per cent. Technological samples of the nearby Damir iron ore deposit indicate the cobalt grade from 0.008 to 0.013 per cent.

The sulpho-arsenic-cobalt mineralization within the South Dashkesan (Pirsultan) iron ore deposit, except that of cobalt-pyrite, is characterized also by lenses, impregnations and rarely by streaks of cobaltite among magnetite skarns. Five lens-shaped bodies of cobaltite ores were found to occur in the lower section of magnetite skarns deposition downward of cobalt-bearing pyrite ores. The mineral composition is dominated by cobaltite followed by pyrite, chalcopyrite, glaucodite, hematite, saffolorite and cubanite. Cobalt content of sulpho-arsenic-cobalt ores varies from 0.041 to 0.925 per cent reaching a grade of 3 per cent in separate blocks.

The Amamchay cobalt deposit

The Amamchay cobalt deposit is located to the south-west from the South Dashkesan deposit. The character of ore mineralization has common features with that within the "North" and "North-Eastern" deposits. The deposit is hosted by marbled limestones of the Tusitanian suite of the Upper Oxfordian – Lower Kimmeridgian age up to 250 metres thick. Limestones are underlied by a tuffogenous-sedimentary sequence of the Calloyian stage and overlapped by volcanogenic rocks of the Kimmeridgian stage.

Magnetite skarns series occurs in the upper section of limestones being cut by numerous dykes of porphyrites of the north-western and, rarely, north-eastern directions. In some places, brecciated and fractured matrix of dykes is substantially replaced by magnetite exposed to chloritization, epidotization, carbonatization and pyritization, with associated cobalt mineralization. Some zones contain only cobalt mineralization along dykes without magnetite skarn mineralization. The most intensive cobalt mineralization up to 30 metres thick has been found to occur in tectonically-crushed and reworked areas of the deposit being a result of intensive tectonic activity and cross-cutting dykes. Cobalt grade varies from 0.004 to 0.95 per cent. Cobaltite is met in a disseminated form, as fissure fillings and separate crystallic aggregates. Other ore minerals are pyrite, chalcopyrite, saffolorite, hematite and molybdenite.

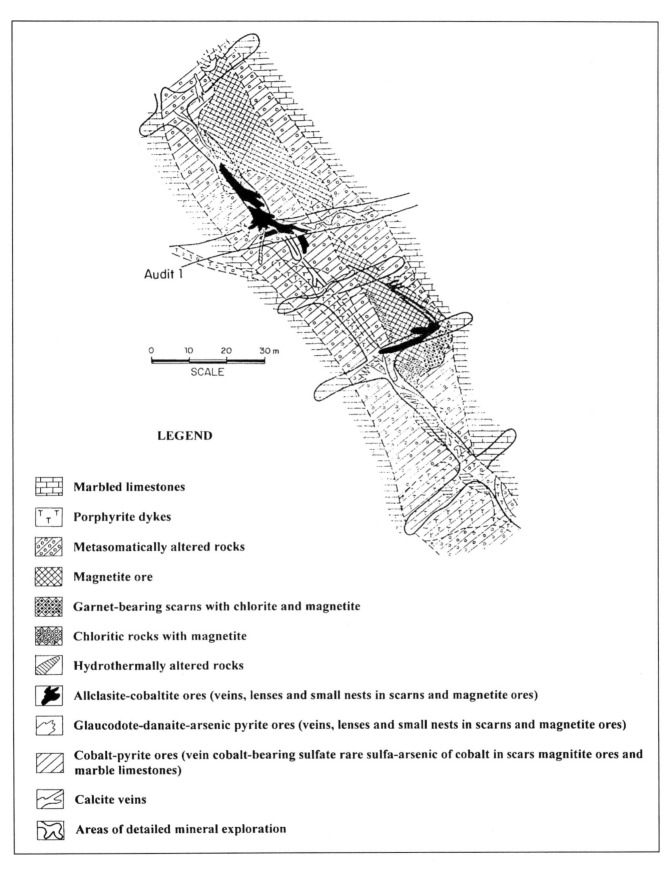

Audit 1

0   10   20   30 m

SCALE

LEGEND

Marbled limestones

Porphyrite dykes

Metasomatically altered rocks

Magnetite ore

Garnet-bearing scarns with chlorite and magnetite

Chloritic rocks with magnetite

Hydrothermally altered rocks

Allclasite-cobaltite ores (veins, lenses and small nests in scarns and magnetite ores)

Glaucodote-danaite-arsenic pyrite ores (veins, lenses and small nests in scarns and magnetite ores)

Cobalt-pyrite ores (vein cobalt-bearing sulfate rare sulfa-arsenic of cobalt in scars magnitite ores and marble limestones)

Calcite veins

Areas of detailed mineral exploration

Figure 21. Geological map of the south-eastern area of the South Dashkesan iron-cobalt deposit

The Qazakh cobalt occurrence

Cobalt mineralization of the Qazakh occurrence is associated with hydrothermal ore complex of the Upper Cretaceous volcanics of the Dashkesan ore region where it was found among manganese ores of the Dashkesan occurrence. The ore district occurs in volcanogenic and pyroclastic rocks of the Upper Coniancian – Lower Santonian and extrusive rocks of the Upper Santonian age being represented by the albitophyres and liparite-porphyres, benthobnite and benthonized rocks. This volcano-tuffogeneous formation is overlapped transgressively by limestones of the Campanian – Maastrichtian age.

Cobalt-manganese mineralization is most likely of hydrothermal genesis, relates paragenetically to extrusive volcanism. The ore-bearing zone up to 3 metres thick is confined to a fracture zone of the marginal part of a small intrusive body. The mineralization is represented by hydroxide of manganese in a form of dendrites and stains saturating debris of albitophyres and liporite-porphyres. Cobalt content in elizavgete and rancierite varies from a range of 0.03-0.04 per cent to 0.68-1.32 per cent.

The Geychay-Hakera metallogenic belt

Cobalt mineralization within this metallogenic belt has been identified in all types of magnesite schists of ultrabasic rocks development in the Kelbadjar region, where the cobalt content varies from 0.001 to 1 per cent. It has been found that an increase of cobalt content in ultrabasic rocks is associated with an increase of magnesite. The maximum cobalt concentrations have been observed in olivine and less in enstatite. The increased cobalt content has been also observed in serpentinites in comparison with source peridotites.

The Ordubad-Zangezur metallogenic belt

Cobal mineralization of the Kilit-Ketan occurrence in the Ordubad ore region has been found in exocontact of the Megri-Ordubad granitoid massif. The cobalt occurrence is hosted by the Upper Cretaceous sandy-argillitic series of the Lower Turonian, marly-argillitic series of the Lower and the Upper Coniacian, limestones of the Upper Coniacian, tuffogenous series of the Lower Santonian, limestones of the Upper Santonian, and marly-argillitic series of the Campanian age. Metasomatic rocks such as marbles, hornfels skarns and epidosites were formed as a result of intensive magmatism in a strip from 200 to 1,000 metres long.

Cobalt-bearing suphide mineralization is confined to the external margin of the Upper Cretaceous rocks surrounding the Megri-Ordubad intrusive massif, where mineralization has been traced over a distance of 2.5 kilometres. Copper-cobalt mineralization is associated genetically with the post-magmatic activity of the Megri-Ordubad pluton. Epidote-garnet skarns of the most promising Ketam zone contain lenses, nests and impregnations of sulphides. Mineral exploration by underground horizontal adits has been terminated due to security instability on the territory of the Nakhchivan Autonomous Republic.

(c)   Molybdenum

The deposits and occurrences of molybdenum ores in the Lesser Caucasus are concentrated within the Ordubad and Dalidag ore regions (Baba-zade and others, 1990; Geology of the USSR, 1976; Kerimou, 1974). The majority of ore deposits of the copper-molybdenum formation is concentrated within the Megri-Ordubad intrusive complex confined to a large geoanticlinal uplift and representing the median massif in the definite stages of the geologic evolution. Molybdenum mineralization is mainly developed in intersection of longitudinal and north-western faults with cross faults of the north-eastern direction. The large Misdag, Alchalig and Diakhchay copper-molybdenum deposits of industrial type are mainly characterized by stockwork type of mineralization with the leading copper component.

Deposits with industrial molybdenum mineralization with a dominant molybdenum component of vein type are represented by either quartz veins and fissure fillings or veinlets and stockworks with impregnated mineralization. The thickness of veins and veinlets vary from 0.1 to 1.0 metre reaching a thickness of up to 2 metres in swelling. The molybdenum content varies from 0.2 to 1.1 per cent. Associated ore minerals are copper (0.02-1.73 per cent), renium (0.04 per cent in molybdenite), selenium (0.06 per cent) and tellurium (0.02 per cent). The molybdenum deposits, unlike the copper-molybdenum deposits of the region, have limited reserves from 100 to a range of 1,500-2,000 tons of molybdenum metal.

The Paragachay deposit

The Paragachay molybdenum deposit is located in the central part of the Ordubad ore region and hosted by gabbro-diorites, diorites, and dykes of lamprophyres and diorite-porphyres (figure 22). The mineralization is tectonically controlled by sublatitudinal (NW – 280°-310°) and submeridional (NE – 20°-60°) faults. The mineralization in the form of veins and veinlets is concentrated in sublatitudinal faults. Ore-bearing gabbro-diorites and diorites have been subjected to intensive hydrothermal-metasomatic alteration. The formation of ore mineralization at the deposit has occurred in the following five stages: (a) quartz-molybdenite early stage productive for molybdenum; (b) quartz-molybdenite-chalcopyrite stage productive for molybdenum and copper; (c) quartz-pyrite-chalcopyrite stage productive for copper; (d) quartz-gaiena-sphalerite stage; and (e) most latest carbonate stage. Four quartz-molybdenite veins of industrial importance, namely, Glavnaya, Novaya, Pyataya and Srednya have been exploited within the Paragachay deposit.

The Glavnaya (Bash or Major) vein is striking north-west at 270°-320° and dipping to the south-west with an angle from 55°-60°. The south-eastern part of the vein contains molybdenum mineralization and the north-western part that of copper. The average thickness of the vein in its south-eastern part is 0.7 metres with a range from 0.1 to 2.5 metres. The vein has been explored on two horizons by adits and some drilling wells. The vein is accompanied by a dyke of spessartite and has an apophyses with industrial mineralization. The reserves are unknown.

The Novaya (Yeni or New) vein strikes north-west at 280°-300° and dips to the south-west with the angle 70°. It has been explored on nine horizons by mining openings and drilling wells. The north-western part of the vein along the near-latitudinal tectonic fault contains copper mineralization, and the rest of the vein molybdenite. The average thickness of the vein is 0.6 metres. The average grade of molybdenum is 0.7 per cent. Data on reserves are not available.

The Pyataya (Besh or the Fifth) vein tends north-west at 290°-310° and dips to the south-west at the angles from 60° to 80°. Similar to the Bash vein, the south-eastern part of this vein contains molybdenite and has been explored on four horizons by adits and drilling wells. The surfacial and upper horizons of the vein does not contain any industrial mineralization. The thickness of the vein is from 0.2 to 0.3 metre on the average. The thickness and molybdenum content tend to increase with a depth. The vein apophyses have been explored on two horizons and proved to contain industrial molybdenum mineralization with an average grade of 0.8 per cent. Further prospects of increasing molybdenum reserves are associated with mineral exploration of the lower horizons of the vein on its north-western flank. The reserves are unknown.

The Srednya (Orta or Middle) vein occurs between the above Bash and Yeni veins. The vein tends north-west at 290°-300° and dips south-west at angles from 30° to 70°. The vein is represented by a zone of hydrothermally-altered rocks of 0.1-0.2 metre thick with quartz stringers from 0.05 to 0.1 metre with a molybdenum content up to 0.02 per cent. The vein has been explored on four horizons by mining openings and drilling wells proved to contain industrial mineralization in the middle horizons. The main ore forming minerals are pyrite, chalcopyrite and molybdenite. The mineralization has been found in the form of impregnation, fissure fillings and selvages in coarse-grained milky quartz together with fine-grained quartz. Ores have banded, rarely brecciated texture. Pinches and swells substitute each other forming lens-shaped structure.

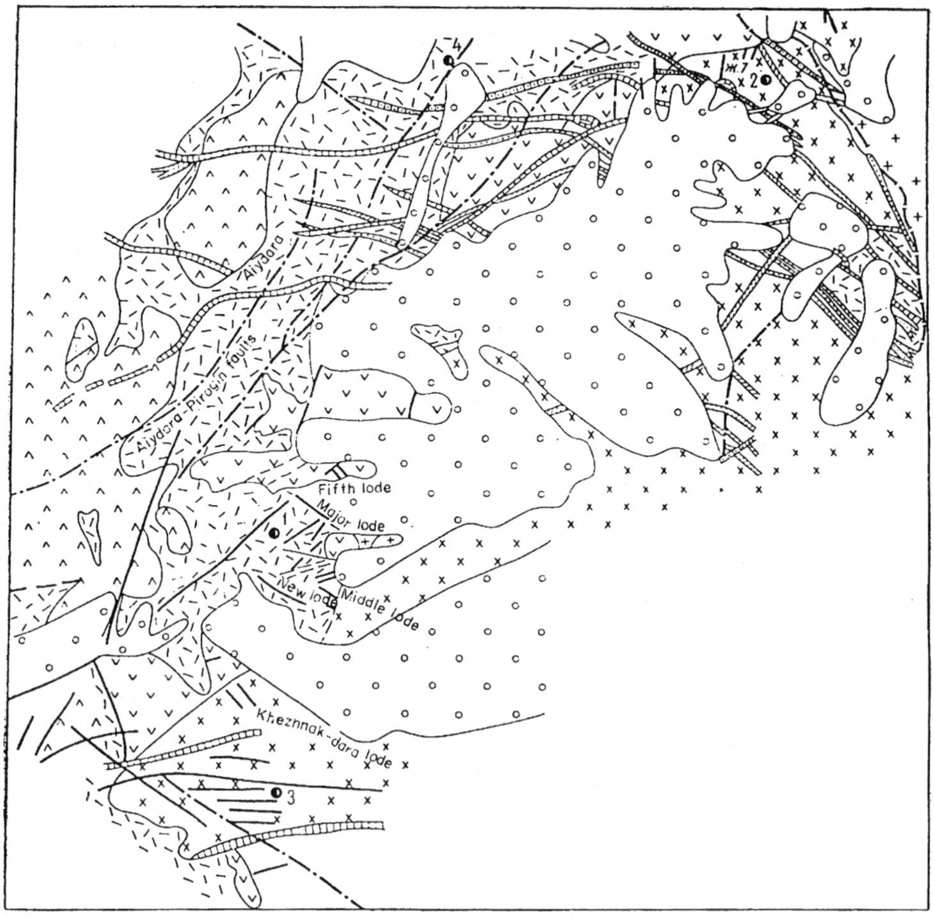

LEGEND

▢	Glacial deposits
▢	Andesites, diabase porphyrites, dacites
▢	Diorites, gabbro-diorites, gabbro-hornblends (I phase)
▢	Quartzose syenite-diorites, porphyry quartzose syenite-diorites and granosyenite (II phase)
▢	Porphyry granodiorites (III phase)
▢	Granodiorites-porphyres (II phase)
▢	Granodiorite-porphyres (III phase)
▢	Diorite-porphyrites, lamprophyres (III phase)
▢	Secondary quartzites
▢	Copper-molybdenum-bearing veins
▢	Faults
▢	Deposits of the Paragachay ore field: 1-Paragachay (Mo); 2-Kapudjik (Cu, Mo); 3-Madanidzor (Cu, Mo); 4-Paragachay (rutile)

Compiled by M.A. Agasein, R.R. Agakishibekova

Figure 22. Geological map of the Paragachay copper-molybdenum deposit

Unlike the Glavnaya (Bash or Major) vein, where the dyke-related mineralization demonstrates its continuity, the mineralization in the last three veins discontinues along their strike. The prospects of the Paragachay molybdenum deposit are associated with the lower horizons of the Yeni and Besh veins which can be opened by mine or adit from 2 to 2.5 kilometres long. At present, due to unfavourable economic-technical conditions the exploitation works have been suspended. The remaining mineable reserves of molybdenum as of 1 January 1999 on $B + C_1$ category are 54,000 tons of molybdenum ore or 256 tons of molybdenum metal.

The Gapidjig occurrence

The Gapidjig molybdenum occurrence was found in the watershed part of the Zangezur ridge, dividing the basins of Paraga and Vohchi rivers. The area is known to contain 16 quartz-molybdenite-bearing veins. The occurrence is hosted by rocks of granosyenite intrusive phase being complicated on the north by a narrow strip of fissures and secondary hydrothermal alteration. Rocks of vein type represented by spessartites, diorite-porphyrites and granite-porphyriters are widespread. The extended fractures of the north-east and north-west limbs are widely developed in the area of the Gapidjig occurrence. Five ore-bearing zones of fissure fillings were found in fractures of the north-western direction.

Ore-bearing zones with an average thickness of 0.35 metre with frequent pinches up to a few centimetres and swells up to 1.5-2 metres are represented by crushed, fractured and quartzose syenite-diorites with a thin impregnation of molybdenite. Ortoclase and biotite areals around zones have been distinguished. Two stages of mineralization are the major high-temperature quartz-molybdenite stage and the minor quartz-chalcopyrite-molybdenite stage. Fractures of the north-eastern direction are nearly barren having in some places very thin selvages and rare impregnations of galenite. It enables to suggest that a low-temperature quartz-sphalerite-galena stage has pronounced there on a very limited scale. The most promising veins of the deposit are the Gapidjig and No. 7 and 9 veins of clear selvages and lens form.

The vein No. 7 tends north-western at 330°-350° and dips to the south-west with a variable angle from 50° to 70°. The average thickness of the vein is 0.38 metre. On the surface, it is represented by yellow coarse-grained quartz with secondary minerals of molybdenum and iron. Mineral exploration on three underground horizons by adits and two drilling wells indicates the average thickness of the vein of 0.92 metre. The average content is 0.63 per cent of molybdenum and 1.24 per cent of copper.

The Gapidjig vein is situated on the north-eastern slope of the Zangezur ridge at around 800 metres from the vein No. 7. The vein tends north-west at 340° and dips to the south-west at angle 45°. The average thickness of the vein is 0.4 metre; the average grade is 0.06 per cent of molybdenum and 0.9 per cent of copper. The occurrence has been studied by short adits and one drilling well. The main minerals are pyrite, chalcopyrite, molybdenite and lode milky coarse-grained quartz. All the minerals, typical for the copper-molybdenum formation, are met in ores. Due to limited reserves, the Gapidjig occurrence does not have any independent industrial importance, however, it can be used as additional raw material base of the Paragachay deposit.

The Urumis molybdenum deposit

There are known to exist ten quartz-molybdenum veins distributed in the endocontact zone of the Megri-Ordubad pluton. The deposit occurs in gabbro-diotites, granodiorites and quartz syenite-diorites with cutting dykes of granodiorite-porphyrites, diorite-porphyrites, lamprophyre, aplite and pegmatites. Tuffs and tuffites of the Eocene in the south-eastern part of the deposit have been changed into secondary quarzites in the contact zone with the intrusion.

The veins strike to the west-north-west at 270°-290° and dip to the south-west at the angle from 50° to 70°. The average thickness is 0.4 metre. The molybdenum content is from 0.001 to 0.1 per cent and that of copper from 0.06 to 0.7 per cent. The veins consist of milky-white quartz containing impregnations of pyrite, chalopyrite, and molybdenite. Secondary hydrothermal alterations are expressed by silicification and sericitization. The veins have a banded texture and lens-shape structure.

The north-western part of the deposit contains mainly copper vein mineralization, which has been explored by short underground adits. The tense concentration of copper-bearing quartz veins within a narrow strip of 400 metres wide and a shallow erosion depth suggest good development prospects. Mineral exploration also expects a possible increase of thickness and content of molybdenum in the south-eastern flank of the deposit where mineralization has not been effected by erosion.

The Gekgyundur deposit

The deposit is hosted by intrusive rocks of the Megri-Ordubad pluton represented by rocks of the early adamellite intrusive phase and late quartz syenite-diorites and porphyry granosyenites being cross cut by dykes of diorites and granite-porphyries. The tectonic structure of the deposit is defined by the major Ordubad fault which divides two intrusive phases and the Vardanichay fault of meridional direction with adjacent zones of hydrothermal alteration.

The thickness of these zones with molybdenum mineralization varies from 0.5 to 1.2 metres where molybdenum content is from 0.01 to 2.5 per cent. The zones are composed of loose chloritized and epidotized rocks. The molybdenuium mineralization, except zone No. 1, is being controlled by the Vardanichay fault. The mineralization at zone No. 1 was traced up to 360 metres deep on four horizons every 60 metres by adits and by underground drilling wells. In some intervals of two horizons, this zone contain the industrial accumulations of molybdenum. The average thickness is 1.1 metres and the average grade of molybdenum is 0.44 per cent. Reserves are so far limited, while the identified further exploration is required to judge its economic prospects. The stockwork type of molybdenum-copper mineralization was suggested at a depth in the area of the Vardanichay fault, where the molybdenum content in individual samples from quartz stringers varies from 0.01 to 2.5 per cent and that of copper from 0.2 to 2.5 per cent.

The Dalidag ore region

Molybdenum mineralization of this region is closely associated with the post-magmatic activity of the Dalidag intrusive massif. The early copper-molybdenum and more later polymetallic ore formations have been distinguished within the deposit. Structural position and localization of these ore formations are defined by a series of dykes which separated the enclosing rocks into two blocks (figure 23).

The typical Teymuruchandag molybdenum deposit of the Dalidag ore region is confined to the north-western exo-contact of the Dalidag granitoid intrusive massif composed of porphyry granosyenites, quartz syenite-diorites and syenite-diorites. The regional west-north-west tending fault of a thrust nature with an amplitude of 400 metres was traced by the Istisu mineral springs and confined to the axis of the Dalidag anticlinorium. The deposit is subdivided into the north-western and south-eastern blocks by a meridional fault. The most part of a subsided block is covered by thick flows of the Quaternary andesite-basaltic lava. Quartz molybdenum veins are confined to ruptures of shearing and fissures along the fault within the uplifted north-western block.

Altogether, 41 quartz veins and zones of hydrothermally altered rocks have been identified within the deposit. The veins strike north-east with a variable limb from 30° to 85° and dip to the south-east and sometimes to the north-west at angles from 50° to 90°. Ore veins are mainly controlled by pre-ore dykes of diorite porphyrite composition. The thickness of veins and zones varies from 0.1 to 1.8 metres. Molybdenum content varies from 0.01 to 0.2 per cent, copper from 0.01 to 0.3 per cent, lead from 0.001 to 1.83 per cent and zinc from 0.01 to 0.74 per cent.

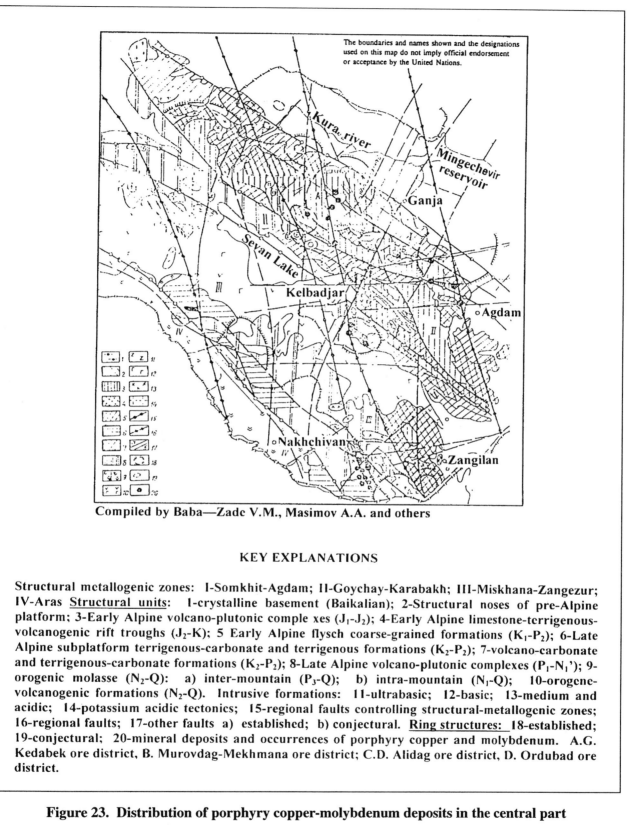

The boundaries and names shown and the designations used on this map do not imply official endorsement or acceptance by the United Nations.

Compiled by Baba—Zadc V.M., Masimov A.A. and others

KEY EXPLANATIONS

Structural metallogenic zones: I-Somkhit-Agdam; II-Goychay-Karabakh; III-Miskhana-Zangezur; IV-Aras <u>Structural units:</u> 1-crystalline basement (Baikalian); 2-Structural noses of pre-Alpine platform; 3-Early Alpine volcano-plutonic comple xes (J_1-J_2); 4-Early Alpine limestone-terrigenous-volcanogenic rift troughs (J_2-K); 5 Early Alpine flysch coarse-grained formations (K_1-P_2); 6-Late Alpine subplatform terrigenous-carbonate and terrigenous formations (K_2-P_2); 7-volcano-carbonate and terrigenous-carbonate formations (K_2-P_2); 8-Late Alpine volcano-plutonic complexes (P_1-N_1'); 9-orogenic molasse (N_2-Q): a) inter-mountain (P_3-Q); b) intra-mountain (N_1-Q); 10-orogenc-volcanogenic formations (N_2-Q). **Intrusive formations:** 11-ultrabasic; 12-basic; 13-medium and acidic; 14-potassium acidic tectonics; 15-regional faults controlling structural-metallogcnic zones; 16-regional faults; 17-other faults a) established; b) conjectural. <u>Ring structures:</u> 18-established; 19-conjectural; 20-mineral deposits and occurrences of porphyry copper and molybdenum. A.G. Kedabek ore district, B. Murovdag-Mekhmana ore district; C.D. Alidag ore district, D. Ordubad ore district.

Figure 23. Distribution of porphyry copper-molybdenum deposits in the central part of the Lesser Caucasus

Veins of a lens from are separated in some places by stepped faults with an amplitude of displacement from a range of 0.5 to 2.0 metres up to 10 metres. Veins are composed mainly of quartz; the main ore-forming minerals are pyrite, molybdenite, galenite and sphalerite. Mineralization is represented by nests and stringers in quartz mass. Veins have brecciated and banded texture owing to imposition of late quartz-polymetallic and quartz-carbonate stage on quartz-molybdenite stage of mineralization. The secondary minerals are chalcopyrite, secondary copper sulphides, bornite, covellite, chalcosine, anglesite, cerussite, malachite, azurite and limonite. Mining, technological, hydrogeological and the relief conditions of the deposit are favorable enabling to develop the deposit by horizontal underground mining.

(d)   Alunites

Alunite resources are known to exist in the Zaglic deposit and the Seifali and Dugli occurrences (Geology of USSR, 1976).

The Zaglik deposit

The Zaglik alunite deposit is confined to the north-eastern side of the Dashkesan syncline composed of volcanogenic and sedimentary formations of the Middle and Upper Jurassic being intruded by the polyphase Upper Jurassic granitoid massif. The deposit is known since the Middle Ages, when alum has been produced from alunites. The host volcano-sedimentary sequence upwards includes the Upper Bajocian porphyrites, agglomeratic lava, yellow tuff-sandstones, tuff-conglomerate and tuff-sandstones which is overlain by a thin bed of argillites and sandstones. The cross-section is followed by carbonate rocks of the Oxfordian and Lizitonian suites being covered by yellow tuffites and extrusive-effusive diabase porphyrites (figure 24). The topmost volcanogenic section is subdivided into lower tuffogenic, lower effusive, upper tuffogenic and upper effusive series with a total thickness of 600 metres. The lower tuffogenic series of 250 metres thick was subjected to intensive metasomatic reformations during the intrusive magmatism.

The composition of metasomatic rocks is changing over a distance from the intrusive massif reflecting the changes of a temperature regime. The metasomatic rocks a direct proximity to the intrusion host magnetite skarns mineralization. Westward, these rocks transfer to silicified rocks, and then into the alunites series with some prophyllitization in the transition zone. Based of this zonation, the deposit has been subdivided into (a) north-western alunite-iron ore area; (b) Alunitdag alunite-siliceous area; (c) Kirvadag alunite-prophyllite area; (d) Zaglik alunite area; and (e) Western Zaglik kaolinite-alunite area.

The alunite series of rocks has a gentle (10°-15°) dip to the south-west. Thrusts up to 30 metres uplifted the southern blocks in relation to the northern ones. Based on degree of alunitization, morphology, composition and admixtures of ores, eight textural and structural types of mineralization have been distinguished in the alunite series of rocks. Besides alunite, the primary minerals of alunite rocks are kaolinite, prophyllite, quartz, hematite and limonite. The secondary minerals are chalcedony, opal, monothermite, zunyite, pyrite, diaspore, halloysite, corundum, fluorite, magnetite, ilmenite, ilmenite, ceticite, chlorite and barite.

Alunite occurs in a form of microscopic to large (4.5 centimetres) amygdules or interlayers up to 15 centimetres size. The dominant alunite colour is cream; in some places, however, depending on admixtures, yellowish, greenish and pink varieties are present. Chemical composition of ores is associated closely with a degree of rocks' alunitization and is consistent over a depth and strike. Based on geochemical exploration, two stratabound ore bodies have been distinguished. The alunite beds are separated by a barren bed from 3 to 10 metres thick.

The thickness of the upper alunite section varies from 4 to 39 metres with an average thickness of 19 metres. It has a limited distribution and pinches out within a short distance. The lower alunite section of the deposit has a wide distribution. Main minerals of industrial significance are alunite and quartz (95 per cent of

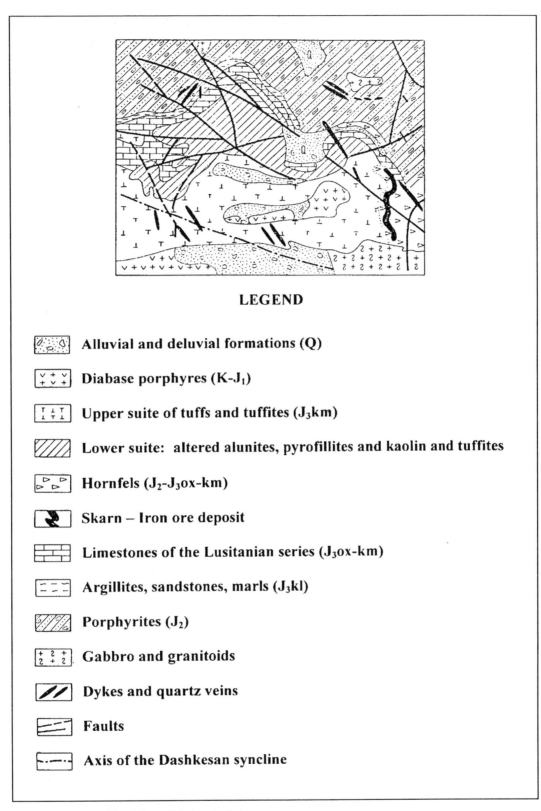

LEGEND

▦	Alluvial and deluvial formations (Q)
▦	Diabase porphyres (K-J$_1$)
▦	Upper suite of tuffs and tuffites (J$_3$km)
▨	Lower suite: altered alunites, pyrofillites and kaolin and tuffites
▦	Hornfels (J$_2$-J$_3$ox-km)
◣	Skarn – Iron ore deposit
▦	Limestones of the Lusitanian series (J$_3$ox-km)
▦	Argillites, sandstones, marls (J$_3$kl)
▨	Porphyrites (J$_2$)
▦	Gabbro and granitoids
▨	Dykes and quartz veins
▦	Faults
▦	Axis of the Dashkesan syncline

Compiled by Kashkay M.A., 1965

Figure 24. Geological map of the Zaglik-Dashkesan group of alunite deposits

the volume), and clayey minerals (5 per cent) represented by kaolinite, dickite and halloysite. Less important weakly-alunitized rocks are represented mainly by quartz, clayey minerals, volcanic glass and hematite. Hydromicas, chlorite, calcite and pyrite are observed in some places. Due to economic and technical reasons, the exploitation of the Zaglic alunite deposit is currently suspended. The remaining reserves as for 1 January 1999 on the categories $A + B + C_1$ are 161,806,000 tons.

The Seifali alunite occurrence

This occurrence is located in the Shamkhir region and confined to hydrothermally altered rocks of the Middle Jurassic (Bathian) of the Alabashli iron ore deposit (figure 25). Similar to the above Zaglic deposit, the alunite mineralization is likely to be hosted by the Upper Jurassic rock series. Major genetic types of mineralization are (a) titanium-magnetite sandstones; (b) intensively hematitized volcanogenic rocks; and (c) alunitized and kaolinized volcanogenic rocks. The cross-section of this occurrence demonstrates a vertical zonation with distinguished downward inlayers of (a) alunite-quartz with little content of dickite and kaolinite; (b) alunite-dickite-kaolinite-quartz; (c) argillite-sericite, and (d) propyllites. Gradual transitions are observed between these zones. The alunite content varies in a wide range from 9.52 to 57.0 per cent.

(e)   Bauxites

On the territory of Azerbaijan, bauxites have been initially found in the Sadarak region of the Nakhchivan Autonomous Region in the Arpachay river basin. The mineral exploration within this river basin has identified the existence of the Geransgalasi, Gabakhyal, Myunkhbala-ogl, Gabakdag, Sadarak, Danzik and Kyarki bauxite occurrences. The occurrences are hosted by terrigenous-carbonate formations of the Devonian and Carboniferous systems and carbonate formations of the Permian and Triassic systems. Magmatism is weakly pronounced and represented by dykes and layered injections of diabase and gabbro-diabase. Bauxites and bauxite-bearing rocks are confined to the lower section of the Permian formation occurring on various rock formations of the Lower Carboniferous. The Bauxe-bearing section is overlapped and underlied everywhere by carbonate rocks and outcrops on the surface in a form of two strips.

The specific feature of bauxites and bauxitic clays is their red and reddish-brick colour, clearly distinguished on a background of dark grey and black limestones. Bauxite-bearing rocks of grey and light-grey colour are also met. The main morphologic type are layers with lens-shaped bodies. Leguminous, oolitic and polytomorphic structures are typical. Conglomerate and brecciated varieties are met in some places. The bauxite-bearing layer has been traced over a distance from 1.5 to 2 kilometres with a thickness from 2 to 13 metres.

The Geran-galasi occurrence

The occurrence has been found on the left bank of Arpachay river, south of Ashagi Yaidji village in the periclinal part of the anticlinal fold. Two outcrops of bauxites are represented by red, reddish-brown, grey and greenish-grey varieties in the upper part of bauxite-bearing section. The bauxite-bearing lateritic profile is represented by clayey, loose and conglomerated rocks with typical leguminous, leguminous-oolitic and pelitomorphic structures. The thickness of the profile varies from 2 to 8 metres depending on a volume of loose sediments. The distribution of bauxites in the bauxite-bearing section is uneven. The lower part of the section is dominated by red bauxitic clays which tend to increase gradually upward reaching the even ratio with legumes in the middle part of the section. In the upper part, legumes dominate over cementing material. Bauxites with a silica module over 2.1, allites and sialites are the major rocks in the section. The content of Al_2O_3 varies from 30 to 57 per cent. Mineralogically, bauxites of the Nakhchivan region are of metaporphyrised type where the large part of geothite transformed into hematite, gibbsite discontinued to exist as trihydrate of aluminum and beohmite – diasporic association with corundum admixture had originated in bauxites. This occurrence is of mineralogical interest only.

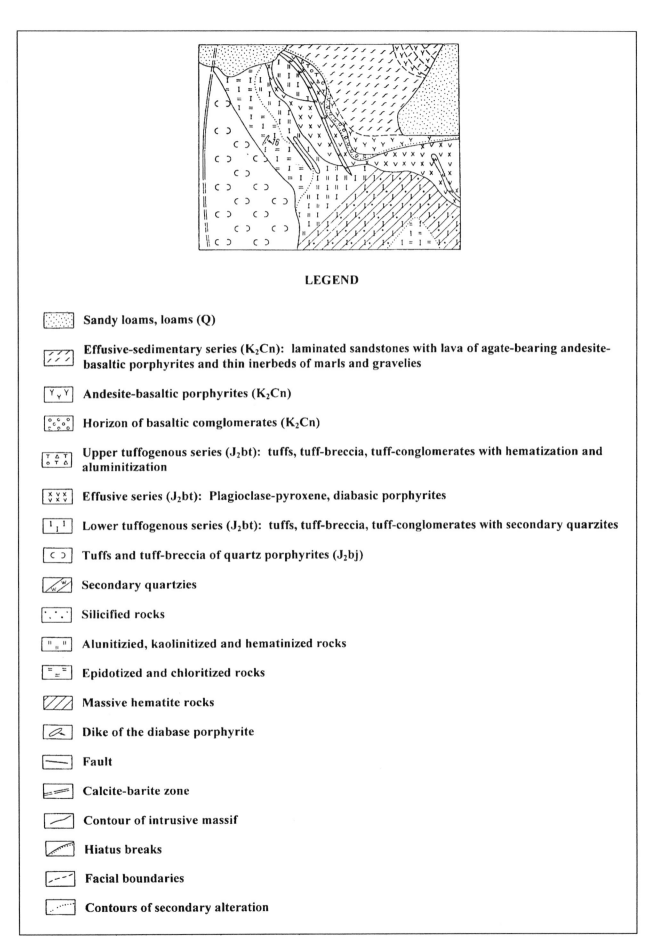

LEGEND

▢ Sandy loams, loams (Q)

▢ Effusive-sedimentary series (K₂Cn): laminated sandstones with lava of agate-bearing andesite-basaltic porphyrites and thin inerbeds of marls and gravelies

▢ Andesite-basaltic porphyrites (K₂Cn)

▢ Horizon of basaltic comglomerates (K₂Cn)

▢ Upper tuffogenous series (J₂bt): tuffs, tuff-breccia, tuff-conglomerates with hematization and aluminitization

▢ Effusive series (J₂bt): Plagioclase-pyroxene, diabasic porphyrites

▢ Lower tuffogenous series (J₂bt): tuffs, tuff-breccia, tuff-conglomerates with secondary quarzites

▢ Tuffs and tuff-breccia of quartz porphyrites (J₂bj)

▢ Secondary quartzies

▢ Silicified rocks

▢ Alunitizied, kaolinitized and hematinized rocks

▢ Epidotized and chloritized rocks

▢ Massive hematite rocks

▢ Dike of the diabase porphyrite

▢ Fault

▢ Calcite-barite zone

▢ Contour of intrusive massif

▢ Hiatus breaks

▢ Facial boundaries

▢ Contours of secondary alteration

Figure 25. Schematic geological map of the Seifali alunite deposit

(f)   Copper

Copper mineralization is the most widespread type of mineralization in the metallogenic provinces of the Azerbaijan part of the Greater and Lesser Caucasus. Copper deposits are involved in all stages of metallogenic development of Azerbaijan and are characterized by a wide range of formational types. The most productive types of copper mineralization are pyrite and porphyry copper types. Copper deposits on the southern slope of the Greater Caucasus are of massive pyrite type. Copper deposits within the Lesser Caucasus are typical to all tectonic zones of Azerbaijan except the Geychay-Garabag zone with its ophiolite belt where pyrite and porphyry copper formation types are dominant.

The metallogenic province of the Greater Caucasus

Copper deposits within the metallogenic province of the Greater Caucasus are concentrated mainly in the Zakataly-Balakhan ore region. The proven reserves and resources of copper ore are associated with massive pyrite and copper-lead-zinc-pyrite types represented by stratiform deposits in sandy-shale formation of Jurassic age (Agayev, 1982; Akberov and others, 1982; Geology of the USSR, 1976; Kurbanov, 1982; Kurbanov and others, 1967).

The Zakataly-Balakhan ore region proved to host the large Filizchay and medium Kasdag and Katekh deposits of pyrite-polymetallic ores of the copper-lead-zinc-pyrite type. Mineable reserves of the Sagator and Karabchay deposits of copper-zinc ores of the copper-zinc-pyrite type have also been estimated. More detailed data on these deposits is given in the lead and zinc section. The industrial development of these copper deposits will be feasible only by integrated utilization of large reserves of pyrite-polymetallic deposits. The extensive mineral exploration programme for copper-pyrite mineralization within the southern slope of the Greater Caucasus has been launched following the discovery of the Mazimchay deposit.

The Mazimchay copper-pyrite deposit

The Mazimchay copper-pyrite deposit is located 20 kilometres from Balakhan city of Azerbaijan near the confluence of Balakhanchay and Mazimchay rivers at the altitude from 1,500 to 2,200 metres. The deposit occupies an area from 6 to 7 kilometres in a highly mountainous area with relief uplifts from 200 to 1,200 metres. The Mazimchay deposit is located within a distance of 500-600 metres to the south from the Kasdag pyrite-polymetallic deposit. The combined proved reserves of these two deposits can serve as the additional raw material base of the Filizchay mining and processing enterprise in the future.

The Mazimchay deposit has been known as a copper occurrence of the Kasdag deposit since 1962. Its greater copper prospectively has been proved by detailed mineral exploration work during 1981-1985. Calculation of inferred copper reserves on C_2 category and projected resources on R_1 category was conducted in 1985.

Tectonically, the Mazimchay deposit is located at the intersection of the Tufan and Sarbash tectonic zones of the Greater Caucasus being separated by the Kekhnamedan deep-seated fault of overthrust nature of 1.5 kilometres wide. Numerous cross-cutting sills and dykes of diabase porphirites, liparite-dacites and gabbro-diabase hosting copper-pyrite and pyrite-polymetallic ores have been found within the deposit. The deposit is confined to the southern overturned limb of the Kasdag anticline composed of sandy-shaley formations of the Kasdag series of the Pleinsbachian and Toarcian suites of the Lower Jurassic. Coarse-laminated rocks of this series are saturated by magmatic formations such as lava-basalts, spilites and diabases and have been subdivided into three seams.

The lower seam is represented mainly by dark-grey clayey shales with separate beds of laminated sandstones. In the top of the seam, there are pockets of thin flysch. The middle seam consists of clayey shales enriched by accumulations of concretions, syngenetic with sedimentation, and globular segregations of pyrite and pirrhotite of economic interest. The upper seam is characterized by rhythmic intercalation of sandstones, aleurolites and clayey shales with an increased thickness of sandstones upwards of the section. The total thickness of the section varies from 1,950 to 2,200 metres.

The structure of the deposit is tectonically complex. Rocks of the Kasdag series are crumpled in longitudinal linear folds and cross flexures intensively complicated by cleavage along axial plane, zones of plastic flow and tectonic faults. Faults of sublatitudinal and north-western extension are united into two systems. The sublatitudinal faults are generally conformable with a lamination of overthrusts being concentrated in a strip of 500 metres wide in parallel to a large Kekhnamedan fault, passing to the south of the deposit. Upthrusts-overthrusts with a large thickness enclose dykes and sills of diabase and ore-bearing zones including that of the Mazimchay deposit. The thick ore-bearing zone of the Mazimchay deposit is confined to a zone of hydrothermally-altered and crumpled rocks with a stringer-impregnated mineralization of pyrrhotite-chalcopyrite composition. This mineralized zone of sub-latitudinal direction has been traced over a distance of 5 kilometres with distinct swells and pinches along its strike and dip. The thickness of two separate ore bodies of vein type with saturated stringer and fissure-filling mineralization varies from 0.6 to 14 metres.

Lens-shaped bodies of massive ore have also been observed within this zone. As a rule, massive pyrrhotite-chalcopyrite ores transform into stringer and fissure-filling/impregnated ores of the same composition along the strike of this zone. Morphologically, ore bodies have tape and lens form with slightly-pronounced contacts and metasomatic processes within enclosing rocks. The grade of copper in ore-bearing dykes is higher than that in ores of sandy-shaley formations.

The mineralization process in dykes was accompanied by chloritization, sericitization and silicification. The distinguishing feature of ore bodies is the presence of swells and pinches changing each other on the extent and dip. Accumulated increase of ore minerals in swells is noticeable. The ore bodies on eastern and western flanks have been explored in detail over a distance of 2,500 metres on strike and for 550-600 metres along the dip. Copper-pyrrhotite and quartz-sulphide ores have been found prevailing within the deposit.

Pyrrhotite in association with chalcopyrite have been observed as stringers and small lens-shaped bodies, and pyrite in a disseminated form. The share of quartz, calcite, ankerite, biotite and other rock-forming minerals in the fissure-impregnated types of ores is at a range of 80-85 per cent. The grade of major mineral component, copper, varies from 0.55 to 13.3 per cent with an average grade of 2.33 per cent. Associated minerals are cobalt, bismuth, gold, silver and sulphur. Technological feasibility study on flotation enrichment of a 500 kilograms sample has proved recovery of 97.6 per cent of copper in 27.2 per cent copper concentrate and pyrrhotite-pyrite product with 37 per cent of sulphur content and 38.1 per cent of sulphur extraction. The associated metals of copper concentrates are 50.2 per cent of gold, 59.1 per cent of silver, 73.5 per cent of bismuth and 63 per cent of cobalt. The combined share of noble metals (gold, silver) and bismuth in copper concentrate substantially increases the value of this product.

The detailed mineral exploration has been conducted by a combination of underground mining openings and adits, drilling and underground geophysics. The inferred reserves of copper ore and copper metal have been estimated on the C_2 category and the projected resources under P_1 category. By reserve/resource categorization scheme, the deposit is rated as a medium class copper deposit. The deposit is planned for development by underground mining upon availability of investment.

The metallogenic province of the Lesser Caucasus

The metallogenic province of the Lesser Caucasus hosts the copper deposits of massive copper-pyrite and porphyry copper types as well as polymetallic deposits with a major copper component of various genetic types (Aliyev, 1976; Baha-zade and others, 1990; Geology of the USSR, 1976; Kerimov, 1974; Kerimov and others, 1986; Kerimov and others, 1996; Kerimov, 1962).

The Lesser Caucasus is generally characterized by a complex polymetallic and polycyclic metallogeny being defined by various patterns of spatial distribution of various metals including copper, lead, zinc, molybdenum, mercury, antimony and gold. The Lesser Caucasus is known as one of the ancient areas of copper ore development. At present, numerous places of ancient production and reworking of copper ores at the Alaverdi, Shamlig, Miskhana, Gedabek, Zangezur and Shanardara ores are known to exist within the Azerbaijanian part of the Lesser Caucasus.

The Gedabek deposit of gold-copper ores was one of the major centres of copper production in the Pre-Revolutionary Russia. High grade copper-pyrite massive ores grading more than 2.5 per cent of copper have been developed by the German company "Siemens".

In the proximity to the Azerbaijanian part of the Lesser Caucasus, development of the Gafan and Alaverdi copper-pyrite, Gafan and Agarak copper-molybdenum deposits in Armenia and the Madneul copper deposit in Georgia is being continued. The large scale geological mapping and mineral exploration programmes within the Azerbaijanian part of the Lesser Caucasus have proved high prospects for copper and copper-bearing polymetallic mineralization. Based on the results of these works, the following prospective metallogenic zones have been delineated:

★　　The Somkhit-Agdam metallogenic belt includes the Qazakh, Gedabek, Dashkesan, Murovdag, Mekhmana and Garabag ore regions hosting the Gedabek, Garadag, Khar-Khar, Goshgarchay, Gizilbulag, Damirli, Khachinchay and Zardaryn deposits of massive copper-pyrite, porphyry copper and complex polymetallic ores.

★　　The Geychay-Hakera metallogenic belt includes the Kelbadjar and Lachyn ore regions.

★　　The Kelbadjar-Gochaz metallogenic belt with its Dalidag ore region.

★　　The Gafan metallogenic belt.

★　　The Ordubad-Zangezur metallogenic belt with the Ordubad ore region hosting the Diakhchay, Shalala, Gey-gel, Paragachay and other deposits of porphyry copper and copper-molybdenum ore.

Brief overview of major types of copper deposits in the above ore regions of Azerbaijan is provided below.

The Gedabek ore region

The Gedabek copper-pyrite deposit with associated gold is located to the north-west of Gedabek district centre in the exo-contact zone of the Gedabek granitoid massif of the Jurassic-Early Cretaceous age and gabbroids of the Late Jurassic age (figure 26).

The deposit is hosted by volcanogenic formations of the Lower Bajocian, the Upper Bajocian series of quartzose plagioporphyres, effusive pyroclastic formations of the Bathonian stage, strongly schistosed tuffogenous-sedimentary deposits of the Callovian-Oxfordian stage and carbonate deposits of the Luzitanian stage. As a result of magmatic activity, the carbonates of the Luzitanian stage have been transformed into vesuvian-garnet-wollastonite and mixed skarns. The process was accompanied by formation of quartz diorites and numerous dykes of plagioclase, diorite and diabase porphyrites and rarely, of aplite and kersantite. Tectonically, the deposit is confined to the anticlinal fold of the north-western direction complicated by parallel faults and fractures. The complex tectonic position of the deposit has favoured concentration and localization of various mineralization. The mineralization was mostly found in secondary quarzites of mono-quarzites of mono-quartz, quartz-sericite and quartz-kaolinite facies and, partially, hornfels around a local volcano-plutonic structure. These ore-bearing secondary quarzites of sedimentary and subvolcanic nature are overlaid by a series of epidotized, keratinized and chloritized formations and their pyroclasts, frequently with impregnated sulphide mineralization represented mainly by pyrite, and rarely, chalcopyrite.

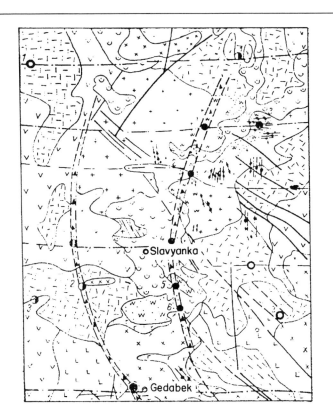

LEGEND

Recent fluvial deposits
Sandy fragmental limestones (J_3^{oxf+km})
Andesite-porphyrites and their tuffs (J_2bt)
Quartz-plagioporphyrites and their tuffs (J_2bj)
Andesite-porphyrites and their tuffs (J_2bj_1)

INTRUSIVE FORMATIONS:

Gabbro, gabbro-diorites, gabbro-diabase (J_3-K_1)
Granodiorites, quartz-diorites, diorites
Plagioclase-dyke complexes
Diabase and diabase-porphyrites
Quartz-diorites, diorite-porphyrites
Lamprophyres
Secondary quartzites

FAULTS:

Sublongitudinal ore-controlling faults
Sublatitudinal
Other faults

MINERAL DEPOSITS AND OCCURRENCES:

Gedabek copper-pyrite field
Porphyry copper deposits (1-Karabakh; 2-Charchar; 3-Jagirchay; 4-Siny-yar; 5-Maarif; 6-Bouk-Kalachy)
Copper-polymetallic deposits (1-Perizamanly; 2-Maschit; 3-Novo-Spasov)
Sulfo-pyrite deposits (1-Dashbulag; 2-Kiziljadag; 3-Shekerbek)
Bittibulag copper-arsenic deposit

Figure 26. Geological map of the Gedabek copper ore district

Morphological types of ore bodies are stocks and lenses of high grade massive pyrite ores and large stockworks of stringer-impregnated-fissure-fillings ores of poor grade. Stocks and lenses of massive ores are represented by covellite-bornite-chalcosine-chalcopyrite-pyrite association of minerals, sometimes with galenite and sphalerite. Stringer-impregnated ores of large stockworks contain chalcopyrite-chalcosine-quartz-pyrite association, in some places, with barite, covellite, bornite- and native copper. Major metals of copper-pyrite ores are copper, gold and silver and associated minerals are lead, zinc, molybdenum, cobalt and others. Six individual stocks with a length from first tens to several hundred metres and a width up to several tens of metres are known within the deposit. These stocks have been developed by Siemens company before 1917. The stringer-impregnated type of mineralization with relatively poorer grades of metals in stockworks usually frame stocks of high grade ores. Limonite, sulphur, melakonite, manganese oxides, malachite, azurite, chrycolla, gypsum, melanterite and epsiolite are found in the oxidation zone of ore bodies. A zone of cementation is rather distinctive containing covellite, rare chalcosine and native copper with native silver and cuprite in some places. Substantial remaining reserves of gold, copper and silver have been evaluated in mine dams and tailings of ancient and old mining workings of the deposit.

The scale of stringer-impregnated type of mineralization with a presence noble metals, favourable geographycal, economic and mining-technical conditions define high prospects of the Gedabek deposit for mining investment.

The Novo-Gorelovka deposit

The Novo-Gorelovka deposit of copper-zinc ores is known since the end of the nineteenth century in the Gedabek region. The deposit is hosted by the Upper-Bajocian quartz plagioporphyres as well as volcanoclastic and volcanic formations of the Bathonian stage of the Middle Jurassic with a total thickness up to 600 metres. This volcanogenic formation is intruded by the Novo-Gorelovka Late Jurassic granitoid massif composed mainly of quartz diorites (figure 27). In the exo-contact zone of this massif, rocks of the Bathonian suite are intensively silicificated, sericitized, epidotized and ferrunginated. Tectonically, the deposit is confined to the anticlinal fold of the second order, dislocated by the Novo-Gorelovka fault of a dome structure. The fault is likely to play an essential role in localization of mineralization.

The ore body of a stock shape contains mainly sphalerite and chalcopyrite. Marcalite, pyrrhotite, galenite, chalcosine and hydro-ferrum oxide are the secondary minerals. Quartz and barite are major cementing minerals. The texture of ore is massive. Chalcopyrite forms nests and stringers. The deposit is genetically associated with post-magmatic activity of the Novo-Gorelovka intrusive massif. The deposit requires additional mineral exploration to judge its economic prospects.

The Battibulag copper-mercury deposit

The Battibulag copper-mercury deposit is known to occur in the Gedabek ore region since 1850. Mineral explozation has been conducted by Siemens company during 1910-1911 and 1916-1917. The deposit occurs in volcanogenic formations of the Lower Bajocian suite with a thickness more than 300 metres being intruded by the Pre-Bathonian Atabek-Slavyan plagiogranites. Intensive hydrothermal alteration of volcanogenic formations are represented by sericitized, silicificated, kaolinized and epidotized rocks. Rocks of vein type are represented by dykes of diabase porphyres, and rarely, of diabase. Tectonically, the deposit is confined to the northern limb of anticlinal fold of latitudinal direction. The Gedabek ore-controlling fault of submeridional direction plays an essential role in the structure of the deposit and localization of mineralization.

The impregnated type of ores is mainly of quartz-pyrite composition and that nest-vein type of enargite-barite composition. Impregnated ores are widespread though the intensity of mineralization is gradually decreasing with a depth. Major ore minerals are chalcopyrite and enargite. The nest-vein type of mineralization forms irregular nests, lenses and veins among quartz-sericite rocks. The main ore minerals are enargite and pyrite;

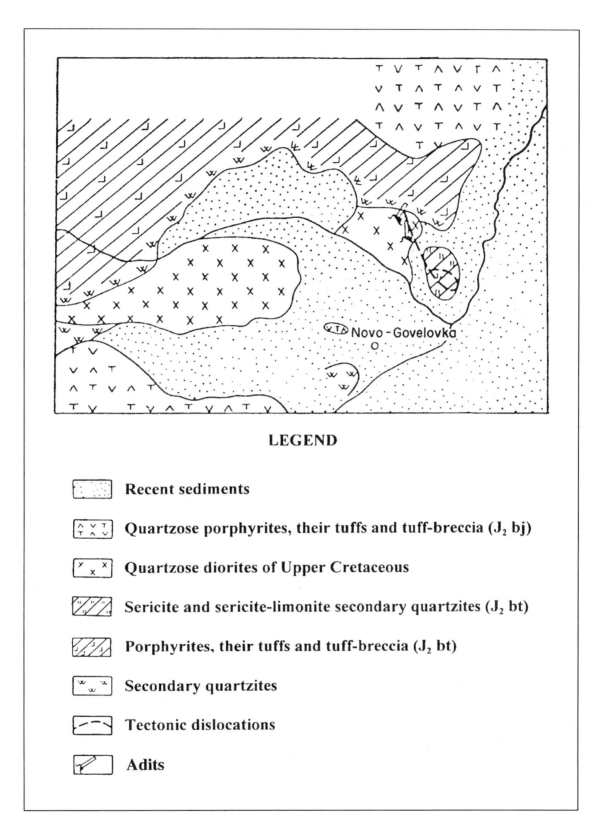

LEGEND

Recent sediments
Quartzose porphyrites, their tuffs and tuff-breccia (J_2 bj)
Quartzose diorites of Upper Cretaceous
Sericite and sericite-limonite secondary quartzites (J_2 bt)
Porphyrites, their tuffs and tuff-breccia (J_2 bt)
Secondary quartzites
Tectonic dislocations
Adits

Figure 27. Schematic geological map of the Novo-Gorelovka copper-zinc deposit

chalcopyrite, galenite, sphalerite and barite are found rarely. Main cementing minerals are sericite, rarely quartz and kaolinite. Enargite-barite ores are characterized by a limited development on a depth yielding to impregnated pyrite ores. The deposit requires further exploration to identify its economic prospects.

The Garadag porphyry copper deposit

The Garadag porphyry copper deposit is located in the Gedabek ore region, 600 metres to the west-south-west of Chanlibel village and 30 kilometres from the adjacent Shamkhor railway station. The deposit is confined to the eastern part of the large Atabek-Slavyan massif of plagiogranites which serves as an intrusive frame of porphyry copper system. The area of the deposit is characterized by a complex geological structure and is composed of andesites, andesite-porphyrites, liparite-dacite porphyres and their rudaceous facies of the Upper Bajocian age. These volcanic rocks are intruded by the Atabek-Slavyan massif of plagiogranites, small stocks of quartz-diorite porphyres and subvolcanic bodies of liparite-dacite porphyres and are cross-cut by a series of dykes of diabase and quartz-diorite porphyrites. Tectonically, the area of the deposit is confined to the knot of intersection of the Maarif-Khar-Khar-Chanlibel fault of submeridional extent with faults and fractures of the north-eastern and the north-western orientation, which defined its stockwork inner structure.

The Garadag porphyry copper deposit is subdivided into the Central, Eastern, and Khar-Khar areas. The mineralization is enclosed into hydrothermally-reworked plagiogranites, diorites and quartz-diorite porphyrites, which have eventually been transformed into secondary quarzites. Secondary quarzites are composed of mono-quarzites, quartz-kaolin and quartz-sericite facies. Mineralization is typical to that of all porphyry copper deposits of the world being represented by stringer-impregnated and fissure-filling types.

The morphology of the ore body is irregularly isometrical. Stringer and disseminated type of mineralization is determined by a stockwork structure of the ore body. The vertical zonation of the deposit distinguishes upward a zone of leaching, a zone of secondary pyrite enrichment or cementation and a zone of primary ores. The boundary of the oxidation ore leaching zone and the zone of secondary pyrite enrichment is rather distinct. The boundary of the cementation zone and primary ores is characterized by gradual transition of chalcosine-pyrite ores into chalcopyrite-pyrite association. Rocks of the oxidation zone are intensively limonitized and kaolinizated, and rarely, malachitized. The thickness of oxidation zone varies from 10 to 100 metres. The zone of secondary pyrite enrichment is represented by kaolinitized, rarely limonitized secondary quarzites with insets, stringers and rarely, small nests of pyrite, pyrite-melnikovite-chalcosine, and more rare chalcopyrite, molybdenite, bornite and covellite.

The thickness of the cementation zone varies within 20 to 80 metres reaching 130 metres in some places. The zone of secondary pyrite enrichment is of economic interest. The grade of copper and molybdenum varies from 0.4 to 1.0 per cent and from 0.001 to 0.1 per cent respectively. Small nests and stringers of turquoise of practical interest have been observed at the boundary of the zone of leaching and the zone of cementation. The zone of primary ores is represented by secondary quarzites, partially silificated diorites-porphyrites, plagiogranites with impregnated thin stringers and small nests of pyrite, rare chalcopyrite and more rare molybdenite.

The major metals of economic interest are copper and molybdenum, with associated gold and silver. Exploration drilling has contoured the ore body with a variable barite copper grade from 0.3 to 0.45 per cent. The thickness of the productive section varies from 200 to 250 metres with an average content of copper from 0.64 to 0.68 per cent and that of molybdenum from 0.005 to 0.006 per cent. By reserves/resources categorization scheme, the deposit is regarded as a medium by its reserves and as a large deposit by its projected resources. Feasibility studies on floatation scheme of ore enrichment indicate the extraction of combined copper-molybdenum concentrate with a recovery of copper at 88 per cent and molybdenum at 50 per cent with associated gold and silver. Laboratory tests on heap-leaching of ores of the Garadag deposit indicate a good recovery of copper with low grades.

The deposit is planned for development by open pit mining. Favourable geographical and economic conditions place the deposit into a category of highly prospective targets for investment of exploitation works. The Gedabek ore region also hosts the Maarif, Beyuk-Kalachy, Maschit and other small occurrences of porphyry copper.

The Maarif occurrence

The Maarif occurrence of porphyry copper is located to the south-east from the Karabad deposit and confined to the intersection of the Maarif-Khar-Khar-Chanlibel fault with the Maarif-Bittibulag anticlinal structure. The occurrence is composed of volcanogenic-pyroclastic formations of the Bajocian stage of the Atabek-Slavyan plagiogranite massif with cross-cutting dykes of diabase porphyres. The occurrence is enclosed in a zone of intensively silicificated and kaolinized rocks, in some places, being transformed into secondary quarzites. The zone in a submeridional direction extents over a distance of more than 2 kilometres with a width from 650 to 800 metres. Two zones of mineralization are confined to selvages of fault of more than 1.5 kilometres long with a thickness from 80 to 210 metres. While a grade of molybdenum remains constant, the grade of copper is increasing with a depth. Major ore minerals are pyrite, chalcopyrite and molybdenum with associated gold grading 1 gram/ton. Increased contents of copper and molybdenum are observed in secondary quarzites at deeper intervals of the mineralized section.

The Beyuk-Kalachy occurrence

The Beyuk-Kalachy occurrence of porphyry copper is located 2 kilometres to the north-west from Soyutlu village in the Gedabek ore region. The occurrence was found among secondary quarzites formed from the Bajocian volcanic rocks of mainly ryolite-porphyry composition.

The Beyuk-Kalachy occurrence is structurally complex being confined to the intersection of faults of the north-eastern and submeridional direction. Porphyry copper mineralization is associated with quartz-sericite facies of secondary quarzites. Zones of oxidation and leaching are characterized by a presence of secondary minerals of copper being represented by selvages and stains of malachite and azurite. The grade of copper varies from 0.2 to 1.0 per cent and that of molybdenum does not exceed 0.005 per cent with a minor associated gold. The low grades of copper and molybdenum on the surface are likely to be linked with a process of intensive leaching. The mineralization has not been studied at a depth.

The Maschit occurrence

The Maschit occurrence of porphyry copper is located in the Novo-Gorelovka village of the Gedabek region and confined to the north-eastern limb of the Maarif anticlinal fold of the north-western direction. The anticline is composed of volcanogenic formations of the Bajocian-Bathonian age being intruded by a stockwork body of quartz-diorite-porphyrite and dykes of basic, intermediate and acid rocks. The structure of the Maschit occurrence is complicated by the intersection of the Novo-Gorelovka-Khar-Khar and Arikhdam-Beyuk-Kalachi faults. The porphyry copper mineralization is confined to a series of closed steeply-dipping-faults of the north-western direction and is localized in quartz-sericite-kaolinite facies of secondary quarzites (figure 28).

Porphyry copper mineralization is spatially linked with copper-polymetallic – mineralization wherein high values are also typical for zinc, lead and molybdenum. The ore-bearing zone extent for 1,200 metres with a total thickness up to 800 metres. The zone consists of six parallel subzones including the first subzone being traced for 600 metres with an average thickness of 28 metres.

An average content of copper in this subzone is 0.74 per cent and a grade of molybdenum varies from 0.001 to 0.005 per cent. The rest of subzones are less extended and of lesser grades being traced over a distance from 350 to 500 metres with a thickness from 40 to 50 metres and an average copper grade of 0.55 per cent. The occurrence has been targeted for further mineral exploration at a depth to judge its economic prospects.

112

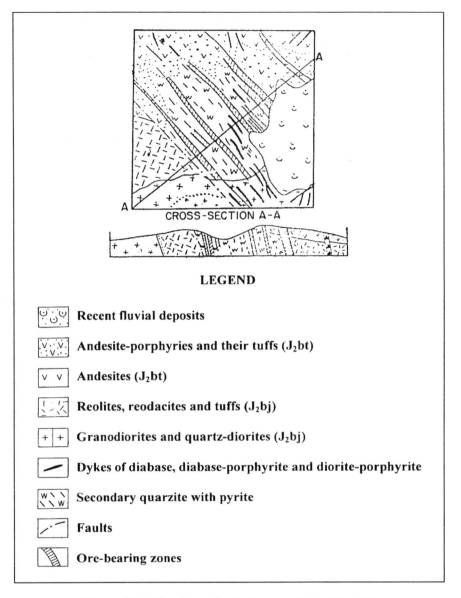

CROSS-SECTION A-A

LEGEND

Recent fluvial deposits	
Andesite-porphyries and their tuffs (J₂bt)	
Andesites (J₂bt)	
Reolites, reodacites and tuffs (J₂bj)	
Granodiorites and quartz-diorites (J₂bj)	
Dykes of diabase, diabase-porphyrite and diorite-porphyrite	
Secondary quarzite with pyrite	
Faults	
Ore-bearing zones	

**Figure 28. Sketch geological map of the Maschit
copper-polymetallic occurrence**

The Murovdag ore region

The Murovdag ore region hosts a number of copper and molybdenum, lead, zinc and other mineral deposits and includes the Goshgarchay and Gizil-Arkhach ore fields. The Goshgarchai ore field includes the Goshgarchay deposit, Goshgardag occurrence of porphyry copper and the Chanakhchi and Zivlyan occurrences of copper-pyrite ores. The Gizil-Arkhach ore field hosts the Gizil-Arkhach, Kechaldag, Djamilli, Elbekdash and other occurrence of porphyry copper.

The Goshgarchai ore field

The Goshgarchay ore field is located in the central part of the north-western flank of the Murovdag anticlinorium made up of the Lower Bajocian andesite-basalt subformation and differentiated basalt-andesite-ryolitic formation. The Goshgarchay porphyry copper deposit of this ore field is a typical example of porphyry copper mineralization of the whole Murovdag ore region.

The Goshgarchay deposit

The Goshgarchay porphyry copper deposit is located within a distance of 10-12 kilometres to the south-west from Khoshbulag village of the Dashkesan region. The deposit is mainly composed of the Bajocian volcanogenic formations being intruded by rocks of the Goshgarchay granitoids massif (figure 29). Rocks of volcanogenic series are represented by effusive plagioclase-pyroxene, plagioclase and diabase basalts, andesite-basalts, andesites and their pyroclasts. Intrusive rocks include gabbro, gabbro-diorites, diorites, quartzose diorites and porphyry granodiorites. Steeply-dipping multiple dykes of diorite, quartz-diorite and gabbro-diabase porphyrites are cutting the above intrusive and volconic rocks.

The deposit is structurally associated with a system of plumage fractures and fissures of the main ore-controlling fault being accompanied by silicified, sericitized, chloritized and epidotized metasomatic rocks hosting porphyry copper and polymetallic mineralization. Zones of hydrothermally-altered rocks are traced over a distance of up to 1,000-1,200 metres with a thickness from 30 to 40 metres, and rarely, more than 100 metres.

Three gradual metasomatic zones have been distinguished around ore-generating intrusive massif of porphyry structure. The internal metasomatic zone covers endo-contact and apical part of the porphyry intrusive being represented by intensively silicified rocks which have been almost transformed into secondary quarzites. The quartz core which is usually typical for porphyry copper systems has not been observed within this deposit.

The intermediate zone consists of quartz-sericite-chloritic facies of secondary quarzites, occupying an area of 1,200 metres in length by a range of 400 to 600 metres in a width. Porphyry copper mineralization of vein-impregnated type is distinctly superimposed on this facies of secondary quartzites. The third external zone is represented by propylitic facies of secondary quarzites hosting streaky-impregnated stockwork ores and quartz and carbonate veins with disseminated pyrite, chalcopyrite and molybdenum mineralization.

The stockwork body of the central part of the deposit occupies an area of 0.4 square kilometres in the apical and peripheral parts of the intrusive massif of porphyry structure hosting ten enriched areas of copper mineralization with a copper grade above 0.3 per cent. The largest area is of 0.12 square kilometres in size. These mineralization zones are hosted and intercalated by barren and slightly mineralized rocks with copper grading up to 0.2 per cent. These enriched areas on the surface are likely being combined at a depth into an inified ore body of a stockwork type with a complex morphology.

The grade of copper varies from 0.2 to 2.5 per cent with an average grade of 0.4 per cent with associated molybdenum, gold, silver and cobalt. The grade of gold in some intervals is more than 1.0 g/t and that of silver is from 2.5 to 40 g/t, which are well correlated with a copper content for porphyry type deposits.

Along with a stockwork type of mineralization in the southern and south-eastern parts of the deposit, the vein type of copper mineralization indicates some prospects of buried porphyry mineralization. The rare "Mantas" type of mineralization typical for numerous porphyry copper deposits of Peru and Chile is represented by chalcosine in association with quartz, calcite and epidote which fill cavities has been observed in the deposit. The vertical profile of mineralization varies from 600 to 700 metres. This deposit of economic interest is a target for investment and development.

The Goshgardag occurrence

The ore-bearing zone of the north-eastern limb occupies an area of 0.3 square kilometres. The mineralogy of the Goshgardag occurrence is similar to that in the above Goshgarchay deposit consisting mainly of pyrite, chalcopyrite, molybdenite, rare sphalerite and galenite. The geochemical exploration within the Goshgarchay ore region has identified numerous complex geochemical anomalies of certain elements being confined to concrete structures. These anomalies in combination with the known deposits and occurrences are substantially increasing

114

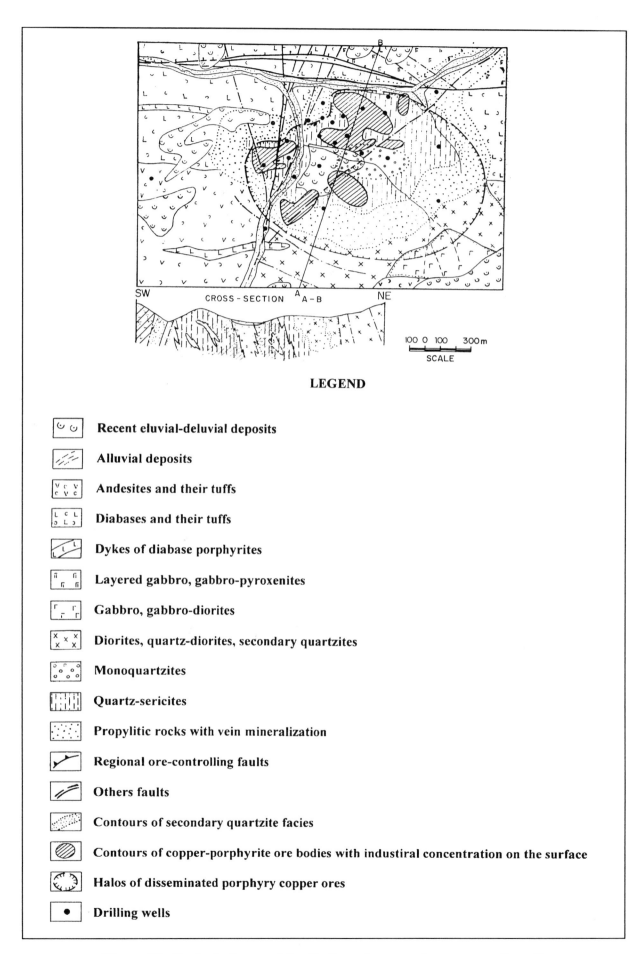

LEGEND

	Recent eluvial-deluvial deposits
	Alluvial deposits
	Andesites and their tuffs
	Diabases and their tuffs
	Dykes of diabase porphyrites
	Layered gabbro, gabbro-pyroxenites
	Gabbro, gabbro-diorites
	Diorites, quartz-diorites, secondary quartzites
	Monoquartzites
	Quartz-sericites
	Propylitic rocks with vein mineralization
	Regional ore-controlling faults
	Others faults
	Contours of secondary quartzite facies
	Contours of copper-porphyrite ore bodies with indusiral concentration on the surface
	Halos of disseminated porphyry copper ores
	Drilling wells

Figure 29. Geological map of the Goshgarchay porphyry copper deposit

prospects of the Goshgarchay ore region for future discovery of large porphyry copper and porphyry copper molybdenum deposits.

The Garabag ore region

The Garabag ore region includes the Gizilbulag, Mekhmana, Gyulyatag, Damirli, Khachynchay, Agdara and Gazanchai porphyry copper and the Khazinadag copper-pyrite deposit and occurrences. The ore region is located in the south-eastern part of the Somkhit-Agdam tectonic zone and confined to a knot of intersection of the Agdam anticlinorium and the Dalidag-Mekhmana uplift. The Garabag ore region is characterized by a spatial linkage of varies genetic and morphological types of sulphide mineralization. The ore region is hosted by the Middle-Upper Cretaceous sedimentary and volcanogenic-sedimentary rocks dislocated by faults of the north-western, north-eastern and sublatitudinal directions and by intrusive massifs. The Damirli, Gyulatag, Khachinchay and Agdara deposits and occurrences of porphyry copper are confined to exo- and endo-contact zones of the Djanyatag intrusive massif of gabbro-diorite-granodiorite formation which intruded the Jurassic volcanites and, in some places, is unconformably overlain by more recent Cretaceous formations.

The Damirli porphyry copper deposit

The Damirli porphyry copper deposit is located within two kilometres to the south-east from Damirli village of the Ashderin district. The deposit is confined to the endo-exo-contact zone of the Djanyatag intrusive massif. The mineralization is hosted by silicified, kolinized and pyritized rocks of the granitoid massif and volcanic rocks of intermediate composition. These rocks are intruded by subvolcanic bodies of andeste-dacite and liparite-dacite porphyres being transformed into secondary quarzites. The structure of the deposit is complex being crossed by a series of closed faults of the north-west-submeridional and north-east-sublatitudinal directions with cross-cutting dykes of granodiorite-porphyres, liparite-dacites, andesite-dacites and diorites (figure 30).

The deposit is represented by stockwork bodies of fissure filling-impregnated type with pyrite-molybdenite-chalcopyrite association, sometimes with chalcosine, bornite and covellite. The area of development of copper mineralization is around a range of 5-6 square kilometres being from 1.8 to 2.2 kilometres wide and more than 3 kilometers long. The deposit also includes six quartz-vein zones with gold sulphide mineralization traced over a distance from 4.5 to 8 kilometres. The grade of gold is up to 5 g/t and that of silver is up to 91 g/t. The grade of copper in fissure filling and disseminated types of ore varies from 0.1 to 0.8 per cent, molybdenum from 0.001 to 0.2 per cent, gold from 0.1 to 0.2 g/t, and silver from 4 to 6 g/t.

Mineral exploration by drilling and geophysics has proved the extension of fissure filling and disseminated types of copper and molybdenum mineralization to a depth over 300 metres. Given the large reserves of copper ore despite its relatively low grades, the deposit constitutes a target for open pit mining in the future.

The Khachinchay porphyry copper deposit

The Khachinchay deposit of porphyry copper is located within 9 kilometres to the north-west from Agdam city in the south-south-eastern contact zone of the Djanyatag granitoid massif. The deposit is confined to the archy part of the local Eddikhirman brachyanticline of the Garabag uplift composed of intermediate and acid volcanics of the Middle and Upper Jurassic being intruded by stocks of granitoids. The mineralization is hosted by quartz diorites and diorites of the southern endo-contact zone of the Djanyatag granitoid massif, and partly, by the Early and Middle Bathonian andesite-dacites and liparite-dacite porphyres.

The deposit is represented by a stockwork body of low-graded copper-molybdenum ores with associated gold and silver of higher grades confined to an area of conjunction of faults of the north-western and north-eastern directions. Numerous dykes of andesites, diorite-porphyrites, liparite-dacite porphyres and liparite, as well as hydrothermally-altered rocks have been found within the deposit's area. The secondary hydrothermal

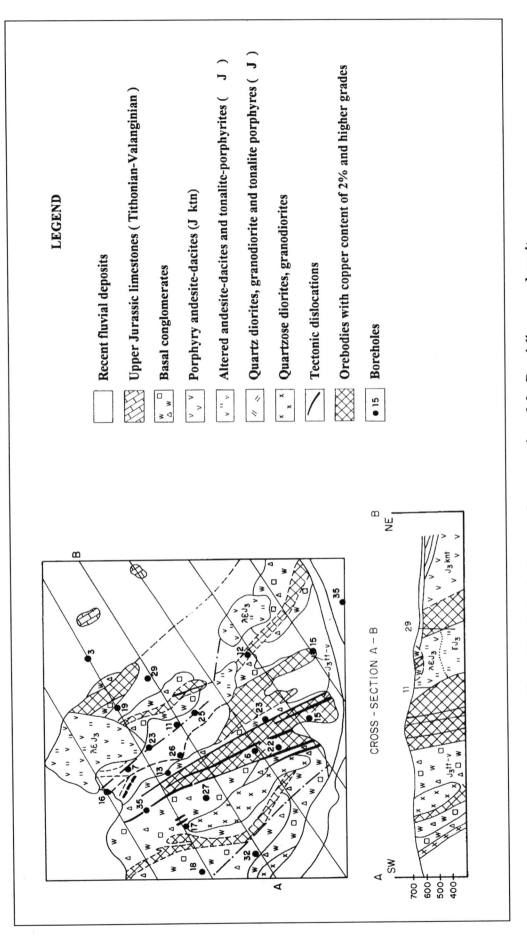

LEGEND

Recent fluvial deposits

Upper Jurassic limestones (Tithonian-Valanginian)

Basal conglomerates

Porphyry andesite-dacites (J ktn)

Altered andesite-dacites and tonalite-porphyrites (J   )

Quartz diorites, granodiorite and tonalite porphyres (J   )

Quartzose diorites, granodiorites

Tectonic dislocations

Orebodies with copper content of 2% and higher grades

Boreholes

CROSS - SECTION A - B

Figure 30. Geological map and cross-section of the Damirli copper deposit

alterations are pronounced by silicification, pyritization, chloritization, kaolinization and sericitization. The major ore mineral of fissure filling and disseminated types of mineralization are covellite, bornite, chalcosine, molybdenited, chalcopyrite and pyrite. Copper hydrocarbonates (malachite, rarely azurite), covellite and hydro-ferrum oxide are observed in the oxidation zone.

The total area of distribution of fissure filling-disseminated types of sulphide of mineralization is around 0.8-1.0 square kilometres and that of the mineralized stockwork is 800-1,000 metres by 300-400 metres. Copper grade varies from 0.1 to 0.6 per cent, molybdenum from 0.003 to 0.02 per cent, gold is 2.2 g/t and that of silver up to 30-40 g/t. The deposit did not undergo a detailed mineral exploration, however, given the intensity and character of sulphide mineralization, prospects of enclosing volcanic rocks for future discoveries of porphyry copper mineralization are very high. The other porphyry copper occurrences in the Garabag ore region are very similar to the Damirli deposit. Given a widespread distribution of porphyry copper mineralization in exo-and endo-contact zones of the Djanyatag intrusive massif, favourable tectonic and geologic environment as well as positive results of geological, geophysical and geochemical exploration, the Garabag ore region represents one of highly prospective targets for discovery of new porphyry copper mineralization of large scale.

The Ordubad ore region

The Ordubad ore region constitutes a part of the Mikhmana-Zangezur tectonic subzone hosting a number of known porphyry copper and molybdenum deposits. The region is sharply distinguished from other zones of the Lesser Caucasus and includes the known copper-molybdenum belt part of which is observed on the territory of the Nakhchivan Autonomous Republic of Azerbaijan.

Porphyry copper deposits of the Ordubad ore region were localized within the western part of the Megri-Ordubad granitoid massif, where the Paragachay, Diakhchay, Misdag, Gey-gel, Geydag, Gekgyundur, Shalalag and other deposits were found (figure 31). The detailed mineral exploration and estimation of reserves on category C_2 has been completed only within the Paragachay deposit. The reserves and prospects of the rest of the deposits are unkhown. At present, the exploitation of the Paragachay copper-molybdenum deposit has been suspended due to economic problems.

The Diakhchay deposit

The Diakhchay porphyry copper deposit is located in the central part of the Diakhchay ore field in the upper streams of the Ordubadchay river. The deposit is enclosed in monzonites, granodiorites, quartz diorites, granosyenites, quartz syenite-diorites and granodiorites-porphyres being intruded by cross-cutting dykes of granite-porphyres and diorite-porphyres. The mineralization is tectonically controlled by the Ordubad deep-seated fault being accompanied by a zone of metasomatic rocks from 1.2 to 1.5 kilometres wide (figure 32). The major stockwork zone represents a system of fractures, fissure fillings and impregnation of molybdenite, chalcopyrite and pyrite in quartz syenite-diorites in a contact area in the south with hydrothermally-altered gabbro-diorites and adamellites.

The stockwork zone is elongated along dykes of granodiorite porphyry or along a contact of intrusive rocks of various phases over a distance of up to two kilometres. The thickness of the zone tends to increase in the areas of dykes jointing. Relatively intensive hydrothermal-metasomatic changes in the form of local feld-spartization, biotitization, silicification and sericitization are observed in tectonically reworked parts of the zone along contacts with dykes. The major ore minerals are copper and molybdenum of fissure filling and disseminated types. On the surface, the zone has been traced over a distance of 600 metres. A width of the mineralized zone is 140 metres with the most intensive mineralization from 40 to 100 metres.

Mineral exploration of the deposit by drilling and adits indicates a copper grade on the surface from 0.66 to 1.3 per cent up to 2.0 per cent and that of molybdenum from 0.001 to 0.003 per cent. The grades of copper and molybdenum tend to decrease with a depth with 0.7 per cent of copper and 0.0022 per cent of molybdenum.

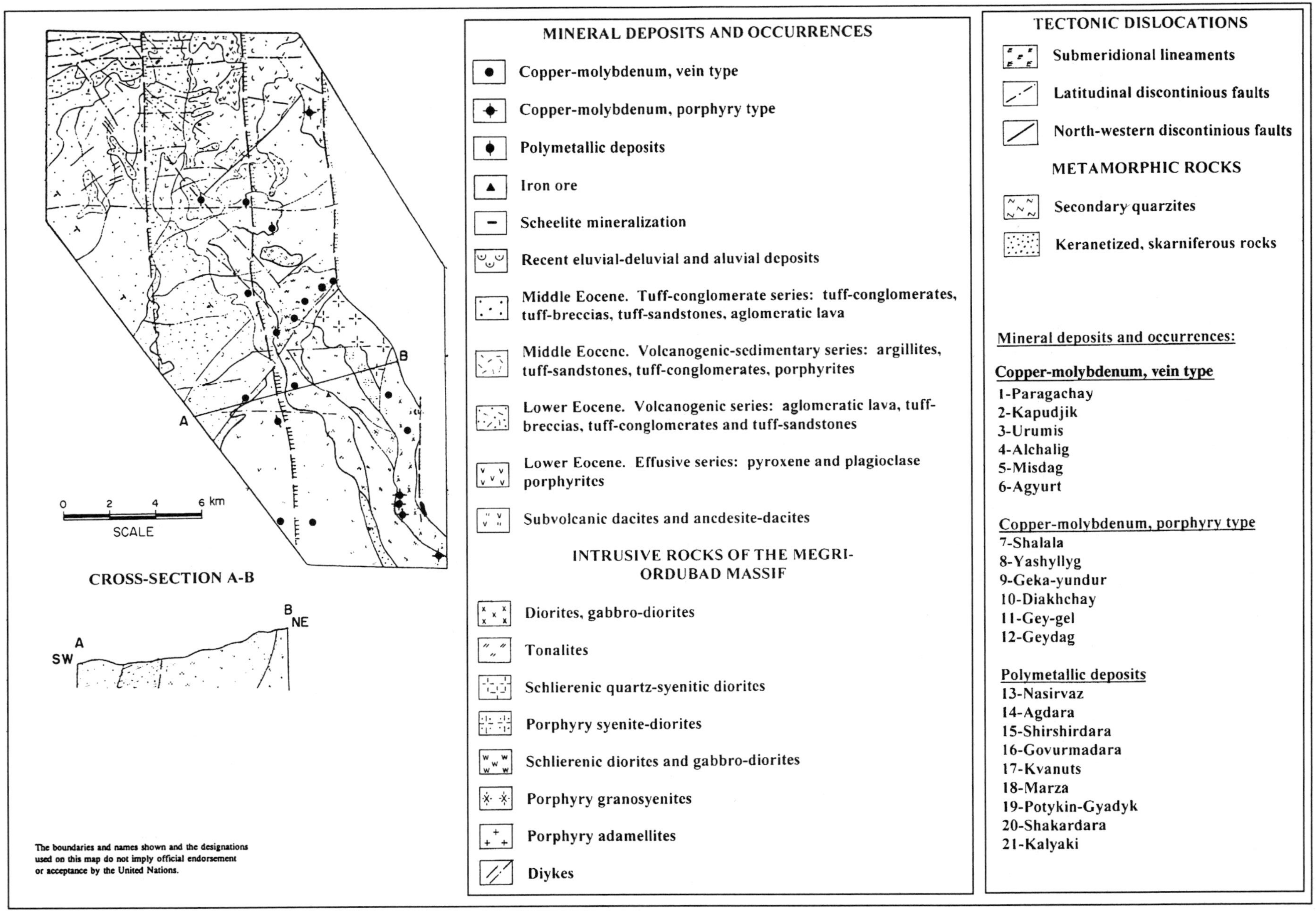

TECTONIC DISLOCATIONS

Submeridional lineaments

Latitudinal discontinious faults

North-western discontinious faults

METAMORPHIC ROCKS

Secondary quarzites

Keranetized, skarniferous rocks

Mineral deposits and occurrences:

Copper-molybdenum, vein type

1-Paragachay
2-Kapudjik
3-Urumis
4-Alchalig
5-Misdag
6-Agyurt

Copper-molybdenum, porphyry type

7-Shalala
8-Yashyllyg
9-Geka-yundur
10-Diakhchay
11-Gey-gel
12-Geydag

Polymetallic deposits

13-Nasirvaz
14-Agdara
15-Shirshirdara
16-Govurmadara
17-Kvanuts
18-Marza
19-Potykin-Gyadyk
20-Shakardara
21-Kalyaki

MINERAL DEPOSITS AND OCCURRENCES

Copper-molybdenum, vein type

Copper-molybdenum, porphyry type

Polymetallic deposits

Iron ore

Scheelite mineralization

Recent eluvial-deluvial and aluvial deposits

Middle Eocene. Tuff-conglomerate series: tuff-conglomerates, tuff-breccias, tuff-sandstones, aglomeratic lava

Middle Eocene. Volcanogenic-sedimentary series: argillites, tuff-sandstones, tuff-conglomerates, porphyrites

Lower Eocene. Volcanogenic series: aglomeratic lava, tuff-breccias, tuff-conglomerates and tuff-sandstones

Lower Eocene. Effusive series: pyroxene and plagioclase porphyrites

Subvolcanic dacites and ancdesite-dacites

INTRUSIVE ROCKS OF THE MEGRI-ORDUBAD MASSIF

Diorites, gabbro-diorites

Tonalites

Schlierenic quartz-syenitic diorites

Porphyry syenite-diorites

Schlierenic diorites and gabbro-diorites

Porphyry granosyenites

Porphyry adamellites

Diykes

CROSS-SECTION A-B

SCALE

0   2   4   6 km

A
SW

B
NE

The boundaries and names shown and the designations used on this map do not imply official endorsement or acceptance by the United Nations.

Figure 31. Geological map of the Ordubad porphyry copper ore district

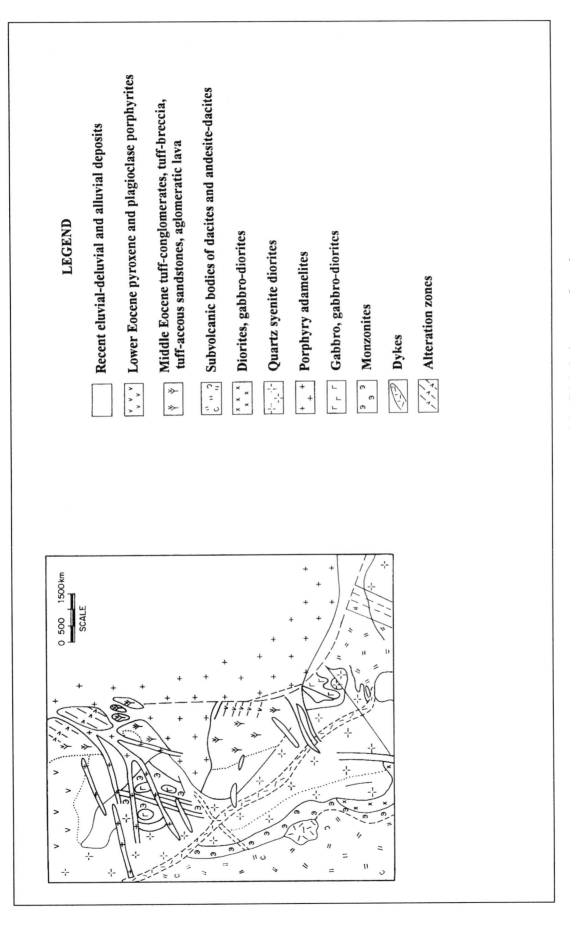

LEGEND

Recent eluvial-deluvial and alluvial deposits

Lower Eocene pyroxene and plagioclase porphyrites

Middle Eocene tuff-conglomerates, tuff-breccia,
tuff-aceous sandstones, aglomeratic lava

Subvolcanic bodies of dacites and andesite-dacites

Diorites, gabbro-diorites

Quartz syenite diorites

Porphyry adamelites

Gabbro, gabbro-diorites

Monzonites

Dykes

Alteration zones

Figure 32. Schematic geological map of the Diakchai copper deposit

The mineralization has been traced up to a depth from 350 to 400 metres. The inferred reserves of copper and molybdenum have been estimated on C_2 category.

The Sarkidag and Fakhlidara occurrences of copper-molybdenum ores were found in the north-western and south-eastern parts of the Diakhchay ore field respectively. The occurrences are represented by stockwork zones with a variable copper grade from 0.4 to 2.44 per cent and a molybdenum grade from 0.01 to 0.02 per cent. The proximity of these occurrences to the Diakhchay deposit increases the economic prospects of the Diakhchay copper-molybdenum ore field for future development.

The Misdag deposit

The Misdag deposit is located in the Ordubad region on the south-western slope of the Zangezur ridge in the upper streams of the Vanandchay river. The deposit is confined to the endo-contact of the Megri-Ordubad granitoid massif and is basically composed of quartz, monzonites, monzonite diorites, diorite syenites, diorites and gabbro-diorites. Major structural elements are tectonic faults and associated fractures of submeridional and north-western directions (figure 33). The mineralization tends to be associated with separate fractures, dykes and zones of jointing of the north-eastern direction. The deposit is represented by a series of numerous closed steeply-dipping ore zones including 18 prospective zones concentrated within an area of 0.3 square kilometres. The distance between zones varies from a range of 15-20 to 100-150 metres. On the surface, the mineralized zones have been traced from 300 to 700 metres with a variable thickness from 0.5 to 10 metres. Most of the zones strike in the north-eastern direction and dip at 60°-85° north-west. On the recent erosion level, these zones were traced to a depth of more than 350 metres. Ore bodies are represented by veins and stockworks characterized by frequent swells and pinches of veins. The thickness of lenticular ore bodies in swells is increasing up to 40 metres and is reducing up to 0.5 metre in pinches.

Distribution of major metals in the ore bodies is irregular. The grade of copper varies within a wide range from 0.2 to 7.2 per cent with an average grade from 1.3 to 2.5 per cent. Associated metals of economic importance are molybdenum, cobalt and gold in some veins. Major ore minerals are magnetite, chalcopyrite, sphalerite, galenite, pyrrhotite and cubanite and those of the oxidation zone are malachite, azurite, bornite, chalcosine, limonite, goethitte and hydro-ferrum oxide. A high content of copper in veins and fissure zones is accompanied by accumulation of disseminated copper mineralization in host rocks with a copper grade from 0.1 to 0.4 per cent that substantially increases the economic prospects of the deposit. Due to complex mining and geological conditions, the deposit has not been studied at a depth.

The Geygel deposit

The Geygel deposit is located within 8 kilometres to the north-east from Nyurgyut village in the watershed of the Zangezur ridge. The deposit is subdivided into the northern, central and southern areas (figure 33). Mineralization of stockwork type is confined to rocks of the granodiorite-porphyry phase of the Megri-Ordubad intrusive massif being intruded by dykes of granodiorite porphyres. The deposit is tectonically controlled by a system of faults and fractures of sub-meridional (20° NE) and north-western (270°-290° NW) direction being healed by dykes of diorite porphyrites and granite-porphyres respectively. More intensive mineralization has been observed within the central part of the deposit containing five ore-bearing zones of sublatitudinal direction and several hundred metres long. Almost all stages of mineralization typical for porphyry copper deposits of the Ordubad ore region are present in this deposit. The central area of the deposit is considered to be of economic interest owing to commercial concentration of porphyry copper-molybdenum mineralization.

The Geydag deposit

The Geydag porphyry copper deposit is located in the confluence of the Alindjachay and Gilyanchay rivers. The area of the Geydag deposit hosts the Khanaga-Ortakend and Bashkend occurrences as well as the major

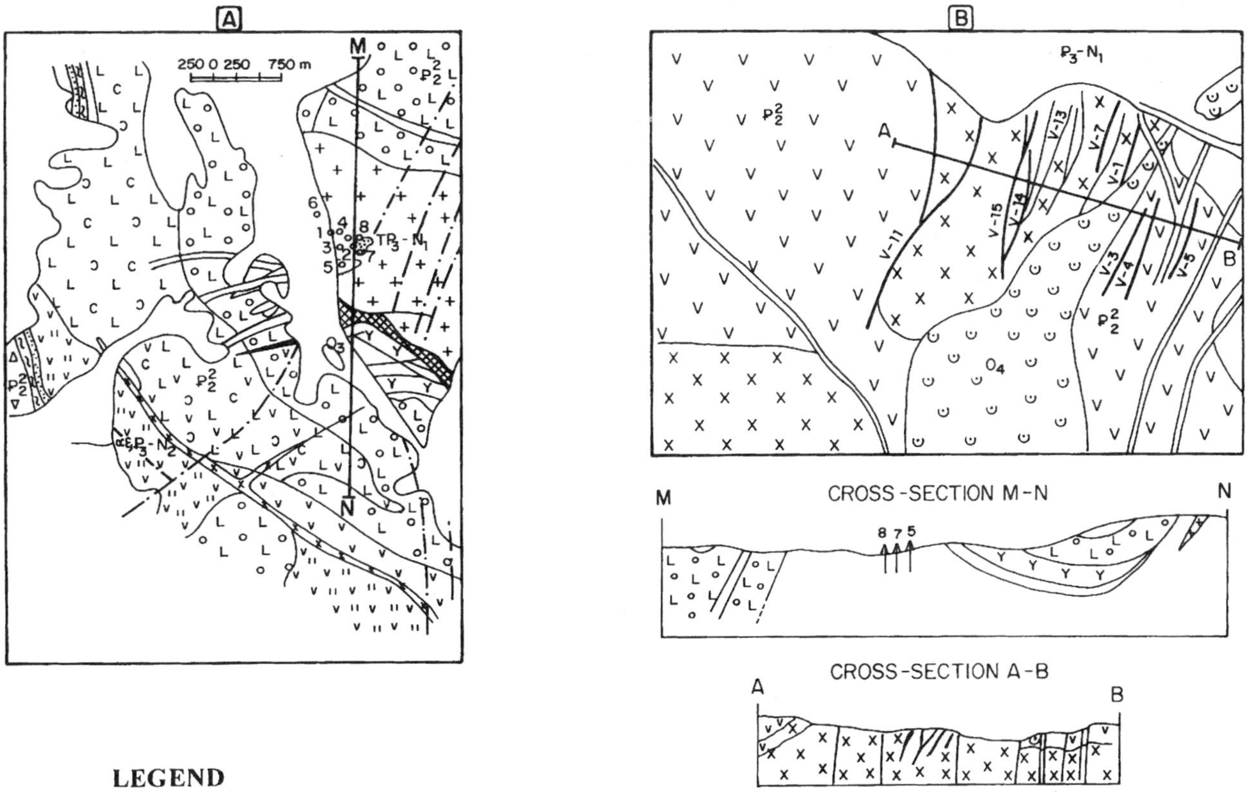

LEGEND

⌣ ⌣	Recent fluvial deposits (Q₄)

Recent fluvial deposits (Q$_4$)

Middle Eocene volcanogenic rocks (P$_2^2$)

Middle Eocene subvolcanic facies of basalts and andesite-basalts (P$_2^2$)

Middle Eocene volcanics (P$_2^2$)

Middle Paleogene volcanics (P$_2^2$)

Middle Paleogene basalts and andesite-basalts

Upper Paleogene-Middle Neogene volcanics (P$_3$-N$_2$)

Porphyry granites and granadiorites of the Megri-Ordubad intrusive massif

Granodiorites, quartz diorites and diorites of the Megri-Ordubad intrusive massif

Dykes of diorite porphyrites

Dykes of granite porphyres

Boreholes

Quartz-sulfide veins

Faults and fractures

Figure 33. Schematic geological map and cross-section of the Geygel (A) and Misdag (B) copper occurrences

Djadakhli, Dikyurt, Muradkhanli and Gyumushdara individual stockwork ore bodies localized in intensively dislocated and hydrothermally-altered andesite-dacite porphyrites, quartz-syenite-diorites, tuff-sandstones, tuff-gravelites and other rocks. The length of ore bodies varies from 390 to 500 metres and the width from 200 to 470 metres. Copper-molybdenum mineralization has been traced at a depth from 420 to 680 metres. The average content of copper in ore bodies varies from 0.28 to 0.66 per cent and that of molybdenum from 0.008 to 0.011 per cent. Associated lead-zinc mineralization is confined to selvages and dykes of diorite-porphyres. Galenite and sphalerite are mainly of fissure filling and disseminated tyhpes. A thickness of mineralized intervals varies from 16 to 50 metres grading 0.35 per cent of lead, and 1.19 per cent of zinc. The inferred reserves of copper have been estimated under C_2 category. The deposit requires additional mineral exploration to judge its economic prospects.

The Gekgyundur deposit

The Gekgyundur deposit is confined to a zone of intensive jointing along the main Ordubad and Vardanichay faults composed of rocks of early adamellite phase of the Megri-Ordubad intrusive massif and late quartz syenite-diorites, porphyry granosyenites being intruded by dykes of diorite and granodiorite-porphyres. The ore-bearing zone is confined to a contact area of granodiorites and was traced from 1,200 to 1,500 metres long and from 480 to 600 metres wide. Mineralization is presented by stringer-impregnated, stockwork and vein types. The major stockwork of the deposit with copper mineralization reaches a thickness up to 168 metres grading 0.85 per cent of copper.

On the south-west flank of the deposit, the thickness is decreasing being splitted into several steeply-dipping bodies with a thickness from 14.5 to 28 metres found at a spacing interval from 200 to 300 metres. The grade of copper in these bodies varies from 0.53 to 0.65 per cent and that of molybdenum does not exceed 0.001 per cent. Similar situation is observed on the north-eastern flank of the deposit where three individual bodies have been traced from 300 to 500 metres with a thickness from 10 to 20 metres. The grade of copper is from 0.74 to 0.77 per cent and that of molybdenum is up to 0.001 per cent. Such a morphology of the stockwork deposit is defined by its tectonic position and peculiarities of internal structure of the ore-bearing zone of the deposit. Chalcopyrite, molybdenite and pyrite are the basic ore minerals. Secondary minerals of copper are covellite, bornite, malachite and chrysocolla. Copper reserves are unknown.

The Shalala deposit

The Shalala deposit is hosted by quartz and syenite-diorites of the second intrusive phase of the Megri-Ordubad granitoid massif. The deposit is represented by a zone of stockwork mineralization of up to 300 metres wide and 800 metres long hosting four closed ore bodies of a complex morphology with a thickness from 7 to 100 metres. Basic ore minerals, chalcopyrite, bornite, molybdenite and pyrite form impregnations and stringers. The content of copper in the ore bodies varies from 0.11 to 7.8 per cent. The most intensive mineralization was found in an isolated ore body of up to 300 metres from 410 metres deep with an average thickness of 41.5 metres. The average grade of copper is 0.5 per cent and that of molybdenum is 0.006 per cent. Two zones with a thickness of 30 and 14 metres were found in inter-dyke interval running in parallel to the major ore body. The grade of copper is up to 0.84 per cent an that of molybdenum is from 0.005 to 0.025 per cent. Further mineral exploration is likely to lead to new discoveries of porphyry copper-molybdenum mineralization of economic interest.

The Darridag-Paradash ore region

This region represents the area of development of the Oligocene-Early Miocene volcanism associated with concentration of numerous small scale occurrences of ferrous metals. Copper mineralization in this region is close to one of the most productive copper sandstones types. Numerous occurrences of copper of the Asadkyaf group are confined to rocks of volcano-sedimentary series of the Oligocene age along the north-north-eastern flank of the Nakhchivan superimposed trough being controlled by the Nakhchivan fault. Three copper-bearing beds within the Oligocene rocks form a copper belt of up to 60-70 kilometres long hosting around twenty areas with a high copper mineralization. The number of copper-bearing beds within this belt varies from one to four with a variable thickness from 0.6 to 9.0 metres. The grade of copper in beds varies from 0.25 to 1.56 per cent. Impregnated copper mineralization is represented by native copper, cuprite, chalcosine, azurite and malachite. The Asadkyaf group of occurrences is of potential economic interest owing to a polymetallic character of mineralization.

(g)   Mercury

Mercury mineralization is present in all metallogenic provinces of Azerbaijan, but its intensity is uneven in various zones due to tectonic faults separating various structural and formational zones of the Greater and Lesser Caucasus (Geology of the USSR, 1976, Kashkay and others, 1970; Kashkay and Nasibov, 1985; Suleimanov and Baba-zade, 1974). Mercury deposits are traced in the form of isolated zones or chains along the extended folded and tectonic structures of the Lesser Caucasus. Based on a distribution pattern of mercury mineralization, the Southern, Central and the Northern zones of mercury mineralization have been distinguished within the Lesser Caucasus (figure 34). Analysis of numerous data on distribution patterns of mercury mineralization identified the stratigraphic-lithologic, structural and magmatic factors.

Mercury mineralization has been found in rocks of various lithology and stratigraphic intervals. The oldest mercury mineralization is associated with the Middle Jurassic volcanogenic formations, and the most recent with the Mio-Pliocene tuffs and dykes of liparite-dacites. The intensity of mercury mineralization tends to increase from the Middle-Upper Jurassic – Lower Cretaceous deposits to the Upper Cretaceous formations. The Lower Cenonian volcano-sedimentary formations overlain by the Upper Jurassic limestones has been proved to be the most productive stratigraphic section hosting around 70 per cent of known mercury deposits in Azerbaijan. The major lithological varieties of the Upper Cretaceous interval are magnesite schists, limestones, conglomerates, rudaceous tuffs, sandstones, breccia and clayey-siliceous rocks. Distribution of mercury deposits and occurrences in the Lesser Caucasus is shown in figure 35. Classification of mercury deposits and occurrences of Azerbaijan is given in table 2.

The Shorbulag deposit

The deposit occurs in volcanogenic formations of the Bathonian suite, sedimentary-volcanic rocks of the Lower Cenonian stage and intrusive rocks of ultrabasic, basic and acid composition. Ultrabasites are represented by serpeintinized dunites and peridotites of a lens shape elongated along tectonic faults of the north-western direction. Mercury mineralization is controlled by tectonic dislocations of thrust type and hosted by tectonically-reworked, crushed, schistose and loose rocks being subjected to intensive silicification, carbonatization and other hydrothermal metasomatic alterations. The major enclosing environment of mercury mineralization are hydrothermal metasomatic carbonate rocks. In some areas, cinnabar is confined to crushed and altered porphyrites, argillites as well as talcose and carbonatized serpentinites. Cinnabar is the main ore mineral with a limited presence of chalcopyrite and pyrite. Steeply-dipping fissure fillings and thin veins of calcite and, more rarely quartz, cut mercury-bearing zones in various directions.

In ore-bearing zones, cinnabar is observed in the form of impregnations, small nests, selvages, stringers, and other accumulations of various shapes. Among seven ore-bearing zones of the deposit, the first, third and fourth zones have been found to be the most prospective. The position of the first zone is closely controlled by a tectonic fault along a contact of serpentinites with sedimentary-volcanogenic rocks of the Lower Cenonian hosting a lens of magnesite schists with intensive cinnabar mineralization. The structural position of the third zone is very similar to that of the first zone. Mineralization here is represented by frequent impregnations and thin and short stringers of cinnabar in hydrothermal metasomatic carbonate and quartz rocks and altered porphyrites. Mineralization of cinnabar in the most extended fourth zone is confined both to listvenites and dykes of diabase porphyrites occurring among listvenites. Ore-bodies have irregular complex pillar and column

124

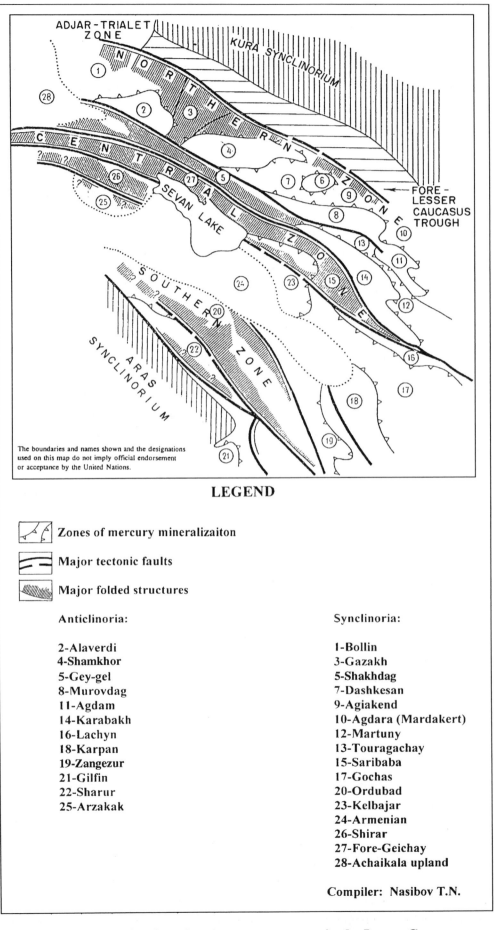

The boundaries and names shown and the designations used on this map do not imply official endorsement or acceptance by the United Nations.

LEGEND

Zones of mercury mineralizaiton

Major tectonic faults

Major folded structures

Anticlinoria:

2-Alaverdi
4-Shamkhor
5-Gey-gel
8-Murovdag
11-Agdam
14-Karabakh
16-Lachyn
18-Karpan
19-Zangezur
21-Gilfin
22-Sharur
25-Arzakak

Synclinoria:

1-Bollin
3-Gazakh
5-Shakhdag
7-Dashkesan
9-Agiakend
10-Agdara (Mardakert)
12-Martuny
13-Touragachay
15-Saribaba
17-Gochas
20-Ordubad
23-Kelbajar
24-Armenian
26-Shirar
27-Fore-Geichay
28-Achaikala upland

Compiler: Nasibov T.N.

Figure 34. Distribution of major mercury zones in the Lesser Caucasus

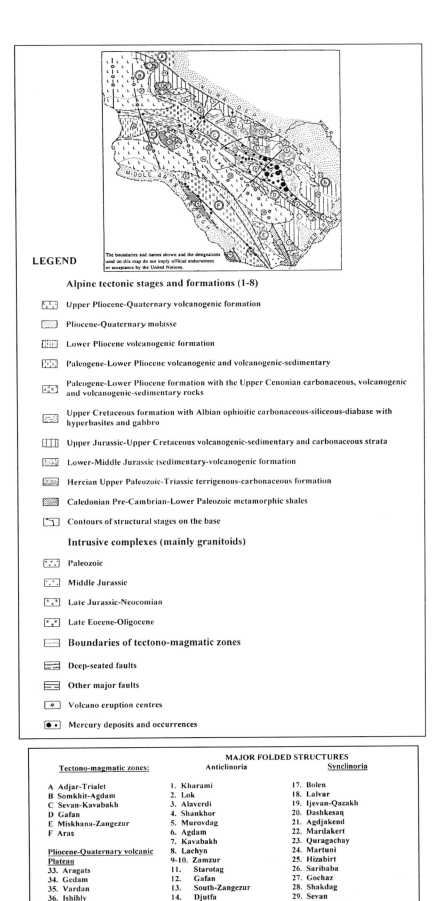

LEGEND

Alpine tectonic stages and formations (1-8)

Upper Pliocene-Quaternary volcanogenic formation

Pliocene-Quaternary molasse

Lower Pliocene volcanogenic formation

Paleogene-Lower Pliocene volcanogenic and volcanogenic-sedimentary

Paleogene-Lower Pliocene formation with the Upper Cenonian carbonaceous, volcanogenic and volcanogenic-sedimentary rocks

Upper Cretaceous formation with Albian ophioitic carbonaceous-siliceous-diabase with hyperbasites and gabbro

Upper Jurassic-Upper Cretaceous volcanogenic-sedimentary and carbonaceous strata

Lower-Middle Jurassic (sedimentary-volcanogenic formation

Hercian Upper Paleozoic-Triassic terrigenous-carbonaceous formation

Caledonian Pre-Cambrian-Lower Paleozoic metamorphic shales

Contours of structural stages on the base

Intrusive complexes (mainly granitoids)

Paleozoic

Middle Jurassic

Late Jurassic-Neocomian

Late Eocene-Oligocene

Boundaries of tectono-magmatic zones

Deep-seated faults

Other major faults

Volcano eruption centres

Mercury deposits and occurrences

	MAJOR FOLDED STRUCTURES	
Tectono-magmatic zones:	Anticlinoria	Synclinoria
A Adjar-Trialet	1. Kharami	17. Bolen
B Somkhit-Agdam	2. Lok	18. Lalvar
C Sevan-Kavabakh	3. Alaverdi	19. Ijevan-Qazakh
D Gafan	4. Shankhor	20. Dashkesaṇ
E Miskhana-Zangezur	5. Murovdag	21. Agdjakend
F Aras	6. Agdam	22. Mardakert
	7. Kavabakh	23. Quragachay
Pliocene-Quaternary volcanic	8. Lachyn	24. Martuni
Plateau	9-10. Zamzur	25. Hizabirt
33. Aragats	11. Starotag	26. Saribaba
34. Gedam	12. Gafan	27. Gochaz
35. Vardan	13. South-Zangezur	28. Shakdag
36. Ishihly	14. Djutfa	29. Sevan
37. Achalkala	15. Sharur	30. Yerevan-Ordubad
	16. Arzakan	31. Kelbadjar
		32. Leninakan

Compiled by: Nasibov T.N. and Allakhver-diev G.I.

Figure 35. Distribution of mercury deposits and occurrences in the Lesser Caucasus

Table 2. Classification of mercury deposits and occurrences of Azerbaijan

Formational type	Mineral type	Typical mineral associations	Host rocks	Structural and morphological types	Shape of ore bodies	Hydrothermal alterations	Sample of deposits and occurrences
Mercury	Magnesite-carbonaceous	Cinnabar, pyrite chalcopyrite, bornite, orpigment, magnetite, millerite, quartz, calcite, dolomite, dikkite, alkerite.	Serpentinites, magnetite schists, andesite-dacite, sandstones, argillites.	Lenses and veins in tectonically-reworked areas along and in intersection of faults and structural zones.	Lenses, veins.	Magnesite schists, silicafication, argilization.	Shorbulag, Agkaya, Agyatag Sarydash, Kamyshly, Nagdolychay, Chilgyazchay, Guneyplin.
Mercury	Carbonate-cinnabar	Cinnabar, pyrite, chalcopyrite, realgar, quartz, calcite	Limestone	Lenses and veins along steeply-dipping tectonic dislocations and fractures	Lenses and pillars of complex morphology	Silicafication, pyritization, calcitization.	Narzali, Arzuni, Dumanli, Millin and other deposits
Antimony-mercury	Quartz-carbonate-antimony-cinnabar (jasper type)	Cinnabar, antimony, pyrite, realgar, barite, orpigment, chalcopyrite, quartz, calcite, dolomite, dikkite, hydromica kaolinite.	Limestones, volcanogenic rudaceous rocks, sandstones.	Lenses-bearing veins and pillars along steeply-dipping thrusts and interbeds' fractures.	Stratiform and pillar-like veins.	Silicafication, pyritization, argillization, jasperization.	Levchay, Novolev, Eliz-gel.
Antimony-arsenic		Realgar, antimony, quartz.				Horfelns, selicitization, silicafication.	Deveboyin, Turschsuin

shape elongated along to main ore-controlling fault dipping gently to the south-east. The grade and reserves of mercury in this deposit are not available.

The Agkaya deposit

The deposit is hosted by volcano-sedimentary sequence of the Lower Cenonian represented by silicified brown argillites with interbeds of tuff-sandstones, porphyrites, tuffs and quartz-sericite-chlorite shales and thick pelitomorphic limestones of the Upper Cenonian age outcropped in the north-western part of the deposit. Intrusive rocks are represented by serpentinized periodites, gabbroids, stockwork bodies of diorite porphyrites, granodiorites and the recent Mio-Pliocene andesites, andesite-dacites and rare liparites forming dykes and stockworks. The deposit occupies a small part of the Agkayachay anticlinorium and is confined to a zone of intersection of tectonic faults dividing the Geydara-Almali anticline and the Chichekli-Kongur syncline located to the north.

Mercury mineralization has been found in listvenites and metasomatic varieties of listvenites. In six ore-bearing zones discovered in the Agkaya deposit, only three ore bodies have been studies on the surface. The grade, reserves and prospects of the deposit are unknown.

The Agyatag deposit

The deposit contains three areas of mercury mineralization confined to the Agyatag tectonic block. The first mineralized area is composed, mainly, of the Santonian tectonic breccia, jasperous brown argillites, dacites, serpentines and listvenites. The distribution of mercury mineralization of stringer-disseminated type within the only ore body in this area is very uneven. The second ore area is also confined to a crossing tectonic block and composed, mainly, of tectonic breccia, listvenites and dacites. Similar to the first area, the mercury mineralization of irregular stockwork shape is being structurally controlled by tectonic fault of upthrust-overthrust nature. The geologic and tectonic environment of the third mineralized area is very similar to that of the above two areas. The morphology of ore bodies within the deposit is rather complex reflecting an uneven distribution of mercury mineralization. In most cases, ore bodies are of column, pillar, lens or irregular complex shape.

The major textural types of mercury ore are brecciated, impregnated, massive, crustal, veined and earthy, where the first four types are dominant. Main ore mineral of the deposit is cinnabar, with quartz and calcite as cementing minerals. Secondary minerals are pyrite, arsenopyrite, rare chalcopyrite, sphalertie, hematite and schwazite. Hypergene minerals are represented by metacinnabarite, linolite, scorodite, malachite, eruzite, chalcosione and covelline. The grades and reserves of the deposit are unknown.

The Gamishli deposit

The deposit is located at a distance of 1.5-2.0 kilometres to the south from Gamishli village of the Kelbadjar region on the left bank of the Levchay river. The deposit occurs in schistose, silicified, and partially brecciated sandy-calcareous-clayey deposits of the Santonian suite dislocated by numerous longitudinal and rare near-meridional faults with accompanied schistose serpentinites and gabbroids.

The deposit is confined to a recumbent contact of the Garabag fault of upthrust-overthrust nature, where mercury mineralization in a form of scattered small impregnations of cinnabar was localized in silicified, brecciated and pyritized listvenites being traced in latitudinal direction along the overthrust strip dipping at (60°-80°) to the north. A total thickness of a zone of altered, schistose and unconsolidated rocks varies from 50 to 100 metres reaching 200 metres. This zone has been traced over a distance of 10 kilometres running via the Tala occurrence till the middle stream of the Bulandyhsu river.

With a wide dissemination of mercury mineralization within this zone, two small ore bodies were identified on the surface. The first ore body in the north-western part of the deposit occupies an area on the surface of 200 square kilometres. The average mercury content in the ore body is 0.13 per cent. The ore-body dips to the north-east at 50°-60° being composed of silicified, strongly brecciated and pyritized listvenites hosting fine disseminations, small nests and thread stringers of cinnabar. The proved mercury reserves of this ore body up to a depth of 30 metres are 20 tons.

The size of the second ore body on the surface is 140 square kilometres and the average mercury content is 0.17 per cent. Mercury mineralization is hosted by silicified and brecciated listvenites bearing everywhere fine disseminations and impregnations of cinnabar, rare chalcosine, chalcopyrite, pyrite, ezurite and malachite. A hanging side of the ore body is composed of silicified, brecciated and pyritized argillites, and a recumbent side of schistose serpentinites. The proved mercury reserves of this ore body up to a depth of 36 metres are 22 tons.

The Chilgyazchay deposit

The deposit is located in the mid-stream of the Chilgyazchay river basin to the south-east from the Mt. Agkaya. The geologic environment of the deposit in its south-western part consists of the Cenomanian sandy-clayey sequence overlain by a seam of fine-and medium clastic conglomerates. The mineralization is being controlled by the Nagdalichay upthrust hosting a thick zone of ore-bearing breccias overthrusted on tectonically-reworked argillites. Industrial concentrations of mercury mineralization are confined to feathering fractures of the Agyatag-Nagdalichay fault with a pronounced role of structural-lithologic factors. The tectonic features of the deposit are mostly of the dominated Caucasian and cross-cutting meridional directions. These dislocations are accompanied by silicification, kaolinitization, limonitization, brecciation and crushing of host rocks. Mercury mineralization within the deposit is confined to tectonic breccias, mainly formed by red jasperous argillites of the Santonian age. A lens-shaped body along the Chilgyazchay fault of up to 40 metres thick has been found.

Separate nest-shaped and irregular accumulations of cinnabar with a rich mercury content were distinguished in knots of intersection of longitudinal ore-distributing fractures with the cross-cutting faults of the Caucasian direction. Massive solid aggregates of cinnabar have been found in a form of small nests of rounded shape with a size from 3 to 5 centimetres in diameter. Altogether, three ore-bearing intervals have been identified on the surface and eleven mercury-bearing seams have been traced at a depth. Major hypogeneous minerals of the Chilgyazchay deposit are cinnabar, chalcopyrite, arsenopyrite, pyrite, quartz and calcite and hypergeneous minerals are limonite, goethite, malachite and dickite. Grades and reserves of mercury have not been reported.

The Narzali deposit

The deposit is located 350-400 metres to the east from the Kalafalikh village on the eastern flank of he Chilgyaz syncline. The deposit is hosted by coarse-grained terrigenous formations of the Coniacian – Santonian age, terrigenous – carbonaceous series of the Campanian and Maastrichtian ages of the Upper Cretaceous, and by clayey-carbonaceous formations of the Paleogene. Coarse-grained terrigenous series of the Coniacian – Santonian age have been intruded by undifferentiated serpentinized ultrabasic rocks and gabbroids. Two close outcrops of small stocks of diorite, quartz and plagiogranite have been observed in the north-eastern part of the deposit. Metasomatic rocks are represented by listvenites and listvenitized rocks observed in the northern and north-eastern part of the deposit along a tectonic zone and in a contact zone of serpentinized ultrabasic rocks with the Santonian terrigenous rocks. The deposit is spartially related to a zone of the Sultangoyunuchan (Kalafalikhchay) upthrust being characterized by a complex tectonic structure. Mercury mineralization of high grades was found in several small ore bodies occurring among limestones. These ore bodies are being controlled by steeply-dipping faults and fractures of different directions. Morphologically, ore bodies of stratabound, nest, lens, vein and irregular types have been found in various sections of a limestone interval along the strike. Grades and mercury reserves have not been reported.

The Levchay deposit

The Levchay deposit is located in the central part of the Garagaya-Elizgel anticlinal zone and composed of intensively dislocated and partially crushed sandy-clayey and calcareous rocks of the Upper Cenomanian age and subvolcanic formations (andesite-dacites, liparite-dacites) and their tuffs of the Mio-Pliocene. Rich accumulation of mercury was observed in the western part of the deposit coinciding with a submergence of the Aghdash anticlinal fold to the west. Three ore bodies with mercury and one ore body with antimony mineralization have been delineated and evaluated in the in the upper sections of the central part of the deposit.

All these bodies of stockwork, complex lens or irregular shape and morphology are confined to a submerciable part of the anticline. The archy part of the anticline is composed of crushed limestones transformed into jasperoids along a zone from 50 to 150 metres wide. The ore bodies are confined to knots of intersection of meridional and latitudinal faults. Main ore minerals are cinnabar, antimonite, stibcinite, valentinite, realgar, orpigment and metacinnabarite. Other minerals are calcite, quartz, bitumen and gypsum.

The Yeni-Lev antimony-mercury occurrence

The occurrence is located in the south-eastern continuation of the Levchay deposit and confined to contact of subvolcanic formations with the Cretaceous carbonaceous formation. The northern and southern mercury-bearing zones were delineated on the surface. The length of the southern zone is up to 500 metres with a variable thickness from 3 to 10 metres. The northern zone extends over a distance of 200 metres with a thickness from 1 to 8 metres. Antimonite mineralization in a form of small nests of 3 x 5 metres in size was found at a depth of 2-3 metres from the surface in crushed jasperoids in the western flank of the occurrence. The occurrence is confined to the axial part of the Levchay anticline at the intersection of tectonic faults of the north-eastern and north-western directions. The grades and reserves of mercury and antimony have not been reported.

(h)   Tungsten

The distribution of wolfram mineralization on the Azerbaijan territory is rather limited. There are known to exist several occurrences of tungsten near the Kilit village of the Ordubad ore region of the Nakhchivan Autonomous Republic as well as in the central part of the Lesser Caucasus region in the Geydara, Konurdag, Sarigash, Nadirkhanli and Nadjafli districts. The mineralization tends to be associated with the hyperbasitic belt development with adjacent outcrops of metal-bearing small intrusions of the Neogene age and skarn type mineralization in contact zone of the Dalidag granitoid massif. The mineralization is represented, mainly, by scheelite in quartz veins, aplites and veins of the Kilit and Dalidag granitoid massifs. Heavy concentrations of scheelite have been panned in the Kelbadjar region in the basin of the Terter river and in upper streams of the Ildrimsu river and in the Nakhchivan Autonomous Republic in the Kilitchay-Pazmarachay area.

The Kilit tungsten occurrence

The Kilit occurrence is located near the Kilit village in keratinized calcareous sandstones and marly shales of the Upper Cretaceous. Three steeply-dipping quartz veins with sulphide mineralization vary in a thickness from 0.05 to 0.7 metre. The first vein was transected by three horizons of adits wherein the wolfram mineralization is partially attributed to its western recumbent selvage. The thickness of wolfram-bearing crust of the vein varies from 3 to 6 centimetres. Quartz is white, often pectinal, in some places weakly crystallized. The main ore minerals are manganese, wolframite (hubnerite), chalcopyrite, pyrite, tetrahedrite, sometimes arsenopyrite, sphalerite, and rare galenite. Wolframite is represented by long crystal aggregates. The rest of minerals in the vein are observed as sporadic small nests and stains. Hydrothermal alteration of 2-3 centimetres thick is represented by silicification. Chlorite is usually observed in hornfels near ore zones.

The grade of WO_3 varies from 0.01 to 0.82 per cent reaching 1.08 per cent. An average grade of WO_3 in the first vein is 0.32 per cent. The grade of copper varies from 0.05 to 0.1 per cent, zinc from 0.006 to 0.1 per cent, lead is 0.04 per cent with traces of arsenic and antimony. The wolfram prospects of the other two quartz veins of the occurrence are minor.

The Dalidag tungsten occurrence

Tungsten-bearing quartz veins and veinlets of the Dalidag occurrence are confined to hornfelses, keratinized tuff-sandstones and tuff-conglomerates of the Upper Eocene with rare interbeds of tuffites. A part of sulphides-tungsten bearing veins is also located in the endo-contact zone of the Dalidag intrusive massif among porphyry quartz syenites, which in some places, have been transformed into granosyenites and syenite-diorites. A length of veins varies in a wide range from 50 to 400 metres. Altogether, 81 quartz veins have been discovered in the area of the Dalidag occurrence including 47 veins which have been proved on the surface by mining openings.

Mineralization is represented by wolframite and scheelite which form irregular aggregate accumulations in close association with chalcopyrite, pyrite, galenite, sphalerite, pyrolusite, polianite and anglesite. The grade of tungsten varies from 0.1 to a range of 2.3 per cent. The Dalidag occurrence and a skarn belt of the northern part of the Dalidag granitoid massif has not been studied well for tungsten mineralization. A wide distribution of tungsten lode mineralization including known scheelite mineralization in quartz veins of the Pliocene and small intrusions occurring among listvenites and ultrabasites in the Kelbadjar region all indicate high prospects of the area for further discoveries of tungsten mineralization.

(i)   Arsenic

Besides the Darridag realgar-orpiment deposit, the arsenic mineralization is known to exist in the Salvarty and Paradash occurrences in the Nakhchivan Autonomous Republic and in the Deveboynu occurrence in the Lachyn region of Azerbaijan. The arsenic mineralization of economic interest has been also found among sulphide-arsenic cobalt ores of the Dashkesan deposit and copper-arsenic ores of the Bittibulag deposit in the Gedabek region.

The Darridag (Djulfa) arsenic deposit

The deposit is hosted by the Campanian and Maastrichtian limestones and marls, sandstones and clays of the Danian stage and the Pliocene, tuffogenous-sedimentary rocks with basal conglomerates of the Middle and Upper Eocene and volcanogenic-rudaceous rocks of the Lower and Middle Oligocene, which construct the Darridag anticlinal fold of the north-western strike. The north-eastern limb of this anticlimal fold hosts interbedded intrusive massif of hornblende diorites. The mineralization in the northern part of the deposit is represented by realgar-orpiment ores of stockwork type, in the central part by antimonite ores of nest type, and, in the southern zone near arsenic source, by realgar of disseminated type. Arsenic mineralization tends to be controlled by fractures of near-meridional direction.

Main proved reserves of the deposit are concentrated in the south-western part of the Darridag mountain ridge in the Campanian-Maastrichtian and the Eocene marls and sandstones being controlled by a tectonic fault crossing the axial part of the Darridag anticlinal fold. The ore body is represented by a nearly vertical stockwork which tends to widen with a depth. Four main mineral types of ores have been distinguished within the deposit. The first type is represented, mainly, by realgar with slight admixture of antimonite. The second mineral type has the highest quality of ores, but observed more rarely than the first one. Orpiment predominates in mineral composition with minor realgar. The third mineral type of high quality of ores is observed rarely. Mineralogically, it is represented by finely-disseminated orpiment of yellowish-greenish colour with films of black earthy melnikovite. The fourth mineral type of low quality of ores and of any industrial importance is represented by slightly enriched host rocks.

Structurally, the first three mineral types of mineralization are confined to the main fracture of the fault running across the center of the ore zone. Another two ore zones, were distinguished within tectonic faults parallel to the main fault zone. Main ore minerals are realgar, orpiment and rare antinomite; secondary minerals are arsenopyrite, arsenic melnikovite and pitticite. Arsenic-bearing hot mineral springs were found on the surface within a distance of 1-1.5 kilometres from the deposits being generated by arsenic ores. This part of the deposit has not been explored yet. Antimony and mercury mineralization of large extent, which was found within the Darridag deposit enhances the economic prospects of the deposit.

The Salvarty occurrence

The Salvarty arsenic occurrence is located in the Salvarty mountain among andesites and their pyroclasts of the Lower Pliocene age. Ore mineralization is confined to a fault of the north-eastern direction (330°-340°) of 12 metres thick. The main ore minerals are realgar, orpiment, pyrite, antimonite and rare sphalerite. Secondary minerals are valentinite, limonite, melantorite and, sometimes, earthy sulphur. Other minerals are quartz, kaolinite and opal. The occurrence requires mineral exploration to judge its prospects.

(j)   Antimony

Antimony mineralization is known to exist in many places of Azerbaijan, however, the mineralization is so far of a mineralogical interest only and economic prospects are unknown yet. The mineralization is distributed along the Darridag-Ortakend-Bashkend-Salvarty belt where it is met in paragenetic association with realgar and orpigment described in the previous chapter. Mineralization of the same genetic type was found in the Deveboylu area in the central part of the Lesser Caucasus and in the upper streams of the Levchay river among the Levchay group of antimony occurrences. Antimony was also found in other mineral associations with arsenic in the Bittibulag deposit of enargite as famatinite, and in association with cobalt in the Dashkesan deposit. In the Kelbadjar region, the occurrence of antimony minerals was found on the Zod mountain pass.

The Djulfa (Darridag) deposit

The geologic and structural position of the deposit is in "Arsenic" section above. Antimonite mineralization within the Djulfa deposit was found in three areas of the deposit where it is paragenetically associated with arsenic and other mineralization. The north-western area of the deposit hosts the main reserves of arsenic ores where antimonite is observed in a form of small admixtures. The antimony grades in this area are very poor. The south-eastern area is represented by mineral springs where antimonite is accompanied by realgar and orpigment. The antimony hydrogen (SbH_3) content in arsenic-bearing mineral springs of the Darridag deposit is about 0.005 per cent, and that in mineralized host rocks is minor. The central area of the deposit hosts nests, impregnated and disseminated types of ore where the grade of antimony reaches 8 per cent. In the mineral composition of antimony ore, realgar has a subordinate position; secondary minerals are anhydrous and complex oxides of antimony represented by valentinite, servantinite and stibcinite.

The Levchay deposit

The geologic and structural position of the Levchay deposit is given under "Arsenic" section above. Antimony mineralization was found in significant concentrations in a form of minor admixtures in mercury ore bodies and in independent accumulations. The antimony ore body of 1.5 metres thick has been open by adit No. 1. The thickness of the ore body tends to increase with a depth reaching a range of 8-10 metres at a depth of adit No. 6 which is 50 metres downward from the level of the first adit. The main mineral of the ore body is antimonite which forms solid veins, stringers, lenses and impregnations. The secondary minerals are cinnabar realgar, valentinite and servantite. Quartz is the main vein mineral. Calcite in a form of stringers in silicified limestones is subordinate. Bitumens and clayey minerals are observed somewhere. The antimony content is about 5 per cent.

The Fazil occurrence

The occurrence is located in the eastern flank of the Levchay deposit. The antimony-bearing vein is confined to a steeply-dipping tectonic fault which cross-cuts the southern limb of a symmetric syncline composed of silicified limestones of the Upper Cenonian. Numerous occurrences and points of antimony mineralization in association with mercury, arsenic and other minerals within the Levchay mercury-bearing zone and in other areas of ophiolites development suggest prospects for discovering new antimony and complex antimony-mercury, antimony-arsenic and other deposits in the central part of the Lesser Caucasus.

(k)   Bismuth

The mono-mineral deposits and occurrences of bismuth are unknown in Azerbaijan, however, it has been indicated as an associated metal in ores of many polymetallic deposits of the country. The examples are polymetallic ores of the Mekhmana deposit and the Bashkend-Ortakend occurrence of the Nakhchivan Autonomous Republic where the grade of bismuth reaches a range of 0.03-0.04 per cent. A presence of galeno-

132

bismuthite has been observed in molybdenum ores of the Paragachay deposit. A high grade of bismuth from 0.01 to 0.1 per cent has been also indicated at the Vejnali gold-sulphide-quartz veins deposit. Traces of bismuth have been also reported from sulphide ores of the Chiragideresi and Gedabek deposits and in chalcopyrites of the Dashkesan deposit. In polymetallic ores of the Bayan occurrence, a grade of bismuth varies from traces to 0.01 per cent, and that in the Molla Gasanli occurrence of the Dashkesan ore field reaches 0.1 per cent. Overall, bismuth mineralization in Azerbaijan is of meralogical interest only.

3. Precious metals

(a)   Gold

Gold mining in the Transcaucasian territory including the Lesser Caucasus has been known for a long time. According to historical data, some gold-bearing areas were developed in VI-I centuries BC. Geological research, mapping programmes and mineral exploration have led to a discovery of gold deposits and occurrences and associated genetic presence of gold in ores of copper-pyrite, porphyry copper and copper-polymetallic deposits of Azerbaijan (Abdullayev and others, 1979; Baba-zade, 1967; Hasanov and Aliyev, 1984; Kerimov and others, 1983; Kerimov and others, 1996; Kurbanov and others, 1981; Mansurov, 1998; Suleimanov and Baba-zade, 1986; Soleimanov and others, 1986).

In the Azerbaijanian part of the Lesser Caucasus, gold mineralization is typical for the following metallogenic belts:

❑   The Somkhit-Agdam belt: gold-sulphide and gold-sulphide-quartz mineralization;

❑   The Geychay-Hakera belt: gold-sulphide-carbonate-quartz and gold-sulphide-quartz mineralization;

❑   The Kelbadjar-Gochaz belt: gold-sulphide quartz mineralization;

❑   The Ordubad-Zangezur belt: gold-sulphide and gold-quartz mineralization;

❑   The Gafan belt: gold quartz mineralization.

The Lesser Caucasus region is characterized by spatial combination of development of gold, copper, lead and zinc, silver, molybdenum and other mineralization typical for regions with rejuvenated tectonic activity and magmatism. Due to this spatial overlapping of gold, porphyry copper, copper-pyrite, copper-polymetallic and other types of mineralization, the Lesser Caucasus is treated as a polymetallic gold-bearing metallogenic province with a complex polycyclic metallogeny. A spatial and genetic relationship of gold mineralization with subvolcanic magmatic formations of various composition has also been identified.

An important role of structural control in localization of gold in fractured zones and blocks of volcano-plutonic constructions has been noted and proved. There are some prospects of discovering of new types of gold-sulphide mineralization in jasperoids and dolomites of carbonate series, carbonaceous shales and secondary quarzites. Major morphological types of gold mineralization are steeply-dipping veins and stockworks and those of gold-sulphide mineralization are gently-dipping interbedded bodies and stockworks. The following four formational types of gold and gold-bearing complex ores have been distinguished: (a) gold deposits of gold-sulphide, gold-sulphide-quartz, gold-sulphide-carbonate-quartz and gold-quartz ore formations; (b) gold-bearing deposits of complex copper-gold ore and gold-copper-polymetallic ores where gold is one of the basic components; (c) deposits of copper sulphides, massive copper and porphyry copper types with substantial associated gold; and (d) porphyry copper deposits with gold traces.

The most productive terrains are magmatic formations of geosynclinal and orogenic stages of the Alpine cycle associated with concentrations of polymetallic, copper and molybdenum ores. The geochronologic dating of gold mineralization indicates a wide range in a concentration of gold ore found in all stages of the Alpine metalogenic epoch and pronounced in the Lesser Caucasus metallogenic province from the Bajocian to the Pliocene. Several small gold placers are represented by scattered alluvial, fluvial terrace and alluvial-proluvial types being characterized by irregular gold distribution. The most prospective Qazakh, Gedabek and Garabag gold-bearing districts with proved gold reserves were found within the Azerbaijan part of the Somkhit-Agdam metaligenic belt. Highly-prospective occurrences of gold and complex gold-bearing ores were identified within the Dashkesan, Gey-Gel and Murovdag ore regions and the Shusha-Fizuli potential area.

The Qazakh ore district

The Qazakh ore district is located in the north-west of the Azerbaijanian segment of the Somkhit-Agdam zone covering the north-eastern part of Ijevan-Qazakh transformal gold-bearing fractured zone from 26 to 30 kilometres long. This ore district includes the Dagkesaman gold-copper-polymetalic deposit gold occurrences, numerous points of gold mineralization, geochemical halos and small gold-bearing placers.

The Dagkesaman gold deposit

The deposit is represented by steeply-dipping gold-bearing quartz veins containing ore intervals of a "pillars" type with a high content of gold. Gold is associated with quartz and pyrite, chalcopyrite, sphalerite, galenite and others sulphides. More close association of gold is with quartz and chalcopyrite. The basic metal is gold with associated silver, lead, zinc and copper. The ratio of gold to silver within the deposit is 1:4. Favorable geologic and structural position of the deposit, the intensity and scope of gold ore mineralization all indicate high prospects for its economic development.

The Gedabek ore district

The district belongs to the northern part of the Megri-Gedabek gold-bearing structure of a submeridional direction. The district incorporates the Gosha gold-sulphide and Gedabek copper-gold deposits with estimated gold reserves, the Garabag and Khar-Khar, Maarif, Gizildja, Barum-Barsum and Berezin deposits of fissure-filling and disseminated types in porphyry copper deposits as well as the Itgirlan, Mundjukhlu, Badakend and other occurrences of gold and gold-silver ores.

The Gedabek copper-gold deposit

The deposit of copper-pyrite type is known to occur in secondary quarzites being represented by fissure fillings-disseminated sulphide-quartz mineralization of chalcopyrite-pyrite-quartz polymetallic formation of stockwork type, and partly, by stocks and lenses of massive copper-pyrite ores. The major ore body of stockwork type and large size contains adjacent ore bodies with high copper and gold grades. The major metals are copper, gold and silver. A more detailed description of the Gedabek deposit is given in "Copper" section. Given the favorable geologic and structural position of the deposit, the intensity and scope of mineralization, grades and reserves, the Gedabek deposit constitutes the primary target for open pit mining.

The Gosha gold deposit

The Gosha gold-sulphide deposit is confined to the Gosha anticline located on the north-west flank of the Shamkhor uplift. The deposit is hosted by layered porphyrites intercalated with bands of their pyroclasts, quartz porphyres and their tuffs. The volcanic section is intruded by quartz-diorites and a subvolcanic body of liparite-dacites of the Upper Jurassic age. Cross-cutting dykes of diabases, andesites and, rarely, liparite-dacites are widely developed within the deposit. The deposit is structurally controlled by a dense network of faults and fractures of the north-western, north-eastern, sub-meridional and sub-latitudinal directions with gold-bearing metasomatites.

Ore bodies are represented by extended subparallel hydrothermally-altered zones, quartz-sulphide veins, stockworks and fissure filling-disseminated types of mineralization. Higher grades of gold were found in quartz-sulphide veins, mineralized zones and stockworks. The main ore minerals are pyrite and native gold; secondary minerals are sphalerite, chalcopyrite, galenite, bornite and coverlite. Other minerals are quartz, carbonate, sericite, chlorite and kaolinite. Hydrothermal alterations are represented by schistosity, kaolinization, sericitization and chloritization. The basic precious components are gold and silver having irregular distribution patterns. Gold mineralization was traced over 400 metres deep by underground mining.

Reserves of gold and silver have been proved to be economic for development by underground mining. The adjacent Itgirlan, Mundjukhly, Shikhabat and other gold and gold-silver occurrences on the flanks of the Gosha deposit enhance the prospects of the deposit. The Gedabek ore district is made up of the Paleozoic carbonaceous shales containing steeply-dipping multiple quartz veins with sulphide mineralization and is considered potentially prospective for discovering of gold mineralization of black shales type. A wide distribution of geochemical halos of gold and hydrothermal metasomatites including gold-bearing secondary quarzites enhance the prospects of the Gedabek ore district for new discoveries of complex polymetallic deposits of base and precious metals.

The Garabag ore district

The Garabag ore district represents a part of the Somkhit-Agdam metallogenic zone being confined to the Khachinchay-Terter uplifted isolated block of the north-eastern part of the Dalidag-Mekhmana transformal uplift. The ore district has been developed in the Middle Upper in the Jurassic volcanogenic, volcano-sedimentary and the Cretaceous terrigenous-carbonaceous formations. Mineralization is genetically associated with intensive volcanic activity during the Jurassic time being traced by numerous volcano-structural constructions. The most typical Djanyatag intrusive massif is composed mainly of quartz diorite, banatites, tonalites and its varieties. Dykes of granite-porphyry, liparites and granodiorite-porphyres are widely developed within the massif. A rather intensive gold mineralization has been superimposed on massive sulphide, copper-polymetallic and porphyry copper mineralization. A clear zonation and distribution of porphyry copper, gold, gold-copper-polymetallic, copper-gold deposits has been noted from the east to the west within the Garabag ore district. The Garabag ore district incorporates the Cizilbulag and Gizilbulag copper-gold and Mekhmana gold-copper-polymetallic deposits, the Damirli porphyry copper deposit, the Khatinbeili, Sampas and Eddikhirman groups of gold-sulphide-quartz occurrences, gold-bearing placers in the valleys of the Terter, Kabartichay, Gyulyatagchay and Khachinchay rivers, as well as numerous halos of gold, copper, lead, zinc, molybdenum and other metals.

The Gizilbulag deposit

The Gizilbulag copper-gold deposit is hosted by sedimentary-volcanogenic formations of the Middle-Upper Jurassic represented by polimiktic conglomerates, tuff-sandstones of the Callovian-Oxfordian stage, lithoclastic tuffs of andesites of the Bathonian stage and covers and lithoclastic tuffs of liparite-dacites and andesite porphyrites of the Bajocian stage (figure 36). This volcano-sedimentary sequence is intruded by subvolcanic bodies, dykes of andesites, andesite-basalts and liparite-dacites and small intrusions of quartz diorites and diorite porphyrites of the Late Jurassic age. A dense network of faults and fractures has defined a block structure of the deposit. Mineralization is confined to a thick zone of crushed and schistose rocks in liparite-dacite porphyrites and their detrital facies. Two ore bodies are represented by elongated irregular stockworks hosting dense fissure-filling stringer, impregnated and nest-shaped mineralization. Ores are mainly represented by pyrite, pyrite-chalcopyrite and quartz-pyrite-chalcopyrite mineral associations. The basic ore minerals are chalcopyrite, pyrite, native gold; secondary minerals are sphalerite, bornite, galenite, marcasite, melnikovite and arsenopyrite. Gold of irregular and isometric form has been found in chalcopyrite and pyrite as inclusions. The basic precious components are gold, silver and copper.

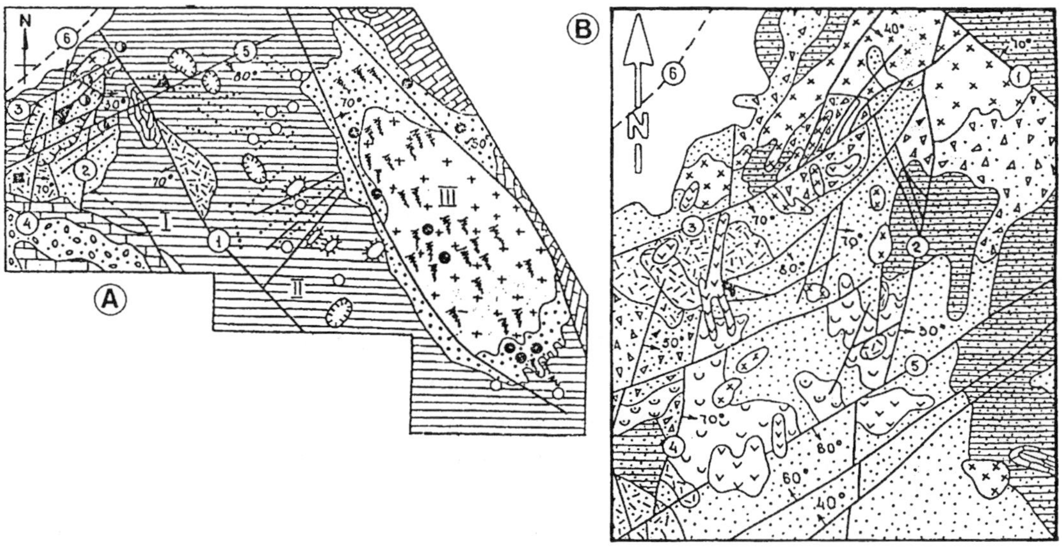

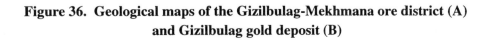

LEGEND

Recent deposits

Upper Cretaceous; fine-crystalline limestones

Upper Jurassic tuff-pebble stones, tuff-gritstones, tuffites

Upper Jurassic limestones

Upper Jurassic tuffs of andesites, tuff-breccia, tuff-sandstones, tuff-pebble stones

Middle Jurassic tuff-sandstones, tuff-gritstones, tuffs, tuff-lava of andesites

Middle Jurassic tuff-aglomerates

Middle Jurassic dacites, liparite-dacites and their tuffs

Middle Jurassic lava breccia, liparite-dacites

Middle Jurassic andesite-porphyrite flows

Upper Jurassic subvolcanic dacites, andesite-dacites

Upper Jurassic andesite-basalts

Late Jurassic diorites and quartz-diorites

Late Jurassic plagiogranites, granodiorites, granosyenites, tonalites

Dykes of dacites, andesite-dacites, syenite-diorites

Silicificated, kaolinitized rocks and secondary quarzites with copper and molybdenum mineralization

Quartz veins and stockworks

Faults

Ore bodies

Porphyry copper mineralization

Gold mineraliation

Polymetallic mineralization

Gold-sulphur mineralization

Copper-pyrite mineralization

Caldera

Contours of jpositive volconic structures

Contours of negative volcanic structures

Faults:

1) Mekhmana

2) Fault of 824.3 metre altitude

3) Kizildag

4) Gizlbulag

5) Yaiji

Tectonic blocks:

I-Gizilbulag

II-Block graben

III-Djanyatag

Figure 36. Geological maps of the Gizilbulag-Mekhmana ore district (A) and Gizilbulag gold deposit (B)

Feasibility studies on technological properties and enrichment of ores in laboratory and semi-industrial conditions have proved the applicability of gravitational-floatation technology of ores reworking for obtaining of conditional gravitational gold-bearing and floatational copper-gold concentrates. Mineral exploration by underground mining and drilling has proved the existence of reserves of gold, silver, copper and other associated minerals of industrial categories suitable for development by open pit mining. Stripped rocks of overburden have been found suitable raw material for production of rock aggregates and vitrified ceramic products.

The Mekhmana deposit

The Mekhmana gold-copper-polymetallic deposit contains more than 30 ore-bearing veinlet zones and veins (figure 36). The detailed mineral exploration has been carried out over four major veins. Calcite-quartz veins contain galenite and sphalerite mineralization of disseminated, nest types and stringers of massive sulphide ore. Ores are mainly of gold-silver-copper and lead-zinc-bearing types. The major metals are lead, zinc, silver and gold with associated cadmium, selenium and tellurium. More detailed description of the Mekhmana deposit is given in the "Lead and Zinc" section and that of the Damirli porphyry copper deposit in the "Copper" section. Given the intensity and scope of mineralization, the Garabag ore district is referenced as one of the highly prospective targets for noble and complex polymetallic deposits of the Lesser Caucasus region.

The Geychay-Akera metallogenic zone

This zone is located southward from the Somkhit-Agdam metallogenic belt conciding with the ophiolite belt of the Lesser Caucasus. The geological structure and mineralization are defined by abyssal fault being traced by outcrops of ophiolite rocks. The zone is characterized by development of early, middle and late stages of endogenous mineralization of the Alpine epoch being represented by chromite, gold-sulphide-quartz and arsenic-antimony-mercury formations.

The Azerbaijanian part of the Geychay-Akera metallogenic belt contains a part of the Zod and Tutkhun deposits, the Soyutluchay, Gilichli-Alchalilg and other groups of gold-sulphide-quartz and gold-sulphide-carbonate-quartz occurrences and the small Soyutluchay placer gold deposit. The zone is potentially prospective for discovery of deposits of finely dispersed gold in jasperoids and antimony-mercury deposits and occurrences. The larger part of gold reserves of the Zod gold-sulphide-quartz deposit is located in the Kelbadjar district of Azerbaijan on the border with Armenia.

The Tutkhun deposit

The Tutkhun gold-sulphide-quartz deposit is also located in the Kelbadjar district and includes the Gazikhanli, Agzibir, Gizilistan, Zargulu and Galaboynu group of gold-bearing areas. The deposit is confined to the area of junction of the Geycha-Garabag tectono-magmatic zone with the Dalidag-Mekhmana transformal uplift. Gold mineralization was found along the longitudinal Agyatag-Zod strip of hyperbasites and granitoids. The deposit occurs in volcanic rocks of intermediate and alkaline composition and terrigenous-sedimentary rocks of the Cretaceous and Paleogene age being intruded by complex ultrabasic and basic intrusions of the pre-Upper Cretaceous and alkaline magmatic rocks of the post-Middle Eocene. Widely developed metasomatites are represented by quartz-kaolinite, quartz-sericite and mono-quartz facies of secondary quarzites.

The dominant part of gold-sulphide-quartz veinlets and veins is confined to granitoid massif. Ore bodies in steeply-dipping vein zones of pillars and pipe shape are confined to areas of junction of faults and fractures of various limbs. The basic ore minerals are quartz, pyrite, galenite, sphalerite, tetraedrite, native gold, molybdenite, antimonite and burnonite and secondary minerals are carbonates, chalcopyrite, sericite and chlorite. The major economic components are gold with associated silver, tellurium, bismuth and antimony. Despite limited mineral exploration, the geologic and structural position of the deposit coupled with the intensity and scope of gold mineralization, wide distribution of metasomatic rocks and a presence of gold occurrences on the flanks of the deposit contribute all to high prospects of the deposit for gold and complex polymetallic gold-silver-bearing ores.

The Azerbaijanian part of the Kelbadjar-Gochaz metallogenic belt is located south-west of the Geychay-Akera zone and includes the Dalidag ore district within the Kelbadjar superimposed trough. The trough is filled up by volcanogenic rocks of the Middle Eocene-Anthropogene formations. The Dalidag ore district is confined to areas of junction of the Kelbadjar-Gochaz longitudinal zone with the Dalidag-Mekhmana uplift with a wide development of batholith intrusive of granodiorite-granite and subvolcanic andesite-dacite formations. Intrusive rocks are represented by monzonite-syenite-diorite and granite-diorite series of the Dalida missif and quartz diorites, diorites and diorite porphyrites of the Zaglik outcrop similar by mineralization to the Megri-Ordubad pluton. The Dalidag ore district incorporates the Agduzdag gold and Dalidag copper-gold deposits, small placer gold deposit, several gold occurrences as well as gold-silver-bearing secondary quarzites, which are widely developed in the area of the district.

The Agduzdag deposit

The Agduzdag deposit occurs in the upper streams of the Zarchay river in the Kelbadjar district. Mineralization is located in andesites, andesite-dacites, liparite-dacites and their detrital facies. Morphologically, ore bodies are represented by steeply-dipping vein zones and veins. Three major veinlet zones out of more than 30 vein zones and veins have been identified within the deposit. Hydrothermal alterations are expressed by schistosity, sometimes by kaolinization, carbonitization, sericitization and, in some places, by fine-dispersed pyritization. The main minerals of ore bodies is quartz, which occupies from 80 to 95 per cent of the volume being followed by calcite and kaolinite. Ore minerals are rare being represented by pyrite, magnetite, chalcopyrite, sphalerite and other minerals. The major metal is gold with associated silver. Distribution of gold and silver is extremely uneven. Gold mineralization has been estimated by geophysics to extend to a depth from 600 to 800 metres. The deposit has been explored on the surface and by underground mining up to a depth from 80 to 120 metres. Based on estimated reserves of gold and vein quartz suitable for fluxes raw material, the prospects of the deposit for economic development are quite high. The Dalidag ore district incorporates several gold-copper-molybdenum and gold-sulphide-quartz occurrences of vein type, and gold-copper-bearing area in secondary quarzites (monoquarzites). Given the favorable geologic position, scale and intensity of mineralization, the prospects of the Dalidag ore district for development of gold and complex gold-bearing ores are very high.

The Ordubad ore district

The Ordubad ore district is located in the Ordubad-Zangezur metallogenic belt of the Nakhchivan Autonomous Republic occupying a vast territory of the western endo-exo-contact zone of the Megri-Ordubad granitoid massif with multiple phases of magmatic activity. This ore district is characterized by a rather intensive complex polymetallic mineralization, forming substantial concentrations and various combinations of copper, molybdenum, lead, zinc, gold and silver metals. The Agdara, Nasirvaz and other deposits and occurrences of gold-copper-polymetallic formation and the Aport (Agyurt), Piyazbashi, Shakardara, Munundara and other deposits and occurrences of the Ordubad group of gold-sulphide-quartz formation are the major targets for economic development within the Ordubad ore district.

The Aport (Agyurt) deposit

The deposit is confined to the area of intersection of the major Ordubad fault of the north-western direction and the Vanandchay-Misdag fault of the north-eastern direction. The area of the deposit is composed of rocks of the Megri-Ordubad intrusive massif represented by granosyenites, quartzose and quartzless syenite-diorites, and aplite-diorites. Quartzose syenite-diorites are prevalent. Ore bodies within the deposit are represented by zones of veins in hydrothermally-altered rocks and by quartz-carbonate veins. Eight zones of veins out of twenty ore zones, which were identified within the deposit, have been studied in detail.

By its mineral composition, the deposit corresponds to gold-sulphide-quartz formation. The basic ore-forming minerals are pyrite and chalcopyrite; secondary minerals are magnetite, pyrrhotite, tennatite-tetraedrite, native gold, sphalerite, molybdenum and others. Gold in ores is characterized by extremely irregular distribution. The basic economic metals of ores are gold, silver and copper. Gold mineralization was traced to a depth of over 400 metres by mineral exploration. The reserves of gold and silver have been evaluated under C_2 category. A gravitational-floatation technological scheme of ore processing has been worked out. A wide distribution of gold-bearing metasomatites, presence of a number of deposits with proved silver and gold reserves and adjacent prospective occurrences in a favorable geological setting all substantiate high prospects of the area of the deposit for discovering new deposits of gold and gold-bearing complex polymetallic ores. By mining, technical and geological conditions, the deposit is suitable for underground mining.

The Gafan metallogenic belt

The Gafan metallogenic belt is located in the south-western part of Azerbaijan on the border with Armenia and includes the Vejnali ore district. Copper-polymetallic mineralization of stringer-impregnated type was found on the extent of ore-bearing zones of the Gafan deposit including the Vejnali quartz-gold deposit.

The Vejnali deposit

The Vejnali deposit is located on the territory of the Zangelan district on the border with Armenia and incorporates twenty-five gold-bearing vein zones. Proved mineable reserves have been so far evaluated within six vein zones. Ore veins and zones of the deposit are mainly represented by quartz-sulphide and, rarely, by quartz-carbonate-sulphide veins and hydrothermally altered disintegrated and brecciated rocks. Sulphides are dominated by pyrite with subordinate chalcopyrite. Arsenopyrite, tennantite, sphalerite, tellurium-bismuthite, and native gold are met in low grades. Basic components of commercial value are gold, silver with associated copper, tellurium and bismuth. A gravitational-floatation technological scheme of ores processing has been worked out enabling to obtain a high percentage of gold (96.5 per cent) and silver (97.4 per cent) extraction.

Preliminary exploration by underground mining openings on four exploration levels have proved mineable reserves of gold to be worked out by underground mining. A presence of numerous gold-bearing veins and zones, which have not been explored at a depth coupled with known deposits with proved gold mineable reserves enhance the prospects of the Azerbaijanian part of the Lesser Caucasus for discovering new economic deposits of gold and complex gold-bearing copper ores with foreign participation in mineral exploration and mining projects. Prospects for discovery of new gold deposits on the Azerbaijan territory are not limited by the Lesser Caucasus region. A new type of finely-dispersed gold mineralization in black shales of the Jurassic age has been proved to be prospective by mineral exploration works on the southern slope of the Greater Caucasus within the Durudja structure.

C. Non-metallic minerals

Azerbaijan possesses abundant resources of non-metallic minerals which play an essential role in economic development of the country and constitute a substantial part of the mineral resources base in terms of a number of explored deposits, proved and potential reserves and a variety of mineral types. The main genetic types of deposits of non-metallic minerals on the territory of Azerbaijan are endogenous, exogenous and metamorphogenic, but a majority of the deposits belongs to a group of exogenous-sedimentary origin incorporating rock salt, gypsum and anhydrite, phosphorites, all kinds of carbonate raw material, clays, sands and sand-gravel deposits. Reserves of major non-metallic minerals and construction materials of Azerbaijan are provided in table 3. A distribution of non-metallic deposits and occurrences in Azerbaijan is shown in figure 37.

Table 3. Reserves of non-metallic minerals and construction materials in Azerbaijan

No.	Non-metallic minerals	Unit	Number of deposits	Reserves
1	2	3	4	5
1	Gypsum	Million tons	2	40.3
2	Anhydrite	Million tons	1	18.1
3	Alum	Million tons	5	5.6
4	Benthonite clay	Million tons	2	99.3
5	Saw-stone, including	Million cubic metres	65	570.2
	limestone,	Million cubic metres	54	512.7
	sandstone,	Million cubic metres	1	0.44
	tuff and tuff-sandstones,	Million cubic metres	9	51.0
	travertine	Million cubic metres	1	6.1
6	Facing stone, including	Million cubic metres	23	58.3
	limestone,	Million cubic metres	2	7.4
	marbled limestone,	Million cubic metres	13	27.6
	porphyrite,	Million cubic metres	1	0.92
	travertine,	Million cubic metres	2	14.42
	tuffs,	Million cubic metres	1	0.94
	gabbro,	Million cubic metres	1	2.03
	conglomerate,	Million cubic metres	2	3.23
	teschenite	Million cubic metres	1	1.76
7	Cement raw mineral, including	Million tons	10	373.7
	limestones,	Million tons	4	242.02
	clay,	Million tons	4	120.07
	trass,	Million tons	1	4.56
	volcanic ash	Million tons	1	7.05
8	Rock salt	Million tons	4	1 301.6
9	Dolomites	Million tons	2	10.02
10	Quartz and quarzites	Million tons	2	7.59
11	Flux limestones	Million tons	1	50.8
12	Limestone for soda production	Million tons	1	244.6
13	Zeolite	Million tons	1	12.5
14	Quartz sands	Million cubic metres	3	20.0
15	Ceramic raw material	Million tons	2	19.0
16	Barite	Million tons	2	0.38
17	Pyrofillite	Million tons	1	6.5
18	Porcelain stone	Million tons	1	3.4
19	Bituminous sands	Million tons	3	3.5
20	Building stone, including	Million cubic metres	26	152.6
21	Clays	Million tons	94	191.7
22	Gravel-sand	Million cubic metres	68	1 059.3
23	Building sand	Million cubic metres	16	68.0
24	Perlite-pumice	Million cubic metres	2	6.6
25	Mineral pigments	Thousand tons	2	46.4
26	Iodine-bromine water	Thousand cubic metres/day	5	250.5
27	Fresh underground water	Thousand cubic metres/day	59	6 758.9
28	Mineral water	Thousand cubic metres/day	29	19.8

140

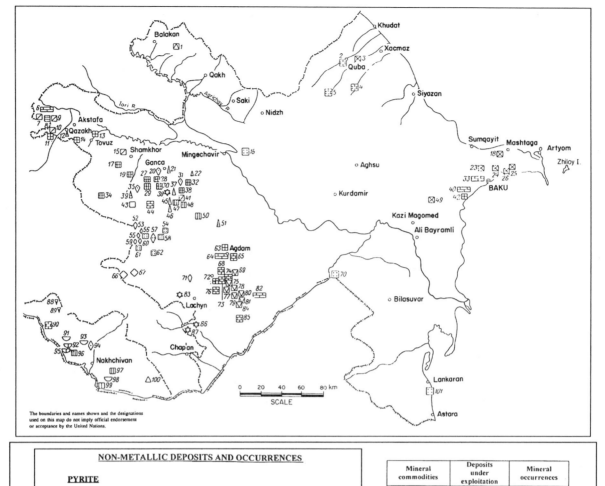

NON-METALLIC DEPOSITS AND OCCURRENCES

PYRITE
45. Chiragidzor deposit
37. Chiragidzor-Toganali deposit
46. Toganali deposit

PHOSPHORITES
89. Geran galasi occurrence
88. Gumushlug occurrence

ROCK SALT
98. Nekhram deposit
93. Nakhchivan deposit
91. Pusyan deposit

DOLOMITE
99. Nekhram deposit

BENTONITE
10. Dashsalakhli deposit
9. Ali Bayramli deposit
7. Kaimakhli deposit
41. Upper Agdjakend deposit
15. Shamkhor deposit
18. Shikhandag deposit

FLUX LIMESTONE
43. Khachbulag deposit

KAOLIN AND REFRACTORY CLAYS
17. Chardakhli deposit
19. Gotul deposit
34. Kara-Murad occurrence
29. Anshapur deposit
28. Agekhush deposit
30. Danaer deposit
27. Zaglik occurrence
38. Mirzik deposit
32. Karabulakh deposit

SECONDARY QUARTZITES
20. Kizildjin deposit
31. Getashen deposit
35. Chovdar deposit

PYROPHILLITE
39. Kirvakar (Sharukar) Deposit

ANDALUSITE
100. Paragachay deposit

SERPENTINE
53. Geidara zone
55. Zaidara zone
59. Nikolaev zone
60. Kiazimbin zone

TUFF-SANDSTONES
94. Daralin deposit

TUFF
57. Kilisalin deposit

MARBLED LIMESTONE AND MARBLE
90. Ulya-Novashen deposit
68. Vararak deposit
73. Zariinbakh deposit
74. Gorov deposit
85. Arakul deposit
5. Kazma-Kryg deposit
2. Akhchai deposit
4. Tengin deposit
44. Dashkesan deposit
76. Shushin deposit
65. Gulabli deposit

SAND AND GRAVEL
70. Bagramtapin
101. Lenkoran deposit
16. Mingechaur deposit
61. Boglypain occurrence
58. Khovatayoccurrence
54. Adjaris occurrence
62. Dzhamard occurrence
56. Leusky occurrence

ASBESTOS
71. Ipyak occurrence
52. Geidara occurrence

LIMESTONE AND CLAYS
42. Karadang deposit
11. Dash-Salakhlin deposit
14. Upper Oksuzli deposit
63. Chobandag deposit
13. Aidag deposit
72. Shushikend deposit

TRASS, VOLCANICASH, PUMICE
8. Kaimakhli deposit

GYPSUM
47. Upper Agdjakend deposit
48. Monashid deposit
50. Dostagir deposit
96. Shakhtakhtin deposit
97. Azazin deposit

CALCIUM CARBONATE
21. Kirovabad deposit
51. Mardakert deposit
12. Kazakh occurrence
22. Khailar occurrence

DIMENSTION AND FACING STONE
33. Guzdek deposit
40. Karadag deposit
82. Dovlyaterlin deposit
6. Dashsalakhlin deposit
64. Shakhbulag deposit

TRAVERTINE
95. Shakhtakhtin deposit
92. Buzgov deposit

PERLITE AND OBCIDIAN
67. Kechaldag deposit
66. Deve-gezu small deposit (obcidian)

GLASS SAND AND QUARTZ FOR GLASS INDUSTRY
49. Adjavelin deposit
3. Cuba deposit
24. Khyrdalan deposit
23. Geokmalin deposit
26. Kirmakin deposit
25. Stepan Rasin deposit

OPTICAL MINERALS
78. Martunin occurrence
75. Minishend (Archinprak) Occurrence
77. Ningin occurrence
69. Agkend (Siptakshen) Occurrence
79. Aranzamin occurrence
84. Tsakur deposit
80. Bagyin-Bashin area
81. Eoku area

CRYSTALLINE QUARTZ
1. Khavanchai, Komsomolsk Group of occurrences

AGATE
36. Adjikend group of deposits
87. Eivazlin deposit
86. Gurdzhulu occurrence
83. Gara-kishlak occurrence

Mineral commodities	Deposits under exploitation	Mineral occurrences
Pyrite	Δ	Δ
Rock salt	▽	▽
Dolomite	⊞	⊞
Phosphorite	▼	▼
Bentonite	⊠	⊠
Flux limestone	▢	▢
Kaolin and refractory clays	⊞	▤
Seconday quartzlites	◊	◊
Pyrrophillite	▲	▲
Andalusite	△	△
Serpentine	◇	◇
Asbestos	◊	◊
Building materials and expanded clays	⊟	▤
Trass, volcanic ash, pumice	⊟	▤
Gypsum	⊡	⊡
Calcium Carbonate	▲	▲
Dimension and facing stones	⊟	▭
Travertine	▽	▽
Tuff-sandstones	◊	◊
Tuff	◊	◊
Marbled limestone	⊞	⊞
Gravel, sand	▣	▣
Perlite and obcidian	◇	◇
Ballasts	△	△
Craft and semi-precious stones (agante)	◆	◇
Optical minerals	⊠	⊠
Crystalline quartz	◤	◤
Glass sand and quartz for glass industry	⊠	⊠

Compiled by: Bairamov A.A., Gadzhiev T.G., Agakishibekova R.R. and Nagiev A.N.

Figure 37. Distribution of non-metallic mineral deposits and occurrences in Azerbaijan

1. Chemical raw materials and salts

The deposits of chemical raw materials group incorporate sulfuric pyrite, rock salt, dolomites, phosphorites and barite .

(a)   Sulfuric pyrite

Sulfuric pyrite is contained in all ore widespread formations of the Lesser and Greater Caucasus of Azerbaijan. The deposits of sulfur-pyrite, polymetallic and copper-polymetallic ores of pyrite formation have an economic value. The deposits where sulfuric pyrite is the constituent of complex ores have been described in the section "Metallic minerals" above. All known large sulfuric pyrite deposits are concentrated within the Lesser Caucasus and confined to positive structures. These deposits are characterized by similar conditions of formation being confined to a series of quartz plagioporphyres of the Upper Bajocian age. Accumulations of sulfuric-pyrite ores of this series are linked with subvolcanic facies of the Upper Bajocian volcanism being represented by plagiogranite-porphyres.

The ore-enclosing quartzose plagioporphyres and their subvolcanic facies are distinguished by a high intensity of hydrothermal-metasomatic changes which have led to a formation of secondary quarzites. The formation of sulphur-pyrite deposits has occurred simultaneously with post-magmatic hydrothermal-metasomatic processes. The largest accumulation of sulfur-pyrite ores in Azerbaijan belongs to the Chiragideresi-Toganali group of deposits. The Chiragideresi, Chiragideresi-Toganali and Toganali deposits and some occurrences are closely connected with each others owing to similar geologic and structural positions, chemical and mineral composition. The deposits differ from each other by morpholopy of ore bodies and textural types of ores. The deposits are hosted by volcanogenic-sedimentary rocks of the Middle Jurassic represented by quartzose plagioporphyres and being overlaid by the Cretaceous volcanogenic and volcanogenic-sedimentary formations. The deposits of sulphuric pyrite ores are confined exclusively to quartzose plagioporphyres.

The Chiragideresi deposit

Sulfuric pyrite ores of this deposit with a high sulfur content are enclosed in stockworks of complex irregular shape and are widespread within the deposit. The contours of ore bodies are easily distinguished by a sharp decrease of a sulfur content. Other morphologic types of mineralization are nests and lenses. Out of seven ore stockworks known within the deposit, four ore stockworks have been mined out during the periods from 1905 to 1918 and intermittedly from 1923 to 1968.

The Toganali deposit

Ore bodies of the Toganali deposit are localized in the upper part of quartzose plagioporphyres series near a contact with overlapping rocks of volcanogenic series. Mineralization of high grades and finely-disseminated and impregnated types is concentrated in the upper sections of the quartzose plagioporphyres series and decreases with a depth. Small nests of massive pyrite mineralization are observed in some places.

The Chiragideresi-Toganali deposit

Ore bodies of the Chiragideresi-Toganali deposit represent a transition type of mineralization from impregnated ores of the Toganali deposit to massive ores of the Chiragideresi deposit forming stratobround a lens-shaped deposits of 120-300 x 100-400 metres size. Sulphide mineralization in the above three deposits is basically represented by pyrite, with an exception of the Chiragideresi deposit wherein a presence of copper-zinc ores (chalcopyrite, sphalerite, tetrahedrite) has been observed. Marcasite, magnetite, ilmenite, hematite and galenite are found sporadically. Massive and brecciated textures are typical for continuous ores and vein and impregnated textural types for discontinued mineralization with lower grades.

Besides, the above mentioned deposits, the Slavyan, Gandzazar and Gyulyatag sulfuric pyrite occurrences are known to exist in the Agdara district of the Lesser Ccucasus. Mineralization is represented by vein-impregnated types with rare veins and lenses. The grade of sulfur varies from 15 to 18 per cent reaching 30 per cent in areas of continuous mineralization. A widespread distribution of ore-bearing quartzose plagioporphyres on the territory of Azerbaijan suggest high prospects for discovering of new deposits of sulfuric pyrite ores.

(b)   Rock salt

All known deposits of rock salt in Azerbaijan are located on the territory of Nakhchivan Autonomous Republic in the south-eastern part of the known Miocene salt-bearing basin of 300 kilometres long and from 15 to 20 kilometres wide. The major deposits of this basin are the Nekhram, Pusiyan and Nakhchivan. Salt-bearing formations are traced by a narrow strip along the Nakhchivan trough westward from the Alindjachay river up to the border with Armenia. Stratigraphically, salt-bearing formations are hosted by rock series of the Upper Oligocene-Miocene. The Nekhram and Pusiyan deposits of rock salt of economic importance are confined to a basement of the Karagan suite which conformably overlies rocks of the Tarkhan-Chokrak suite being represented by alternation of rocks of sandy-clayey and calcerous-marly facies.

The distinguishing feature of the latter suite is the appearance of interbeds and lenses of gypsum in its upper part. During the Karagan time, a process of salt accumulation has reached a halite stage, but turned to be unfinished due to a slow subsidence of the basin's bottom, its contraction, shoaling and desalination. In the late stage of the Middle Sarmatian of the Upper Miocene, the role of hydrochemical sediments is gradually increased reaching a halite stage in the Nakhchivan deposit at the end of the Middle Sarmatian. The Nakhchivan deposit of rock salt is structurally confined to flexures of the north-eastern direction, which originated in areas of transformal troughs of the basement with a follow up accumulation of halogenous deposits of a great thickness. The description of known salt deposits of the Nakhchivan Autonomous Republic is provided below.

The Nekhram deposit

The Nekhram deposit is located in the south-east of the Nakhchivan depression at a distance of 10-12 kilometres from Nakhchivan city. The lower section of the rock salt-bearing formation contains greenish-grey fine-bedded clays which transform on the extent into greenish-grey sandstones with inclusions of anhydrite and rare crystals of rock salt of 12-13 metres thick. The thickness of the medium rock salt section of the deposit is being increased from the south-east to the north-west of the deposit from 44.5 to 85.8 metres. The rock salt section of the Nekhram deposit of 13.5 square kilometres size is overlain by the section of gypsum and anhydrite. The thickness of all above section including the rock salt beds is decreasing towards the central part of the deposit. The rock salt section contains admixtures of terrigenous material as small-dotted inclusions and interbeds of anhydrite.

The average chemical composition of salt is 91.61 per cent of $NaCl$, 0.16 per cent of $CaCl_2$, 0.13 per cent of $MgCl_2$, 2.87 per cent of $CaSO_4$, 4.78 per cent of undissolved sediments, and 0.28 per cent of gygroscopic moisture. According to the content of sodium chloride, salts of the deposit don't meet the requirements of the State's standards for table salt. The content of magnesium is within these standards. The Nekhram salt has a delicious taste due to a low content of magnesian salts. The calcium content is close to standards for the second grade of salts. An increased content of undissolved sediments deterriorates salt quality and its usage in a natural form. The proved reserves of the Nekhram rock salt deposit according to $B + C_1$ category were approved by the State Commission on Reserves of the former Soviet Union in 1972. There are good prospects for increasing the reserves. The deposit has not been exploited so far.

The Pusiyan deposit

The Pusiyan deposit was discovered in 1955 near the Pusiyan village of the Sadarak district of the Nakhchivan Autonomous Republic. By external appearance and chemical composition, rock salts of the Pusiyan deposit are similar to those of the Nekhram deposit. The deposit has not been explored in detail, however, due to the equal thickness of rock salt section, the reserves of the Pusiyan deposit are likely of the same order with those of the above Nekhram deposit.

The Nakhchivan deposit

The deposit is located 12 kilometres to the north-west from Nakhchivan city in the Upper Cretaceous and Quaternary formations. The Upper Cretaceous formation is represented by sandstones and sands with interbeds of limestones, marls, aleurolites and volcanic ashes. The Quaternary sediments are represented by a cover of shingles and conglomerates of 70 metres thick. Out of five seams of rock salt that have been distinguished within the deposit, the only two upper seams have the industrial importance.

Chemical composition of rock salt of the upper stratum is as follows: NaCl is from 95.24 to 95.79 per cent, $MgCl_2$ is 0.04 per cent, $CaCl_2$ is 0.001 per cent, Na_2SO_4 is from 0.30 to 0.31 per cent, $MgSO_4$ is 0.21 per cent, $CaSO_4$ from 2.01 to 2.34 per cent and undissolved sediments from 3.23 to 4.01 per cent. The chemical composition of salt of the Nakhchivan deposit is almost similar to that of the Nekhram deposit with a presence of sodium sulfate indicating lesser degree of brine metamorphism in the Nakhchivan rock slat deposition in comparison with the Nekhram deposit.

The main deficiency of the Nakhchivan salt is considerable admixtures of terrigenous material and calcium sulfate. The density of salts is 2.13 grams/cubic centimetres. The deposit is being developed by columnar mining since 1928. The produced salt is used mainly for food industry. The mining losses are reaching 70 per cent due to unusable chips during the extraction of lump salt. The proved reserves were estimated according to A + B + C_1 reserve categories in 1964. Due to economic crisis, the salt production at the deposit has been slow down.

Besides the rock salt, there are known to exist small deposits of natural salt brines in the Absheron peninsula of Azerbaijan. A salt crust from 5 to 10 centimetres thick occupies the area from 0.25 to 0.3 square kilometres in the Masazir lake, 16 kilometres to the south from Baku. The annual salt production for domestic needs is from 3,000 to 5,000 tons. In the Beyukshor lake, 10 kilometres to the north-east from Baku, the thickness of a salt layer is from 6 to 10 centimetres. In the lakeside part of the deposit, there are two/three salt layers of 5-7 centimetres thick each. The size of the salt crust area is 0.5 square kilometres. Annual salt production is from 10,000 to 15,000 tons. These lakes also contain a terapeodic muds used for medical treatment.

(c)   Dolomites

Large deposits of dolomites of industrial importance occur in carbonaceous rocks of the Lower Mesozoic, which construct the north-eastern limb of the Sharur-Djulfa anticlinorium of the Aras tectono-magmatic zone.

The Nekhram deposit

The Nekhram deposit in the Nakhchivan Autonomous Republic is confined to the upper group of the Triassic system composed of dolomites. The deposit is located near the Nekhram railway station where dolomites extend along the left bank of the Aras river for five kilometres forming the hills and cliffs from 100 to 500 metres above river level. The deposit has been originally explored for refractory raw materials. Laboratory studies of dolomites had proved their application as the first class of refractories. Chemical composition of dolomites is as follows: MgO from 19.95 to 20.95 per cent, CaO from 28.5 to 29.6 per cent, Al_2O_3 from 0.91 to 1.12 per cent, SiO_2 from 2.14 to 2.9 per cent, Fe_2O_3 from 0.5 to 1.73 per cent, $CaCO_3$ is 54.08 per cent and $MgCO_3$ is

43.06 per cent. Technological studies have not been carried out. Proved reserves of dolomites for refractory purposes have been evaluated on B + C₁ category of reserves.

The Nekhram deposit has been also explored for highly durable rock aggregates for road construction. The proved reserves of dolomites as rock aggregates were evaluated according to A + C₁ reserve categories. The chemical composition of dolomites within explored reserves meets the requirements of the State's standards for production of calcium soda. A usage of dolomites in soda production has good prospects for obtaining of associated magnesium oxide and periclase. Dolomites of the Nekhram deposit have been also studied by metallothermic technology as raw materials for metallic magnesium. The technology enabled to extract 91-92 per cent of magnesium with a purity of 99.98 per cent. Current exploration works on reserve evaluation of dolomites are being carried out in the Gobustan dolomite occurrence.

(d)   *Phosphorites*

Despite the absence of large deposits of phosphorites on the territory of Azerbaijan, an increased phosphorization has been identified in terrigenous-carbonaceous formations of the Middle and Upper Devonian in the Nakhchivan Autonomous Republic, in the Upper Cretaceous formations in the area of the south-eastern submersion of the Greater Caucasus and in the Maikop suite of the Shdmakha-Gobustan area. A weak phosphorization was been observed in the Middle Jurassic sandstones and the Upper Cretaceous conglomertes in the southern slope of the Greater Caucasus. Detailed exploration on the territory of the Nakhchivan Autonomous Republic has identified a presence of phosphorites in a cross-section of the Famennian and Frasnian stages of the Upper Devonian in the East Arpachay river basin. The sequence is represented by alternation of clayey shales, limestones, quartzites and sandstones. The interbeds of phosphorites are confined to beds of clayey shales with a variable thickness from 5 to 40 metres.

Five neighboring areas of phosphorite-bearing rocks have been distinguished within the Arpachay river basin. Phosphorite-bearing seams strike in concordance with enclosing series of rocks in the north-western direction at the angle of 320°-340° dipping to the south-west with the angle from 25°-45°. In some areas, the number of phosphorite-bearing beds varies from 3 to 17 with a thickness from 0.2 to 0.7 metres each. Three natural types of phosphorites, namely, the dominant oolitic, nodules, and phosphoritized host rocks were distinguished within this area. The content of P_2O_5 varies in wide ranges for different strata from 1.17 to 15.75 per cent. The content of P_2O_5 in the most representative Geranigalasi occurrence varies from 3 to 8 per cent in eight phosphozite-bearing intervals, from 5 to 8 per cent in three intervals of the Gumushlug occurrence and 15.75 per cent in the fourth seam of the Aivazan occurrence.

Phosphorites are represented by homogeneous sediments which were formed in a shallow sea basin of a normal salinity on considerable distance from a coastal line. Concentration of phosphoritic grains in sediments has occurred as a result of benthonic intervals. A deposition of phosphoritic beds is confined to a replacement of carbonaceous facies by siliceous rocks in connection with pulsated vibrations of a basin's bottom on background of stable geoanticlinal regime. Besides the above Upper Devonian phosphorite-bearing occurrences, the Middle Devonian, Upper Carboniferous and Permian phosphorite-bearing formations are potential targets for further exploration of phosphates.

(e)   *Barite*

Around twenty barite deposits and occurrences that have been found on the Azerbaijan territory are represented by a vein type and often confined to marginal parts of anticlinoria in volcanogenic formations of the Middle Jurassic. The Chovdar, Gushchu, Zaglik, Bayan and other barite deposits are located within the Shamkhor anticlinorium. The Chaikend, Azad, Bashkishlak and other deposits are confined to the Gey-gel uplift and the Tonashen barite deposit was found within the Agdam anticlinorium.

A distribution of barite mineralization is controlled by relatively large faults and adjacent fractured zones, originated in archy zones of anticlines and in axial planes of folds. These fractured and compression zones of 5-6 metres thick are often accompanied by brecciation and intensive hydrothermal alteration pronounced by silicification, kaolinizition, sericitization and chloritization. Typical morphological types of barite mineralization are veins and fissure-fillings. A total number of barite-bearing veins within the barite deposits of Azerbaijan varies from ten to twenty, except the Chovdar and Bashkishlak deposits where the number of veins varies from 30 to 45. The veins of mainly north-western direction are normally steeply dipping with variable angles from 40° to 85°. A thickness of veins varies normally from 0.15 to 2.0 metres with an increased thickness in swellings of the Chovdar deposit up to 6 metres. A general length of veins varies from 200 to 500 metres with an exceptional length of some veins at the Chovdar exposit from 1,000 to 1,500 metres.

A specific feature of barite-bearing veins at the Chovdar, Bayan and some other deposits is their clear morphology stipulated by an alternation of barite veins with barren intervals. Hydrothermal alterations of host rocks along bartie-bearing fractures are represented by quarzitization, calcitization, epidodization, sericitizatrion and chloritization. Textural varieties include foliated, latticed and cellular types of barite in upper sections of ore veins and crypto-crystalline and dense varieties in the lower sections. Well-formed crystals of barite are rare. Barite is the major ore mineral and rarely-associated minerals are quartz, calcite, fluorite and fine-disseminated galenite. Within the Chovdar, Bashkishlak and Bayan deposits, the concentration of galenite increases noticeably in the lower sections of barite-bearing veins. Minor pyrite, chalcopyrite, tennantite-tetraedrite, and sphalerites are observed in paragenesis with galenite.

A vertical zonation in all barite deposits is being traced by a dominant barite mineralization in the upper parts of veins through gradual transition to a lead-barite mineralization in the middle part to a completely polymetallic mineralization in the bottom sections of veins. Downward, barite is gradually replaced by quartz and, partially, by calcite and in lower sections by noticeable fluorite in association with polymetallic mineralization. The content of $BaSO_4$ varies from 70 to 95 per cent, density from 3.7 to 4.5 gram/cubic centimetres, CaO from 5 to 10 per cent, SiO_2 up to 10 per cent, Fe_2O_3 from 1 to 2 per cent.

Proved reserves at the Chovdar and Bashkishlak barite deposits have been evaluated by detailed mineral exploration according to $A + B + C_1$ reserve categories. These deposits have been exploited until 1955. Despite long-standing ongoing mineral exploration programmes for barite mineralization, no major deposits of industrial importance were found so far. The barite mineralization, however, was studied mainly to a depth from 40 to 50 metres and down to 200 metres in separate sections. A close paragenetic association of barite with lead, zinc and copper mineralization suggests a common initial source of barite and sulphide mineralization and a possibility to find concentrations of lead, zinc and copper in deeper sections.

(f)   Zeolites

Zeolites are widely used in industry as sorbents, molecular sieves, catalysts for drying and refining of gas, extraction of valuable admixtures, filters of natural water and other purposes. Among natural zeolites, the most valuable industrial varieties are highly siliceous clinoptilolites, mordenites, erionites and chabasites. These minerals of zeolite group are widespread in Azerbaijan in volcanogenic-pyroclastic and sedimentary rocks of the Upper Cretaceous and Tertiary age. Fine-grained vitrified tuffs of acid composition which are subjected easily to replacement by zeolites were found in the north-western part of Azerbaijan in the Upper Cretaceous volcanogenic-carbonaceous formations of the Qazakh and Agdjakend troughs and in the Shamkhr uplift. A composition and structure of these formations in variable. The presence of fine rudaceous tuffs and tuffites of liparites and lioparite-dacites in the Qazakh trough with alternating limestones suggests good prospects for zeolite raw material in these geologic structures.

The Aidag zeolite deposit

The deposit has been found seven kilometres to the north-west from Tauz town near the Baku-Tbilisi railway in carbonaceous-tuffogenic rocks of the Campanian stage of the Upper Cretaceous. The zeolite-bearing strata is represented by massive fine-grained heat tuffs of light, light-cream and light-green color, which has been raced over a distance of 2,000 metres with a variable thickness from 10 to 80 metres with a dipping angle from 15° to 40°. The main minerals are clinoptilonite, quartz and calcite with associated biotite and chlorite. The detailed mineral exploration has contoured two beds of zeolite-bearing tuffs with proven reserves of 10 million tons.

The average content of clinoptilolite is 30.4 per cent in the upper layer and 63.3 per cent in the lower bed. The central part of the deposit shows a high content of clinoptilolite from 60 to 99 per cent. The average chemical composition of the productive strata is 60 per cent of SiO_2, 1.24 per cent of MgO, 11.92 per cent of Al_2O_3, 2.12 per cent of K_2O, 1.4 per cent of Fe_2O_3 and 5.77 per cent of CaO.

A lead content varies from 0.001 to 0.01 per cent. High effective industrial applications of natural zeolites of the Aidag deposit had been studied and proved in laboratory and experimental/industrial conditions. These zeolites are used for: as molecular sieves (desiccant in double-glazing; air-braking systems in trucks; drying natural gas). Ion-exchange properties depend on the fact that certain loosely bonded ions can be exchanged for other ions relatively easily cleaning radioactive, sewage, agricultural waste; detergent builder; aquaculture; pet litter; fertilizer and soil amendment; animal feed supplement. Zeolite's affinity for water allows it to adsorb and de-adsorb water pet litter; carriers for herbicides, fungicides, and pesticides. The large surface pores and interior cavities of zeolites allow it to be used as a catalyst or a catalyst carrier petroleum cracking (fluid cracking catalyst or FCC); isomerization, hydrogenation and dehydrogenation, methanation, and dehydration. Adsorption properties are used for purification, bulk separation, and drying (pet litter, desiccant; odor control). Zeolites are inert and white or near white and can be used as a filler in the paper industry and as a mild abrasive in toothpaste.

There are good prospects for increased reserves of zeolite-bearing heated tuffs at the Aidag deposit and the Upper Cretaceous trass bluish tuffs within the Koroglu deposit in the Qazakh district. A chain of zeolite occurrences similar to the Aidag deposit was traced on the north-eastern slope of the Lesser Caucasus. The presence of large reserves of analcimite enhances the value of these occurrences for zeolite production. Besides the Upper Cretaceous formations, the Tertiary formations of the Talysh mountain area contain zeolites in volcanogenic-sedimentary formations of the Paleogene-Neogene age. Beds of heated tuffs, tuffites and trasses among the Pliocene rocks are of special interest for zeolites. Prospects for zeolites are also associated with the Paleogene volcanogenic-sedimentary rocks in the Nakhchivan fold area and in the Kelbadjar superimposed trough.

(g) *Mineral pigments*

Geologic prospecting for mineral pigments on the territory of Azerbaijan has succeeded by discovering the large Danaeri and Chovdar deposits in the Dashkesan district and the Mirzik deposit in the Khanlar district. The deposits are hosted by hydrothermally-altered rocks of volcanogenic series of the Middle Jurassic age. Pigments are related to a group of ferrum-oxide pigments corresponding to clayey ochre.

The Chovdar deposit

The deposit is located at a distance of 19-20 kilometres to the south-west from the Ganja railway station spartially coinciding with the Chovdar barite deposit. Technological properties of mineral ochres, occurring in stratified layer from 4 to 8 metres thick, comply with the State's standards. The remaining reserves of ochers grading 32 per cent of Fe_2O_3 are 38,000 tons.

The Mirzik deposit

The deposit is located on the southern end of Mirzik village of the Khanlar district. The deposit of clayey ochre of golded colour is confined to a large tectonic fault of the north-western direction and gentle dip from 10° to 20°. A faults zone is filled with limonitized epidote-chlorite disintegrated rocks of lemon-golded-yellow colour. Enclosing rocks as a result of supergenous processes have been completely reworked and transformed into dispersial ochre mass. Technological tests of paints made from the above pigments have showed good gentle coverage and susceptibility of vanish. The remaining reserves of the deposit are 8,000 tons of ochre with a content of Fe_2O_3 from 40 to 49 per cent. The detailed mineral exploration for increasing the reserves has identified the new Danaeri and Sariyal deposits of orches with a variable Fe_2O_3 content at the Danaeri deposit from 35 to 50 per cent. Other target for development of mineral orches are pigments of secondary origin known in the Jabrail district near Sumgayit city.

The Dashveisal occurrence

The occurrence is located 2.5 kilometres to the north-west from the Jabrail district centre in delluvial-elluvial sediments. A pigment-bearing layer from 0.5 to 3 metres thick consists of detrital material with a clayey fraction of 48.57 per cent. The minerals are hydromicas, quartz, kaolinites, aportite, hematite, limonite and calcite. The chemical composition is 46.88 per cent of SiO_2, 19.62 per cent of Al_2O_3, 9.38 per cent of Fe_2O_3, 8.44 per cent of CaO, 4.13 per cent of MgO, and 1.23 per cent of SO_3. Pigments of this occurrence are clayey ochre which is a raw material for dark-red paints of covering ability 20.4 g/m^2 and oil capacity of 27.18 per cent. A light-pink cement resistable to atmospheric erosion was obtained by pigments addition to white clinker in quantity from 2.5 to 10 per cent. Proved reserves are estimated at 40,000 tons.

The Sumgayit occurrence

The occurrence is located on the right slope of the Sumgayit river valley, 20 kilometres to the north-west from the Khirdalan town being represented by red clays of the Tertiary age. The seam of clays with a thickness of 8 metres is traced over a distance from 2.5 to 3 kilometres. Clays are compact, of a red colour with various shades; a clayey fraction is 98 per cent. Chemical composition is 54.88 per cent of SiO_2, 18.52 per cent of Al_2O_3, 7.78 per cent of Fe_2O_3, 3.13 per cent of MgO, 0.81 per cent of CaO and 1.17 per cent of SO_3. Covering ability is 2.25 g/m^2 and oil capacity is 25.3 per cent. Pigments of this occurrence are related to clayey red types suitable for production of coloured cement and linoleum. Proved reserves are estimated at 1 million tons. Other prospective areas of Azerbaijan for mineral pigments of various types, colours and shades are coloured varieties of the Tertiary clays of the Shamakah-Gobustan foothill zone, hematites of the Alabashli area in the Shamkhor district and limonitized clays of the Nakhchivan Autonomous Republic.

2. Semi-precious and ornamental stones

The semi-precious stones that are known on the territory of Azerbaijan are amethysts, garnets and epidotes in skarns of the Dashkesan iron ore deposit, rock crystals in the Alpine veins of the Greater Caucasus, turmaline in exo-contact of porphyry granites of the Atabek-Slavyan intrusive massif and chalcedone, agate and heliotrope in rocks of volcanogenic series of the Santonian suite. The craft stones are widespread and include agate, jasper, serpinitine, vesuvian, agalmatiolite, obsidiane, marble onix, aleuritic onix, listvenites, gypsum, alabastr, marble, some rocks of porphyry structure and transparent varieties of copal. A turquoise mineralization was found in altered secondary quarzites in a form of nests, stringers and almonds within the oxidation zone of porphyry copper deposits in the Gedabek region.

(a)   *Heliotrope and chalcedone*

Accumulations of heliotrone, jasper and chalcedone are closely associated with agate deposits of the Todan-Adjikend group confined to the highly fractured Upper Cretaceous cover of andesite porphyrites of 70 metres thick. Accumulations of heliotrope, jasper and agate form almonds and geodes from 1 to 15 centimetres size unevenly distributed in rock mass, as well as vein accumulations, fissure-fillings and stringers of irregular shape. The average content of heliotrope is 137.6 g/m^3 on rock mass, and up to 160 g/m^3 in separate areas. The chalcedone content in the same areas is from 20 to 200 g/m^3.

(b)   *Iridescent obsidiane*

Iridescent obsidiane was found in obsidiane-bearing strata of the Kechaldag deposit of perlites and obsidianes located in the Kelbadjar district. Distribution patterns are very complex. Major varieties are nearly black, dark grey, grey and silvery of banded and spotted texture or a combination of two or three of the above varieties. Silver-grey or mother-of-pearl obsidian was observed in black obsidians in some areas. Iridescence is observed in oblique cuts and maximal irisdescence in cuts parallel to banding. The iridescence colour is greenish-grey, silvery-light blue, violet and rare dark-blue of various intensity. The iridescent obsidians of the Kechaldag deposit have a high decorative quality. The possible reserves are estimated at 20,000 cubic metres and there are good prospects to find new deposits in the areas of recent young volcanism development in the Kelbadjar and Lachin districts.

(c)   *Agate*

Agate of practical interest was found in the Khanlar, Agdjakend and Qazakh districts in the north-eastern foothills of the Lesser Caucasus and in the Gubadli district of the Bazarchay river basin. The Khanlar-Qazakh agate occurrences are hosted by rocks of volcanogenic series of the Santonian age within the Agdjakend and Qazakh troughs. The enclosing almond-shaped andesite porphyrites form covers with a variable thickness from 20 to 100 metres in the middle part of the Lower Santonian section or in the upper part of the Santonian suite. Agates are met as secretions, geodes, almonds, stringers and lenses. Agate bodies are subdivided into three types: (a) almond-shaped in gaseous cavities; (b) nests and geodes in cavities of solution and (c) veins in fracture-fillings. The vein type of agates has no practical importance because of its limited thickness. The size of almonds and geodes vary within from several millimetres to 20 centimetres, sometimes reaching a range of 30-40 centimetres. The weight varies from 0.2 to 8 kilograms. By texture, agates are sub-divided into (a) jewelry type including the Uruguay type with flat parallel layers and (b) technical-banded chalcedony of evenly-distributed colour.

The Adjikend agate deposit

The deposit is located in the Khanlar district in andesite porphyrites of the Santonian age. The exploration by drilling and mining openings have identified three prospective agate-bearing areas. The content of agate is from 110 to 148 g/t. Proven reserves are 286.8 tons including 65.87 tons of jewelry agate.

The Bazarchay agate-bearing field

The field is located within the Gochaz syncline and the north-eastern limb of the Gafan anticlinorium in the watershed of the Bazarchay and Hakera rivers. The agate accumulations of various sizes are confined to tarry-black andesite porphyrites and tuff-breccias. Six agate-bearing areas of the agate field were distinguished and delineated within the *Eivazli* agate deposit. These areas were studied up to a 10 metres depth. By quality, agates of the Eivazli deposit correspond to the best grades of agates from the above Adjikend deposit. The Khanlar-Qazakh agate occurrences and the Bazarchay agate-bearing field are the typical products of the hydrothermal formations of low temperature being originated on small depths during the post-volcanic hydrothermal autometamorphism.

(d) Marbled onyx

Marbled onyx represents a dense, fine-grained variety of aragonite which is easily subjected to processing and polishing. Major colours of pale tones are milky-white, greenish, yellowish, bluish, brownish and others. Onyxes of practical interest originated from travertines were found in the areas of young volcanism development within the Kelbadjar district and in the Nakhchivan Autonomous Republic.

In the Nakhchivan Autonomous Republic, travertines were found in the area of the Sirab group of mineral springs being confined to a fault of the north-western extension. In travertines, onyxes form interbeds from 15 to 25 centimetres thick and also stringers from 5 to 20 centimetres thick. The inferred reserves have been estimated within 50 tons. Onyx is of high decorative quality. The colour is lemon-yellowish to pale-greenish.

In the Kelbadjar district, the occurrence of marbled onyx is confined to travertines forming thick deposits in the area of mineral springs on the left bank of the Tutkhun river. Onyx-bearing interbeds are distributed in the area of 0.2 km^2. Onyx output varies from 720 to 1,630 g/m^3. The share of first grade onyx is from 10 to 12 per cent. The colours are white and yellow of very beautiful banded varieties. The recent discovery of the occurrence of marble onyx was made in travertines within the southern slopes of the Greater Caucasus. The thickness of onyx-bearing seam is from 0.3 to 0.6 metres. The colour is pale-yellow and brownish-yellow with a good polishing ability.

(e) Copal

Intensive mineral exploration programme for copal-bearing deposits has been carried out in 1950s for usage in the vanish-paint industry. At present, this problem is not actual anymore owing to usage of artificial tars. Large concretions of copal up to 30 centimetres thick of semi-transparent and transparent varieties of amber, red, yellow and orange colours are used, however, in the jewelry industry. Copal-bearing seams are hosted by the Cenomanian sandy-clayey suites of the Upper Cretaceous overlying transgressively the Lower Cretaceous or Upper Jurassic formations in the Somkhit-Agdam and Geychay-Garabag tectonic zones. Proved reserves of copal-bearing rocks at the Yukhari-Agdjakend deposit of copal in the Geranboi district are over 3.0 million cubic metres with an average content of copal of 200 g/m^3. The neighboring Gyulistan copal deposit has similar estimated reserves. The copal-bearing suite of clayey sandstones of up to 25 metres thick was found near the Gorchu village in the Lachyn district. A size of inclusions of transparent copal of amber-yellow colour reaches 10 centimetres.

(f) Jade

Jade is observed in a form of veins and stringers. Jades have good decorative qualities and polishing ability. The colours are milky-white, light-blue, greenish-dark blue, light-green and light pink. Output of a good quality jade is from 10 to 20 per cent.

(g) Nephrite

Nephrites of a high decorative quality and polishing capacity are met as veins, lenses and lenses-veins in contact zones of serpentinites with limestones. The colours are dark-green and grass-green. The output of a good quality nephrite is from 5 to 60 per cent.

(h)   Listvenites (magnesite schists)

Listvenites are observed in a form of veins, lenses, lenses/veins and stockworks. Listvenites or magnesite schists have a high decorative quality and polishing capacity. The output of a good quality listvenites is up to 80 per cent.

(i)   Demantoides and topaz

These stones were observed in open fractures and cavities. The stones are of high decorative and jewelry qualities. The colours are grass-green for demantoide and honey-yellow for topazolite.

(j)   Jasper

Jaspers of a high decorative quality and good polishing capacity were met as stratified beds, lenses, nests and concretions. The output of a good quality jasper is from 30 to 50 per cent.

(k)   Crystal quartz

Crystal quartz forms druses consisting of separate crystals with an average size of 3 x 10 centimetres. The output of conditional quartz is from 130 to 550 g/m^3.

(l)   Agate-aleurolite

Agate-aleurolites were met in a form of stratified beds hosting almonds of carbonaceous-tuff-aleurolite composition. The stone has a high decorative quality and polishing ability. The output of conditional stone is 12 kg/m^3. In general, the geologic and metallogenic environment of the territory of Azerbaijan is favourable for industrial accumulations of semi-precious and decorative stones.

3. Ceramic and glass raw materials

(a)   Clays

Clays for ceramics, bricks and roof tiles are widely distributed in the territory of Azerbaijan being confined to continental and, rarely to marine facies of the Recent and Pliocene formations. Continental clayey formations include alluvial, alluvial-deluvial, deluvial and alluvial-proluvial agloporites and homogeneous mud breccias of mud volcanoes. Agloporites are loessy, calcareous and contain large inclusions of various rocks including gypsum and chlorite salts.

Marine clayey deposits of the Lower Absheron stage within the Absheron peninsula are being developed to produce building bricks and keramsite. Homogeneous clays of the Absheron and Pontian stages are developed by the Garadag cement plant to produce drilling muds. The majority of clayey deposits are being worked out on a small scale by local enterprises and artisans. Proven reserves of ceramic clays are over 3 million cubic metres. The proven reserves of 94 deposits of clays for brick-tile production are over 190 million cubic metres.

(b)   Silica sands and quartz for casting

Silica sands of a low quality and limited usage in the glass industry are known to occur among the Neogene deposits of the Gobustan and Absheron peninsula and the Quba district. The deposits of the Gobustan and Quba regions are of the Miocene age, and those of the Absheron peninsula are of the Pliocene age. In the Gobustan, silica sands are confined to the Chokrak suite of a maximal thickness from 450 to 500 metres in the south-western Gobustan containing beds of silica sands with a variable thickness.

The Adjiveli deposit

The Adjiveli deposit of silica sands is located at a distance of 1.5-2.0 kilometres to the south from the Adjiveli village. Silica sands are traced on the northern side of the Adjiveli anticlinorium over a distance of 8 kilometres. The bed of silica sands in the central area of the deposit with a thickness from 35 to 50 metres has been traced over a distance of 3.3 kilometres. Silica sands are grey and yellowish-grey, fine-grained, homogeneous, with rare interbeds and lenses of brown clays. The granulometric composition shows the share of the fractions from 3 to 0.5 mm at 25 per cent and that from 0.25 to 0.05 mm from 60 to 75 per cent of a total mass. Major minerals are quartz (88-92 per cent) and feldspar (3.0-8.5 per cent). A heavy fraction from 6.5 to 2.0 per cent consists of brownish iron ore, magnetite, muscovite, glaukonite, disthene and other minerals. A volume mass of silica sands is 1.62 tons/cubic metre.

Chemical composition of silica sands in percentage is as follows: SiO_2 - 90.22, TiO_2 - 1.0, Al_2O_3 - 1.90, Fe_2O_3 - 2.45, CaO - 1.12, MgO - 0.41, Na_2O - 0.44, K_2O- 0.95; SO_3 - 0.59, and H_2O - 0.70. Technological enrichment studies were conducted in laboratory on two samples with a content of SiO_2 at 89.5 and 94.3 per cent and Fe_2O_3 content at 1.02 and 0.8 per cent. The obtained concentrate from two samples contains 96.08 and 97.26 per cent of SiO_2 and 0.13 and 0.09 per cent of Fe_2O_3 respectively.

The Zeid deposit

The deposit is located in the Quba district at 34 kilometres to the south-west from the district's centre near the Zeid village. Silica sands are represented by three beds of fine-grained sands being separated from each other by thin beds of clays. Chemical composition of silica sands is SiO_2 from 90.4 to 94.8 per cent, Fe_2O_3 from 1.5 to 3.5 per cent and TiO_2 from 0.13 to 0.5 per cent. Technological studies in laboratory and semi-industrial conditions have proved their feasibility for glass production. The inferred reserves were estimated at a range of 10-12 million tons. The deposit is currently undergoing a detailed mineral exploration.

Silica sand deposits of the Absheron group

The Khirdalan, Sulutapa, Gekmali and Kirmaki deposits of the Absheron group are confined to the Upper Kirmaki suite and the "hiatus" suite of the productive series. Sands of these deposits are fine- and medium-grained of grey and yellowish-grey colour. The chemical composition is from 83 to 93 per cent of SiO_2, from 1.5 to 4.5 per cent of Al_2O_3 and from 1 to 3.5 per cent of Fe_2O_3. The proved reserves are 4 million tons. In some regions of Azerbaijan with a high demand for glass containers, other kinds of raw material, such as secondary quarzites were used for glass production owing to absence of glass sands. The prospective areas for glass production from quarzites were identified within the Gumushlug lead-zinc deposit in the Nakhchivan Autonomous Republic. Fine-grained thin-banded quarzites of light-grey colour form beds from 6 to 8 metres thick occurring in limestones of the basement of the Frasnian stage of the Upper Devonian. Secondary quarzites were traced over a distance of 700-800 metres dipping at 40°-45° to the south-west. Chemical composition of secondary quartzite is as follows: (%): $SiO2$ - 90.12, Al_2O_3 - 2.18, TiO - 0.36, Fe_2O_3 - 2.96, CaO - 0.57, MgO - 3.62, SO_3 - 0.05, K_2O - 0.36 and Na_2O - 0.04.

Current exploration programmes are aimed at discovering crystalline and lump quartz suitable for production of glass with specific properties to be used in optical, electro-technical, chemical and other industries. More prospective area for this kind of raw materials in Azerbaijan is the southern slope of the Greater Caucasus, where monomineral quartz veins were found in rocks of the Jurassic sandy-shaley series in the past. The majority of quartz veins tend to confine to sandstones of the Khinalug suite of the Bajocian age. The feasibility study on one sample of quartz from the Khavanachay deposit has proved the suitability of quartz for casting. The colour is milky-white. Chemical composition is 98.57 per cent of SiO_2, 0.58 per cent of CaO and 0.08 per cent of SO_3.

4. Optical raw materials

(a)   Iceland spar

The deposits and occurrences of iceland spar were found within the Somkhit-Agdam tectono-magmatic zone and in the Talysh Mountain. In the Somkhit-Agdam zone, optical calcite is associated with spheroid lava, basaltic mandelstones and the Tithonian limestones. The Mirishen, Ningin, Agkend, Aranzamin, Pirdjaman and Abdul deposits of iceland spar are located within the Garabag region and hosted by the Santonian volcanogenic formations. The morphogenetic types are interspheroid pockets and nests, intraspheroid geodes, interbed pockets and tectonic pockets.

The most widespread type is interspheroid pockets and nests filled mainly by coarse-grained milky-white calcite. Crystals of calcite which are usually turbid, cracked and fractured were found in the central parts of pockets and nests. Sizes of pockets and nests vary from 5 x 12 to 50 x 60 centimetres. Optical calcite is accompanied by small crystals of analcime natrolite, geilandite, desmine and mordenite. Analcime and mordenite are met as inclusions in crystals of spar. Intraspheroid geodes are subdivided into multiple and single-chambered geodes. The sizes of multiple chambered geodes in mandelstones are from 1.2 x 1 x 1 metres to 2 x 1.65 x 1.5 metres.

Single-chambered closed geodes are located in central parts of spheroid blocks of mandelstones varying in sizes from 15 x 16 x 18 centimetres to 70 x 60 x 100 centimetres. Crystals of iceland spar in single-chambered geodes are framed by large crystals of analcime and by grained and fibrous varieties of milky-white calcite. Crystals of iceland spar in these geodes have a minimum of initial and secondary cracks and inclusions. Interbed pockets are met near contacts of mandelstones with limestones and between xenolites of carbonaceous rocks. Their sizes are 4 x 0.1 x 0.5 metres. The size of crystals of calcite varies along edges from 3 to 20 centimetres. Crystals of iceland spar are oblate and compressed, so clear scalenohedrons were not observed. Tectonic pockets of the ellipsoid shape and 4 x 3 x 2 metres size are filled with large druzes and monocrystals of calcite up to 10 centimetres size on edge. The output of optically-suitable crystals doesn't exceed 1-2 per cent. Iceland spar of this genetic group is associated with hydrothermal activity of basaltic lava. The Tsakur and Sarkishen deposits represent the second genetic group of iceland spars.

The Tsakur deposit

The deposit is located in the Fizuli district in the Tithonian crushed limestones. Crystals of iceland spar of yellowish colour and with a clayey shirt were found in loose clayey mass. Local and dispersed mud inclusions and fractures are observed in crystals. The monorhombohedron crystals of a good quality are often observed among enriched crystals.

The Sarkishen group of occurrences

The Sarkishen group of iceland spar occurrences includes three separate areas. The Bagin-bashi spar-bearing zone is confined to the Tithonian limestones. In the Baku area, the spar-bearing pockets and calcite veins with crystals of iceland spar are tectonically-related. In the Gyadyk area, calcite veins with a thickness from 0.5 to 0.7 metres and from 10 to 20 metres long are confined to sandy limestones. Calcite crystals constructed nests, filled by brown clay. In general, the Tsakur-Sarkishen group of occurrences and the whole area of development of the Tithonian limestones of the Garabag are prospective for discovering new deposits of optic calcite.

(b)   Calcite

The Kosmolyan deposit

The Kosmolyan calcite deposit is located within the Talysh structural and formational zone in andesites, basalts and their tuffs, tuff-breccias, tuff-conglomerates, covers of andesite-basalts, small dolerite and hypoabyssal intrusions of the basic composition of the Kosmolyan and Peshtasar suites of the Eocene age. The variable morphology of crystal-bearing bodies depends mainly on the type and origin of host fractures enclosing veins. The typical feature of calcite-bearing bodies is a presence of numerous cracks and cavities of various geometric forms up to 0.3 metre size. The size of calcite crystals sometimes reach a range of 20-25 centimetres along the edge. Four types of spartization were distinguished within the deposit.

The first nest type includes nests and cavities of irregular geometry, which originated in a space between debris of volcanogenic rocks and spheroid bodies of andesite-basalts. The second geode type is often confined to the upper sections of volcanic cover, and to basalts and andesite-basalts. The third vein type is confined to volcanic rocks of basic composition and includes a monomineral milky-white and grey calcite. The fourth type incorporates crystal-bearing zones of hydrothermally altered rocks. Among crystals of spar, twins of growth and mechanical twins are widely distributed. Laboratory studies had proved crystals of iceland spar to be a very good optical material. The output of optical material is from 20.95 to 167.5 gr/m^3. Current detailed exploration is being carried out in some of the above areas.

(c)   Piezoelectric quartz

Geological mapping and mineral exploration programmes have identified the Komsomol deposit and the Kulunusu, Suvagil, Nourbashi, Agkamal, Magmaldag, Ktekchay and Guton occurrences of piezoelectric quartz all located on the southern slope of the Greater Caucasus of Azerbaijan. Crystal-bearing veins of quartz, and sometimes, of quartz-carbonate composition with a thickness from 1.5 to 5 metres occur mainly in sandstones and, rarely, in clayey shales of the Jurassic age. Lens-shaped veins pinch out rather quickly with a depth. Druzes and monocrystals of transparent, semi-transparent and milky-white rock crystals are met in cavities and bag pockets. The morphogenetic types are intravein or residual cavities, mineralized cracks and fractures and cavities of leaching.

Crystal-bearing cavities in a form of elongated lenses, ellipses and tubs vary in size from 2 x 2, 2 x 2.5, 30 x 40 to 40 x 50 centimetres. The size of crystals varies from 1 x 2 to 6 x 8 centimetres reaching 8 x 13 centimetres. The size of transparent crystals varies from 0.5 to 5 centimetres and the weight is from 4 to 50 grams. The size of semi-transparent varieties of crystals is from 2 to 13 centimetres and the weight is from 6 to 900 grams. The quality of majority of crystals complies with standards, however, sizes are small for piezooptical products. The output of piezooptical quartz is from 18 to 57 per cent. The chemical composition is 98.57 per cent of SiO_2, 0.58 per cent of CaO, 0.08 per cent of SO_3 and 0.1 per cent of H_2O. The content of pigments' admixtures is 0.001 per cent of Mn, 0.006 per cent of Sn, 0.01 per cent of Cu, 0.001-0.003 per cent of Ti, 0.01 per cent of Ni, 0.01 per cent of Fe and 0.03 per cent of cromium. Genetically, crystal-bearing veins are associated with hydrothermal processes.

5. Refractory minerals

(a)   Flux limestones

Flux limestones are widespread in the area of the Dashkesan iron ore deposit.

The Khoshbulag deposit

The Khoshbulag deposit of flux limestones is located at six kilometres southward from Dashkesan city and hosted by a thick series of marbled limestones of the Luzitanian age with steeply-dipping (60° - 80°) dykes of diorite, diabase and, rarely, andesite porphyrites. The average chemical composition of limestones is as follows (%): SiO_2 - 1.7, Al_2O_3 - 0.33, Fe_2O_3 - 0.26, CaO - 53.9, MgO - 0.36, SO_3 - 0.012 and VnO - 0.025. The density varies within a range of 2.65 - 2.85 g/cm^3 with the average density of 2.76 g/cm^3 and humidity of 0.20 per cent. The average durability of limestones by compression in air dry conditions is 740 kgs/cm^2. Limestones were used for pellets' production from iron ore concentrates of the South Dashkesan deposit. Proven reserves of flux limestones are 51.7 million tons. Owing to technological substitution of flux limestones by bentonite clays, the deposit is not exploited.

The Zangelan deposit

The Zangelan deposit of limestones of the Barremian age is located in the Zangelan district. The deposit has been explored for raw materials of soda ash production. Limestones comply with requirements of soda ash production, corresponding to technical conditions of converter limestones. The chemical composition is as follows (%): CaO - 54.6; MgO - 0.4, $SiO_2 + Al_2O_3$ - 1.16, S – 0.024 and P_2O_5 - 0.015. The durability's limit is more than 300 kgs/cm^2. Proven reserves are 129.8 million tons. Limestones of the Zangelan deposit can be used as low phosphorous fluxes for converter production in the ferrous metallurgy. The deposit is not exploited.

(b)   Kaolin and refractory minerals

Raw materials for ceramic production and refractory applications are abundant on the territory of Azerbaijan and include kaolin, refractory clays, secondary quarzites, pyrophillites, andesite, quarzites and serpentinites. Except serpentinites, all the deposits of refractory raw materials are concentrated within the Somkhit-Agdam tectonic zone of the Lesser Caucasus representing products of hydrothermal-metasomatic changes of the Horgskian volcanogenic rocks. The deposits and occurrences of kaolin and fireclays are known within the Shamkhor anticlinorium and the Dashkesan synclinorium. The Chardakhli deposit of kaolin clays and the Chovdar deposit of feldspar were found in the course of mineral exploration.

The Chardakhli deposit

The Chardakhli deposit is located within three kilometres southward from the Chanlibel village of the Shamkhor district. The deposit is represented by a series of steeply-dipping tectonic zones of the north-eastern direction in quartzose plagioporphyres which were transformed into secondary quarzites. The deposit includes six zones of kaolin, fireclays and kaolinized rocks containing from 20 to 40 per cent of kaoline. These zones from 5 to 14 metres thick have been traced from 250 to 800 metres. Mineral exploration up to a 60 metres depth has identified proven reserves of kaolin at 500,000 tons. Besides, there are some prospects in the Gedabek ore region for discovering new deposits of sericite and kaolinite facies of secondary quarzites to be used as a raw material for porcelain and ceramic industry.

The Garamurad kaolin occurrence

The Garamurad occurrence in the Dashkesan region is represented by lenses and veins of pure kaolin and kaolinized zones in secondary quarzites on quartzose plagioporphyres. Prospects are limited.

The Chovdar feldspar deposit

The Chovdar deposit of feldspar is located in the Dashkesan region within 1.5 kilometres northward of the Chovdar village and 13 kilometres from the "Gushch Bridge" railway station. The deposit is composed of ryolites and ryodacites of the Lower Bajocian age which have underwent intensive hydrothermal alteration along the tectonically-crushed and reworked zone from 500 to 700 metres thick and from 1.5 to 2 kilometres long. The identified depth of kaolinites is 60 metres. The thickness of weathering profile is from 3 to 5 metres. Major minerals are quartz, kaolinite, sericite, hydromicas and some carbonates. The chemical composition is as follows (%): SiO_2 - 73.14, Al_2O_3 - 10.09, Fe_2O_3 - 2.21, TiO_2 - 0.29, CaO - 1.72, MgO - 2.31, S - 1.26, SO_3 - 2.28, P_2O_5 - 0.10, FeO - 0.70, Na_2O - 0.63 and K_2O - 1.61. The basic harmful admixtures are FeO_3 and TiO_2. Ferrum is present in hematite and limonite and, at a depth, in the content of sulphides.

Technological scheme of raw material enrichment including floatation and subsequent acid processing of floatation product enabled to obtain 75 per cent of quartz-feldspar product corresponding to the requirements of the Republic's standards. The detailed mineral exploration has proved the reserves of 3.4 million tons of feldspar. Despite favourable mining and technical conditions, the deposit is not exploited.

(c) Bentonite clays

Major deposits of bentonite clays in Azerbaijan were found in the Cretaceous and Paleogene formations. Bentonite clays of the Cretaceous system are mainly confined to volcanogenic-sedimentary formations of the Coniacian-Santonian and partly the Companion stages of the synclinal troughs in the north-eastern foothill of the Lesser Caucasus.

The Khanlar deposit had been exploited since 1956. Mining operations are currently ceased with remaining reserves of 0.42 million tons. The largest Dash-Salakhli deposit of bentonites is located in the Qazakh district within the north-eastern foothills of the Lesser Caucasus. The deposit is composed of volcanogenic-pyroclastic formations of the Santonian stage with dominant lava and subvolcanic formations. Thick beds of bentonite clays are mainly confined to the upper section of the above Santonian formation.

The deposit is subdivided into the northern, central and southern areas being located at a distance of one kilometre from each other. In the central area, the bentonite bed of 66 metres thick was traced over a distance of 900 metres and that in the southern area of 35 metres thick for 1,300 metres. The width of the deposit is from 250 to 380 metres. The deposit outcrops partially on the surface, but the largest part of bentonite interval is overlain by agloporities with debris of tuffs and limestones. The thickness of overburden is from 6 to 20 metres. Bentonite clays are underlied by tuffs, tuffites, tuff-sandstones and tuff-conglomerates. The bentonite bed contains two layers being distinguished by colour and density. Bentonite clays were formed in a cause of hydrothermal reprocessing of tuffs. The basic mineral of production section is montmorillonite (70-85 per cent) with associated calcite, tridimite and rare gypsum. Bentonites are alkaline with a coefficient of alkalinity from 0.42 to 10.24 with an average alkalinity of 2.3. The expending capacity clays in air dry conditions is from 2 to 19 times. Based on the above natural properties, alkaline highly-dispersed bentonites with a high expending capacity and comparatively low-dispersed with sand admixtures and a low expanding capacity of bentonite clays were distinguished within the deposit.

Bentonites of the first type are suitable for production of pellets of iron ore concentrates and for production of clayey solutions of high quality. Bentonites of the second type are used for oil refining, production of keramzite, separation of gasoline fraction of oil and other purposes. Proven reserves of bentonite clays are 107 million tons. The deposit is being exploited since 1974 by the State Enterprise "Metallurgy". The remaining reserves are 99 million tons.

Other potential contributors to a resource base of bentonites in Azerbaijan are the Ali Bayramli and Kaimakhli occurrences in the vicinity of the above Dash-Salakhli deposit, the Upper Agdjakend occurrence in the Shamkhor district and a group of bentonite deposits and occurrences in the Shemakha-Gobustan region in the area of the south-eastern subsidence of the Greater Caucasus. The latter bentonite clays are confined to the lower sections of the Kounian suite of the Eocene. The Paleogene group contains numerous deposits and occurrences of bentonite clays including the Shikhandag group of the Shikhandag, Kyashkuryak and Beilyar deposits. The results of chemical assay of bentonite clays in Azerbaijan are shown in table 4.

Table 4. Chemical composition of bentonite clays in Azerbaijan

Unit: per cent

Name of deposits	SiO_2	Al_2O_3	FeO_3	TiO_2	CaO	MgO	Na_2O	K_2O	Moisture	P.H.
Dash-Salakhli	53.3	14.2	4.23	0.4	9.7	2.62	1.5	1.2	7.1	7.0
Ali-Bairamli	62.5	14.3	2.0	0.3	2.1	2.1	2.2	0.7	-	8.6
Shikhandag group	57.6	16.4	4.8	0.45	2.0	4.1	5.1	1.07	8.34	5.1

The Beilyar bentonite deposit

The Beilyar deposit is located within a distance of 4-5 kilometres southward from the Agdara village of the Shemakha district. Two production bands of intercalating bentonites with bentonite clays and argillites from 15 to 30 metres thick each were noted within the deposit. Bentonites are accounting from 80 to 85 per cent of the total thickness of each band and were traced over a distance of several kilometres. Mineral exploration is being conducted by drilling. The inferred reserves are from 10 to 12 million tons. These reserves of bentonite clays can be substantially increased at the expense of the Shikhandag and Kyashkuryak deposits. A high quantity of bentonites enables their application in medical and perfume industries, production of drilling muds as well as in bleaching of oil and vegetable oils.

(d)   Secondary quarzites

Secondary quarzites represent a product of hydrothermally-metasomatic changes of acid volcanogenic rocks of the Jurassic and Paleogene formations widespread in the most regions of the Lesser Caucasus. The most known secondary quarzites of the Somkhit-Agdam tectonic zone were formed from quartzose plagioporphyres and their tuffs in the areas of active subvolcanic intrusions of the same composition and age.

From a variety of secondary quarzites, an intensively-kaolinized type suitable for fire clay production and substantially quartzose secondary quarzites are prevalent. The occurrences of intensively-kaolinized rocks are known in the Gedabek, Dashkesan, Khanlar, Qazakh and other regions. The Kyurakchay deposit of quartzose plagioporphyres in the Khanlar district has been explored for raw material in production of refractory materials. Quartzose plagioporphyres were met at a cliff slope of the Kyurakchay river being overlain by tuff-sandstones and porphyrites of the Bathonian stage. Chemical composition (in %) is as follows: SiO_2 from 67.57 to 79.54, Al_2O_3 from 12.28 to 18.72, CaO from 1.22 to 1.46 and Fe_2O from 1.58 to 3.25. Proven reserves are 4.0 million tons.

The Poladbulag deposit in the Khanlar district consists of kaolinized quartzose plagioporphyres and their tuffs of 300 metres long and from 70 to 80 metres wide. The average content of Al_2O_3 is 20.6 per cent and the content of Fe_2O_3 is from 0.47 to 1.44 per cent. The inferred reserves are around 2 million tons. The Gizildja, Sarisu and Chovdar deposits belong to a group of secondary quarzites.

The Gizildja deposit is situated near the Gizildja village on the left bank of the Goshgarchay river. Secondary quarzites have a monolith structure. Alunitized varieties are dominant in the lower part of the section. Secondary quarzites are suitable for brick production. The deposit is being developed by open pit mining. Proven reserves were evaluated at 3.4 million tons. The Sarisu deposit of secondary quarzites is located in the Khanlar district. Secondary quarzites are pure and dense. Proved reserves of secondary quarzites are 0.7 million tons. The Chovdar deposit of secondary quarzites is located in the Dashkesan region. Secondary quarzites are mainly represented by kaolinized and ochrous types. Proven reserves estimated in 1944 are 4.1 million tons.

Technological studies have proved a suitability of secondary quarzites of the above three deposits for production of bricks. Other potential areas of a special interest are contact-metasomatic secondary quarzites of the Paleogene complex in the Ordubad region of the Nakhchivan Autonomous Republic. Chemical composition of secondary quartzites and physical and mechanical properties of finished products are shown in table 5.

Table 5. Chemical composition of secondary quarzites and properties of finished products in Azerbaijan

Name of deposits	Chemical composition						Physical and mechanical properties of finished products		
	SiO_2	Al_2O_3 + Fe_2O_3	CaO	MgO	H_2O	p.p.p.	Density, g/cm^3	Water-absorbing capacity, per cent	Mechanical strength, kgs/cm^2
Gizildja	94.64	2.50	2.20	No	0.11	0.3	2.41	16.6	295
Getashen	94.04	2.16	2.40	No	0.60	0.8	2.39	20.1	275
Chovdar	94.46	2.15	2.05	No	0.52	.6	2.43	12.8	310

(e)   Pyrophyllites

Pyrophyllites are widely used owing to their high thermal stability and a high alkaline and acid-proof resistance. The only known Kirvadag deposit of pyrophyllite in the Dashkesna district is represented by a series of hydrothermally altered tuffs of the Kimmeridgian age which enclose the known alunite deposit. A total thickness of hydrothermally-altered tuffs varies within 16 to 84 metres with an average thickness of 40 metres. The deposit was studied in detail in 1951 for a raw material of inertial fillers for insecticides.

A degree of pyrophyllitization is being defined by chemical analysis. Pyrophyllitized and alunitized varieties are distinguished by SO_3 and SiO_2 contents. The intensively pyrophyllized varieties contain from 58 to 64 per cent of SiO_2 and from 0.16 to 1.40 per cent of SO_3 and the alunitized varieties from 44 to 48 per cent of SiO_2, from 18 to 27 per cent of SO_3 and more higher content (from 2.5 to 5 per cent) of alkalines. Pyrophyllites form two beds with a thickness of 10.5 and 11.7 metres being separated by 10-15 metres bed of substantially alunitized and hematized tuffs. Reserves of pyrophyllites are estimated at around 6-6.5 million tons. Application of pyrophyllites as fire-proof raw material requires an appropriate enrichment in removing harmful admixtures.

(f)   Serpentinites

Serpentinites are widely developed within the ophiolite belt of the Lesser Caucasus. Massifs of ultrabasic and basic rocks represented by peridotites, harzburgites, dunites and pyroxenites are controlled by abyssal fractures. Peridotites and dunites were subjected to metamorphism and transformed into serpentinites. Dunites and serpentinites are the basic types of magnesia-silicate rocks, which can be used for production of forsterite refractors. In some areas, dunites form lens-shaped schlieren isolations among serpentinized peridotites. The large thickness of dunites-serpentinites was noted in chromite occurrences. Isolated massifs of dunites of isometric or elongated form are widely developed in the area of middle streams of the Terter river basin in the Kelbadjar district. No special research on usage of serpentinites as a raw material for production of refractors has been conducted. Laboratory studies have proved a possibility of their use in agriculture for increasing productivity of sowing plants. Numerous small occurrences of asbestos are associated with serpentinites. The content of asbestos of the Ipyak occurrence of chrysotile-asbestos in the Lachyn district is from 2 to 3 kg/ton and that in the Geydara occurrence of tremolite-asbestos in the Kelbadjar district is 20 per cent. Mining of serpentinites can be accompanied by associated production of asbestos raw material. Reserves of dunite-sepentinites are practically inexhaustible.

6. Construction and building materials

The territory of Azerbaijan hosts nearly all kinds of building materials and resources required by construction industry except of high-quality sands. Construction materials are dominated by carbonaceous rocks widely spread in the Lesser Caucasus and in the areas of the south-eastern submersion of the Greater Caucasus.

Limestones of the Upper Cretaceous have more special importance in the Lesser Caucasus, where they are met in composition of thick volcanogenic-sedimentary series of the northern and eastern foothills of the Lesser Caucasus. Limestones of the Neogene have been mapped in the Shemakha, Gobustan and Absheron regions of the south-eastern submersion of the Greater Caucasus. Limestones are mainly used for cement, building stone and lime production and marbles as facing and dimension stones. Gravel-sandy deposits of recent and paleo-river terraces are used as fillers for concrete. The Quaternary clays and loams are used in concrete production and as brick-tile raw materials.

Altogether, 237 deposits of building materials of varios kinds were found on the territory of Azerbaijan. These include 8 deposits of concrete raw materials, 5 deposits of gypsum, anhydrite and alum, 20 deposits of facing stones, 22 deposits of building stone including 11 deposits of calcareous raw material, 33 deposits of dimension stones, 83 deposits of clays including 75 deposits for brick-tile production, 5 deposits of keramzite and algoporite, 3 deposits of refractory ceramics, 55 deposits of sandy-gravel admixture and 11 deposits of building sands.

(a)   Raw materials for the cement industry

Azerbaijan possesses a resource-base of all components for cement and concrete production. Main resources of raw materials are carbonaceous and clayey-carbonaceous rocks of the Cretaceous and Neogene age. The Quaternary loams are used as clayey component and the Cretaceous volcanic ashes and trasses as hydraulic fillers. Gypsum, anhydrite, alum shales and calcareous raw materials are widely used in production of stringent building materials. Proven reserves on A + B + C reserve categories have been evaluated for ten deposits as follows: 242 million tons of carbonates, 120 million tons of clayey rocks, 4.6 million tons of hydraulic fillers (trasses) and 7 million tons of volcanic ash. Currently, the only operating Garadag cement plant in Azerbaijan works on the resource-base of limestones and clays from the Garadag deposit and trasses of the Kerogliy deposit. The rest of the above resource-base for cement production can be used by the Touuz and Agdam cement plants, which are not currently operating.

(b)   Gypsum, anhydrite, alum

The deposits of gypsum are known to exist in the north-eastern part of he Lesser Caucasus and in the Nakhchivan Autonomous Republic. In the north-eastern part of the Lesser Caucasus, the gypsum-bearing deposits are confined to volcanogenic-sedimentary rocks of the Kimeridgian-Tithonian age. Gypsum-enclosing rocks are tuffs, tuff-breccias, tuff-sandstones, porphyrites and limestones. Formation of gypsum deposits took place in lagoonal conditions during some stages of regression of the Upper Jurassic sea. The Yukhari-Agdjakend, Monashid and Dastagir deposits belong to this group of gypsum deposits.

In the Nakhchivan Autonomous Republic, gypsum deposits are confined to a salt-bearing section of the Miocene age. Gypsum beds are confined to the lower part of the section of the Karagan suite made up of clays, aleurolites and sandstones. The typical examples of this group are the Aras and Shakhtakhti gypsum deposits. Alum accumulations which are represented by fine-grained mixture of gypsum, clay, carbonaceous and siliceous minerals, are widely spread in foothills and flat valley regions among the Quaternary deposits. Proved total reserves of eight deposits of gypsum, anhydrite and alum are 64.3 million tons.

The Agdjakend gypsum mine with large reserves produces raw materials mainly for stringers and gypsum products at the Baku plant of gypsum products. Current exploration programme is being carried out for gypsum and alum in the Gobustan area based on numerous occurrences of gypsum identified in the past by geological mapping and mineral prospecting programmes.

7. Dimension and facing stones

(a) Building stones

Similar to any other mountainous country, the people of Azerbaijan widely use natural stones for civil and industrial construction. In terms of distribution and industrial usage, the leading role belongs to shelly limestones. Shelly limestones of the Pontian and Absheron stages and, partially, of the Khazarian stage of the Upper Neogene are widely distributed in the Kura depression and in the Absheron peninsula.

Organogenic and pelitomorphic limestones of the Tithonian stage of the Upper Jurassic and Campanian-Maastrichtian stages of the Upper Cretaceous are widely spread in the area of the north-eastern foothills of the Lesser Caucasus. In some regions of the Nakhchivan Autonomous Republic, Lenkaran and Astara districts of Azerbaijan where there is a lack of limestones, tuffs, sandstones and travertines are widely used for building blocks in civil and industrial construction. Altogether, 65 deposits of building stones including 54 deposits of limestones, tuffs, sandstones and travertines with total reserves of over 570 million cubic metres have been explored in Azerbaijan. Practically, the industry of building materials of Azerbaijan is secured by proved reserves for many years ahead.

(b) Facing stones

Rocks of various genetic types which can be used as natural facing materials are widely spread on the territory of Azerbaijan. The magmatic series of rocks includes gabbroids, diorites, granodiorites and plagiogranites of the Somkhit-Agdam zone of the Jurassic age, gabbro-teschenites and andesites of the Mountain Talysh, monzonites and granosyenites of the Megri-Ordubad intrusive massif of the Terriary age and the Eocene volcanic tuffs of the Aras zone.

Intrusive rocks and volcanic lava and tuffs have variable textures and colours from light-grey, pink, red to dark-grey, greenish and nearly black. Other souses of facing stones are the Mesozoic and Paleozoic deposits of marble and marbled limestones and also the recent travertines and dense varieties of the Absheron limestones. Marbles and marbled limestones are confined to carbonaceous formations of the Oxfordian and Tithonian stages, carbonaceous deposits of the Lower Cretaceous and lower sections of the Upper Cretaceous, as well as to the Paleozoic deposits of the Aras zone.

The Oxfordian crinoidal limestones and marbles of the Dashkesan deposit have a light-grey colour with increasing whiteness in areas of intensive recrystallization. Reddish tints of variable intensity and shades from gentle-pink to flesh-red and mixed red-grey are typical for the Tithonian marbled limestones. Crystalline and slightly marbled limestones of the Cretaceous age are characterized mainly by grey, greenish-grey, and reddish-grey colours.

The resource base of raw materials for facing stones of Azerbaijan is represented by 22 deposits of marble, marbled limestones, porphyrites, travertines, tuffs, conglomerates, teschenites and limestones with total reserves of over 66 million cubic metres. Some domestic construction organizations and companies in Azerbaijan are widely using quarrying damps and tailings of marble chips and sands for local decorative purposes and export.

(c) Rocks for stone casing

Rocks which can be used for stone casting are widely spread on the territory of Azerbaijan. The laboratory studies have proved that the most suitable rocks are andesite-basalts of the Quaternary age widely spread within the Kelbadjar superimposed trough. From five to eight flows of andesite-basalts with a variable thickness from

6 to 55 metres each were distinguished in the volcanic section of up to 370 metres thick. The upper flow with a thickness of 40 metres was studied in more details. Chemical composition of andesite-basalts in the upper flow is as follows (%): SiO_2 from 51 to 54, Al_2O_3 from 15 to 18, TiO_2 - 10.5, Fe_2O_3 from 7 to 8, CaO from 6 to 8 and MgO from 4 to 6 per cent. Laboratory and experimental industrial studies have proved that andesite-basalts can be used for stone casting on condition that serpentinite, chromite and carbonate components will be added.

Optimal composition of blast-furnace burden is 80 per cent of andesite-basalt, 10 per cent of serpentinite, 10 per cent of burned dolomite and 3 per cent of chromite iron stone. The obtained products comply completely with the technical standards. Resources of andesite-basalts are practically inexhaustible, however, most of the resources are located in remote areas at around 300 kilometres from the nearest railway. Other sources of rocks for stone casting are being explored in the well-developed Dashkesan, Ordubad and Lenkaran districts.

8. Fillers and ballasts

(a) Gravel, sand and rock aggregates

On the territory of Azerbaijan, the deposits of detrital materials are represented by alluvial, alluvial-proluvial, deluvial, eolian and marine sediments. Alluvial deposits are confined to recent flood plains and older terraces of rivers from the Greater and Lesser Caucasus and Talysh mountains. A lens-shaped form of deposits elongated along water streams is typical for these deposits. The Quaternary alluvial-proluvial deposits are similar to alluvial sediments constructing cones of river drifts and occupying vast areas in foothills of mountains. The deposits of both genetic types are usually represented by gravels and pebbles with admixtures of boulders, sands and clayey material. Rock source materials are granodiorites, porphyrites, diorites, limestones, marls, sandstones and other sedimentory and magmatic rocks. A degree of roundness is variable. Sand's content varies from 15 to 35 per cent of a total mass. The composition of sand material is quartz, carbonates, feldspar, ortoclase, hornblende, garnet, pyroxene, barite, epidote and various ore minerals.

Gravels and sands are being dredged simultaneously. Their thickness in various deposits varies from 0.5 to 17 metres with a thickness of overburden up to 5 metres. Total resources of 74 deposits of sand and gravel are 1,086 million cubic metres. Mining operations are ongoing on twenty deposits of boulder-gravel-sandy mixture and one deposit of sands.

(b) Perlites and obsidians

In Azerbaijan, the deposits of perlites and obsidians are known in the Kelbadjar district where they are confined to the upper horizons of the Kechaldag and Kichik Devegezu liparite domes of the Pliocene age. The Kechaldag dome is composed of glassy liparites being characterized by alternation of perlites and obsidians of a variable thickness. Thin alternating perlites and obsidians are sorted easily. Perlites are characterized by a dense micro-structure, fluidal dense or grained micro-composition and specific jointing. The Kechaldag dome has a vertical zonation with glassy rocks in the upper part of the dome, sphelorite-glassy and spherolite-semi-glassy rocks in the middle part and liporites with interbeds and lenses of glass in the lower section of the dome. Obsidians are homogeneous, of black or grey colour with glassy glitter and abrasive properties. Perlites' colours are whitish, yellowish and light-grey with pale-violet shades. Perlites are characterized by silk glitter and glassy structure.

Chemical composition of obsidians is as follows: SiO_2 from 73.99 to 76.37 per cent, Al_2O_3 from 13.48 to 14.22 per cent, Fe_2O_3 from 1.04 to 1.20 per cent, FeO from 0.60 to 1.78 per cent, MgO from 0.14 to 0.36 per cent, CaO from 0.53 to 1.90 per cent, Na_2O from 2.92 to 4.53 per cent, K_2O from 1.94 to 9.87 per cent and SO_3 from 0.18 to 0.41 per cent. Chemical compositional of perlites is as follows: SiO_2 - 75.12 per cent, Al_2O_3 - 15.08 per cent, Fe_2O_3 - 1.90 per cent, FeO - 0.28 per cent, CaO - 2.22 per cent, Na_2O - 2.02 per cent, K_2O - 0.65 per cent and SO_3 - 1.24 per cent.

Swelling of perlites starts at a temperature within 760°-860° with a swelling coefficient from 15 to 20 times. Rocks with grain size from 3 to 5 mm should be furnaced during 10 seconds at a temperature of 1,000°C to obtain 12-14 multiple swelling. Further increase of temperature leads to cracking. Swelled small particles are characterized by a little volume mass (60-80 kg/m^3) and a high fragility. The density of obsidian is 2.28-2.29 g/cm^3 and that of perlites is from 1.34 to 1.61 g/cm^3. The porosity of obsidians is from 0.4 to 1.3 per cent and that of perlites from 30 to 42 per cent.

Obsidians and perlites of Azerbaijan are raw materials suitable for obtaining of light swelling materials and can be of wide usage as light fillers for concrete and heat-isolation materials. The deposits of perlites and obsidians were explored at a shallow depth from the surface. Proved reserves of perlites and obsidians are 4.5 million cubic metres.

(c)   Expended clay aggregates

Geological prospecting and technological tests have identified the sources of raw material for expended clay aggregates which include continental loams and agloporites of the upper sections of the Khvalin stage in the Lenkaran zone, clays of the Absheron stage in Khizi-Devechi zone, the Quaternary loams in the Khachmaz district and clayey shales of the Jurassic age in various regions of the southern slope of the Greater Caucasus. Six deposits of suitable clays include two deposits in the Khizi district, one deposit in the Mugan-Salyan zone, two deposits in the Lenkaran zone and one deposit in the Nakhchivan Autonomous Republic. Total resources are over 20 million cubic metres. Currently, expanded clay aggregates are produced only at the Baku brick plant from clays of the Khizi deposit. Annual production is 184,000 cubic metres. The rest of the deposits are not developed.

Chemical composition of clays suitable for expanded clay aggregates' production is as follows: SiO_2 from 54.6 to 62.68 per cent, Fe_2O_3 from 5.12 to 7.80 per cent, Al_2O_3 from 15.2 to 19.38 per cent, TiO_2 from 0.49 to 0.84 per cent, CaO from 1.33 to 7.54 per cent, MgO from 1.99 to 3.54 per cent, $K_2O + Na_2O$ from 1.33 to 5.22 per cent, SO_3 from 0.21 to 0.41 per cent, p.p.p from 4.56 to 9.20 per cent. Optimal temperature of swelling is from 1,170° to 1,200°C. The swelling interval is from 40° to 135°C. The density is from 0.39 to 0.93 g/cm^3.

III. CURRENT STATUS AND FUTURE TRENDS OF PETROLEUM AND MINING INDUSTRIES

A. Current status of petroleum, mining and mineral-based industries

For over one century, Azerbaijan has been an oil and gas producer, with a petroleum refining industry. Azerbaijan is also a producer of iron ore, alumina, copper and molybdenum ore, lead and zinc ore, precious stones and industrial minerals including iodine, bromine, clays, gypsum, limestone, marble and other decorative and building stones. The country's most significant deposits are its oil reserves, and a number of foreign firms are currenty involved in projects to develop these reserves. The mineral resources base is able to meet the current and future demand for raw materials of various industrial sectors including refinery, chemical, petrochemical, energy, metallurgical and construction industries.

1. Oil and gas industry

The development of oil production in the Absheron peninsular goes back centuries. Azerbaijan, however, became particularly famous for its "Black gold" at the end of the 19th and the beginning of the 20th century. In 1901, eleven million tons of oil were produced. This figure represented more than half of the world's output. Offshore oil production in the Caspian Sea started in 1921 on Piralakhi Island and in the Biby-Eibat Bay. However, the Caspian oil potential wasn't intensively developed until the fifties with the opening up of the massive Dashlari oil field. It was here that the world's first offshore pile trestles were erected. A common characteristic of all the oil fields is the complexity of their tectonic structure. This is typified by their multi-stratal oil and gas saturation and the unpredictable variability of their geological exploitation parameters by section and area.

The 1998 year can be characterized as the turning point in Azerbaijan oil policy and strategy: five production sharing agreements were signed and entered into force, oil production under the "Contract of the Century" as well as "early" oil transportation has begun via the northern route of the Baku-Grozny-Novorossiysk export pipeline (figure 39). President Heydar Aliyev has also established a working group for export pipeline development (Guluzade, 1998).

A doubtless victory of the Azerbaijan Government's five years of work is the signing of nine production sharing agreements for offshore hydrocarbon exploration in the Azerbaijan section of the Caspian Sea. It is planned to invest some $30 billion under these agreements. If several new agreements are signed the investments could reach $35-40 billion. In general, the agreements have been scheduled up to the years 2024-2032, and over 1,500 million tons of oil are expected to be produced during the 25-30 years of operations.

According to different estimates, commercial reserves in the Azerbaijan an sector of the Caspian Sea amount to a range of 4-10 billion tons of oil. Even assuming that they are as low as 4 billion tons, it is clear that about 37 per cent of the total of Azerbaijan's commercial reserves of oil are to be produced under these agreements, whereas 7 per cent will be produced by the Azerbaijan's State Oil Corporation (SOCAR). The estimate is based on the average annual production of 9 million tons. Therefore, Azerbaijan can offer for development the remaining 56 per cent or 2,200 million tons of its offshore oil reserves.

Generally, 67 oil and gas deposits have been discovered in Azerbaijan during its oil and gas industry history. Currently, 37 onshore and 17 offshore fields have been developed in the country, with a total production of 1,400 million tons of oil and over 450 billion cubic metres of gas extracted from its reservoirs. One hundred forty-five prospective blocks have been found in the Azerbaijan in sector of the Caspian Sea of which 40 occur at a sea level down to 60 metres, 33 structures at a depth from 60 to 200 metres, and 72 below 200 metres of the water column (Guluzade, 1998) (figure 38).

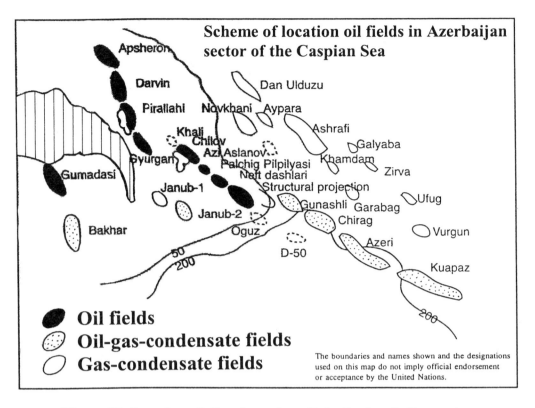

Figure 38. Location of oil and gas deposits in the Azerbaijan sector of the Caspian Sea

By 1 May 1998, sixty seven oil and gas fields had been opened up, of these fifty five fields are today in production. In total 1,365.5 million tons of oil and condensate and 443.8 billion cubic metres of gas have been recovered, including 435.5 million tons of oil and 318.7 billion cubic metres of gas extracted from offshore oil fields. Azerbaijan's highest oil production figures were achieved in 1941, when 23.4 million tons of oil were produced (a figure which accounted for 75 per cent of the whole of the Soviet Union's output), and in 1981 around 15 billion cubic metres of gas were produced, 12.8 billion cubic metres of which came from offshore fields (Yusifzade, 1998). At present, the majority of Azerbaijan's offshore and onshore oil fields are in the final stages of exploitation. In the last decade, the oil and gas output levels of these fields has been steadily decreasing. Over the last ten years, Azerbaijan's oil output has decreased from 13.8 million tons in 1987 to 9,022 million tons in 1997.

The main reasons for this drop in oil and gas output are the exhaustion of onshore oil fields and the long service of offshore fields, the limited opportunities for full oil recovery from deep-seated offshore reservoirs over 100-150 metres under the sea due to the lack of the requisite technology, the sharp reduction of oil exploitation and the worsening of the quality of work on existing wells. The sharp decrease in production drilling was caused by the curtailment of capital investment in drilling due to the limited financial resources and technological facilities made available to SOCAR at the time of breaking up of economic ties between the republics of the former Soviet Union.

Today, there are forty-two known onshore oil and gas fields in Azerbaijan and of these thirty-seven are under production. The total output from these onshore oil and gas fields is 931.5 million tons of oil and 129 billion cubic metres of gas. All these deposits with the exception of two or three fields are at the final stages of their working lives. The recovered oil and gas from these onshore deposits were an impressive 87 per cent of the initial recoverable reserves. The highest onshore oil production figures were achieved in 1941 when 23.4 million tons of oil were recovered. The top year for onshore gas production was 1961 when 6.0 billion cubic metres of gas were extracted.

In 1998, the onshore oil and gas production was 1.6 million tons of oil and 260 million cubic metres of gas. Currently, many of the onshore fields are producting a 50 per cent higher output than in previous years. However, such low production levels don't necessarily mean that these onshore fields are completely exhausted. The rennovation of more than four thousand idle wells in combination with artificial pressure on the strata can increase oil output by one and a half to two times. In addition, there is a large potential to discover onshore untapped reservoirs in the deeper sections of the Mesozoic system. Exploration work to be carried out will offer renewed opportunities of increasing onshore oil production, however, this will require modern technology and considerable investment. Foreign companies have already shown interest in a number of onshore sites (Guluzade, 1998).

In terms of its oil and gas reserves, the Caspian basin is an extremely promising area. It would be difficult to find a single area in the whole region, which would not be worth prospecting. In total, 166 structures have been found in the Azerbaijan sector of the Caspian Sea (figure 38). Twenty five oil and gas fields have been opened up and of these eighteen are in production, two are no longer in production, five are yet to go into production, and there are still 141 structures, which have not yet been prospected (table 6).

Table 6. Status of exploration and development of oil and gas structures in Azerbaijan sector of the Caspian Sea as of 1 May 1998

Status of exploration and development of oil and gas structures in the Azerbaijan sector of the Caspian Sea	Number of structures	Sea Depth		
		0-60 metres	60-200 metres	Above 200 metres
1. **Discovered structures ready for exploration drilling or under exploration drilling total:**	**141**	**41**	**27**	**73**
Including				
Apsheron archipelago	32	15	17	–
Baku archipelago	29	20	9	–
Near Caspian – Kuba area	7	6	1	–
Middle Caspian/Deep Waters	4	–	–	4
Southern Caspian/Deep Waters	69	–	–	69
2. **Discovered Structures – total:**	**113**	**27**	**16**	**70**
Including				
Apsheron archipelago	16	8	8	–
Baku archipelago	21	14	7	–
Near Caspian – Kuba area	6	5	1	–
Middle Caspian/Deep Waters	4	–	–	4
Southern Caspian/Deep Waters	66	–	–	66
3. **Structures prepared for exploration drilling – total:**	**22**	**10**	**9**	**3**
Including				
Apsheron archipelago	12	5	7	–
Baku archipelago	6	4	2	–
Near Caspian – Kuba area	1	1	–	–
Southern Caspian/Deep Waters	3	–	–	3
4. **Structures under exploration drilling – total:**	**6**	**4**	**2**	**–**
Including				
Apsheron archipelago	4	2	2	–
Baku archipelago	2	2	–	–

The production rate of the recoverable reserves extracted from the total reserves of the offshore oil fields comes to about 60 per cent. The highest production figures ever achieved for the Caspian region were 12.9 million tons of oil in 1970 and 14.1 billion cubic metres of gas in 1982. It was during this period that a number of large shallow water oil fields were opened up. In the consequent years, oil production output decreased for a number of reasons. Firstly, a large part of the Caspian shelf was placed out of bounds for exploration by the State environmental agencies. Secondly, the industry lacked the necessary technology to produce deep water oil at a depth of over 40 metres.

In 1998, 7.5 million tons of oil and condensate and 6.0 billion cubic metres of gas were produced in the Caspian region by 1,430 wells at an average daily output of 20,000 tons.

At present, a high level of oil recovery is being maintained at the main oil fields. For example, at the Neft Dashlari oil field which has initial recoverable reserves of 176 million tons of oil and 13.2 billion cubic metres of gas, 158.6 million tons of oil and 12.4 billion cubic metres of gas have been recovered. This puts the oil output coefficient here at an impressive 0.49. This was close to the projected figures and that is something, which is not often achieved, in practice anywhere (Guluzade, 1998).

Out of all the new oil fields, the main volume of oil produced comes from the Guneshli oil field with initial recoverable reserves of 175 million tons of oil. The Guneshli field was first exploited on an industrial level in 1980. By 1 May 1998, the oil field had 12 deep-sea fixed drilling rigs, and 151 wells of which 135 are working. During the period of exploitation up to 1 May 1998, 77.6 million tons of oil and over 19.9 billion cubic metres of gas were recovered, in addition 14.6 million cubic metres of water were injected. Due to the limited volume of water injected, the development of the deposit is actually on a depletion drive.

One of the most important results of the exploration work carried out over the last decade is the opening up in the Azerbaijan sector of the Caspian Sea of a series of large oil fields at a depth of 80-350 metres with recoverable reserves of approximately 700 million tons of oil and 200 billion cubic metres of gas. Over the next 20-30 years, the prospects of the country's energy and fuel industry will depend on the development of these oil fields. Indeed the main volume of oil output today comes from one of these fields, namely the Guneshli oil field.

In 1985, the Chirag deep water oil field was opened up. This structure covers an area of 13 x 2.5 kilometres. The depth of the sea in this area varies from 120 to 250 metres. Exploration work has underlined the similarity of geological characteristics, and tectonic position of this area with those in the Guneshli filed. Two years after the opening up of the Chirag deposit, the Azeri oil and gas field was opened up to the south-east of the Chirag field on an extension of the Absheron-Balakhan uplifts. In 1998, the Kyapaz oil field was discovered in a fold covering an area of 27 x 3 kilometres. The area of the fold is slightly uplifted and the depth of the sea varies from 85 to 125 metres. At the same time, the opening up of these deposits were delayed due to the lack of the necessary equipment and technology.

Currently, the oil and gas industry of Azerbaijan is operated by the State Oil Company of Azerbaijan Republic (SOCAR) which represents a powerful industrial and financial governmental structure. The SOCAR includes 77,000 of personnel, oil producing ventures, refinery capacity of 20.6 million tons per year, natural gas refining plant with its annual capacity of 6.5 billion cubic metres, eight machinery plants, deep water construction engineering plant for construction of permanent drilling platforms to be installed at 200 metres depth and deeper, maritime fleet that includes 300 various vessels and numerous floating drilling rigs, including 5 semi-submersible and 8 self-submersible drilling platforms. Major parametres of SOCAR's industrial production in 1990-1998 are shown in table 7.

In 1997, SOCAR began its reorganization. The company's board decided to prepare its "social infrastructure" and several other facilities for privatization. In fact, the first step towards splitting up this industrial giant into several functional units has been made. The SOCAR reorganization is closely connected with the

Table 7. Major parameters of industrial production of the State Oil Company of Azerbaijan Republic (SOCAR), 1990-1998

Activities and products	Measure unit	1990	1991	1992	1993	1994	1995	1996	1997	1998
Oil production inclusive condensate	Thousand tons	11 512.8	11 741.9	11 084.2	10 295.0	9 562.7	9 161.3	9 100.3	9 021.8	9 052.2
Condensate production	Thousand tons	511.3	468.1	388.5	323.7	254.3	215.6	209.9	202.8	177.0
Gas production including condensate	Million cubic metres	9 925.7	8 621.1	7 871.8	6 378.7	6 378.7	6 643.9	6 304.6	5 963.9	5 589.5
Natural gas production	Million cubic metres	7 803.0	7 123.9	6 501.0	4 996.4	4 996.4	4 498.9	4 228.9	3 956.1	3 255.1
Oil local consumption	Thousand tons	404.6	384.5	394.7	320.7	170.6	179.5	194.6	192.4	192.7
Total oil losses	Thousand tons	156.2	144.1	138.3	128.7	90.6	92.3	107.9	109.1	108.9
Exploitation losses	Thousand tons	90.7	94.5	90.6	84.1	58.9	51.5	61.0	59.5	59.2
Transportation losses	Thousand tons	65.5	49.6	47.7	44.6	31.7	40.8	46.9	49.6	49.7
Gas losses	Million cubic metres	37.2	57.0	73.3	36.9	57.8	20.7	16.4	15.6	164.1
Gas burned in torshers	Million cubic metres	1 252.5	1 430.7	1 295.0	1 534.2	1 061.0	99.2	178.1	247.3	174.4
Oil refining	Thousand tons	16 331.6	15 820.1	11 936.0	9 974.5	9 350.2	8 923.1	8 718.7	8 642.6	8 254.3
Production: benzine	Thousand tons	2 009.7	1 761.9	1 216.0	1 246.5	1 268.9	1 039.1	1 022.2	1 108.4	836.7
Kerosine	Thousand tons	24.6	24.8	29.8	71.5	148.8	94.6	150.3	130.9	172.0
Jet fuel	Thousand tons	1 285.0	1 230.0	442.0	438.0	419.0	509.0	525.0	576.0	523.7
Diesel fuel	-do-	3 898.8	3 634.9	3 158.8	2 324.0	2 261.0	2 189.5	2 090.0	2 142.1	2 042.4
Black oil	-do-	6 852.8	7 421.2	5 514.9	4 930.3	400.4	4 220.1	3 957.3	4 066.3	4 202.4
Bitumen	-do-	145.6	113.1	89.8	82.1	65.9	53.6	39.8	21.3	25.0
Lubricating oil	-do-	817.5	762.6	397.6	208.0	229.6	1 246.4	124.0	98.8	81.7
Coke	Thousand tons	166.2	161.3	96.5	59.9	39.5	4.1	59.1	48.2	29.8
Black oil used in refining plant	Thousand tons	166.4	193.3	108.8	174.3	148.3	183.9	234.2	198.2	244.8

general reform in the Azerbaijan power industry. The establishment of the fuel and power industry expected in 1997 has not occurred yet, and the Government focused its efforts on the development of the general concept for the future ministry. Generally, the existing situation, when reform and investment should cover the entire power industry, requires the creation of a state body responsible for overall coordination.

In the SOCAR's management reorganization, there were expected a creation of a new expanded division based on SOCAR's Foreign Investment Management Department (FIMD), which will coordinate the realization of joint projects and prepare new contracts, and desisnation of the future affiliated companies representing SOCAR's interests in the majority of the signed agreements.

The affiliates could become joint-stock companies, issuing bonds convertible on international securities markets. The Government will participate in planning of SOCAR's future transformation into a joint-stock company and even the privatization of the company or its units. The final strategy development was supposed to take two years, 1998 and 1999. The reform will also touch the oil income distribution. It was planed to establish an Azerbaijan Petroleum Fund by the end of 1998. Supported by governmental bodies, the Fund will coordinate the receipt and distribution of profits to which the country is entitled under the joint projects.

In 1997-1998, SOCAR's main business fields were:

❏ Onshre and offshore oil production;

❏ Oil refining at Azerneftyag and Azerneftyanadzhag;

❏ Oil products export;

❏ Crude oil export to international markets (starting at the end of 1997).

In 1997, SOCAR successfully accomplished its task of producing 9 million tons of oil and even exceeded the planned production rate. Having maintained its annual production rate at 9-9.1 million tons over the last three years, SOCAR plans to continue this tradition. This can be considered as a real achievement of the SOCAR administration: before 1994 the production rate decreased by 10 per cent a year. However, it is still difficult for the state company to match the planned production levels of natural gas . In 1995, $50 million of investments was required to improve the natural gas industry's sustainability. The money was intended for buying equipment to drill new wells and rehabilitate old wells having some potential. The Government, however, has not found any free capital for this investment. It is supposed that the country's gas production level will be increased with further development of old gas fields, development of new ones, and associated gas production on the oil fields exploited under the joint projects.

In 1998, SOCAR planed to produce 9 million tons of oil and 6,000 million cubic metres of gas. Beginning from 1999, the rate was planned to gradually decrease to 6.15 million tons by the year 2000 at old non-contract fields. This is also true for old gas fields: the production level there will drop to 4,150 million cubic metres by 2010 (Guluzade, 1998).

Currently, for about the last two years, SOCAR's processing facilities have been forced to produce black oil only, adversely affecting the oil refining processes. In general, their state leaves much to be desired: only 40-45 per cent of the capacities or 20 million tons a year is used currently. The reason is the lack of the main raw material, oil. The reduction in the production rates observed in Azerbaijan during the last decade has resulted in the degradation of both the country's power and fuel potential and the refined product quality (Guluzade, 1998).

Earlier, the lack of domestic raw materials was covered by oil imported from Turkmenia, Western Siberia, and Kazakhstan. Refining plants in Baku have been nearly smashed by the breach of the economic links with CIS countries, and by the blockade of Azerbaijan's northern communications. Another serious problem is the lack of an adequate and sound market for the refined products. In 1998, SOCAR planned to export 480 thousand tons of oil to international markets (40 thousand tons a month), and to receive minimum $60 million. Oil products export will, probably, remain stable. The most important event in 1997 was the beginning of crude oil export by SOCAR to international markets. On 25 October 1997, the first 120,000 tons of Azerbaijan oil were transported via the northern main pipeline to port Novorossiysk (figure 39). In recent decades, oil, petroleum products and gas have become the most important elements of development of the world's energy sector. Azerbaijan is among the countries, which enjoy great power and fuel resources, developed oil and gas transportation systems, and power generation facilities. Today, the country's energy complex is considered as a guarantee of overcoming the crisis faced by the country, and sustaining Azerbaijan's economic development. Oil refining gives products used in many industries and in many spheres of human activities. Thus, overcoming the crisis in oil refining and ensuring its efficient functioning is among the top priorities at the current stage of the nation's development. An analysis of the current situation in Azerbaijan's energy sector has shown that recreation and development of the fuel and power sectors, including the oil refining industry, requires huge material and financial resources which are beyond the country's capabilities. The development of the sector is hardly possible without the creation of a full-value energy market ensuring an inflow of foreign capital and technology. The established legal framework has enabled the Government to direct its economic policy towards introduction of market relations and attraction of investments into the country, especially foreign direct investment.

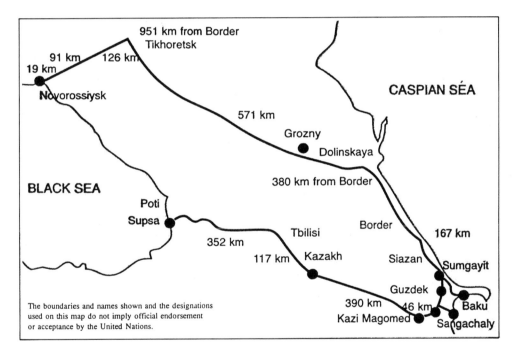

Figure 39. Oil pipeline routes in the Caucasus

Azerbaijan's oil refining industry has been souring for a number of years. Its radical reconstruction, which began in the late seventies, was interrupted in the late eighties and had not, finalized as yet. The industry, which in 1997 accounted for 40 per cent of the total energy sector, is operating well below of its capacity owing to outdated technology and equipment, low amounts of oil to be refined, and lack of a clear strategy for development of the industry which would ensure a good return on investment. Currently, over one-third of the oil refining plants installed about two and half decades ago have become obsolete. The poor state of the equipment, transportation and storage facilities, which are on average 70 per cent worn-out results in substantial losses of oil and oil products. Less than 60 per cent of the facilities meet any modern standards of consumption of power, raw materials or reagents, not to mention environmental safety. The existing facilities can hardly enable production of any high quality products. The oil refining rate has been gradually dropping from more than 22 million tons in the late eighties to the current 9 million tons or even less. Hence, 50 per cent of the processing capacities remain idle. The situation as to employment of secondary processing capacities is even worse being complicated by the higher rate of the equipment attrition.

Due to the shortages in fuel supply in the country, the domestic market consumes all the black oil produced in Azerbaijan. A rather low local price for the black oil reduces the general profitability of the refining industry. The high production cost also decreases the efficiency of oil products export, which is a large share of the total country's exports. Currently, a great inflow of oil is expected owing to the signing and successful implementation of the Contract of the Century and other major oil projects. The share of oil to be refined is also expected to increase. The practice indicates that in case of rational and efficient oil refining, the income from refined products is more than double that received from the sale of crude oil. While it appears to be impossible to achieve the required level of efficiency currently, it may be achieved by the time of the increased oil production.

To realize the goal, an upgrade of the existing facilities and construction of new plants for secondary refining is required. This will enable to increase the degree of refining, quality of oil products and general performance indicators of the industry. Currently, the refining degree is under 50 per cent, where just a one per cent increase achieved by processing the oil waste is equivalent to refining of 0.5 million tons of oil. Modernization of the existing secondary refining will produce a growth of the refining degree to 65-70 per cent or even to 75-80 per cent in the case of construction of new secondary refining units.

World experience proves that non-waste technologies allow for a refining degree as high as 100 per cent, which maximizes the profitability. Therefore, the target is to develop a clear concept of development of Azerbaijan's oil refining industry. This concept will provide the basis for designing process flows, which should include both the existing plants and new capacities for the anticipated increase in the amount of oil to be refined. It appears that the oil potential of Azerbaijan can be used fully. A far-sighted approach to resolving this problem will make the refining industry's modernization to up-to-date standards quite realistic and ensure efficient functioning for the beginning of the next century. In the course of realization of such a programme, the demand for related products (additives, inhibitors, catalysts, etc.) will increase, and joint ventures with world leaders in the industry are expected to be established. In general, oil refining in Azerbaijan, having a substantial share in the country's energy sector, as well as its comprehensive R & D base, and the status of the sole supplier of different oil products to many industries, has a great potential for strengthening the national economy.

2. Mining and mineral-based industries

The country has 350 non-fuel mineral deposits containing ore resources defined under the classification system used in the former Soviet Union, 168 of which are under development. Azerbaijan also has numerous other mineral resources, including such metals as aluminium in alunite, arsenic, cobalt, copper, chromite, iron ore, lead and zinc, manganese, mercury, molybdenum and tungsten; industrial minerals such as barytes, clays, refractory-grade dolomite, gypsum, kaolin, limestone, pyrite, salt and zeolites, and semi-precious stones, including amethyst, andalusite and garnet (Levine, 1998).

Azerbaijan's mining and metallurgical industry is controlled by the state company Metallurgiya, composed of eighteen enterprises including mining companies, the Gyandzha alumina refinery, the Sumgait aluminium smelter, aluminium rolling and wire drawing enterprises, powder metallurgy production facilities, and scrap metal units for ferrous and non-ferrous metals. Mineral productions, import, export and demand for metallic mineral products in Azerbaijan is shown in table 8.

(a)   Aluminium

According to Metallurgiya, foreign investment is particularly needed in the aluminium production sector. Although Azerbaijan produces alumina from both bauxite and domestic alunite ore, the 450,000-tons/year Gyandzha alumina refinery, originally built to process alunite, was expanded in the late 1970s to process imported

Table 8. Production, import, export and consumption of major mining and metallurgical products in Azerbaijan, 1990, 1995, 1998

Unit: thousand tons

Type of activity	Year	Mineral products			
		Iron concentrate	Steel pipes	Primary aluminium	Aluminium oxide
Production	1990	460.2	492.6	26.8	239.0
	1995	1.5	9.8	3.6	26.0
	1998	6.6	3.1	3.4	6.6
Import	1990	–	50.0	1.0	–
	1995	–	7.0	0.3	–
	1998	–	40.7	0.14	–
Export	1990	410.0	410.0	22.4	186.0
	1995	–	5.6	3.3	17.9
	1998	–	2.1	3.0	2.5
Consumption	1990	50.2	132.6	5.4	53.0
	1995	1.5	11.2	0.6	8.1
	1998	6.6	41.7	0.54	4.1

bauxite rather than alunite. Presently, there is only one 100,000 tons/year section at Gyandzha processes alunite. The alumina from Gyandzha was shipped to the Sumgait aluminium smelter in Azerbaijan and to the Tajik aluminium smelter in Tajikistan. Revival of the aluminium industry would require full integration of processes from the mining of alunite through to the smelting of aluminium. Political unrest in the Caucasus, however, has interfered with shipments to Tajikistan and sharply reduced the amount of alumina shipped there.

Trans World Metal of the United Kingdom of Great Britain and Northern Ireland, one of the major foreign firms involved in the production and sales of Russian aluminium, took control of the Gyandzha alumina refinery, which supplied the Sumgait smelter and other aluminium smelters. The Gyandzha refinery, however, was at a standstill throughout much of 1996. It produced 26,100 tons of alumina in 1995. Azerbaijan also has an aluminium smelter at Sumgait with capacity to produce about 60,000 tons/year of aluminium.

The Sumgait smelter was only producing at the rate of 15,000 tons/year in 1994. Azerbaijan was engaged in a project with Kaiser Engineering to double the capacity at Sumgait and which from Soderberg to prebake technology. According to the plans to renovate Sumgait, during the first two-and-a-half years of renovation, 50 per cent of the plant's pots would be shut down. Full production was to be achieved after four years. Plans also called for upgrading the Gyandzha alumina refinery to improve the quality of the alumina, but not to increase capacity. Half of the alumina is now being shipped to plants in the Russian Federation, and it is planned to continue these shipments.

The city of Sumgait, with some 300,000 inhabitants and located 100 kilometres from Baku, is Azerbaijan's major manufacturing centre and is considered one of the most polluted cities in the FSU. It is the centre of Azerbaijan's petrochemical and oil equipment manufacturing industries and the site of Azerbaijan's aluminium smelter, the management of which has been entrusted to the Trans-World Group of the United Kingdom.

A United Nations Development Programme plan was formed to resurrect the economy of Sumgait and correct its pollution problems. The plan calls for declaring Sumgait a special economic zone, which will offer large tax incentives and subsidies to investors while at the same time engaging in a major infrastructure overhaul. Investors will be expected to introduce environmentally cleaner technology and to contribute to an environmental clean up fund. The creation of a free economic zone in Sumgait, a major industrial centre, will be one test as to how well Azerbaijan is currently positioned to attract foreign investment outside of its oil sector.

(a)   Gold

Plans call for the construction of Azerbaijan's first bullion plant in Baku that will produce gold of 99.9 per cent purity, with the capacity to produce 5,000 kilograms/year of bullion. Other precious metals, including silver, also will be produced at this plant. The plant is projected to produce at design capacity in three to four years.

The United States-Canadian firm International Gold Resources was planning to establish a joint venture with Azergold, an association of exploration, mining and construction companies, to develop gold lode deposits in Azerbaijan with reported reserves of 50-55 tons and perspective reserves of up to 500 tons. It was projected that Azerbaijan could produce up to 5 tons/year of gold. The gold reportedly could only be refined economically in Azerbaijan and therefore, it would also be necessary to construct refining facilities. Financing was being sought for this planned joint venture (Levine, 1998).

(b)   Ferrous and non-ferrous metals

Iron ore was mined at the Dashkesan open pit, Azerbaijan's sole source of iron ore. The disintegration of economic relations resulted in the suspension of iron ore mining in the Dashkesan deposit. Earlier, this deposit was operated by a large concentration works with an annual output of 700,000 tons. The main product is concentrated ore with a 60.3 per cent iron content.

Azerbaijan plans to increase iron ore output, but currently lacks customers for its ore. Its former customer, the Rustavi steel mill in Georgia, has halved its output. Azerbaijan has one steel mill in Sumgait, but the steel mill is only operating at one-third capacity. Reserves at Dashkesan are reportedly 230 million tons to back-up the mining operations during 80-90 years. The total investment required for ferrous metallurgy is US$ 920 million. Azerbaijan's non-ferrous metallurgy which is specializing in local alunite metals, gold, silver, and copper refinery industry requires another US$ 700 million of investment (Levine, 1998). The mineral production of Azerbaijan for 1996-1997 is shown in table 9.

Table 9. Mineral production of Azerbaijan, 1996-1997

Unit: tons unless otherwise stated

Mineral Commodity	1996	1997
Aluminium, primary	812	4,717
Caustic soda	33,000	23,000
Cement	223,000	314,700
Fertilizers	1,900	5,400
Natural gas (million cubic metres)	6,305	5,961
Petroleum, crude ('000 tonnes)	9,100	9,027
Steel, crude	2,725	24,607
Rolled	2,000	16,400
Pipes	3,100	13,000
Sulphuric acid	31,000	52,500

Source: US-Azerbaijan Chamber of Commerce. Investment Guide to Azerbaijan, Interfax.

3. Construction materials industry

There is a widespread resource base of raw materials for construction materials industry, which operates using both domestic and imported minerals to meet the demand of civil and industrial construction.

Despite a strong diversified mineral resource base and historical achievements, the mining industry of Azerbaijan is encountering problems in performance, efficiency, transportation and utilization. The industry operates much below of its full capacity and is plagued by outdated technology and equipment, rising production costs, capital, energy and severe infrastructure problems. Attempts to boost domestic minerals supply in the republic so far have progressed slowly because of economic difficulties. The republic lacks the financing required to initiate new, large-scale development projects. The production of construction materials and related products is shown in table 10.

Table 10. Production of construction materials and related products in Azerbaijan

Construction materials and products	Unit	1990	1995	1997	1998
Cement	Thousand tons	989.9	195.9	314.7	199.1
Construction lime	Thousand tons	44.0	3.0	0.5	0.2
Gypsum	Thousand tons	65.6	5.5	2.0	3.3
Natural building blocks	Million pieces of conventional bricks	1,317.0	161.0	98.0	95.2
Bricks	Million pieces	132.0	26.0	14.8	13.2
Window glass	Million square metres	5.32	1.07	1.12	0.64
Light aggregates	Thousand cubic metres	122.7	6.0	6.4	6.42
Natural facing stones	Thousand square metres	1,088.5	108.9	51.2	61.1
Ceramic facing material	Thousand square metres	620.0	82.0	36.8	12.0
Ceramic floor tiles	Thousand square metres	539.0	88.3	28.8	6.6
Linoleum (floor coatings)	Thousand square metres	4,880.7	56.1	–	–

The construction sector is a major consumer of construction material products and mineral resources used to produce reinforced concrete and road construction materials. The intensive development of construction industry in Azerbaijan falls in 1970-1980s, when 60 large industrial enterprises have been built to service the societal needs of the country. The number of enterprises engaged in the construction industry has reached 526 in the early 1990s. The break up of the former Soviet Union and a follow-up economic crisis have disrupted the production of construction materials and construction industry in Azerbaijan (table 11).

The analysis of table 11 indicates that a total production of the construction materials sector in 1998 was just 15 per cent of that production level in 1990. The share of construction materials sector in industrial production also reduced from 2.9 per cent in 1990 to 1.3 per cent in 1998. The work force of the sector has also reduced by two times during this period. In line with the economic restructuring programme of Azerbaijan, the construction materials industry is currently being privatized by establishing joint stock enterprises and small private ventures.

B. Development prospects of the petroleum and mining sectors

1. Future trends of the oil and gas sector

Prospective development of the oil and gas industry of Azerbaijan is associated with rehabilitation of major old onshore and offshore hydrocarbon deposits and exploitation of new deposits jointly with foreign

Table 11. Production of major products of the construction industry in Azerbaijan

Products	Unit	1990	1995	1997	1998
Asbestos-cement sheets	Thousand pieces	65.5	8.0	14.4	13.8
Sanitary-ceramic articles	Thousand pieces	56.8	5.6	7.1	2.2
Assembled reinforced concrete and single articles	Thousand cubic metres	1,312.3	90.5	32.3	14.4
Wooden constructions	Thousand square metres	751.0	9.3	17.9	5.2
Asphalt-concrete	Thousand metres	865.0	424.0	51.0	63.0

companies. The remaining reserves of the onshore deposits of Azerbaijan have attracted sizeable foreign investment in seven joint development projects that enables to suggest a stable annual oil production from onshore deposits at a level of 1.6-1.7 million tones.

Primary development prospects of petroleum production are, however, associated with the offshore deposits in the Azerbaijan sector of the Caspian Sea where 145 petroliferous structures have been discovered. Forty structures occur up to a 60 metres water depth, 33 structures at water depths ranging from 60 to 200 metres and 72 structures at water depths over 200 metres containing total estimated hydrocarbon resources from 4 to 10 billion tons of oil equivalent. This resource potential is currently under extensive petroleum exploration programmes. By a period of 2015-2020, the annual exploration drilling is expected to reach 150,000 metres and exploitation drilling up to 460,000 metres. It is planned that such intensive petroleum exploration and development programmes over the next two decades will ensure energy independence and increased export revenue of the country. The projected production of oil and natural gas up to the year 2025 is shown in table 12 and figures 40 and 41.

Table 12. Projected production of oil and gas in Azerbaijan up to the year 2025

Units: Oil in million tonnes
Gas in billion cubic meres

	1999	2000	2005	2010	2015	2020	2025
Total oil production	12.03	13.66	27.72	48.70	50.0	52.5	55.0
Oil production onshore	1.6	1.6	1.6	1.6	1.65	1.7	1.7
Oil production offshore	10.43	12.06	26.72	47.1	48.35	50.8	53.3
Total gas production	6.48	6.45	13.4	17.5	20.6	22.8	25.0
Gas production onshore	0.2	0.2	0.2	0.2	0.3	0.3	0.4
Gas production offshore	6.28	6.25	13.2	17.3	20.3	22.5	24.6

It is estimated that around US$ 45 billion investment including US$ 40 billion of foreign investment will be required for rehabilitation and development of oil and gas industry of Azerbaijan.

The oil and gas pipeline system will be improved to ensure sustainable crude supply to national refineries and supplies of Azerbaijan and transit hydrocarbons from Kazakhstan and Turkmenistan to the world markets. Out of 11 suggested proposals on the routing of export pipelines, the terminals on the Black Sea and Mediterranean have been opted. The most apparent main export pipeline route, which is planned for transmission of the Caspian and Kazakhstan crude oil, is the Baku-Geikhan route going through Georgia and Turkey. Export pipeline routes going to the Black Sea coast (Baku-Supsa and Baku-Novorossiysk) are planned for subsequent transition through Bosforus into the Mediterrahian Sea terminals or crude oil delivery into the Ukraine, Romania and Bulgaria

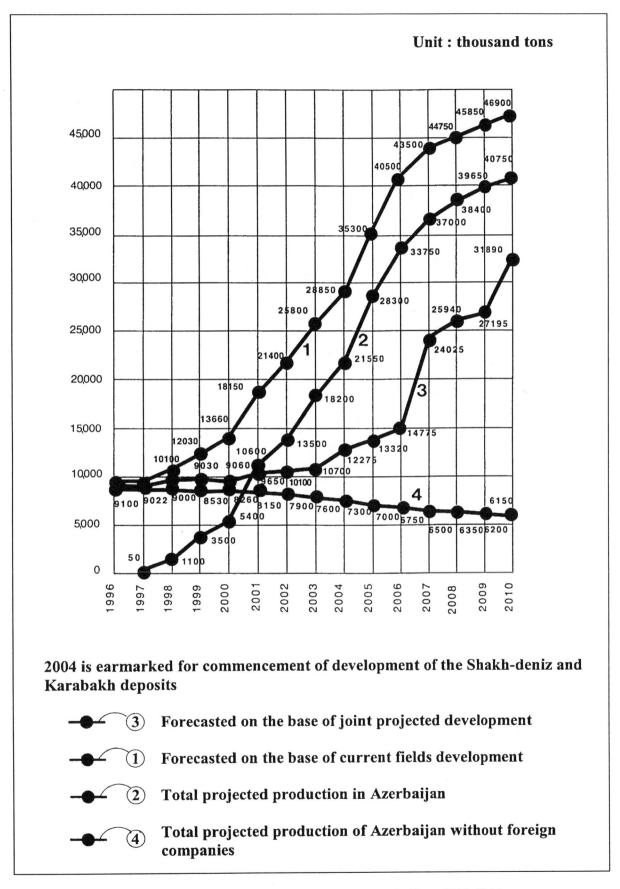

Unit : thousand tons

2004 is earmarked for commencement of development of the Shakh-deniz and Karabakh deposits

③ Forecasted on the base of joint projected development

① Forecasted on the base of current fields development

② Total projected production in Azerbaijan

④ Total projected production of Azerbaijan without foreign companies

Figure 40. Forecast of oil production in Azerbaijan, 2000-2010

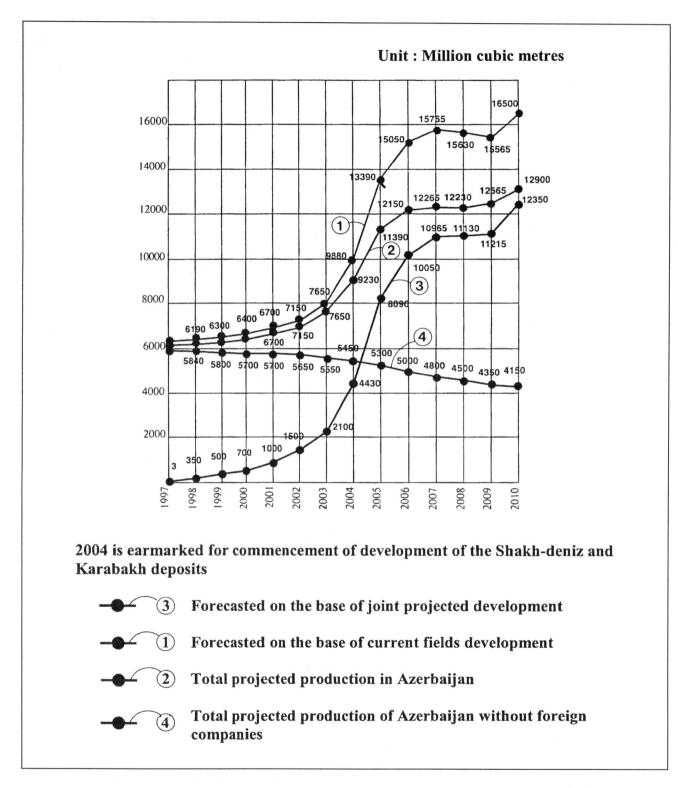

Figure 41. Forecast of gas production in Azerbaijan, 2000-2010

terminals. In view of the petroleum potential of Azerbaijan, Kazakhstan and Turkmenistan, the projected capacity of the export pipeline is planned at around 50 million tons per year with estimated construction cost from US$ 2.5 to 3.0 billion.

The proposed project to build the main transit gas pipeline of 2,000 kilometres long will provide supplies of Turkmenistan and Kazakhstan natural gas across the Caspian Sea floor, Azerbaijan, Georgia and Turkey to the European markets. The expected maximum pipeline capacity is from 30 to 35 billion cubic metres and its estimated cost at about US$ 2.5-3.1 billion. The expected share of Azerbaijan in this project is around US$ 500-600 million. The plan on rehabilitation and improvement of existing gas pipeline system suggest renewal of corroded parts of the gas network, reconstruction and expansion of surface gas storage, updating of gas control and measurement stations and gas losses reduction in gas transportation systems. Total amount of both domestic and foreign investment required for rehabilitation of the gas sector of the country is estimated from $US 350 to 400 million up to the year 2025.

The development programme for the refining of Azerbaijan industry up to the year 2005 requires the Industrial Enterprise "Azneftyanadzhag" to reconstruct and build new crude refining facilities, to increase the extraction rates of installed devices, to renovate catalytic cracking and polymerization units and other actions. It is expected that the implementation of this programme will increase refining capacity up to 14 million tons/ year, engine lubricants production will exceed 69.8 per cent of the total amount of refining product and an extraction ratio will reach a level of 75.3 per cent which is typical for recent refining technologies. Overall reconstruction and modernization of the operating enterprises are being also planned by the Industrial Enterprise "Azneftyag". The implementation of rehabilitation programme for refinery industry of Azerbaijan would require investment over $US 200 million. The refining capacity of crude oil is expected to amount to 15 million tons in 2005 and about 25-30 million tons in the period from 2020 to 2025. In parallel with plans for increased oil and gas production and refining capacities, loss-reduction and efficient energy consumption technologies are planned to be applied in all stapes of petroleum development.

2. Chemical and petrochemical industry

The development prospects of the chemical and petrochemical industry of Azerbaijan are associated with implementation of the following programmes:

❑ Reconstruction, expansion and technical renovation of operating enterprises aimed to increase production for domestic and world markets, as well as to provide various sectors of the economy with new chemical products and materials;

❑ Complete utilization of the capacity of the EP-300 system for integrated processing of liquid pyrolysis products, propane-propylene fraction of the Baku refinery, prior development of relatively low energy-and-water consumption technologies for polymer materials production and construction of new facilities for production of consumer goods;

❑ Upgrading extraction capacities of chemical products;

❑ To reduce dependence of chemical industry from imported chemical raw materials and manufactured products in parallel with restoration of trade of crude and semi-manufactured products from CIS countries;

❑ Sequential reduction of energy consumption;

❑ Improvement of environmental protection management and rehabilitation of chemical enterprises;

❏ Restructuring and decentralization of chemical industry by establishing new small and medium scale enterprises to produce processed plastic articles, lacquers and paints using domestic chemical products and raw materials;

❏ Exploration and development of domestic mineral resource base of raw materials for new and operating enterprises of the chemical industry.

The projected production of the chemical and petrochemical industries based on implementation of the above programmes is shown in table 13.

Table 13. Projected production of chemical and petrochemical industries of Azerbaijan, 2000-2025

Unit: thousand tons

Chemical products	1998	1999	2000	2005	2010	2015	2020	2025
Polyethylene	22	70	80	120	120	150	150	150
Epoxy tar		1	2	10	10	12	13	15
	3	4	5	10	10	10	10	10
Caustic soda	20.8	23	25	50	55	60	60	60
Syntetic washing articles	0.6	1	3	15	17	20	30	40
Sulphuric acid	30	42	100	150	170	200	300	400
Granulated phosphate fertilizers	15	7	20	35	50	80	100	120
Spirit	11.8	12	12	12	15	15	18	20
Isopropylen rubber and latex	0.7	2.6	5	40	50	60	65	70
Automobile tires (thousand pieces)	0.3	35	50	200	350	600	800	1 000
Polypropylene				80	100	100	100	100
Benzol				60	60	60	60	60
Toluol				30	30	30	30	30
Ethyl-benzol					80	80	80	80
Polystyrole					20	25	25	25
Linear polyethylene						200	200	200
Polyvinil chloride						100	100	100
Chloride						200	250	300

3. Mining and metallurgical sector

Azerbaijan possesses a great variety of rich mineral resources. Although comprehensive geological and mineral exploration work has been conducted with technical and financial assistance from the former Soviet Union, large areas of the country still remain unexplored with regard to its mineral potential. Azerbaijan has numerous mineral resources, including such metals and metal ore as alunite used for alumina production, arsenic, cobalt, copper, chromite, iron ore, lead and zinc, gold and silver, manganese, mercury, molybdenum and tungsten, industrial minerals and non-metallic minerals, such as barite, clays, refractory-grade dolomite, gypsum, kaolin, limestone, pyrite, salt and zeolites, and semi-precious stones including amethyst, andalusite and garnet, as well as a range of building materials. Altogether, 350 non-fuel mineral deposits and occurrences have been identified so far, 168 of which have a potential for development. Given the diversified geologic environment, favourable metallogenic development and identified resource base, the mineral sector of Azerbaijan has a strong potential for development. Currently, out of 39 ore deposits with proved reserves the only Dashkesan magnetite scarn deposit and Zaglik alunite deposit are currently being developed on a limited scale.

Iron ore was mined at the Dashkesan open pit, Azerbaijan's sole source of iron ore. The disintegration of economic relations resulted in the suspension of iron ore mining in the Dashkesan deposit. Earlier, this deposit was operated by a large concentration works with an annual output of 700,000 tons. The main product is concentrated ore with a 60.3 per cent iron content. Azerbaijan plans to increase iron ore output, but currently lacks customers for its ore.

The resource base for ferrous metallurgy consists of the deposits with large reserves and high-grade cobalt-bearing magnetite iron ores, bentonite, dolomites and flux limestones, chromite, iron and manganese ores. All these deposits are concentrated on the west of the country within the Qazakh-Ganja-Kelbadjar economic-geographic region with a well-developed energy infrastructure including the Mingechevir, Shamkhor and Enikend hydropower stations and Azerbaijan thermal power station. This resource-base coupled with a well-developed infrastructure provides a good ground for restoration of activities of the Azerbaijan Mining-Processing Combinate and design of a closed production cycle for ferrous metallurgy.

The resource base for non-ferrous metallurgy comprises the deposits of alunite, polymetallic (complex) copper, molybdenum, cobalt, mercury, antimony and other base and rare metals. Over 90 per cent of proved reserves of polymetallic ores are concentrated in the north-west of the country within the Sheki-Zakataly economic region and in the western and south-western regions of Azerbaijan. This resource base suggests a good potential for development of non-ferrous metallurgy in the country other than the aluminium industry. The priority areas in the development of non-fuel mineral sector are:

❏ Establishment of a closed production cycle for ferrous metals and metallurgy articles of steel including ferro-alloys through technical renovation and expansion of the Azerbaijan Mining-Processing Combinate (AzGOK) and construction of enterprises to produce sponge iron using direct reduction technology out of concentrates and electric furnace steel smelting;

❏ Reconstruction and renovation of aluminium production capacities, including increased production of new articles and introduction of innovative anode technology;

❏ Construction of facilities for non-ferrous metal rolling and articles based on supplies from the Filizchay polymetallic-sulphide ore deposits located within the Sheki-Zagatala economic region;

❏ Establishment of exploration-mining-processing enterprises to obtain concentrates of non-ferrous metal ores on the basis of deposits located within the western and south-western regions of Azerbaijan.

The implementation of these plans and programmes will enable to rehabilitate the mining and metallurgical industries and will meet the demand of various economic and industrial sectors of the country and substitute current imports. The projected production of mining and metallurgical sectors of Azerbaijan is shown in table 14.

4. Construction sector

Market economy reforms, which have been initiated in Azerbaijan since 1991, have given a boost to the development of the construction industry in the last two years. Further development of the construction sector would require an intensive exploitation of known deposits and exploration programmes in identifying new resources of construction raw materials. The projected production of construction materials and construction industry Azerbaijan are given in tables 15 and 16.

Table 14. Past and projected production of mining and metallurgical industries in Azerbaijan, 1990-2025

Unit: thousand tons

Mineral commodity or metal products	1990	1995	2000	2005	2010	2015	2020	2025
Steel	27.1	2.4	2.5	1 000	2 000	3 000	5 000	6 000
Finished roll	521.7	11.8	15.0	700	1 600	2 300	4 300	5 200
Steel pipes	492.6	9.8	31.0	200	400	500	600	600
Primary aluminium	26.8	3.6	50	50	90	95	100	110
Copper metal	–	–	–	–	25	28	30	35
Polymetals	–	–	–	–	110	115	125	130
Rolled non-ferrous metals	37.6	0.5	2.0	2.5	40	42	45	50

Table 15. Projected production of construction raw materials in Azerbaijan, 1999-2025

Construction materials	Units	1999	2000	2005	2010	2015	2020	2025
Cement	Thousand tonnes	350	400	2 000	2 400	3 800	3 200	3 500
Construction lime	Thousand tonnes	–	5	200	270	300	350	400
Gypsum, alum	Thousand tonnes	15	20	100	130	180	210	250
Natural building blocks	Million pieces of conventional bricks	300	360	1 000	1 500	2 000	2 300	2 600
Bricks	Million pieces	20	20	150	250	320	370	400
Window glass	Million square metres	0.8	1.0	3.5	4.5	6.0	7.0	7.5
Light fillers	Thousand cubic metres	8.0	10	100	150	230	300	350
Natural facing materials	Thousand cubic metres	70	92	600	1 000	1 200	1 500	1 700
Ceramic facing materials	Thousand cubic metres	15	20	600	800	950	1 100	1 200
Ceramic floor tiles	Thousand cubic metres	8.0	10	500	600	800	1 000	1 200
Linoleum	Thousand cubic metres	–	–	2 000	2 200	2 500	3 100	3 500

Table 16. Projected production of construction industry in Azerbaijan, 1999-2025

Production	Units	1999	2000	2005	2010	2015	2020	2025
Asbestos-cement pipes	Thousand sheets	25	30	120	240	360	480	600
Sanitary-ceramic articles	Thousand pieces	2.8	3.0	50	150	250	300	350
Reinforced cement construction and articles	Thousand cubic metres	50	70	250	400	700	1 000	1 500
Wood constructions	Thousand square metres	6.0	8.5	250	600	850	1 150	1 500
Asphalt-concreate	Million tons	70	80	500	800	1 200	1 500	1 800

C. Foreign investment in the petroleum and mineral sectors

1. Petroleum sector

Azerbaijan is poised to acquire great additional wealth with the development of its offshore oil fields through international consortia. Around 50 oil and gas companies are currently involved in petroleum exploration and exploitation in the country (table 17). The last six years have been earmarked by several achievements in national oil policy and strategy through signing of seventeen production sharing agreements for offshore hydrocarbon exploration in the Azerbaijan sector of the Caspian Sea (figure 42). Oil production under the "Contract of the Century" has commenced together with early oil transportation via the northern route of the Baku-Grozny-Novorossiysk export pipeline. The "Contract of he Century" in the development of the Azeri, Chirag and deep water Guneshli oil fields was signed on 20 September 1994. The Azerbaijan International Operating Company (AIOC) was set up for the execution of the contract activities. The participants in this contract together with the State Oil Company of the Azerbaijan Republic (SOCAR) were Amoco, Unocal, MacDermott (United States), BP (United Kingdom), Statoil (Norway), LUKoil (the Russian Federation), TPAO (Turkey), Delta (Saudi Arabia).

This contract was the first step in the open door policy for foreign companies to come to Azerbaijan and to be more confident in investing in the country's economy. In this sense, the contract played a decisive role not only in the development of Azerbaijan's oil and gas resources but also in the attraction of foreign investors in general. It is worth noting that after the contract was signed such companies as Chevron, Exxon, Mobil, Itochu and others abandoned their previously cautious positions and became actively involved in Azerbaijan (Yusifzade, 1998).

Since the signing of the "Contract of the Century", SOCAR together with AIOC have been conducting planned operations in accordance with the programme and budget with a view to implementing the Early Oil Production Programme. Within the framework of this programme, geotechnical exploration has been carried out on the whole contract area. This included the deep sea area around the fixed drilling rig No. 1 on the Chirag structure and also the oil pipe routing from the deposit to the terminal in the Sangachal region. In the contract area, seismic exploration surveys have been successfully carried out and the data collected were processed and interpreted. Work has been carried out on the modernization of the "Dada Gorgud" semi-submersible drilling rig. With this modernized rig, four exploration wells have been sunk in the Guneshli, Chirag and Azeri blocks. The results from these test wells were positive and confirmed the data that had previously been collected on these deposits.

Table 17. Equity participation of SOCAR and foreign companies in the contracts in force

Prospective structures or deposits	CONTRACTING PARTIES	Share (%) As of the signing contract	Share (%) As of the end of 1998	Date of signing the contract	Effective date of contract commencement
The Azeri and Chirag deposits and a deep water part of the Guneshli deposit	SOCAR	20.0	10.0	20 September 1994	12 December 1994
	Amoco Caspian Sea Petroleum Ltd.	17.0	17.0		
	BP Exploration (Caspian Sea) Ltd.	17.1	17.1		
	Delta Nimir Khazar Ltd.	1.6	1.68		
	Den Norske Stats Olieselscap a.s., d	8.5	8.56		
	S/C LUKoil	10.0	10.0		
	Pennzoil Caspian Corporation	9.8	4.8		
	Ramco Khazar Energy Ltd.	2.0	2.08		
	Turkie Petrollari A.O.	1.7	6.75		
	Unocal Khazar Ltd., d	9.5	10.0		
	Exxon	–	8.0		
	Itochu	–	3.9		
Perspective structure Karabakh	LUKoil International Ltd.	7.5	12.5	10 November 1995	23 February 1996
	Agip Azerbaijan BV.	5.0	5.0		
	LUKAgip N.V.	50.0	45.0		
	Pennzoil Caspian Development Corporation	30.0	30.0		
	ComAfCo SOCAR	7.5	7.5		
Perspective structure Shah-Deniz	BP Exploration (Azerbaijan) Ltd.	25.5	25.5	4 June 1996	17 October 1996
	Elf Petroleum Azerbaijan B.V.	10.0	10.0		
	LUKoil International Ltd.	10.0	10.0		
	Oil Industries Engineering & Construction (Islamic Republic of Iran)	10.0	10.0		
	State Oil Azerbaijan A.S.	25.5	25.5		
	Turkish Petroleum Overseas Company Ltd.	9.0	9.0		
	ComAfco SOCAR	10.0	10.0		
Perspective structures Ashrafy and Dan Ulduzu	Amoco Nord Absheron Petroleum Ltd.	30.0	30.0	14 December 1996	7 March 1997
	Unocal Eastern Hemisphere Exploration Ltd.	25.5	25.5		
	Itochu Oil Exploration (Caspian) Ink.	20.0	20.0		
	Delta Oil Company (Azerbaijan) Ltd.	4.5	4.5		
	NafCo SOCAR	20.0	20.0		
Perspective structures Lencoran Deniz and Talish Deniz	Elf Petroleum Azerbaijan B.V.	65.0	40.0	13 January 1997	25 June 1997
	Total Exploration & Production Azerbaijan	10.0	10.0		
	NafCo SOCAR	25.0	25.0		
	Deminex Azerbaijan Petroleum GmbH	–	10.0		
	Fina Oil Gas S.A.	–	5.0		
	OIIK	–	10.0		
Perspective Azeri block D-222	LUKoil International GmbH	60.0	60.0	3 July 1997	4 November 1997
	NAK SOCAR	40.0	40.0		
Perspective structure Nakhchivan	Exxon Exploration and Production Azerbaijan Ltd.	50.0	50.0	1 August 1997	5 December 1997
	NAK SOCAR	50.0	50.0		
Perspective marine block Absheron	Chevron Overseas Exploration Ltd.	30.0	30.0	1 August 1997	5 December 1997
	Foreign Oil Companies	20.0	–		
	NAK SOCAR	50.0	50.0		
	Total Exploration and Production Azerbaijan	–	20.0		
Perspective marine Oguz structure	Mobil Exploration and Production Azerbaijan Ink.	50.0	50.0	7 August 1997	5 December 1997
	NAK SOCAR	50.0	50.0		

Note: For location of contract areas see figure 42.

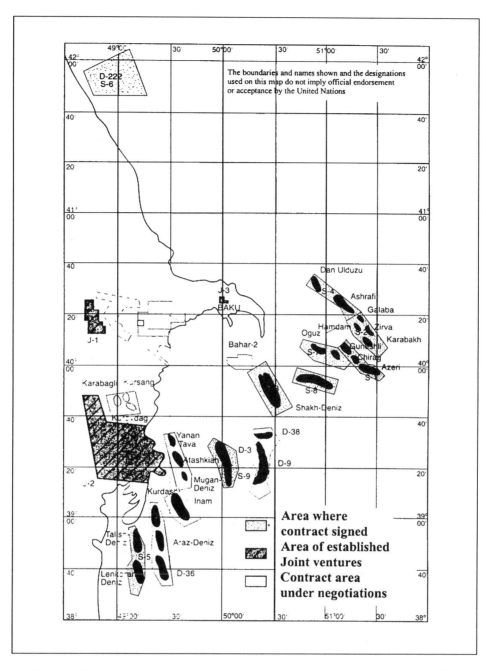

Figure 42. Location of contract areas for petroleum exploration and development in Azerbaijan, 1998

The drilling and completion of the construction work on these wells has always been at the top of SOCAR's priorities, and joint operations and contacts with AIOC were made on an everyday basis. This has created the necessary confidence prerequisite to future exploration work, the final calculation of the oil and gas reserves and the defining of the output levels for the Guneshli, Chirag and Azeri structures.

As far as the question of oil exports from the contract block is concerned, it is worth noting that the first oil from the Early Oil Project was produced on 7 November 1997. In order to achieve the project's aims, work was carried out on the Chirag – 1 drilling rig, the terminal at Sangachal and also along the northern and western export routings of the oil pipelines. On the northern export routing, work was completed on a 530-mm diameter pipeline from the Sangachal terminal which was merged with the SOCAR's existing 720-mm pipeline. On the western route, engineering work was carried out and construction work is still going on.

The implementation of the "Contract of the Century" will not only increase the amount of oil produced in Azerbaijan but will have a positive effect on the whole of the country's economy. The positive results achieved as a result of the signing of this contract has played and will continue to play a very significant role in the expansion of foreign investment in Azerbaijan's oil and gas industry. After the "Contract of the Century", other contracts were later signed on the development of the "Karabakh", "Shah deniz", "Lenkoran deniz-Talysh deniz", "Dan Ulduzu-Ashrafi", D-222, Apsheron, Nakhchivan and Oguz structures. These have all opened Azerbaijan's doors to an ever greater number of foreign investors. From this point of view, the "Contract of the Century" is by far the Azerbaijan's most significant deal.

Unlike the "Contract of the Century", in all nine subsequent contracts, covering more than 18 prospective structures, the areas according to which the agreements were signed are not existing oil and gas oil fields, but prospective fields. In order to open up an oil field, one has to carry out a fair degree of exploration work. This includes drilling deep exploration wells, which require certain risks and paying certain initial costs. This exploration work will be financed to a large degree by foreign companies at their risk.

There is little doubt that the above mentioned contracts signed by SOCAR will significantly increase Azerbaijan's oil and gas production. If in 1997 Azerbaijan produced 9.022 million tons of oil and 5,964 billion cubic metres of gas, the output in 1999 was nearly 280,000 barrels a day, or 50 per cent more then in 1997. Starting from this year oil and gas production levels will steadily increase and by the year 2010 will reach an estimated 46.9 million tons of oil and 16.5 billion cubic metres of gas.

In accordance with the second contract, which was signed in November 1995, the Caspian International Operations Company was formed and started initial work on the Karabakh structure. Engineering, geological and seismic sea survey exploration work was completed on the Karabakh block. The first exploration well was sunk and the geophysical results from this work showed a hydrocarbon presence in the Nadkirmahin sandy member.

In accordance with the third contract which was signed on 4 June 1996 on the joint production of the Shah Deniz structure, work has been carried out to implement a multi-disciplined programme of exploration of the contract area. Engineering, geological and offshore seismic surveys have been completed and the data collected has been processed. Work is likewise in progress on preparing the Shelf-5 rig, which will be used, for drilling exploration wells.

In accordance with the fourth contract signed on 14 December 1996 on the joint production of the Ashrafi and Dan Ulduzu structures, the North Apsheron Operational Company was set up which drilled exploration well No. 1 from the Dada Gorgud semi-submersible drilling rig. During the tests at well No. 1, 620 cubic metres of gas and 70 tons of oil were recovered per day from the Podkirmahin suite and 460 tons of oil per day from the Nadkirmahin sandy member. This represents the opening up of yet another completely new oil and gas deposit in the Azerbaijan sector of the Caspian Sea. This was the first exploration well which SOCAR had ever sunk on a prospective block in collaboration with a foreign company which had produced oil and gas.

In January 1997, the fifth contract was signed in the Elysee Palace in Paris on the joint exploration, development and production sharing of the output of the Lenkoran deniz and Talysh deniz structure with a number of French companies. This was the first oil contract ever signed outside of Azerbaijan. The contract will be in effect for 25 years and testify the expansion and development of economic relations between France and Azerbaijan.

The sixth agreement was signed on 3 July 1997 as a part of President Aliev's official state visit in Moscow. This agreement was on the exploration, development and production sharing on the D-222 prospect in the northern part of the Azerbaijan sector of the Caspian Sea.

During President Aliev's visit to the United States, three contracts were signed in the White House on 1 August 1997 (the seventh, eighth and ninth respectively). These contracts were concluded between SOCAR and leading American oil companies on the exploration, development and production sharing of the Absheron, Nakhchivan and Qguz prospects. Arco, Conoco and Shell are also at the negotiation stage of choosing appropriate sites for collaboration work.

Recently, Japanese oil companies have become much more active in Azerbaijan. The Itochu company has acquired equity participation of the Azeri, Chirag and Guneshli agreements and the contract on the Ashrafi and Dan Ulduzu deposits. The Japanese National Oil Corporation has completed geological and geophysical exploration work on two prospects on the Azerbaijan shelf in the south of the Azerbaijan sector of the Caspian Sea. A memorandum of mutual understanding and the basic principles and provisions for an agreement have been signed on the exploration, development and production sharing on a number of blocks selected by a consortium of Japanese companies. In addition, there is a number of other oil companies from around the world which realized the enormous hydrocarbon potential opportunities that Azerbaijan can offer.

If these new agreements are signed, the investment could reach US$ 35-40 billion. In general, the agreements have been scheduled up to the years 2024-2032, and over 1,500 million tons of oil are expected to be produced during the 25-30 years of operations.

Looking closely at the potential opportunities that Azerbaijan has to offer it is evident that the country's crude oil and gas resources are sufficient to increase oil and gas production up to 45-50 million tons a year over the next few years. This in turn will be sufficient to provide a strong basis from which we can solve Azerbaijan's economic and social problems and ensure sustainable development of its national economy.

2. Mineral sector

At a conference in Istanbul in June 1998, the Chairman of the Azerbaijan State Committee for Geology and Mineral Resources listed deposits for which the country is seeking to attract investors. These proposals include: developing the Filizchay copper, lead and zinc deposits; establishing an enterprise to exploit the Dashkesan group of deposits (including recovery of cobalt and iron ore from the magnetite ore tailings, and constructing a plant to produce bentonite powder); developing the Karadag copper porphyry deposit; establishing a joint venture to mine copper-bearing pyrite ores from the Mazymchay deposit; establishing a plant to produce soda ash based on reserves of dolomite and rock salt in the Nakhchivan district; and establishing a joint venture to develop the Aidag zeolite deposit (Levine, 1998).

Azerbaijan's non-ferrous metallurgy which is specializing in local alunite metals, gold, silver, and copper refinery industry requires around US$ 700 million of investment. According to Metallurgiya, foreign investment is particularly needed in the aluminium production sector. Although Azerbaijan produces alumina from both bauxite and domestic alunite ore, the 450,000 tons/year Gyandzha alumina refinery, originally built to process alunite, was expanded in the late 1970s to process imported bauxite rather than alunite. Presently, only one 100,000 tons/year section at Gyandzha processes alunite. Revival of the aluminium industry would require full integration of processes from the mining of alunite through to the smelting of aluminium.

Azerbaijan did not begin a programme of rapid privatization until mid-1996, and the privatization of medium-and large-scale enterprises did not begin until mid-1997. A large number of enterprises in the mineral sector, including those producing cement, petrochemicals, and oil and gas, were classified as strategic enterprises and can only be privatized with a presidential decree. A presidential decree was issued in early 1998 to privatize the metallurgical enterprises that form the Metallurgiya holding company. These enterprises include the Azerboru association (formerly the Sumgayit steel pipe plant), the Sumgayit non-terrous metals plant (Sumgyaittsvetmet), the Gyandzha Glinozem (alumina) production association, and the Zaglik alunite mines. The Gyandzha Production Association currently employs 2,800 people and, besides alumina, has the capacity to produce 350,000 tons/

year of sulphuric acid and 115,000 tons/year of mineral fertilizer. Production peaked at near capacity in 1987-1988 and has fallen since to about 20 per cent of the capacity.

Azerbaijan has been engaged in an effort to develop its gold resources. The Azerbaijan Geology Department has calculated the country's total gold reserves at 1,500 tons. The government and RV Investment Group Services, a United States consortium, signed a contract for the exploration and development of nine gold lode deposits in the Nakhchivan Autonomous Republic and the Angelan, Kebadzhar, Tauz and Kedabak regions of Azerbaijan. The consortium will finance the exploration and development, and will retain a 49 per cent interest and local company Azergyzyl will own 51 per cent. During the first three years, the partners will explore nine deposits, which are estimated to contain 400 tons of gold, 2,500 tons of silver and 15 million tons of copper ore. However, these estimates include resources on disputed territory with Armenia (Levine, 1998).

In overall, the Government of Azerbaijan is trying to achieve a sustainable and balanced economic development, and for that reason is making efforts to revive its mining and metallurgical industries.

IV. MINERAL POLICY AND REGULATORY FRAMEWORK FOR THE DEVELOPMENT OF THE MINERAL SECTOR

A. Current economic and investment policy

The Government of Azerbaijan supported by international financial and economic institutions has already initiated a series of economic reforms towards (i) liberalization of external economic relations, (ii) implementation of the privatization programme, (iii) achievement of macroeconomic stabilization and (iv) establishment of a friendly environment and incentives for domestic and foreign investment.

During the last six years, Azerbaijan's Parliament has enacted over 60 priority laws to speed up economic reforms and create favourable conditions for foreign investments. The law governing investment activities states that ventures with foreign participants where the share of foreign investment in hard currency, equipment, or raw materials is at least 30 per cent of the registration fund are exempted from the profit tax. Industrial and construction companies enjoy a 5-year tax holiday as of the date of official registration.

Over 1,200 joint ventures with companies from about 60 countries of the world have been registered in Azerbaijan. The registration funds of these ventures exceed US$ 600 million. The total foreign investment in Azerbaijan's economy was US$ 1,307.3 million in 1997, which is 2.5 fold higher than the investment in 1996 wherien direct investment amounted to US$ 1,111.0 million (Abasov, 1998).

Realizing that the current foreign investment flow is not sufficient for sustainable economy, the Ministry of Economy has developed the national long-term priority investment programme, which envisages the attraction of US$ 55 billion including US$ 30 billion in the development of oil and gas sector (Abasov, 1998).

Azerbaijan's government, assisted by the World Bank, has developed and adopted a three-year programme (1997-1999) of investment in the state sector, where the priority is given to the development of infrastructure. The programme is worth US$ 2,042.2 million, of which US$ 595.8 million should be allocated for the power industry, US$ 316.1 million for the oil and gas industry, US$ 382.2 million for the water industry and irrigation, and US$ 221.6 million for the transportation. Such companies as Siemens (Germany), ABB (Kraftwerke Ag, Germany), Nichimen, Mitsui (Japan) are supposed to participate in a number of projects.

According to this programme, the most urgent priority is the reconstruction of the power sector with technical upgrading of the existing power plants, and creation of power facilities in the Nakhchivan Autonomous Republic after being isolated for six years. About 60 per cent of Azerbaijan's power facilities, installed more than 30 years ago, suffer from high consumption of resources and high-energy losses. Foreign investments in the power industry are expected to reach US$ 2.3 billion, and over US$ 30 billion in the oil and gas industry.

Some 3,500 industrial companies operate in machine-engineering, metallurgical and chemical industries including 130 companies in the machine-building industry. Following the privatization programme, the government intends to sell the major share of small, medium-sized and large state-owned enterprises to various companies, including foreign companies. The required investment in industrial development should reach US$ 1.3 billion. Upgrading and establishment of new production facilities is also required by the chemical industry.

The major goal of the industry is to increase the percentage of finished products, which can be achieved by the construction of facilities for production of polymer materials, especially polypropylene. The planned investment in the chemical industry will facilitate the production of hundreds of millions of products, which are highly competitive in the world market. The Italian and Japanese companies such as Nichimen, Chioda, Techniman and others will invest in the development of the chemical industry.

Large investment programmes in the revival of light and cotton industries, agricultural production and food processing industries as well as infrastructure have been also formulated by the government in cooperation and with financial support of the World Bank, the European Union as well as business companies from France, Germany, Israel, Turkey, United Kingdom and the United States.

Although Azerbaijan has been an oil and gas producer for around 120 years, there are still significant undeveloped hydrocarbon reserves offshore in the Caspian Sea. Upon acquiring independence, Azerbaijan has been trying to attract foreign investors to participate in the development of these reserves. A number of major petroleum companies are currently engaged in development of Azerbaijan's oil and gas resources, which will be a significant source of revenue for the country.

The development of Azerbaijan's other mineral industries are more problematic. Aluminium production, for example, which is based in part on domestically mined alunite, may prove unprofitable under market economy conditions. Development of Azerbaijan's other metallic and industrial mineral industries also now will have to be scrutinized in terms of market economic factors, including transport costs that may impede the development of these industries; there still will be domestic markets for a number of Azerbaijan's industrial minerals and also markets in the newly independent states of the former USSR for mineral commodities from Azerbaijan.

Despite a strong diversified mineral resource base and historical achievements, the mining industry of Azerbaijan is encountering problems in performance, efficiency, transportation and utilization. The industry operates well below of its full capacity and is plagued by outdated technology and equipment, rising production costs, capital, energy and severe infrastructure problems. Attempts to boost domestic minerals supply in the republic so far have progressed slowly because of economic difficulties. The republic lack the financing required to initiate new, large-scale development projects.

In an effort to reinvigorate the mining industry, the Government of the Azerbaijan Republic is now encouraging foreign participation in the industry through joint ventures. Having been closed to foreign investors for decades, the Government of Azerbaijan is undertaking intensive work and making great efforts to attract overseas investment. The Government desires to expand its nations' mineral and energy sectors and improve the efficiency of utilization of raw materials in the country by introducing capital, technology and machinery from abroad. This represents the first massive efforts by the leadership of the republic to seek joint ventures in petroleum and mining sectors and a departure from traditional self-sufficiency principles.

Opportunities for foreign participation in mining activities are wide ranging and include, among others, the following:

- ❐ Enhancement of production performance in the ferrous and non-ferrous metals industry;

- ❐ Use of advanced prospecting techniques for the discovery of blind ore deposits;

- ❐ Adoption of improved recovery methods to rework gold tailings and waste rock dups; and

- ❐ Cleaning up of environmental damage.

B. Mining and other related legislation

The Government recognizes the role of the petroleum and mining sector to the economy and has formulated a clear oil and mineral policy and medium/long term national strategic development plan aimed to increase further the share of the mining and oil production. The National Assembly promulgated the new mining law in May 1998 towards its further liberalization to attract foreign investment for modernization and re-equipment of existing mines, benefication and processing plants. A set of relevant legislative acts and regulations (land, groundwater, forestry, mineral resources, environment, investment, etc.) has been translated from the local language to Russian and English and is available for foreign investors on a commercial basis since 1999.

In accordance with the Constitution, natural resources belong to the Azerbaijan Republic; the Mineral Resources Law provides a legal and economic background in regulation of mineral resources use between the State and subsoil resource user.

The basic principles of mineral resources use include an efficient integrated and safe development of mineral resources and environmental protection, increase of raw materials supply favourable conditions for promotion of investment and royalties. The State regulations of mineral resources development are being carried out through licensing procedure, overall control and mine inspection.

The basic principles of the Mineral Resources Law are the following:

- ☐ Subsoil and mineral resources contained therein belong to the State, which can lend them for development. The issues of land access and land use are regulated by appropriate legislative acts including that on private property.

- ☐ Both individuals and legal entities including foreign entities are eligible for exploration and development of mineral resources in any form of property.

- ☐ Subsoil resources are made available for geological studies, mineral exploration and development, reprocessing of mine waste products, building of underground constructions not connected with mineral resources development, establishment of specific geological objects and material collection. The duration of land use is regulated by licencing procedure set up by the Law.

- ☐ Land tenure issues are being regulated by separate legislative, executive and jurisdical entities.

- ☐ The State through its authorized management bodies regulates a process of mineral resources development and protection; monitor the geoscientific data coverage of the territory, mineral resources and reserves, issue licences and monitor mineral titling system, defines charges for subsoil use and mineral resources development, carries out expertise; defines the order of reporting and acquisition, storage and use of geologic data; conrols efficient and complete use of mineral resources; and provides overall implementation of the State policy in the area of mineral resources development.

- ☐ Geological prospecting, mineral exploration and mining activities are being undertaken on the basis of licencing procedure.

- ☐ A licence holder should carry out its activities within the terms and conditions of licence and under the overall objective of rational utilization of mineral resources.

- ☐ Geologic information obtained in a process of mineral resources exploration and development belongs to the State and should be submitted to the State's Geological Fund under the established procedure.

- ☐ A licence holder has a conjunctive right from exploration to mining within the same land area under the established procedure.

- ☐ Geological data on minerals obtained in a process of activities under a licence is a subject to the State's expertise.

- ☐ Royalties and other charges should be paid in a course of mining production.

- ☐ A system of exclusive rights and incentives is applied to stimulate the use of environmentally friendly technologies and to mine highly-demanded minerals located in remote and economically less developed areas.

❐   The State through its designated bodies controls the implementation of activities by a licence holder based on the principles of rational utilization and integrated development of land and its subsoil mineral resource, proper environmental management and mine safety.

The Mineral Resources Law of Azerbaijan provides a legal ground for the development of the mineral sector of the country through promotion of foreign direct investment, best environmental practices and advanced exploration, mining, and processing technologies. The Law and other implementing rules also regulate the licensing procedures in Azerbaijan, which has been enacted by a presidential decree. According to this decree, the State Committee on Geology and Mineral Resources of Azerbaijan was entrusted to issue the licences, and the Cabinet of Ministers has established the licence issuing procedure for (I) geological prospecting and mineral exploration; (ii) exploration and exploitation of groundwater resources; (iii) mining of industrial non-metallic minerals, construction materials, semi-precious, building and ornamental stones.

Mining licences for the development of non-ferrous and precious metals at this stage of economic development are issued by the Government. Foreign investors have the conjunctive right to explore and develop mineral resources within a signed contact on a concession area with the Cabinet of Ministers to be approved by the Azerbaijanian Parliament.

C. Mining taxation and access to land

The issues of mining taxation, royalties and contractor's use of land are governed by the Mineral Resources Law, the Royalty Law, Land Code, Land Taxes Law and other legislative acts of Azerbaijan. The Mineral Resources Law of Azerbaijan provides the imposition of the following taxes into the State budget: royalty, land use occupation fees during exploration and mining, income tax, fees for offshore area use and taxes for obtaining a licence and charges for geologic and other information. The Royalty Law of Azerbaijan regulates royalty charges, which are calculated as rates of production value of various mineral commodities, and other charges as specified above. Fees for land use and subsoil mineral resources development are collected in accordance with the Land Code and Land Taxation Law of Azerbaijan.

The issues of foreign investments in Azerbaijan are handled in accordance with the Foreign Investment Protection Law, Investment Law and international agreements, which aim at attraction and efficient use of foreign investments, advanced technologies and managerial practices in mineral resources development with due consideration to protection of foreign capital and investors' rights. Foreign investors might be citizens of Azerbaijan, residents of foreign countries, foreign states and international organizations. Foreign investments in Azerbaijan are permitted in a form of (i) equity participation in joint ventures and production sharing contracts; (ii) 100 per cent ownership and participation in mining ventures; (iii) share holding of enterprises, properties, buildings and construction projects; (iv) licencing of land and other natural resources; (v) other forms of foreign investments by agreements concluded with juridical and physical persons of Azerbaijan. Foreign investors can also take part in privatization of state and municipal enterprises and incomplete construction projects. Machinery, equipment and other foreign properties brought for the development of these enterprises are exempted from customs duties.

D. Government institutional framework for the development of
petroleum and mining sectors

Geological mapping and mineral exploration on the territory of Azerbaijan are being carried out by territorial geological-prospecting expeditions. These are structurally subordinated and managed by the State Committee on Geology and Mineral Resources which has been empowered by the Government to be a major decision-making body and client of regional geological investigations financed from the State budget. Geological and exploration expeditions can act as Azerbaijan partners in some joint ventures with foreign investors in mineral exploration and geological prospecting projects of prospective areas.

The State Committee on Geology and Mineral Resources under the Cabinet of Ministers of Azerbaijan has over 2,500 employees including 1,100 professionals at Baku as well as at its 11 regional offices. Its services adequately address all areas related to collection of geodata, mineral exploration and geological data support to the mining industry. The Committee is required modern computer equipment and training with the objectives to inventory and digitize in an easily accessible GIS format all relevant geodata available in the country and related international institutions. The organizational structure of the geological and mineral sector of Azerbaijan is shown in figure 43.

The State Oil Company of Azerbaijan Republic (SOCAR) deals with prospecting, exploration, and development of oil and gas deposits including appropriate construction within the offshore areas of the Azerbaijan sector of the Caspian Sea. SOCAR also includes refinery sector, petrochemical enterprises, construction, transportation/shipping and trading structures, that supply crude and oil products to domestic and overseas markets. SOCAR consists of four principle boards on geophysics and engineering geology, onshore petroleum exploration and development, offshore exploration and hydrocarbon production and managing department on foreign relations and international cooperation (figure 44).

Azerbaijan's mining and metallurgical industry is controlled by the State Company Metallurgiya, composed of 18 enterprises including mining companies, the Gyandzha alumina refinery, the Sumgait aluminium smelter, aluminium rolling and wire drawing enterprises, powder metallurgy production facilities, scrap metal units for ferrous and non-ferrous metals and production facilities for mining and processing bentonites and rock salt. The State Company "Azergizil" conducts prospecting, exploration and mining of gold-bearing deposits and occurrences in Azerbaijan. The Joint Stock Company "Promstroy material" is in charge of development of various types of non-metallic minerals and construction materials including their production and marketing. Small-scale enterprises are quarrying and processing building blocks, dimension and facing stones and clays for brick production. The sequential process of mineral resources/reserves evaluation in Azerbaijan is shown in figure 45.

Mineral resources as well as the Geological Survey and mining enterprises belong to the State and have not been subjected so far to privatization. The proved geological and mineral potential of Azerbaijan constitutes a favourable basis for the future development of the petroleum and mining industries, and the Government is undertaking further regulatory measures to attract foreign investment to the mineral sector. The Government's economic restructuring programme and supporting measures have already enabled Azerbaijan to attract sizeable foreign investment in petroleum exploration and exploitation. Foreign investment and direct participation in a wide range of industries is openly invited, especially for exploring, extracting and processing of fuel and non-fuel mineral resources.

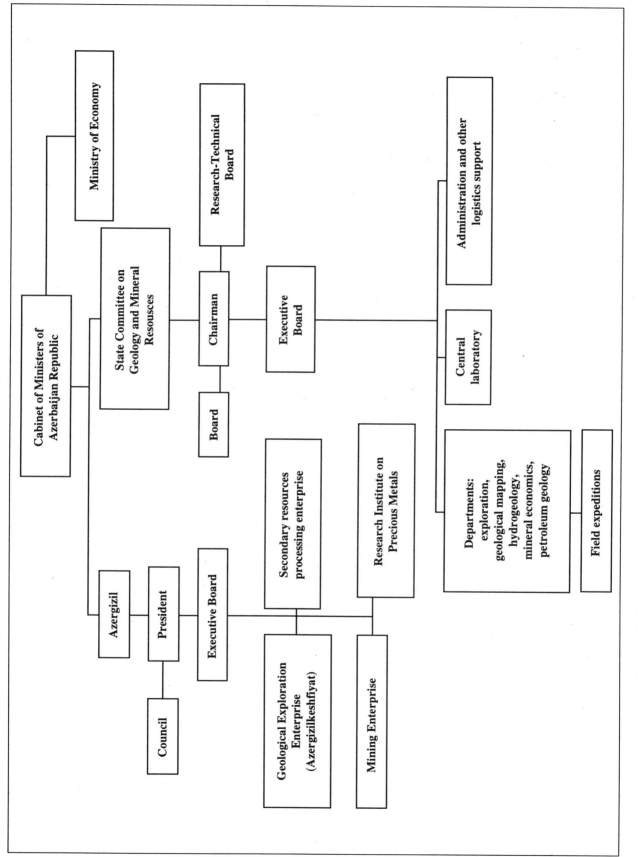

Figure 43. Organizational chart of the geological and mineral sector in Azerbaijan

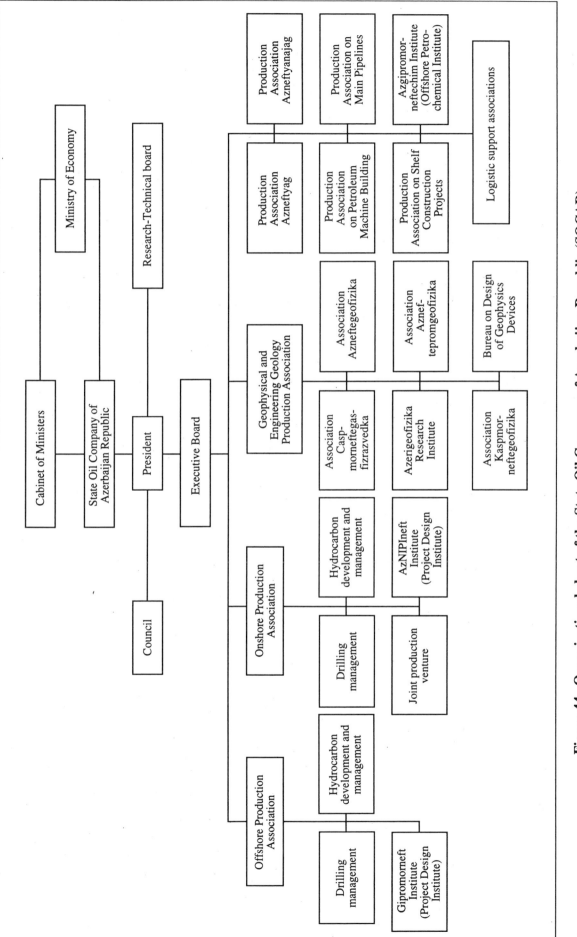

Figure 44. Organizational chart of the State Oil Company of Azerbaijan Republic (SOCAR)

194

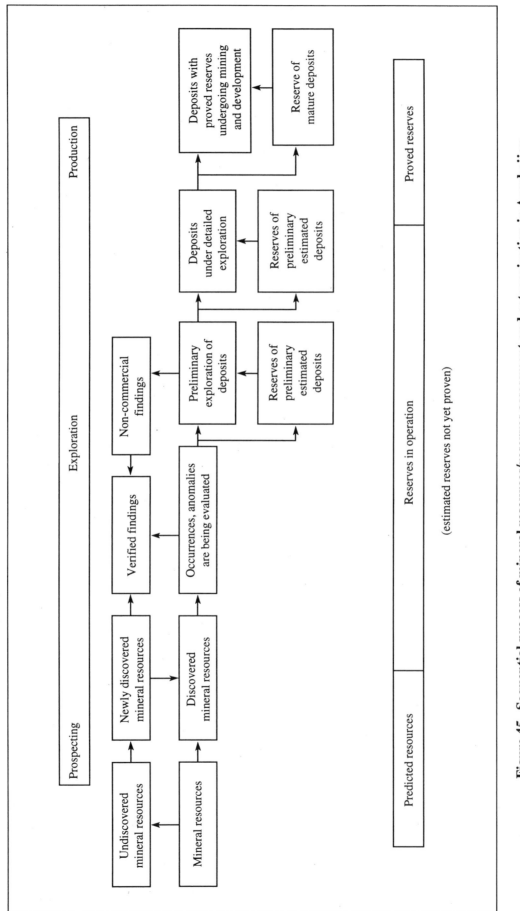

Figure 45. Sequential process of mineral resources/reserves assessment and categorization in Azerbaijan

V. INDEX OF MAJOR MINERAL DEPOSITS AND OCCURRENCES OF AZERBAIJAN

Number on the map	Name of deposit, occurrence or group of occurrences	Location (administrative unit)	Host rocks	Main ore minerals and their content, per cent	Form and size of ore bodies	Category of deposit and reserves
1	2	3	4	5	6	7
	1. FERROUS METALS					
	Iron ore					
1	Dashkesan magnetite deposit	Dashkesan	Volcanogenic-sedimentary	Fe-39%, Co	Stratabound deposit, Length = 0.1-2.0 km Width = 20-60 m	50 million tons
2	South-Dashkesan iron ore (magnetite) cobalt deposit	Dashkesan	Volcanogenic-sedimentary	Fe-42-50%, Co	Stratabound deposit, Length = 0.1-2.0 km Width = 20-60 m	96 million tons
3	Damir iron ore-cobalt deposit	Dashkesan	Volcanogenic-sedimentary	Fe-44%, Co	Stratabound deposit, Length = 0.1-2.0 km Width = 20-60 m	88 million tons
4	Dardara magnetite deposit	Dashkesan	Volcanogenic-sedimentary	Fe-46%, Co	Stratabound deposit, Length = 0.1-2.0 km Width = 20-60 m	3.3 million tons
5	Tatarlin occurrence of magnetite	Touuz	Volcanogenic-sedimentary	Fe, Ti, V_2O_5	Stratabound	
6	Alabashli hematite deposit	Khanlar	Volcanogenic	Fe-17-43%	Stratabound	Large
7	Darvadag magnetite occurrence	Gedabek	Carbonates	Fe-9-15% to 58.2% Co-0.015-0.035%	Lenses, veins of abnormal form	
8	Karikend hematite occurrence	Gedabek	Volcanogenic	Fe	Lenses, stratabound bodies	
9	Magavuz occurrence of magnetite-bearing sandstones	Terter	Volcanogenic-sedimentary	Fe, Ti	Stratabound	
10	Halifali occurrence of magnetite	Jabrail	Volcanogenic-sedimentary	Fe, Ti	Stratabound	
11	Bash-Yurt magnetite skarn occurrence	Ordubad	Skarns	Fe, Cu, Pb	Lenses, mineralized zones	

Number on the map	Name of deposit, occurrence or group of occurrences	Location (administrative unit)	Host rocks	Main ore minerals and their content, per cent	Form and size of ore bodies	Category of deposit and reserves
1	2	3	4	5	6	7
12	Gyuneikend occurrence of magnetite-bearing sandstones	Dashkesan	Volcanogenic-sedimentary	Fe, Ti	Stratabound	
Manganese						
13	Kaimakhli occurrence	Qazakh	Volcanogenic-sedimentary	Mn, Fe	Lens-shaped bodies	
14	Molla Djali deposit	Khanlar	Sandstones, clays	Mn-0.3-16.7% Fe-20.4-42% P_2O_5-1.54%	Lens-shaped bodies Length = 45-200 m Width = 0.3-10 m	Small
15	Kyurakchay occurrence	Khanlar	Carbonates	Mn, Co, Cu, Zn	Lenses	
16	Erkech occurrence	Geranboi				
17	Bichenag occurrence	Shakhbuz	Andesites	Mn-8-22%	Stockwork bodies	
18	Alyagi occurrence	Ordubad	Volcanogenic	Mn-0.0.5-46.8%	Stratabound bodies Length = 50-350 m Width = 2-8 m	
19	Alyagi occurrence	Qazakh	Volcanogenic-sedimentary	Mn-1.8-25% Fe-16-19%, Cio	Lens-shaped bodies Length = 100-200 m Width = 2-12 m	Small
20	Elvar occurrence	Khanlar	Clays	Mn-2-20% Fe-10-15%	Lens-shaped bodies Length = 350-400 m Width = 0.8-2.0 m	
Chromium						
21	Geidara group of deposits	Kelbadjar	Serpentinized dunites	Cr-43.1-52.2% FeO-12.5-16.4%	Stocks, lens-shaped bodies Length = 300-400 m Width = 0.5-15 m	Small
22	Nikolayev occurrence	Kelbadjar	Serpentinized dunites	Cr, Fe	Lenses, stocks, nests	
23	Hatavan occurrence	Kelbadjar	Serpentinized dunites	Cr, Fe	Lenses, stocks, nests	

Number on the map	Name of deposit, occurrence or group of occurrences	Location (administrative unit)	Host rocks	Main ore minerals and their content, per cent	Form and size of ore bodies	Category of deposit and reserves
1	2	3	4	5	6	7
24	Kyazimbina occurrence	Kelbadjar	Serpentinized dunites	Cr, Fe	Lenses, stocks, nests	
25	Gavrilov occurrence	Lachyn	Serpentinized dunites	Cr, Fe	Lenses, stocks, nests	
26	Ipac occurrence	Lachyn	Serpentinized dunites	Cr, Fe	Lenses, stocks, nests	
27	Halifali occurrence	Lachyn	Serpentinized dunites	Cr, Fe	Lenses, stocks, nests	
28	Djomard occurrence	Kelbadjar	Serpentinized dunites	Cr, Fe	Lenses, stocks, nests	
Titanium						
29	Lenkaran deposit of titano-magnetite	Lenkaran	Titano-magnetite sands	Ti, Fe	Stratiform Length = 52 km Width = 50-30 m	Small
2. NON-FERROUS AND RARE METALS						
Copper						
30	Garadag deposit of porphyr copper	Shamkhor	Plagiogranites, secondary quarzites	Cu-0.2-0.8% Mo-0.001-0.008%	Stockwork body	Medium
31	Khar-Khar deposit of porphyry copper-molybdenum	Gedabek	Quartz diorites, secondary quarzites	Cu-0.2-0.7% Mo-0.001-0.01%	Stockwork body	
32	Agdara occurrence	Terter	Pyroclasts	Cu, Mo	Stockwork body	
33	Shamlig occurrence	Terter	Clayey shales	Cu, Zn	Lenses	
34	Beyuk-Gishlak occurrence	Touuz	Sandstones, clayey shales	Cu, Zn, Pb	Veins, zones	
35	Karavellyar occurrence	Touuz	Secondary quarzites	Cu, Zn, Pb	Lenses, mineralized zones	
36	Gyumushlug occurrence	Touuz	Sandstones, clayey shales	Cu. Zn, Pb	Veins, mineralized zones	

Number on the map	Name of deposit, occurrence or group of occurrences	Location (administrative unit)	Host rocks	Main ore minerals and their content, per cent	Form and size of ore bodies	Category of deposit and reserves
1	2	3	4	5	6	7
37	Gadjiallar porphyry copper-molybdenum occurrence	Shamkhor	Volcanogenic	Cu, Mo	Mineralized zones	
38	Nuzger occurrence	Shamkhor	Volcanogenic	Cu, Mo	Mineralized zones	
39	Safarli occurrence	Touuz	Secondary quarzites	Cu, Zn, Pb	Lenses, mineralized zones	
40	Jagirchay occurrence	Shamkhor	Secondary quarzites	Cu, Mo	Stockwork body	
41	Bittibulag occurrence of copper and arsenic	Gedabek	Quartz-porphyres, secondary quarzites	Cu, As		
42	Maarif occurrence	Gedabek	Quartz-porphyres, secondary quarzites	Cu, Mo		
43	Kizijadag occurrence	Gedabek	Secondary quarzites	Cu, Mo, Au	Stockwork body, mineralized zones	
44	Parakendsuin occurrence	Gedabek				
45	Novospasov occurrence	Gedabek				
46	Gedabek gold-copper-pyrite deposit	Gedabek	Secondary quarzites	Cu-0.2-2.5% Au	Large stockwork body with stocks and lenses of massive ores	Large
47	Meidali occurrence	Khanlar	Secondary quarzites	Cu	Veined zones	
48	Chanakhchi occurrence	Khanlar	Metasomatites	Cu	Mineralized zones	
49	Djamillibulag occurrence	Terter	Secondary quarzites	Cu	Mineralized zones	
50	Elbekdash occurrence	Terter	Carbonates	Cu, Pb, Zn	Stratabound bodies, lenses	
51	Maschit occurrence of porphyry copper	Gedabek	Secondary quarzites	Cu-0.2-0.5% Mo-0.001-0.01%	Stockwork body with linear mineralized zones	Small
52	Damirli deposit	Terter	Secondary quarzites	Cu-0.1-0.8% Mo-0.001-0.02% Au, Ag	Large stockwork body with linear mineralized zones	Large
53	Boyahmedli occurrence	Agdam	Quartz diorites, diorite porphyrites	Cu, Mo	Mineralized zones	

Number on the map	Name of deposit, occurrence or group of occurrences	Location (administrative unit)	Host rocks	Main ore minerals and their content, per cent	Form and size of ore bodies	Category of deposit and reserves
1	2	3	4	5	6	7
54	Khachinchay occurrence of porphyry copper-molybdenum	Agdam	Quartz diorites, diorites, secondary quarzites	Cu-0.1-0.6% Mo-0.003-0.02% Au, Ag	Stockwork body Length = 0.8-1.0 km Width = 0.3-0.4 km	
55	Bagirsag occurrence of copper-molybdenum	Kelbadjar	Volcanogenic-sedimentary	Cu, Mo, Zn, Pb	Lenses, nests, stratified bodies	
56	Kaladara group of occurrences	Lachyn	Metasomatites	Cu, Au	Mineralized zones	
57	Bolshoi-Taglar occurrence	Khodjavend	Metasomatites	Cu, Au	Mineralized zones	
58	Khar-Khar occurrence	Shakhbuz	Tuff-conglomerates, tuff-sandstones	Cu-1.0-1.2% Mo-0.023% Co-0.076%	Lenses Length = 200-300 m Width = 2.3-9.0 m	
59	Gey-gel deposit of copper-molybdenum	Ordubad	Granosyenite-porphyres	Cu-0.14-1.5% Mo-0.001-0.005%	Stockwork body	
60	Geydag deposit of copper-molybdenum	Djulfa	Andesites, andesite-cacites, secondary quarzites	Cu-0.3-0.5% Mo-0.001-0.02%	Stockwork body	
61	Misdag deposit	Ordubad	Monsonites	Cu-0.3-11.0% Mo-0.003-0.01% Co-0.001-0.03%	Stockwork body with linear mineralized zones Length = 0.3-2.6 km Width = 0.1-1.3 m	Medium
62	Shalala occurrence of copper-molybdenum	Ordubad	Secondary quarzites	Cu-0.1-0.6% Mo-0.001-0.01%	Stockwork body	
63	Kyalyaki occurrence	Ordubad	Metasomatites	Cu, Au	Mineralized zones	
64	Khanagadag occurrence	Djulfa	Volcanogenic-sedimentary	Cu, Mo	Mineralized zones	
65	Agbend occurrence of copper	Zangelan	Volcanogenic	Cu	Lenses	
66	Diakhchay deposit of porphyry copper-molybdenum	Ordubad	Granodiorites	Cu-0.4-1.14% Mo-0.01-0.025%	Stockwork body	Medium
67	Kilit-Ketam copper-cobalt occurrence	Ordubad	Skarns	Cu, Co	Zones of skarns Length = 2.0-2.5 km Width = 200-500 m	

Number on the map	Name of deposit, occurrence or group of occurrences	Location (administrative unit)	Host rocks	Main ore minerals and their content, per cent	Form and size of ore bodies	Category of deposit and reserves
1	2	3	4	5	6	7
68	Kasmala copper-pyrrhotite deposit	Balakhan	Clayey shales, sandstones	Cu-0.8-1.5%	Mineralized ore zone Length = 1.8-2.0 km Width = 5-12 m	Medium
69	Mazimchay copper-pyrrhotite deposit	Balakhan	Clayey shales, sandstones	Cu-1.2-10.0%	Ribbon-shaped bodies Length = 2 300-2 500 m Width = 3-8 m	Medium
Cobalt						
70	Dashkesan (north) deposit	Dashkesan	Volcanogenic-sedimentary	Co-to 7%, Fe	Mineralized ore zones Length = 200-500 m Width = 0.3-10 m	Small
71	Ketam occurrence	Ordubad	Hornfels, skarns	Co, Cu	Mineralized zones	
Lead and zinc						
72	Tenross pyrite-polymetallic occurrence	Balakhan	Clayey shales, sandstones	Pb, Zn, Cu	Stratabound body	
73	Chugak copper-pyrrhotite occurrence	Balakhan	Clayey shales, sandstones	Pb, Zn	Stratabound body	
74	Sagator copper-zinc deposit	Balakhan	Clayey shales, sandstones	Cu-1.75% Zn-1.84%	Stratabound deposit Length = 1 800-2 000 m Width = 1.3-6.0 m	Medium
75	Bulanlig copper-polymetallic occurrence	Balakhan				
76	Kasdag pyrite-polymetallic deposit	Balakhan	Clayey shales, sandstones		Lens-shaped stratabount bodies	Medium
78	Filizchay polymetallic deposit	Balakhan	Clayey shales, sandstones	Cu, Pb, Zn, Au, Ag, Co, Bi, Se, The, In, Cd	Stratabound deposit Length = 1 200 m Width = 3.0-60.0 m	Unique
79	Cheder pyrite-polymetallic occurrence	Balakhan	Clayey shales, sandstones	Pb, Zn	Stratabound	

Number on the map	Name of deposit, occurrence or group of occurrences	Location (administrative unit)	Host rocks	Main ore minerals and their content, per cent	Form and size of ore bodies	Category of deposit and reserves
1	2	3	4	5	6	7
80	Katekh pyrite-polymetallic occurrence	Zakataly	Clayey shales, sandstones	Pb, Zn, Cu, Ag, Au	Stratabound bodies Length = 200-700 m Width = 2-8 m	Medium
81	Saribash pyrite-polymetallic occurrence	Qazakh	Clayey shales, sandstones	Cu-Pb, Zn, Au, Ag	Stratabound bodies Length = 2 500-3 000 m Width = 4-12 m	
82	Badakend polymetallic occurrence	Shamkhor	Volcanogenic	Pb, Zn, Ag	Veins	
83	Asrikchay occurrence of copper-polymetallic ores	Touuz	Eruptive brecia	Cu, Zn		
84	Novo-Gorelovka copper-zinc occurrence	Gedabek	Quartz plagioporphyres	Cu, Zn	Stock-shaped body	
85	Danaeri polymetallic occurrence	Khanlar	Volcanogenic	Pb, Au, Ag	Veins in mineralized zones	
86	Mekhmana polymetallic deposit	Terter	Volcanogenic-sedimentary	Pb-3.4-6.9% Zn-2.0-5.5% Ag, Au	Veins and veinlet zones	Small
87	Levobagirsag copper-polymetallic occurrence	Kelbadjar	Granosyenites	Cu, Pb, Zn	Mineralized zones	
88	Sultangeidar polymetallic occurrence	Kelbadjar	Granosyenites	Pb, Zn, Cu	Mineralized zones	
89	Danzik polymetallic occurrence	Sharur	Carbonates	Pb, Zn	Lenses	
90	Gyumushlug gold-polymetallic deposit	Sharur	Carbonates	Pb-4.36% Zn-1.43% Au	Veins and lens-shaped bodies	Small (Under conservation)
91	Sarpdaria occurrence of polymetals	Ordubad	Volcanogenic	Pb, Zn, Cu		
92	Bashkend-Ortakend polymetallic occurrence	Djulfa	Volcanogenic	Pb, Zn, Cu		

Number on the map	Name of deposit, occurrence or group of occurrences	Location (administrative unit)	Host rocks	Main ore minerals and their content, per cent	Form and size of ore bodies	Category of deposit and reserves
1	2	3	4	5	6	7
93	Nasirvaz polymetallic deposit	Ordubad	Metasomatites	Pb-1.12% Zn-1.21% Cu-0.37%, Au	Lens-shaped stratabound bodies	Medium
94	Agdara polymetallic deposit	Ordubad	Metasomatites	Pb-1.4-3.5% Zn-1.2-3.2% Cu-0.4-1%, Au	Lens-shaped stratabound deposit	Small (Under conservation)
95	Mazra polymetallic occurrence	Ordubad	Volcanogenic	Pb, Zn, Cu		
Arsenic and antimony						
96	Deveboini occurrence	Lachyn	Carbonates	As, Sb	Mineralized zones, lenses	
97	Goshasu occurrence	Lachyn	Carbonates	As, Sb	Mineralized zones	
98	Salvarty occurrence	Shakhbuz	Marls, argillites	As, Sb	Stockworks, nests	
99	Norashen occurrence of arsenic and mercury	Djulfa	Argillites, marls	As, Sb, Hg	Lenses, nests	
100	Daridag deposit of arsenic and antimony	Djulfa	Argillites, marls	As, Sb	Stockworks, nests	Small (Depleted)
Aluminium						
101	Seifali alunite occurrence	Shamkhor	Volcanogenic-sedimentary	Al_2O_3-9.52-57.0%	Stratified bodies Length = 200-500 m Width = 1.0-8.0 m	
102	Zaglik alunite deposit	Dashkesan	Tuffites	Al_2O_3-10.0-36.0%	Stratabound deposit	Large, 160 million tons
103	Danzik bauxite occurrence	Sharur	Carbonates	Al_2O_3	Stratabound lens-shaped bodies	
104	Sadarak bauxite occurrence	Sharur	Carbonates	Al_2O_3	Stratabound lens-shaped bodies	
105	Gabakdag bauxite occurrence	Sharur	Carbonates	Al_2O_3	Stratabound lens-shaped bodies	
106	Myunkhbala ogly bauxite occurrence	Sharur	Carbonates	Al_2O_3	Stratabound lens-shaped bodies	

Number on the map	Name of deposit, occurrence or group of occurrences	Location (administrative unit)	Host rocks	Main ore minerals and their content, per cent	Form and size of ore bodies	Category of deposit and reserves
1	2	3	4	5	6	7
107	Geran galasi bauxite occurrence	Sharur	Carbonates	Al_2O_3 - 30-57%	Lens-shaped – stratabound bodies Length = 1.5-2 km Width = 2-13 m	
108	Gabakhyal bauxite occurrence	Sharur	Carbonates	Al_2O_3	Stratabound lens-shaped bodies	
Molybdenum						
109	Teymuruchandag (Dalidag) occurrence	Kelbadjar	Porphyrites and their tuffs, quartz syenite-diorites	Mo-0.01-0.2% Cu-0.01-0.3% Pb-0.001-1.83% Zn-0.01-0.74%	Veins and mineralized zones	
110	Kapudjik occurrence	Ordubad	Granosyenites, syenite-diorites	Mo-0.63% Cu-1.84%	Mineralized zone	
111	Paragachay deposit	Ordubad	Gabbro-diorites, diorites	Mo-0.02-0.8% Cu	Mineralized zone	
112	Urumis occurrence	Ordubad	Gabbro-diorites, granodiorites	Mo-0.001-0.1% Cu-0.06-0.7%	Veins	Small (Preserved)
113	Gekgyundur occurrence	Ordubad	Quartz syenite-diorites, porphyry granosyenites	Mo-0.01-2.5% Cu-0.2-2.5%	Veins Length = 300-350 m Width = 0.5-1.1 m	
114	Fakhlidara occurrence	Ordubad	Gabbroids	Mo, Cu	Stockwork body	
Tungsten						
115	Levobogirsagchay occurrence	Kelbadjar	Hornfels	W	Veins, veinlet zones	
116	Kyzyl-Chagli (Kilit) occurrence	Ordubad	Keratenized sandstones	W-0.01-1.08%	Veins	
Mercury and antimony						
117	West-Lev occurrence	Kelbadjar	Jasperoides	Hg, Sb	Stratabound lens-shaped bodies	

Number on the map	Name of deposit, occurrence or group of occurrences	Location (administrative unit)	Host rocks	Main ore minerals and their content, per cent	Form and size of ore bodies	Category of deposit and reserves
1	2	3	4	5	6	7
118	Levchay (Lev) deposit of mercury and antimony	Kelbadjar	Jasperoides	Hg-0.2-0.5% Sb	Lens-shaped bodies Length = 20-70 m Width = 2-7 m	Small Hg-500 tons Sb>100 tons
119	Yeni-Lev occurrence	Kelbadjar	Jasperoides	Hg, Sb	Stratum-lens-shaped bodies	
120	Sarigdash occurrence	Kelbadjar	Listvenites	Hg-0.4%	Lenses, nests	
121	Arhachdar occurrence	Kelbadjar	Listvenites	Hg-0.2-0.5%	Lenses, nests	
122	Kilichli occurrence	Kelbadjar	Listvenites	Hg-0.1-0.5%	Lenses, nests	
123	Chaikend occurrence	Kelbadjar	Listvenites	Hg-0.1-0.6%	Lenses, nests	
124	Shorbulag deposit	Kelbadjar	Listvenites, porphyrites, argillites	Hg-0.2-1.0%	Lenses, nests	Small (Preserved)
125	Bashkend-Mil occurrence	Kelbadjar	Listvenites			
126	Agkaya deposit	Kelbadjar	Listvenites	Hg-0.1-0.5%	Lenses, nests	Small
127	Gyunaipeya occurrence	Kelbadjar	Listvenites	Hg-0.01-0.25%	Lenses, nests	
128	Agyatag deposit	Kelbadjar	Listvenites	Hg-0.1-1.5%	Lenses	Small (Preserved)
129	Elyeri occurrence	Lachyn	Listvenites	Hg-0.01-0.7%	Lenses	
130	Hanlanly-Bashlibel occurrence	Kelbadjar	Listvenites	Hg	Nests	
131	Chilgyaschay deposit	Lachyn	Breccia, listvenites	Hg-0.3%	Lenses, nests	Small
132	Nagdali occurrence	Lachyn	Listvenites	Hg	Nests	
133	"Arzu" occurrence	Lachyn	Carbonates	Hg-0.13-0.3%	Lenses, nests	
134	Narzali (Kalafalikh) deposit	Lachyn	Carbonates	Hg-0.1-1.5%	Lenses, veins and bodies of various shapes	Small
135	"Dumanli" occurrence	Lachyn	Listvenites carbonates	Hg-0.1% Zn-0.36% Pb, Co, Ni	Lenses, nests	
136	Ipac occurrence	Lachyn	Argillites diabases	Hg-0.13-0.28%	Nests, lenses	

Number on the map	Name of deposit, occurrence or group of occurrences	Location (administrative unit)	Host rocks	Main ore minerals and their content, per cent	Form and size of ore bodies	Category of deposit and reserves
1	2	3	4	5	6	7
137	Halifali group of occurrence	Lachyn	Listvenites	Hg	Nests	
138	Darridag occurrence	Djulfa	Argillites	Hg-0.2-0.4% Sb	Nests	
	Gold					
139	Gizilbulag deposit	Terter	Liparite-dacites	Au, Cu, Ag, Se	Stockwork bodies	Medium
140	Shakardara deposit	Ordubad	Metasomatites	Au, Cu	Veinlet zones, stockworks	Medium
141	Dagkesaman deposit	Qazakh	Andesite-dacites, andesite porphyrites	Au, Ag, Pb, Zn, Cu	Veinlet zones	Medium
142	Agyurt deposit	Ordubad	Granodiorites granosyenites	Au, Ag, Cu	Veinlet zones	
143	Tutkhun group of occurrences	Kelbadjar	Granitoids	Au, Ag	Veins	
144	Agduzdag deposit	Kelbadjar	Andesite-dacites, rhyolites	Au, Ag	Veinlet zones	
145	Pyazbashi deposit	Ordubad	Volcanogenic-sedimentary	Au, Ag	Veins	
146	Vejnali deposit	Zangelan	Carbonates, volcanogenic	Au, Ag, Cu	Veins, veinlet zones	
147	Gosha deposit	Touuz	Secondary quarzites	Au, Ag	Veins, veinlet zones	
148	Zod (Soyutlu) deposit	Kelbadjar	Carbonaceous-siliceous, gabbroids	Au, Ag	Veins, veinlet zones	
149	Itgirlan occurrence	Touuz	Secondary quarzites	Au, Ag	Veins, veinlet zones	

VI. BIBLIOGRAPHY

Abasov, Cengiz, 1998. Foreign Investment Policy of Azerbaijan. Ministry of Economy of Azerbaijan, Baku.

Abdullayev R.N., 1963. Mesozoic volcanism in the north-eastern part of the Lesser Caucasus. Baku.

Abdullayev R.N., Ismailov A.I., Kerimov A.F., 1979. Gizilbulag Caldera – the new volcano-tectonic morphostructure in the Mekhmana ore district. Baku. Reports of the Academy of Sciences of Azerbaijan No. 4.

Abdullayev R.N., Mustafayev G.V., 1984. Magmatism and metallogeny of Azerbaijan. In col.: Essay on geology of Azerbaijan. Baku.

Abdullayev R.N., Mustafayev G.V., Mustafayev M.A., and others, 1988. Mesozoic magmatic formations of the Lesser Caucasus and related endogenic mineralization. Baku.

Abdullayev R.N., Mustafayev M.A., Samedov R.A., and others, 1991. Petrology of the magmatic complex on the south slope of the Greater Caucasus (Vandam zone). Baku.

Adamiya Sh.A. and Shavishvili I.D., 1979. Model of tectonic evolution of the Caucasus Earth's crust and adjoining regions (Pre-Alpine stage). Moscow, "Geotectonika", No. 1.

Afanasiev G.D., Abdullayev R.N., Azizbekov Sh.A., and others, 1968. Nature of development of magmatism in folding regions (on the example of Caucasus, Kazakhstan and the Far East). Moscow, Nauka.

Agayev S.A., 1982. On the peculiarity of structure conditions and zonality of Filizchay pyrite-polimetallic field. Proceeding of TSNIGRI. Moscow.

Agayev V.B., 1990. Stratigraphy of the Jurassic deposits of Azerbaijan (Greater Caucasus). Baku.

Akberov M.A., Samedov A.M., Mamedov H.Sh., Mamedov I.A., 1982. On the peculiarities of morphology and natural types of ores in the Filizchai deposit. Proceeding of TSNIGRI. Moscow.

Alikhanov E.H., 1968. Oil fields of the Caspian Sea. Moscow, Nedra.

Aliyev V.I., 1976. Iron pyrite formations of the Lesser Caucasus. Abstracts of doctor degree. Baku.

Aliyev I.D., 1998. On the periodicality of formation and localization of porcelain stones (on the example of the Lesser Caucasus). Abstracts of the paper on the Second Republic Conference. Baku State University. Baku.

Aliyev A.I., Bagir-zade F.M., Bunyat-zade Z.A., and others, 1985. Oil and gas fields and perspective structures of Azerbaijan. Baku, Elm.

Ali-zade A.A., Hasanov H.A., Zeynalov M.M., 1966. Oil fields of Azerbaijan. Moscow, Nedra.

Ali-zade S.A., Akhmedov D.M., Akhmedov A.I., and others, 1981. Main peculiarities of metallogeny of Azerbaijan (Explanation notes to metallogenic map). Baku.

Ali-zade S.A., Bairamov A.A., Mamedov A.V., Shirinov N.Sh., 1978. Geology of the Quarternary deposits of Azerbaijan. Baku.

Arutyunova J.E., Juze B.K., 1968. Oil shales of the eastern part of Azerbaijan. In col.: "Geology of coal and pyroschist deposits of the USSR", Vol. 2. Moscow.

208

Azizbekov Sh.A., 1961. Geology of the Nakhchivan Autonomous Republic. Moscow.

Azizbekov Sh.A., Bagirov A.E., Veliyev M.M., and others, 1979. Geology and volcanism of the Talysh mountains. Baku.

Azizbekov Sh.A., Kashkay M.A., 1952. Magmatism and metallogeny of Azerbaijan. Baku.

Azizbekov Sh.A., Hadjiyev T.G., 1969. Cenozoic magmatism of Azerbaijan. Materials of the First Regional Petrology Meeting of the Caucasus, Crimea and Carpats. Tbilisi.

Baba-zade V.M., Malyutin R.S., 1967. Structure conditions and localization of gold mineralization within the Agduzdag ore field (Lesser Caucasus). Baku, Scientific notes of Azerbaijan State University, Series: Geology-geographic sciences, No. 2.

Baba-zade V.M., Makhmudov A.I., Ramazanov V.H., 1990. Copper and molybdenum porphyrite fields in Azerbaijan. Baku, Azerneshr.

Borsuk A.M., 1979. Mesozoic and Cenozoic magmatic formations of the Greater Caucasus. Moscow, Nauka.

Gamkrelidze P.D., Gamkrelidze I.P., 1977. Tectonic sheets on the southern slope of the Caucasus (within Georgia). Tbilisi.

Geodynamic of Caucasus, 1989. Moscow, Nauka.

Geology of Azerbaijan, 1997. Vol. 1. Stratigraphy. Baku.

Geology of Azerbaijan, 1998. Vol. 2. Lithology. Baku.

Geology of Azerbaijan 1999. Vol. 3. Magmatism. Baku.

Geology of the Greater Caucasus, 1976. (Editor: Ajgerey G.D.). Moscow, Nedra.

Geology of USSR, 1964. Vol. 10. Georgian SSR, Geological description. Moscow, Nedra.

Geology of USSR, 1968. Vol. 9. North Caucasus, Geological description. Moscow, Nedra.

Geology of USSR, 1970. Vol. 42. Armenian SSR. Geological description. Moscow, Nedra.

Geology of USSR, 1972. Vol. 47. Azerbaijan SSR, Chapter 1. Geological description. Moscow, Nedra.

Geology of USSR, 1976. Vol. 47. Azerbaijan SSR, Chapter 2. Mineral deposits. Moscow, Nedra.

Guluzade, Kenan, 1998. Azerbaijan oil market. Baku.

Hasanov M.A., 1982. Peculiarity of structure in the Kasdag pyrite-copper polymetallic deposit. Proceeding of TSNIGRI. Moscow.

Hasanov T.A., 1967. Lower Jurassic of Azerbaijan (Lesser Caucasus). Baku.

Hasanov T.A., 1973. Middle Jurassic of Azerbaijan (Lesser Caucasus). Baku.

Hasanov T.Ab., 1985. Ophiolites of the Lesser Caucasus. Moscow, Nedra.

Hasanov T.Ab., 1996. Geodynamic of ophiolites on the structure of the Lesser Caucasus and Iran. Baku.

Hasanov R.K. and Aliyev A.A., 1984. Some features of structure and mineralogical-geochemical peculiarities of ores in the Gizilbulag field. Proceeding of TSNIGRI. Moscow.

Hasanov R.K., Aliyev A.A., 1981. Issues of mineralogy, geochemistry and petrology of Azerbaijan. Baku.

Kangarly T.N., 1982. Peculiarity of the geological structure of the Azerbaijanian part of the Side Range of the Greater Caucasus. Abstract of candidate degree. Baku.

Kangarly T.N., Shekinsky E.M., Zamanov Yu.D., 1994. Tectonic stratification of the earth's crust of the Great Caucasus and the problems of prospecting of oil and gas and ore deposits. Proceedings of 10th Petroleum Congress and Exhibition in Turkey. Ankara.

Kangarly T.N., Ahundov A.B., Aliyev A.M., Abdullayev V.D., 1994. The depth geological mapping of the oil and gas-bearing regions of the South-East Caucasus. Proceedings of 10th Petroleum Congress and Exhibition in Turkey. Ankara.

Kangarly T.N., 1997. Nappe tectonics of the oil and gas-bearing regions of the South-East Caucasus. Proceedings of the International Seminar: "Neotectonics and its influence on oil and gas-pool formation". Baku.

Kangarly T.N., 1999. Peculiarity of the geodynamic evolution of the Greater Caucasus in the Alpine tectono-magmatic cycle (an example of Azerbaijan). Proceeding of International Conference: "Geodynamics of the Black Sea – Caspian Sea segment of the Alpine folded belt and search for minerals perspectives". Baku.

Karyakin Yu.V., 1989. Geogynamic formation of volcanic complex in the Lesser Caucasus. Moscow, Nauka.

Kashkay M.A., 1947. Basic and ultrabasic rocks in Azerbaijan. Baku.

Kashkay M.A., 1964. Petrology and metallogeny in Dashkesan. Moscow, Nedra.

Kashkay M.A., Aliyev V.I., Mamedov A.I., and others, 1970. Petrology and metallogeny of magmatic formations in the Tutkhun basin. Baku.

Kashkay M.A., Nasibov T.N., 1985. Mercury zones of the Sevan-Akera structure in the Lesser Caucasus. Moscow, "Geology of ore deposits". No. 6.

Kerimov A.D., 1964. Petrology and ore-bearing granitoid intrusive of Mekhmana. Baku.

Kerimov A.D., Kerimov F.A., 1974. Structure-genetic peculiarities of the copper-molybdenum field in the Gey-gel region. Proceeding of the Academy of Sciences of Azerbaijan, No. 2.

Kerimov A.F., Shekinsky E.M., Musayev Sh.D., Zamanov Yu.D., 1983. The types of gold mineralization of Azerbaijan. Abstracts of the Conference paper, Moscow.

Kerimov A.F., Zamanov Yu.D., Musayev Sh.D., 1986. Criterion of mineralization of pyrite-polymetallic deposits in volcanic regions. Materials of Workshop: "Geology, geochemistry and ore-bearings of the Lesser Caucasus and Talysh". Baku.

Kerimov A.F., Aliyev A.A., Hasanov R.K., 1996. Geology-structure peculiarity and conditions of formation of the copper-gold field in Gizilbulag. Baku.

Kerimov H.I., 1962. Petrology and ore-bearing of the Gedabek district (Lesser Caucasus). Vol. 1, Vol. 2, Baku.

Khain V.E., 1984. Regional geotectonics: Alpine Mediterranean belt. Moscow, Nedra.

Khalifa-zade Ch.M., Sultanov K.M., 1968. Rare metallogeny of oil shales of Azerbaijan. Scientific report. Baku.

Khalifa-zade Ch.M., Magomedov A.M., 1982. Middle Jurassic deposits of the east and south-eastern Caucasus. Moscow, Nauka.

Khalifa-zade Ch.M., 1986. Mineralogy and origin of bauxites ore in the Nakhchivan ASSR. Baku, Elm.

Khalilov A.G., 1978. Stratigraphy of Azerbaijan. Baku.

Knipper A.L., 1975. Oceanic crust on the structure of Alpine folding region. Moscow, Nauka.

Kovalev A.A., 1978. Mobilizm and prospecting geology criterions. Moscow, Nedra.

Kurbanov N.K., 1982. Integrated prospecting and principles of complex pyrite-copper-polymetallic deposits in Alpine geosyncline belt of the Greater Caucasus. Proceeding of TSNIGRI. Moscow.

Kurbanov N.K., Zlotnic-Khotkevich A.G., Romanov V.I. and others, 1967. On the peculiarity of pyrite-polymetallic mineralization on the southern slope of the Greater Caucasus. Proceeding of TSNIGRI. Moscow.

Kurbanov N.K., Mamedov F.M., Aliyev A.A., 1981. Cyclical mineral formation (origin) of complex gold-pyrite deposits in of the Lesser Caucasus. Geologic and industrial types of gold-ore fields. Proceeding of TSNIGRI. Moscow.

Levine, Richard, 1998. Azerbaijan. Mining Annual Review, 1998.

Lomidze M.G., 1983. Tectonic situation of geosynclinal volcanism. Moscow, Nedra.

Lomidze M.G., 1977. Magmatic formation of the Caucasus and the South-Eastern European platform. Moscow, Nauka.

Lomidze M.G., 1981. Main peculiarities of magmatism and metamorphism of Azerbaijan (Explanation notes to the metallogenic map of Azerbaijan). Baku.

Makhmudov A.I., 1982. Mineralogy of cobalt ores. Moscow, Nedra.

Mansurov M.I., 1998. Structure and texture peculiarity of ores of the Gosha gold-pyrite field. Abstracts of the Conference paper. In series: Mineral resources of Azerbaijan. Baku State University, Baku.

Materials on geology of north-eastern Azerbaijan. 1957. Baku.

Mesozoic and Cenozoic folding belt, 1977. Vol. 1. Moscow, Mir.

Milanovsky E.E., Khain V.E., 1963. Geological structure of the Caucasus. Moscow, Nauka.

Mustafabeyli M.A., Liberson I.M., Akhmedov D.M., 1964. Main features of distribution of endogeneous fields in the Dashkesan ore zone. In book: "Periodic distribution of mineral deposits", Vol. 7. Moscow, Nauka.

Mustafayev H.V., 1977. Mesozoic granitoids of Azerbaijan and their metallogenic peculiarities. Baku.

Mustafayev H.V., Magriby A.A., Shiraliyev A.B., and others, 1989. Periodic distribution and formation of ore deposits in Azerbaijan. Materials of the Conference dedicated to the 50 anniversary of the Institute of Geology of the Academy of Sciences of Azerbaijan. Baku, Elm.

Paffengols K.N., 1970. Essay of magmatism and metallogeny of Caucasus, 1970. Erevan.

Shekinsky E.M., Zamanov Yu.D., Ibragimov I.M., 1998. Rational utilization of mineral resources and reserve promotion of economic potential of the Azerbaijan Republic. Materials of the Second Scientific-Practical Conference: "Azerbaijan on threshold of XXI century". Baku.

Shikhalibeyli E.Sh., 1956. Geological structure and development of the Azerbaijanian part of the Southern Slope of the Greater Caucasus. Baku.

Shikhalibeyli E.Sh., 1966. Geological structure and history of tectonic development of the Eastern part of the Lesser Caucasus. Vol. 1, Vol. 2. Baku.

Shikhalibeyli E.Sh., Hasanov A.G., and others, 1984. Structure and formations of the South Caspian Trough. In col.: Essay on geology of Azerbaijan. Baku.

Shirinov A.M., 1982. Geologic structure and conditions localization of ores in the Jigien pyrite-copper-polimetallic field. Proceedings of TSNIGRI. Moscow.

Sholpo V.N., 1978. Alpine geodynamic evolution of the Greater Caucasus. Moscow, Nedra.

Sokolov S.D., 1977. Olistostrom strata and ophiolite sheet in the Lesser Caucasus. Moscow, Nauka.

Sokolov S.D., 1983. Some questions of magmatism in Azerbaijan. Baku.

Suleimanov S.M., Baba-zade V.M., 1974. Geology of mercury deposits in the Lesser Caucasus. Baku, Azerneshr.

Suleimanov S.M., Guilyev T.B., 1986. Morphology and structure position of the ore body of the Vejnaly ore field. Scientific notes of the Azerbaijan State University, Series: Geology-geographic sciences, No. 1.

Suleimanov S.M., Sitcovsky I.N., Aliyev M.K., 1986. Gold manifestation in the field of volcanic quartz porphyrites in Touus region. Scientific notes of the Azerbaijan State University, Series: Geology-geographic sciences, No. 3.

Yusufova V.D., Zamanov Yu.D., 1998. Oil shales of Azerbaijan – perspective alternative of oil and gas. Materials of the Second Republic an Scientific-Practical Conference: "Azerbaijan on threshold of XXI century". Baku.

Yusifzade K.B., 1998. SOCAR's collaboration with foreign companies: its prospects and success.

Zamanov Yu.D., 1989. Resources of mineral deposits in Azerbaijan and perspectivity of their development. Abstracts of the Paper in the Conference of the Problems of the South Caspian trough. Baku.

Zamanov Yu.D., Shekinsky E.M., Ibragimov I.M., 1998. Non-traditional sources of energy resources in Azerbaijan. Materials of the Second Republican Scientific-Practical Conference: "Azerbaijan on threshold of XXI century". Baku.

ANNEX: COMMONWEALTH MINERAL RESOURCE CLASSIFICATION SCHEME

A uniform and consistent resource classification scheme was used throughout the former Soviet Union covering all mineral resources that were explored, identified, evaluated and projected. The categorization scheme and related terminology varied significantly from that used in the West and other parts of the world, leading to problems of interpretation, comparison and economic assessment. Given the opening of the economies of the former Soviet republics to foreign investment and technology assistance, particularly with regard to the mining industry, achieving an understanding of how the Soviet classification scheme is organized is becoming increasingly vital to business decisions. As the individual countries of the former Soviet Union have started to modify their own classification schemes, mining companies will need to monitor the changing definitions of terms and reinterpretations of geological conditions.

The former Soviet Union's resource classification scheme underwent major changes six times in 1927, 1933, 1941, 1953, 1960 and 1981. In 1981, the former Soviet Union adopted a new reserve and probable resource classification which incorporated a number of new features, including, for the first time, basic principles of appraisal of probable or prognostic resources, enhanced requirements for accuracy in measuring varying categories of reserves and the use of economic concepts in the qualitative and quantitative evaluation of reserves and probable resources. The former Soviet Union's reserve classification scheme was approved by the USSR Council of Ministers and deemed compulsory for all geological and mining agencies and related scientific institutions. The principles of the classification were used for computing the former Soviet Union's State inventory of reserves and evaluation of probable mineral resources.

As a means of comparison, table 18 illustrates the approximate correspondence of resource categories employed in the former Soviet Union and the United States of America. Direct comparison of the individual reserve and resource categories by the level of geological knowledge in the former Soviet Union and western countries is difficult. This is particularly true for the comparison of categories by mining companies in the West. In the former Soviet Union, a number of conditions had to be met prior to assigning reserves to any individual category, including establishing a geologic grouping of layers, identifying their extent and thickness, evaluating the structure of orebodies and analyzing the quality and usefulness of minerals present. The assignment of reserves to a category was also governed by the level of understanding of how natural conditions (hydrogeological, engineering-geological, etc.) influenced the nature of mining operations.

In the former Soviet Union, reserves of categories A and B consisted of the most highly proven part of explored resources. Reserves in these categories are somewhat arbitrary, however, at least in comparison with measured or proved reserves of the classifications used in the United States and Australia. The category C_1 reserves of the Soviet classification scheme are most comparable with indicated or probable reserves of the United States classification. The sum of A, B and C categories of the Soviet classification corresponds chiefly to the demonstrated reserves of the United States.

The following terminology is used in the former Soviet Union classification scheme:

(a)   Reserves are quantities of economic mineral material revealed, explored and evaluated in place in a certain area in the course of geological exploration, drilling and mining during the development history of a mineral deposit;

(b)   Undiscovered or projected resources are masses of undiscovered minerals forecasted on the basis of general geological knowledge, scientific concepts and preliminary results of geological mapping, geophysical and geochemical surveys.

214

Table 18. Approximate correspondence of resource categories in the United States and the former Soviet Union*

Country	Total resources					
United States	Identified resources				Undiscovered resources	
	Demonstrated reserves		Inferred or possible reserves	Hypothetical resources	Speculative resources	
	Measured or proved	Indicated or probable				
Soviet Union	Explored reserves		Projected resources			
	A + B	C_1	C_2	P_1	P_2	P_3

Source: Bejanova, M.P. and H.P. Piskorsky, 1989, "Classification of hard economic mineral resources and resources: principles and special features". Seminar on Modern Methods of Mineral Prospecting, Tbilisi, Georgia, 30 October-10 November 1989, 21 p.;

United States Bureau of Mines and United States Geological Survey, 1980. "Principles of a resource/reserve classification for minerals". USGS Circular 831 (Washington, DC);

Astakhov, Denisov, and Pavlov, 1994. "Prospecting and exploration in the Soviet Union", in Hans Landsberg, John Tilton and rodderick Eggert, eds. *World Mineral Exploration Trends* (Washington, DC., Resources for the Future).

• A, B, C and P indicate caegories of resources, as discussed in the text of this annex.

Reserves are evaluated according to type and in terms of possible use of minerals at individual deposits, ore fields, basins, regions, economic areas and the country as a whole. Reserves from explored mineral deposits are approved by the various geological surveys or reserve committees in the Commonwealth of Independent States, with reserve data being taken into account in the drafting of State plans for economic development, policies for geological exploration and designs of new mining enterprises. The reserves are calculated in place.

Principal criteria used traditionally in the Soviet classification of reserves and probable resources were as follows: importance for the national economy (technological efficiency, profitability), the level of geological assurance (involvement in exploration) and the importance for use in industrial development. In determining the importance of reserves for the national economy, the Soviet classification separated reserves into the following categories:

(a) *balance reserves* are those that are economically feasible under existing conditions or subject to advance mining and processing technology. The size of balance reserves changes in accordance with price fluctuations, and changes in technology, and the supply of and demand for mineral raw materials;

(b) *out-of-balance reserves* are those that are not economically feasible given existing economic or technology conditions, or the insignificant thickness of a deposit, low grade of mineral components, difficult mining conditions, or unfavourable geographic-economic conditions of the mineral deposit.

However, out-of-balance reserves can be reclassified into balance reserves and targeted for economic development with the introduction of advanced mining and processing technologies or because of improved economic conditions in the area where the deposit is located.

In accordance with the level of geological assurance, four reserve categories are established under the Soviet classification scheme: A, B, C_1 and C_2. Reserves under categories A, B and C_1 are assigned to the proved or explored reserves while those under category C_2 are assigned to preliminary assessed reserves.

Category A

These resources consist of the most highly proven part of explored resources. They have been extensively investigated, and the mode of occurrence, shape and structure of an orebody are known. These data are derived from drilling and mine workings. With "A" category resources, the technological properties of the ore minerals, including the hydrogeological, engineering geology, geotechnical and other natural, environmental features, have been studied in detail, ensuring the acquisition of preliminary data necessary for designing ore processing flow-sheets and compiling a detailed technical report for the development of the deposit. The contour of the mineral reserve is established in accordance with data from boreholes and mine workings.

Category B

These reserves include those deposits whose characteristics have not been studied thoroughly although some of their major characteristics have been delineated. The extent of these resources is determined with the help of information from drilling and mining operations, but their extrapolation is permitted to a limited extent only. With "B" category resources, economic minerals are defined and delineated where possible; in cases where definition is impossible, the spatial distribution of industrial mineral types and grades is established. The technological properties of category "B" minerals are studied to a detail needed for the selection of a basic processing flow-sheet while hydrogeological, engineering, geological, geotechnical and other natural conditions are examined to a degree which enables a qualitative and quantitative characterization of their principal parameters and a determination of their influence on the development of the mineral deposit.

Category C_1

These reserves are even less delineated: only their most general characteristics are known. The changeability and possible discontinuity of mineral bodies are assessed while hydrogeological, engineering, geological and other natural features are studied to a degree, which allows only a preliminary characterization of their main parameters.

Category C_2

Preliminary explored resources under category C_2 are established on the basis of geologic, geophysical and geochemical studies and measurements of the orebody in exploratory activities. Resources in this category can also be estimated by extrapolation of geologic data. With category C_2 reserves, the quality and technological properties of the minerals are determined through analysis of only a few laboratory samples or by analogy with better-studied portions of the same or similar deposits. Hydrogeological, engineering, geological and other natural conditions are assessed based on evidence and observations in mine workings and boreholes from other sites and by analogy with data available from the vicinity of the deposit.

Projected or probable resources consist of an undiscovered portion of the mineral base. Their appraisal is based on geological data from similar and explored deposits elsewhere. In contrast to reserves, probable resources are not computed but evaluated in a numerical form. Projected or probable resources are also known as prognostic resources. Similar to reserves, probable resources are evaluated for an entire country, for economic areas, ore basins and fields and individual deposits. Probable resources provide an indication of the expansion possible of a mineral-raw materials base and form a basis for current and long-term economic planning and defining geological exploration and prospecting activities. Based on the level of geological assurance, probable resources fall into three categories: P_1, P_2 and P_3.

Category P_1

These probable resources are those of explored deposits or those currently being explored as well as the resources of new deposits where prospecting has been completed. Category P_1 probable resources can be reclassified into reserves with an expansion of the mineral distribution area or discovery of new ore bodies at the deposit. The quantitative appraisal of the deposit is based on an understanding of the type of deposit and its origin.

Category P_2

Projected resources of undiscovered deposits are likely to exist on the basis of evidence from geologic surveys, prospecting and geophysical and geochemical tests comprise category P_2. The availability of resources in this category is deduced from the estimation of ore occurrences as well as geophysical and geochemical anomalies whose nature has been determined through the course of large-scale (1:50,000) mapping. Category P_2 probable resources form a basis for planning long-term prospecting and assessment programmes.

Category P_3

These probable resources are those of potentially promising areas, districts, basins and ore fields which do not contain mineable mineral deposits but based on stratigraphic, lithological, tectonic and paleogeographic evidence which can lead to a discovery of new deposits. Quantitative estimates of this resource category are based on analogy with better studied regions, areas and basins, where explored mineral deposits of the same genetic type occur. Category P_3 probable resources form a basis for planning of future large-scale geological mapping and prospecting programmes for mineral deposits.

Comparative analysis of the above reserve and resource classification schemes shows that despite common approaches and objectives, the definitions of individual categories of reserves and resources have certain peculiarities in different countries. The Soviet system of classifying reserves and resources incorporates the geologic, economic and technologic characteristics of minerals as well as their importance to the national economy. The scheme has undergone several modifications in recent years.

Western classifications of resources, notably those of the United States and Canada, characterize resources according to their level of geologic assurance and degree of economic feasibility for mining. Direct comparison of the individual reserve and resource categories between the Soviet and Western classifications is not possible owing to the differences in criteria used in assessing the economic feasibility of mining, commodity prices and the costs of extraction between nations. However, it is recommended that companies assessing opportunities for mining development in the former Soviet republics examine Soviet reserve calculations as a means of comparing sizes and conditions of deposits within the Russian Federation and other Commonwealth States while calculating new reserves using their own techniques and criteria.